Psychological Medicine

Psychological Medicine
AN INTRODUCTION TO PSYCHIATRY

Desmond Curran
C.B.E., M.B., F.R.C.P., D.P.M.
Formerly Lord Chancellor's Medical Visitor.
Formerly Honorary Consulting Psychiatrist to St George's Hospital.
Emeritus Professor of Psychiatry, St George's Hospital Medical School,
University of London,
and formerly Civil Consultant in Psychological Medicine to the Royal Navy

Maurice Partridge
D.M., F.R.C.P., D.P.M.
Formerly Consultant Psychiatrist to St George's Hospital
and to the Royal Marsden Hospital.
Formerly Lecturer and Vice-Dean,
St George's Hospital Medical School

Peter Storey
M.D., F.R.C.P., F.R.C.Psych., D.P.M.
Consultant Psychiatrist to St George's Hospital
and Springfield Hospital, London

NINTH EDITION

CHURCHILL LIVINGSTONE
EDINBURGH LONDON AND NEW YORK 1980

CHURCHILL LIVINGSTONE
Medical Division of the Longman Group Limited

Distributed in the United States of America by
Churchill Livingstone Inc., 19 West 44th Street,
New York, N.Y. 10036, and by associated companies,
branches and representatives throughout
the world.

First edition 1943
Second edition 1945
Third edition 1949
Fourth edition 1955
Fifth edition 1963
Sixth edition 1969
Seventh edition 1972
Eighth edition 1976
Ninth edition 1980

ISBN 0 443 02192 9

British Library Cataloguing in Publication Data
Curran, Desmond
  Psychological medicine. – 9th ed.
  1. Mental illness
  I. Title II. Partridge, Maurice
  III. Storey, Peter
  616.8'9   RC454   80-40029

Printed in Singapore by Singapore Offset Printing Pte Ltd

Preface

In this edition I have continued the process of revision and updating, and have brought in a good deal of new material without significantly lengthening the book.

There is a completely new chapter on psychiatry in the aged, a subject of steadily increasing importance, and the section on psychotherapy has been radically altered. Many other changes have been made throughout the text: for example, more epidemiological data and greater emphasis on psychiatry in relationship to the rest of medicine in Chapter 1; considerable changes in Chapter 6 on organic mental states; more on the aetiology of schizophrenia and factors related to relapse; more detail on the ways in which depression can present with physical disorders, and on the assessment of suicidal risk; and changes also in the sections on mental handicap, anxiety states, alcoholism, drug addiction, and in the chapter on treatment.

Changes have been made partly because new information is available, and partly expressing changing attitudes and approaches to the problems of psychiatry. They have also been made in an attempt to answer the questions put to me by medical students, who are increasingly interested in and sophisticated about psychiatry.

As before I have tried to maintain the clarity of expression and the practical and clinical outlook of this book, for which it was always distinguished in the hands of its previous authors.

London, 1980   P. S.

Contents

MPT→

Reactive Depression.

1

Introductory

Psychiatry is a word derived from two Greek words meaning respectively 'mind' and 'medical treatment'. It has thus an exact meaning: it is that branch of medicine that aims at the treatment of mental ill-health. Its aims are therapeutic and it is an integral part of medicine. In this it differs from psychology, with which it is often confused.

Psychology means 'study of the mind'. Since no experience can come to us without participation of the mind, it is clear that such a study must be vast. Psychology has studied the processes involved in such mental functions as perception, memory and learning. It has studied the nature of intelligence and of personality. It has studied behaviour, both of individuals and of groups. It has applied such studies to different aspects of life with the consequent development of specialities, such as educational psychology, vocational psychology, industrial psychology. Apart from normal processes, it has studied abnormal ones, as in abnormal psychology. But it differs from psychiatry in that it is not an integral part of medicine, though in some way related to it, and its aims are not therapeutic, although it has made incidental contributions to therapy, and more and more clinical psychologists are involved in treatment.

This book provides no synopsis or outline of normal psychology, because we feel the subject cannot usefully be compressed into a small enough space. Several books on the subject are recommended in the bibliography.

Psychiatry may be defined as that branch of medicine the special province of which is the study, prevention and treatment of mental ill-health, however produced. The preventive aspect is often called *mental hygiene*.

The scope of psychiatry
Put in the most general terms, mental ill-health is experienced subjectively as a substantial impairment of comfort and happiness, and is shown objectively as a substantial impairment of efficiency or

of the capacity for satisfactory social relationships. The range of clinical material is thus very wide, extending from those whose conditions are sufficiently severe to call for institutional treatment, through those whose conditions, though less severely disabling, may none the less be potent sources of personal misery and social inefficiency, to the 'social problem group' of maladjusted misfits, delinquents and drunkards.

It may be said with truth that many of these are social rather than medical problems. In practice, however, many of them become the subjects of psychiatric care. Whether they do so or not is determined by practical considerations. It is not a theoretical question of where the boundaries of psychiatry begin and end, but a practical one of who is best equipped to deal with the particular problem that is presented. It is not that psychiatry wishes to make territorial demands, but because delinquency and alcoholism are often bound up with problems of personality and psychiatric illness that such cases are often referred for psychiatric opinion and advice.

Mental health should be seen as a spectrum rather than as a category. At one end we have a rarely realised ideal of health, with emotional stability, an absence of distorting neurotic feelings, personal happiness, and good relations with family, work and society. Few people are in that ideal state the whole time, and most would be represented somewhere along our hypothetical spectrum. At the other end it shades off through varying degrees of unhappiness and difficulties in coping into mental illness. This concept is a gross oversimplification of course: many people function well in certain respects and poorly in others, and some major mental illnesses affect people who otherwise cope quite happily with life.

It is worth noting that in some respects each culture and subculture will have its own views of what constitutes an 'ideal' relationship with, for example, society. This is shown very clearly in the clash of opinion between the U.S.S.R. and the Western world about psychiatric illness as an explanation of political dissidence. Another example currently causing problems in Britain, especially in immigrant families, is the incompatibility of traditional Indian and modern British views about the ideal relationships between children and parents.

The mentally healthy person copes with life and its problems, including those of growing up, without undue subjective distress, and without causing undue distress to others, unless subjected to extraordinary pressures. Even when under great pressure, he or she remains able to recognise what the problem is, and to tolerate much distress, without losing self control or the ability to respond in an adaptive and coping way.

The size of the problem

Mental disturbances are common, and many of them are seriously disabling. Statistics produced in different parts of the world and in different historical periods are very difficult to interpret, because of varying diagnostic practices and different methods of case identification and recording. Even between the U.S.A. and the U.K. there are some big diagnostic differences. For example, in some parts of the U.S.A. quite different criteria for the diagnosis of schizophrenia are in use from those in this country, differences which may not be apparent in, for example, an article about treatment or prognosis. The usual European diagnostic criteria are used in this book, but in the U.S.A. quite different criteria, based on concepts of ego-boundaries and ego-strength derived from psychoanalytic theories, are widely used. As a result schizophrenia is diagnosed more often, and affective illness and personality disorder less often, especially in young adults. Different diagnostic practices should always be allowed for when reading foreign articles or books.

Many people believe that there has been a rapid increase in rates of psychiatric illness in the West, but there is no good evidence for this idea. Rather, we have increasingly elaborate psychiatric services, a decreasing willingness to tolerate distress, and an increasing demand for help—from professionals—with problems and symptoms which in the past were accepted as part of a burdensome life which could not be changed and so must be borne. At present the demand seems limitless.

Nor is there solid evidence that modern urban life is more 'stressful' than rural life, or than life in less developed countries. Although we invoke 'stress' so frequently, in fact it remains a poorly defined concept. We all tend to identify our own problems more than those of others, but when rural communities in underdeveloped countries, for example, are studied adequately, a high incidence of both major and minor mental disturbance is always found; even if to the nostalgic Westerner the life seems peaceful compared to his own.

We have made progress in quantifying some of the factors which lead to schizophrenic relapse and depressive illness, by the use of life events schedules and by studies of the emotional interactions in the families (p. 135), and this field is developing rapidly. It remains difficult to be precise about the relationship of mental or psychosomatic illness to factors such as long working hours, excessive responsibility, frustration, continually suppressed anger, pressure to 'beat the clock', and very many other matters which clinical observation and common sense tell us are frequently relevant. A central problem here is that what to one person is a pleasure is to another a pain.

Frequency of mental illness

There are several different methods of identifying and describing the frequency of mental illness, the details of which would be inappropriate here (see Bibliography) but some of the main findings are worth mentioning.

In an extremely thorough study of a Swedish rural community, in which a psychiatrist examined every individual within a brief period of time, the prevalence figures were: psychoses 1.7 per cent; neuroses (excluding minor disturbances) 13 per cent; mental deficiency 1.2 per cent. The estimated cumulative risk in this population, was that by the age of 60 years, 43.4 per cent of men and 73.0 per cent of the women would have had some significant mental disorder; and that 'severe impairment' would have been suffered by 7.9 per cent and 15.4 per cent respectively of men and women. These are very high rates, but many studies around the world have come up with similar, and often with higher rates. For example, surveying a population in Manhattan, but using a questionnaire method, with very different definitions, 815 out of 1000 people were found to have some psychiatric symptoms, and 234:1000 were considered significantly impaired, and to be 'psychiatric cases'. When the Swedish and American researchers concerned in these two reports did a kind of cross-check study, they found that if the American criteria were applied to the Swedish population, the neurosis rate rose from 13.1 to almost 40 per cent; the mental deficiency rate from 1.2 to 10 per cent; but that the psychosis rate did not change. These details are given as a reminder of the difficulties of making comparisons in this field, and of maintaining a critical attitude when presented with mental health statistics.

In Britain many surveys have also been done. One important general practice study showed that individual doctors varied in their estimates of psychiatric morbidity in their own practices between 37.8 and 323 per 1000. This almost tenfold difference is determined by doctors attitudes, interests, and skills, more than by population characteristics; although emotionally disturbed patients do tend to join the lists of doctors likely to give them a sympathetic hearing.

Socially unstable poor populations also have much higher psychiatric morbidity rates than more settled and prosperous areas.

Mental illness among medical patients

Many studies have concentrated on medical and surgical wards and outpatient clinics, and all find high incidences of psychiatric problems. Again there are major differences depending on the method of study, the criteria used, nationality, and so on. Some examples are: a 51 per cent incidence of psychiatric symptoms in newly referred medical outpatients in a London hospital; a 34 per cent incidence in patients with small intestine disease at another; significant depression in 43 of 150 medical inpatients; and almost 50 per cent of a series of patients with abdominal pain with an alcohol problem.

Very often the psychiatric symptoms of these medical and surgical patients are unrecognised until the special study is made. It is as important for the doctor to take a brief psychiatric history and examine the mental state in *every* patient admitted, as it is to ask about dyspnoea and measure the blood pressure. Not only is suicide a common cause of death, but psychiatric symptoms cause much personal suffering.

In many of the patients picked up in these surveys outlined above, there might be no useful treatment, or the disturbance may be only a transient reaction; but in some, serious mental illness might be usefully treated.

Hospital admission statistics

Hospital admission rates are much higher now than they were twenty years ago, although, as has been pointed out earlier, this does not mean that mental illness is commoner, but rather reflects altered attitudes and improved facilities.

In England and Wales first admissions to psychiatric units of all kinds rose from 98 to 137 per 100 000 of population between 1954 and 1970, an increase of 40 per cent. Total admissions rose from 162 to 374 per 100 000, a 125 per cent increase; which is due at least in part to the high number of readmissions inseparable from our present system of encouraging early return to the community.

Between 1970 and 1975 however, there was a 10 per cent fall in first admissions, the first fall since figures were first collected in 1898. This may well reflect improved treatment by general practitioners and in outpatients, especially with antidepressants, which are now used more skilfully. No figures after 1975 are available at the time of writing.

The chances of an individual being admitted to a psychiatric unit of some type during his or her lifetime therefore fell slightly in 1975 to approximately 1 in 8 women and 1 in 12 men, from the earlier high point of 1 in 6 women and 1 in 9 men. The commonest age for first admission is between 20 and 30 years of age. The rates fall to a minimum at about 60 years old, and rise steeply after 65, as dementia becomes increasingly common.

The normal and abnormal in psychiatry

The word 'normal' is used in different senses. When we say that a person is of normal height, we refer to someone who is neither very small nor very tall, but whose height approximates to the statistically average. But when a dentist says that someone has normal teeth, he means something different; he means that the teeth are without blemish, which is far from statistically average. In general medicine, 'normal' is often used to indicate an absence of physical pathology. In psychiatry, we use the word 'normal' in the first sense, to denote something that is more or less average rather than something that is perfect or ideal. That is to say, the normal can only be judged against its background, and the normality or abnormality of a person thus comes to depend on that person's background. A person is physically abnormal when he shows some special difference in physique from other people, and mentally abnormal when he fails to adapt to his social background as other people do. Even so, the differences between one person and another are so great and so variable that it is very difficult to define the normal.

In considering single characteristics, such as height or colour of the hair, it is clear that we must allow for a wide range of variation; in such a far more complicated matter as behaviour, the range is bound to be even wider. Behaviour that passes as normal in Chelsea or Soho might not be considered so in Cheltenham or Tunbridge Wells. When society is viewed as a whole, therefore, we must allow a very wide range as coming within normal limits. We must not stigmatise as pathological something that merely happens to conflict with our own standards. Whereas in general medicine the criteria of whether the haemoglobin, the gastric juice or the basal metabolic rate is normal may be fairly strictly defined, the criteria of psychiatric abnormality are less exact, although it is true that in both the normal shades into the abnormal by gradual degrees. Extraordinary behaviour in itself is not evidence necessarily of mental illness. The diagnosis of mental illness requires the additional presence of other symptoms so that the whole condition can reasonably be regarded as constituting a psychiatric syndrome. In brief, normal people can behave in extraordinary ways. The statistically abnormal, or merely eccentric person is not necessarily a psychiatric problem. Abnormality leads to psychiatric problems when there is failure to adapt to society and when such failure of adaptation causes either social nuisance to others, or distress to the individual concerned. Such distress usually arises either from inefficiency at work or from inability to make or maintain satisfactory social relationships.

Development of psychiatry
The first flowering in Europe was during the great period of the Greek and Roman Empires, when disciples of Aesculapius and later Hippocrates first claimed to treat the mind, until then the province of mysticism rather than of science. Clinical observation led to the development of therapeutic programmes; the patients were studied as individuals, treated with sedatives, and soothed or stimulated by special baths or music. It is of historical interest that balneo-therapy was revived within our own time and that music again had a therapeutic vogue in the 1950s. But after the decay of the Roman Empire psychiatry, as a clinical study or field of scientific enquiry, virtually ceased to exist until the effects of the Renaissance came very slowly to reach the problem of mental illness more than a thousand years later. It was not until the end of the eighteenth century that psychiatry began to flower again.

In Britain a special fillip was given to this process by a chance but important event, the development of recurrent attacks of sustained and uncontrollable excitement by King George the Third. The picture, as described by Fanny Burney, the authoress, in her diary of 1789, when governess at the Court, is that of mania: the severe insomnia, the intense over-activity of the King, the persistent overtalkativeness until the royal larynx became quite hoarse, the continual pottering and ill-directed bustle, and indeed the erotic pursuit by the Monarch of Miss Burney herself through the shrubberies at Kew. (Recent historical research has suggested porphyria as the cause.) The agitated medical consultations and the difficulty of the treatment aroused public interest so that the progress of the august patient did much to focus attention on the welfare of less eminent sufferers. By the beginning of the nineteenth century scientific enquiry and humanitarianism had again begun to exert effect. The re-birth of psychiatric practice in Europe began less than two hundred years ago.

Attention was paid at first mainly to the major mental illnesses, the insanities. The workers occupied themselves first with introducing a more humanitarian approach. The abolition of restraint was advocated by Pinel in France, and by Conolly in Britain. The provision of suitable forms of occupation was encouraged by Tuke. By about 1850 the custodial care of the patients had been improved altogether beyond recognition. These advances have been continued and extended, even during our own time. The huge barrack-like hospitals of the nineteenth century, though themselves an advance, have been increasingly replaced by others of less obviously institutional design, with the introduction of a series of villas to replace vast blocks and enormous wards.

Following this, the trend has been to have psychiatric units in general hospitals serving a certain district, in the hope that ultimately large mental hospitals would become unnecessary, because chronic patients could be maintained mainly in the community. In 1979, at the time of writing, we can still see a need for long term hospital care of a fair number of chronically ill patients in the future.

Factors other than that of better organisation have helped towards improvements in treatment. Pharmaceutical advances with the provision of better drugs have contributed enormously, especially over recent years; and so has public enlightenment. There have been developments in clinical psychology, psychotherapy, nursing practices, occupational therapy, and in diagnosis and the selection of treatment. The remoteness of the mental hospital from ordinary life has been much reduced, as has the stigma that attached to it. Social workers, acting as a liaison between the patient and his family and between the family and the hospital, and making home visits, the encouragement of visiting, periodic leave and 'open days', the organisation of lay helpers, the trend towards returning the patient to the community as far as possible, the provision by local authorities and charitable organisations of after-care homes and hostels for the recovering or partially recovered patient, and the arrangements for providing suitable employment on discharge, have made great alterations for the better in the psychiatric scene.

At the same time that all these reforms were beginning in the nineteenth century, clinical studies were also afoot, directed at first mainly to observation and thence to the descriptive classification of illness. Here the difficulties were peculiar owing to the wide variations from case to case, the absence of objective signs, and the fluctuations shown by the illnesses in their often very long duration. None the less by the end of the century, and largely under the influence of the German psychiatrist, Kraepelin, the confusion previously surrounding psychiatric illnesses had been largely resolved, a categorisation into differing disease-entities had been established, and a workable classification was mapped out. This was an enormous advance; in view of the difficulties a remarkable one, and far greater than may be generally realised.

The extent of the advance can be gauged by comparing events at the beginning and end of the century. In 1815, Dr Thomas Monro, physician to the Royal Bethlehem Hospital, gave evidence to a Board of Enquiry. Many of his patients had been kept in chains for years, and he described his practice in the following words: 'The patients are ordered to be bled about the latter end of May or the beginning of May according to the weather. And after they have been bled they take vomits daily or every other day for a certain number of weeks. After that we purge the patients. That has been the practice invariably for years, long before my time, and it was handed down to me by my father, and I don't know any better practice'. These routine hit-or-miss methods, indiscriminately applied to fettered patients, may be contrasted with the brilliant lecture-demonstrations, teaching the symptomatology of different illnesses with lucid exposition of the differential diagnostic points, that were given in his humane and enlightened hospital by Kraepelin only seventy-five years later.

The value of these methods of descriptive classification was great. To take a specific example, it would have been impossible without them to have linked general paralysis of the insane to its prodromal condition, primary syphilis. In this way, they have paved the way for the subsequent development of treatments for a variety of conditions. But more generally, they brought order almost for the first time to an otherwise chaotic subject; by emphasising the features held in common, they correctly brought together into a related group the apparently heterogeneous illnesses that we now know under the collective term 'schizophrenia', and by long-term study they showed that the apparently contrasting conditions of mania and melancholia were essentially related to each other as the contrasting phases of the same illness, manic-depressive psychosis. These, and other observations, produced clarity from chaos, and by aiding prognosis made for the more effective management of the various conditions.

However, there were drawbacks. First, there were many points at which the classification broke down, owing to the tendency for mixed states to occur, and for illnesses to change their forms as they progressed. Second, and more formidably, these methods yielded no positive indications either as to aetiology or to specific treatment. Kraepelin's approach to psychiatric illness was that which is traditional in general medicine. He viewed psychiatric conditions as disease entities, with an aetiology, pathology, symptomatology, course and prognosis of their own. On this basis he achieved much, but the aetiology and pathology persistently eluded him—except in general paralysis of the insane. He sought for a pathology in terms of structural lesions of the brain, or of biochemical disturbances affecting cerebral function. He did not find it. He was therefore led to infer that the aetiology and pathology depended on hereditary and constitutional factors of an unknown kind. The inference was probably fundamentally correct, but it did not contribute to the problem of treatment. To that extent, the Kraepelinian approach was sterile. Once the classification, whatever its imperfections, had been more or less generally accepted, it was on that sterility that attention came to be focused, although its enduring value is shown now by the fact that different treatments have specific benefits in diagnostic groups based on those Kraepelin originally described.

Around the turn of the century, therefore, other methods were explored. At this time Sigmund Freud, a Viennese neurologist, came upon a number of cases whose symptoms seemed to date from particular incidents that they were at first unable to remember, but whose occurrence was later elicited under hypnosis. With recovery of the memory and adjustment of the patients' attitudes towards the incidents concerned, some cases improved. From this sprang the concept of the 'unconscious mind'. This was in itself nothing new, for it had been written and spoken of by various nineteenth-century thinkers, such as Samuel Butler, the author of *Erewhon*. But its application to psychiatry initiated a trend away from the formal and traditional concepts of mental illness as a disease process, as in other medical conditions, in favour of viewing such illness in a more dynamic way in terms of reaction to events past or present, conscious or unconscious. This was a new conception, and to some extent a sound one. Further, it was attractive in that it offered therapeutic possibilities. Freud's ideas gave rise to the form of treatment called *psycho-analysis*. In order to explain mental illness in terms of reaction he formed the theory that its symptoms arose from a failure of the normal emotional development. Such failure came gradually and increasingly to be attributed to emotional stresses that were alleged to have occurred in childhood or infancy. This theory was further expanded until it sought to explain even the major illnesses, the insanities, as arising from a failure of normal emotional maturation owing to childhood or infantile experiences.

At about the same time, Adolf Meyer in the Unites States also began to conceive of mental illness in terms of reaction, and developed what he called the *psycho-biological* approach. This was conceived on a wider basis than the psycho-analytic theory, was realistic, and took cognisance of physical factors in mental illness. Its essence was that each patient should be considered as an individual, and his illness interpreted in terms of the effect upon him of the life-situation through which he had passed.

Both psycho-biology and psycho-analysis have made contributions to knowledge, and it is difficult to assess which has had the greater influence. It is possible that Meyer, with his scientific and practical approach, had the greater influence within the profession; it is a mark of this that most standard psychiatric textbooks have for many years taught in terms of 'schizophrenic reaction-types' and 'manic-depressive reaction-types' instead of treating schizophrenia and manic-depressive psychosis as illnesses in their own right, as had Kraepelin. Psycho-analysis, on the other hand, has had a greater vogue amongst people of a less scientific and practical kind. Its concepts have dominated psychiatry in the United States since the Second World War, but are beginning to lose ground to the more medical and biological views current in Europe. Its vogue has been great enough to lead some people to believe that psycho-analysis *is* psychiatry, whereas it is one particular form of treatment, based on a specialised theory.

It is easy to understand how both these schools of thought came to receive a special welcome, since they arose from attempts to solve the aetiological and therapeutic deadlock that had been reached by the traditional medical approach to psychiatric problems. Neither fulfilled the original hopes. Further, in that psycho-analysis came to ignore the physical factors in mental illness, and both ignored, or almost ignored, the hereditary and constitutional factors, they succeeded in diverting attention from some very important aspects. A proper balance of psychological, physical, and constitutional factors remains the ideal way of understanding the patient.

Some popular fallacies of the last sixty years
Ideas, derived from psycho-analytic theory, that if all be laid bare, then various unconscious factors may be revealed hitherto impeding the development and progress of the patient, encourage belief in limitless possibilities of 'cure'. Such belief takes no account of the potentialities, which may be limited, with which the individual started life. Nor should the unconscious be regarded as an explanatory widow's cruse.

But once ideas of the limitless are current, limitless hopes may be raised. In this connection, mention may be made of the recently alleged applicability of psychiatry to politics and international relations, as though wars could be prevented and revolutions outmoded by sexual hygiene or breast feeding. The currency of these ideas has done nothing to enhance the reputation of psychiatry.

Conversely, the fact that the Kraepelinian school was therapeutically unproductive within its time has led to the fallacy, never roundly expressed but often implied, that to say a condition is primarily constitutional is also to say that it is untreatable. This is not the case. In general medicine, pernicious anaemia and diabetes were at one time considered constitutional conditions; in some sense they still are, but they are treatable.

Another common fallacy is that all mental illness is a flight from reality in a conscious or unconscious attempt to find a pleasanter milieu. This may or may not be the case in an individual instance, but as a general proposition it is nonsense. For example, very old people may in fact be out of touch with reality to some extent, but it is absurd to suppose that this is necessarily so because they have wished it, either consciously or unconsciously.

Again, there tends to be a popular idea that the psychiatrist encourages free expression, frowns upon discipline and recommends the utmost licence. This is also nonsense, and seems to have arisen from misinterpretation of the term 'repression' which Freud's translators used in a special sense.

PSYCHIATRY AND THE REST OF MEDICAL PRACTICE

In addition to the psychoses, neuroses, and the various syndromes and reactions described in this book, emotional factors are important throughout the practice of clinical medicine in all its branches. They must be considered in situations ranging from reactions of patients to their doctors, and vice versa; through such problems as the attitude of a patient to his renal dialysis, of a spouse to a colostomy, of a mother to breast feeding; and reactions like those of a child to a grandparents' death or the arrival of a new baby in the family. There are no situations in clinical medicine in which people's feelings are not relevant, and in which emotional reactions of unexpected intensity may not suddenly disturb something outwardly straightforward. We outline in this section some of the more important types of problem which can arise.

The doctor–patient relationship

Doctors are in an unusual position in society, carrying so much personal responsibility, and belonging to a closed professional group with long traditions and a powerful mystique. Few people feel neutral about them or approach them for help as they would a plumber. It might be easier if they did. Accompanying the rational appraisal the patient makes of the doctor, and beneath the surface of the professional interview, many patients have a childlike dependence on, and an idealised image of, their doctor. The more ill the person, or the child or spouse who is the focus of treatment, the more complete is the 'handing over' of responsibility to the doctor and to the profession. It is true that with an increasingly sophisticated population a more criticial view is being taken of doctors, but most people still react when ill as their parents did. This trusting dependence is on the whole welcomed by doctors, and by nurses, as it makes it easier to organise and carry out treatments which often involve discomfort, pain and even danger, as in major surgery; it is also welcomed because it makes people feel valued and respected—something everyone likes.

Doctors are supported in the responsibility they carry by the structure of the medical profession. To the outsider it often seems like a union 'closed shop', and is often criticised and resented, but the profession enables individuals to carry responsibilities and problems under which an unsupported individual would collapse.

Occasionally, perhaps because of some mishap, but more commonly arising from the personalities of the patient and doctor concerned, the relationship is strained or even breaks down. The patient's bitterness and anger are often based not only on the outward reality of what has happened, but often on a sense of betrayal or rejection, more appropriate to the feelings of a child for a parent than of one adult to another. We are then dealing with so-called 'transference' problems.

The term 'transference' is one introduced by Freud. It refers to the way in which emotions are 'transferred' from important childhood figures to people in adult life, where they can seriously distort relationships by bringing in an inappropriate intensity of feeling, often accompanied by an expectation of some strong emotional response—usually of a parental kind. All this happens without the individual concerned clearly recognising the existence of these feelings, never mind their source in earlier life (see p. 372).

Doctors, and most especially psychiatrists, who should know better, are more prone than any other group of people to find themselves in difficult transference situations, which can get completely out of hand unless recognised. For example, if a woman regularly attending her doctor has, in addition to the objective reality of her symptoms or problems, powerful but unconscious feelings for him derived from her feelings for her own father; and if that father had been dearly loved but had abandoned the family for another woman when she was seven years old, then trouble is quite likely. Any steps the doctor takes to end the series of consultations may be experienced as further abandonment, and the violence of the emotions generated can be surprising and disturbing. These situations can be avoided best by recognising that they can and do occur, and openly discussing the possibility with the patient in a calm way, as described in the section on psychotherapy (p. 374).

Doctors being human they too have their own emotional preferences and sympathies, dictated by their own development and experiences; and transference distortions (called 'counter-transference' in psychoanalysis when they refer to the doctor's unconscious feelings for the patient) can also occur. At a day to day level this is often no more than that an individual doctor may be happier dealing with, for example, middle-aged women than with men of his own age, or vice versa.

The special position of doctors, especially male, leads them often to become the object of amorous feelings often inextricably mingled with the kind of transference feeling mentioned above. Their position also facilitates sexual advances by either doctor or patient, and the very strict rules laid down for professional conduct by, for example, the General Medical Council in this country, are a recognition of these dangers. The Hippocratic Oath contains '. . . refraining from all wrongdoing or corruption, and especially from any act of seduction, of male or female, bond or free . . .' which perhaps reflects the same problems in a very different culture.

Reactions to illness

The reactions of patients and their families to illness are usually as expected—appropriate concern and action, and most people can display great fortitude when it is really necessary. Problems may arise unexpectedly when a patient's reactions seem inappropriate to the situation. A common cause of this is the fear of cancer or some grave illness, even if to the doctor there is nothing serious. In other cases the opposite happens, and the patient seems unable to face the reality of a serious situation, failing to consult the doctor about obviously sinister developments such as a lump in the breast or haematuria. People can deny to themselves the reality of intolerable worries not only about physical illness, but about situations such as the impending death of a child, or the probability that the spouse is having an affair. There is in fact a wide spectrum of possible responses, from excessive hypochrondriacal worry, through realistic concern, to total denial.

Nearly all serious illnesses need not only physical resistance and effective treatment, but cooperation by the patient and some spirit and will to live. When someone loses this the prognosis worsens, and people can give up and die unexpectedly. A man to whom this applied was a 50-year-old who had been caring for his hemiplegic wife after a stroke, when he had a myocardial infarct, and consequent renal damage. He coped well with renal dialysis, awaiting a renal transplant, until each of his brothers refused to donate a kidney. He became depressed and apathetic, ceased to cooperate actively, and died a few months later.

It is common for people suffering from chronic painful conditions to become depressed. Chronic rheumatoid and osteo-arthritis, with the limitations they impose on life, and the feeling of hopelessness they engender, are good examples. Depression lowers the individual's capacity to cope, and often leads to an increased awareness of the pain and stiffness, lessens the ability to take an interest in other things, and generally intensifies the patient's suffering. Many of these patients can be helped by antidepressants and by lessening social isolation, and the doctor should always be alert to the possibility of depression, and not regard it as inevitable and untreatable in this type of illness.

Physical symptoms and emotional disturbances

Emotional disturbances and psychiatric illnesses can present with physical symptoms which suggest, or even mimic, physical disease, and can be very misleading. Some of these presentations are briefly mentioned in later sections, as are constipation, anorexia, and weight loss in depression. Usually these are obviously secondary to depression, but sometimes one or more may become the major presenting problem. For example, constipation in an elderly man, in whom the depression is not recognised, may lead to detailed investigation for a bowel neoplasm, and the patient's increasing agitation is then regarded as due to natural worry about cancer. A patient with anorexia and weight loss, again secondary to depression, may be similarly investigated for carcinoma of the stomach. These are natural mistakes, and in fact the clinical picture may demand such investigation. What is a clinical error is to fail to think of depression as a cause after negative investigations, and turn the patient away with reassurances which do nothing for the underlying depression. It is as important for the physician, or surgeon, to be able to examine the mental state briefly, as for a psychiatrist to be able to do a neurological examination.

There are several other very common misleading presentations, and a host of uncommon ones. Palpitations and tachycardia due to anxiety, often associated with chest pain and dyspnoea, are perhaps the most common, and rarely go unrecognised by the doctor after screening investigations, especially for thyrotoxicosis. Unfortunately, many patients experience cardiac symptoms in panic attacks, with a fear of passing out or impending death, and they can be very difficult to reassure. If they fail to improve after reassurance it is not enough to prescribe a benzodiazepine and discharge them. They should be examined psychiatrically and treated appropriately.

A closely related and equally common problem presents when a patient reacts to some organic illness with an abnormal degree of anxiety. This is perhaps most common with cardiovascular disease, when anxiety raises blood pressure, causes tachycardia, dyspnoea, easy fatigue, and other symptoms which could be due either to the illness or to the patient's reaction. The heart has profound connotations as the very mainspring of life and seat of the emotions, and heart disease is a frightening idea to almost everyone.

Many patients after myocardial infarction need psychological rehabilitation as well as appropriate physical treatment. It has been demonstrated that psychological counselling, with discussion of the fears about activity, especially of sexual intercourse and its risks, and similar anxieties, improves functional recovery after myocardial infarcts, and greatly lessens the hypochrondriacal invalidism which is a common sequel.

The role of emotion in the causation of physical disease is considered in the section on Psychosomatic Medicine (p. 342).

There are some very common conditions in which it is almost impossible to sort out organic or physical factors from the patients emotional reactions and problems. As an example we can take a major cause of disability, chronic backache; especially in those cases in young or middle aged people who have lumbar pain, absent or slight radiological evidence of disease, and no neurological signs.

Back pain often has a 'dragging' and wearing down quality, and if severe and long lasting often leads to some depressive feelings. Difficulties in the home or at work, especially if there is much unexpressed resentment, commonly cause emotional tension, which in turn leads to muscular tension. If there is already some spasm of the lumbar muscles the emotional tension increases this, and a vicious circle of increasing pain, irritability, domestic tension and inability to work in comfort, is soon established. This situation is a common one, and responds badly to treatment, especially if the pain began after an industrial accident for which there is a possibility of compensation (see p. 101 for compensation neurosis). The patients involved tend to be tense and resentful people, with a complaining quality, but how much this is basic to the personality, and how much secondary to chronic pain and a lack of relief from treatment by doctors, is uncertain in many cases.

A related problem is chronic neck ache in depressed and tense people, more in older women than in others, in whom there is pain and spasm in the shoulder girdle and posterior neck muscles. The slightly stooping, head bowed posture of the depressive; the presence of strong resentments and tensions in the home—often unexpressed because of fear of the consequences—and some degree of cervical osteo-arthritis, combine to form a very characteristic picture, in which treatment by physical means alone is rarely successful. Several old sayings sum up the role of resentment and other emotions in causing pain, discomfort, and so on. 'He gives me a pain in the neck' and 'you make me sick' are common, and often relevant. How much such emotions can lead to structural pathology is a different matter, considered briefly in the section on psychosomatic medicine, but they can certainly intensify symptoms if pathology is already present.

These few examples are given only to illustrate the kind of inter-relationships of physical and emotional problems which are so common in general practice. In any patient who fails to improve as expected from some straightforward seeming condition, it is worth reviewing not only the diagnosis and the treatment used, but also to consider whether some conflict, important life problem, hidden alcoholism, or depression is delaying recovery.

Reactions to death and dying

It is a common observation that over the past 60 years there has been a reversal of attitudes about death and sex. The public expression of grief and mourning has declined, and people have become embarrassed to show their sadness to the world and to their friends, while the opposite has happened with the overt discussion and almost morbid exploitation of sex.

This is relevant to the care of dying patients, whom it is too easy to avoid as soon as there seems to be no more active treatment to offer, because even doctors and nurses can be uncertain how to approach the patient, and to talk about impending death. Even clergymen are less able to do this now, and rarely attempt to help people 'prepare their souls to meet their Maker', as few have this type of religious belief now, and seem to be more involved in a form of social work.

The dying can become sadly isolated, and in addition to the careful relief of pain and other distressing symptoms it can help to give them the time and encouragement to talk about their situation, feelings, regrets and hopes. Most people dying realise it, even though they may not discuss it with their family, each side sometimes thinking that the other could not cope with it if it were brought out into the open.

Difficulties of the student in psychiatry

The difficulties in establishing the aetiology of the major mental illnesses have been, and are, so great that psychiatry lacks much of the precision found elsewhere in medicine. This, together with the difficulty of measuring mental characteristics and the frequent absence of physical signs, tends to discourage the student who has been rightly imbued with the importance of exact observation, and who expects symptoms to be correlated with signs. The insistence of the curriculum on pathology, in a strictly organic and physical sense, makes the student less at ease when dealing with conditions whose physical pathology cannot be directly demonstrated. Moreover, the sin of 'missing' the organic lesion encourages concentration on the organic aspects with neglect of the psychological ones, rather than viewing the patient as a whole.

The student is also often discouraged by the personality of some neurotic patients who may arouse antagonism by being demanding, critical and ungrateful, or who, through inadequacy or selfishness, may evoke moral disapproval. He is then liable to transfer this attitude to psychiatric patients as a whole; in doing so he may be reinforced by the popular fallacy that all psychiatric illness arises from an unwillingness to face life and is an attempt to escape from difficulty.

As we all have problems, and they may be those of the man in the street, certain students may have difficulty at first in taking an objective view of the patient owing to their own emotional entanglements, and these may lead them either to avoid the issue or to becomes too closely involved in it. Detachment comes with practice.

Such views lead to mental illness being regarded as a stigma, and therefore to reluctance to diagnose it, especially if the patient is of like mind and of a sort to evoke sympathy. The student is tempted in all these ways to shun psychiatry and psychiatric considerations in illness. Then, when he is qualified, he finds himself in the predicament that, if he does make a psychiatric diagnosis, he has no very clear idea of what can or should be done. This in itself discourages him from making it. When, in his turn, he comes to teach, the cycle is repeated as the next generation follows his example. Fortunately, an increasing number of physicians now take an intelligent interest in the psychiatric aspects of medicine, and there is far less danger than there was of these unrealistic attitudes being perpetuated.

Aims of psychiatric teaching

The student should have a working knowledge of psychiatry sufficient for most practical purposes. This is easier to obtain than it was. Psychiatry is no longer confined to mental hospitals, cut off from the world and the rest of medicine by their walls, their reputation and their geographical remoteness. Even so, the facilities for learning are still inadequate and will remain so until psychiatry and general medicine are more closely linked, to their mutual advantage, by teaching. The only satisfactory way to achieve this is by the establishment of psychiatric units, with in-patient accommodation, as an integral part of all teaching hospitals and medical centres. This is steadily in progress in Britain.

There are other aims in psychiatric teaching for medical students. As in general medicine and surgery, he has to learn how to approach the problem, how to gather information, and how to think constructively about it. This is more basic than learning the clinical features and treatment of the main psychiatric syndromes, important though that is. One of the greatest difficulties comes in the gathering of the information, because it needs an openness of mind and alertness to subtle clues to detect the presence of some emotional disturbance during a brief consultation about headache or dyspepsia.

The necessary basic knowledge can be obtained without too much difficulty, and it can be applied to the individual case, if, when the history is taken, a reasonable estimate of the mental and emotional characteristics of the patient is made at the same time as the physical assessment. This need cause no great trouble, as will be shown. It will repay by increasing the accuracy of the diagnosis and prognosis as well as helping in the general management of the case, whatever the nature of the condition that is being dealt with. Such an assessment may not be very exact, but it is a great deal better than none at all. After all, medicine is not an exact science; it is an art which uses scientific methods when it can. The essence of being a good clinician is not to use a calculating machine or ready-reckoner, but to exercise a judgment trained in assessing a large number of variables, amongst which psychological factors are not the least important. Apart from problems that are specifically psychiatric, there is inevitably some psychiatric aspect to every case, and it should never be neglected.

2

The aetiology of mental illness

In psychiatry mind and body are considered inseparable, but this has not always been so. The nature and causes of consciousness have never been fully understood. It seems certain, however, that mental activity does depend on the integrated functioning of the nervous system, and therefore on the physical conditions necessary to sustain that function. For mental activity to be possible, there must be an adequate supply of blood to the brain, the blood must be within certain limits of acidity and alkalinity, and must contain certain quantities of oxygen and sugar. Thus, mental activity depends on physical conditions. For our present purposes, therefore, mind and body should not be considered as separate entities, as in the so-called psycho-physical dualism of the earlier philosophers, but should be considered as together forming a whole.

This concept is necessary for the understanding of mental illness. In every case both physical and mental factors have to be considered. The mental and physical make-up of a person are usually referred to together as the 'constitution'. The constitution is the whole person as he is at any one time, whatever the causes may be. The constitution is not a fixed or immutable thing, but develops and changes as life goes on. It includes not only the hereditary endowments both physical and mental with their innate tendencies, and the intrauterine environment, but also the effects of development and experience as shown by the patterns of behaviour that the person has acquired. In fact, the constitution predisposes the individual to react, both physically and mentally, in certain ways.

In order to understand any mental illness, one has to consider first the patient's physical and mental make-up, i.e. his constitution, second, the psychological and physical stresses imposed by his environment, and third, the effect of those stresses upon that constitution. That is, we have to consider in every case (1) psychological, (2) physical, and (3) constitutional factors. These three groups of factors are invariably present and operative in every case, though their practical importance may vary much from one case to another.

The terms psychological, physical and constitutional, denote only different aspects of the whole individual; they overlap, and their separation under these headings is artificial, but it is convenient for description and understanding.

Causation of mental illness as a process

Just as there is never a single and simple cause for normal behaviour, so there is never a single and simple cause for mental illness, which arises always from a variety of factors that combine to produce their effect. In fact, causation is a process involving physical and mental factors, both past and present.

For example, a person may develop a severe attack of rheumatic fever in childhood and as a result may develop mitral stenosis. His physical constitution has then been altered. If many limitations then have to be placed on his activities at home and at school, these will alter the direction of his interests and his adjustment towards his fellow-children, i.e. they will alter the mental aspects of his constitution also. If the attitude of his family has also been over-solicitous and over-protective, he may tend to take excessive care of himself and thus show unnecessary invalid tendencies. Such a person is then more likely to be disturbed by minor symptoms than the average person would be. Such a person developing palpitations in later life may then become excessively disturbed by them, fearing that they herald further heart disease, even though they may be only the normal products of anxiety in some particular situation. His fears may then lead him to be further anxious, with continuance of the palpitation as a result. Such a case can only be understood by considering the psychological, physical and constitutional factors that are involved, through study of the personal history of the patient.

Again, and apart from mental and physical factors that have occurred in the past, the patient may be affected in many ways by immediate environmental influences that exert both psychological and physical effects. Thus, unemployment may lead, through reducing income, to the physical effect of undernourishment as well as to the mental effect of reducing self-confidence. These two may then combine to lower the resistance to mental stress, leading to a rundown condition that may interfere with the appetite and general metabolism. Here again the case can only be understood by considering all three groups of factors, psychological, physical and constitutional, and it will be realised that such consideration calls for a medical training and a sound knowledge of general medicine, with which psychiatry must always be linked.

Relative importance of psychological, physical and constitutional factors

It has already been said that, though these three groups of factors are present in every case, their relative importance will vary from one case to another. In the first example given above, that of the man who experienced abnormal anxiety over palpitations in relation to his previous experience of heart disease, the principal factors were his fears, i.e. psychological factors, for it was those that caused the palpitations, and therefore the anxiety, to continue; but the physical factor of the mitral stenosis and his constitutional tendency to invalid reactions also contributed. In general, the cases in which psychological factors are aetiologically predominant should be intelligible in the following way. (1) The patients should be in clear consciousness and full touch with their surroundings; (2) their normal intellectual powers should be intact; and (3) they should be free from what are called distortions of content (delusions, p. 54, hallucinations, p. 61, misinterpretations. They should be free from physical lesions that could satisfactorily explain the symptoms. The symptoms should be comprehensible, in the light of the previous history and personality as a reaction to recent or immediate situations. The comprehensibility of the symptoms in these terms may require some judgement, and this question will be referred to later. But at this point it may be laid down as a general rule that where the patient shows (1) a physical abnormality that reasonably accounts for the symptoms, or (2) disturbance of consciousness, or (3) distortions of content, or (4) intellectual deterioration, the psychological factors are unlikely to be of predominant importance, and the principal causes should usually be sought elsewhere.

Now, suppose that we have two patients with typhoid fever, and one develops a delirium in course of it. He becomes confused, does not know the date or where he is, sees the pigs that he has bred running over the end of the bed, and hears the imaginary voices of his relatives calling, while he mistakes the identities of those around him. It would be difficult indeed to explain such a state as a mere psychological reaction. On the contrary, we know from previous experience of such cases that the delirium will pass as the physical condition improves. We recognise it as an accompaniment and ascribe it to the toxic effects of the illness; that is, the physical factors are of predominant importance. But the psychological factors also contribute, for the voices that he hears are the voices of his relatives, the animals that he sees are those with which he is familiar; that is, the individual symptoms are the products of his own personal experiences. These last have not caused the state, however, but have merely lent it individual and personal colouring. They have contributed, but in a way of secondary importance. What of the constitutional factors? These also have contributed, for we had two patients, and though the illnesses were equally severe with equal toxic effect, only one developed the delirium. The inference is that there is some difference in their make-up, which causes one to be more susceptible than the other. Thus, the physical factors are indispensable for the development of the delirium, the constitutional factor allows it to develop given the physical conditions, and the psychological factors supply the individual colouring that will make one person's delirium different from another's.

Again, suppose that an elderly person is brought for advice on account of failure of memory and intellectual grasp. She has left the electric fires on all night, through forgetting to turn them off; she has gone to the shops but on arrival cannot remember what she wants to buy; she has failed to keep appointments because she cannot remember which day is which or where she should go. She herself complains that her memory is bad. On examination, we find that she does not know the date even approximately, that she remembers wrongly the ages of her children, that she cannot recall the dates of many important events in her life, especially the more recent ones. Physically, she shows no signs except peripheral and retinal arteriosclerosis of a gross kind, perhaps with some muscular rigidity such as often occurs in old age. There are no immediate environmental or psychological stresses; the previous personality has not been abnormal. There is no reason why she should wish to be as she is; indeed, it causes her hardship and much inconvenience. We correlate the mental and physical findings, and deduce that the failure of memory is secondary to the arteriosclerosis which has led, through inadequate circulation, to deterioration of the brain. Here, the physical factors are again predominant. We infer that the genetic constitutional factors are of some consequence, because there is a marked family history of the same sort of condition. The psychological factors are represented by her being able to remember some things that are of special significance to her in preference to others that she has forgotten; they partly determine what use she makes of her decayed powers, but they have not caused the decay and, as factors, are relatively unimportant.

Here again the assessment of the relative importance of these three groups of factors is made on a common-sense basis, on scrutiny of the case as a whole, and on comparing it with others in our clinical experience. Where physical factors are predominant, the clinical picture will be (1) one of intellectual deficits, or (2) along the range from clouding of consciousness, through confusion (in the simple sense of putting the left shoe on the right foot, getting into the wrong bed unwittingly as a drunk man might do, or mistaking the obvious use of commonplace objects), and sub-delirious states to full delirium. Such states cannot reasonably be explained in terms of psychological factors mainly; these will always be subsidiary, though lending a personal and individual colouring. Constitutional factors will certainly be present, and in the last analysis may be considered responsible for allowing the development of the condition, as when one patient with typhoid develops a delirium and another does not. But physical factors will be the aetiologically predominant ones.

Let us now consider a more complicated case. Suppose that a youth is referred for advice because, after a few weeks during which he has been moody and failing to get on with his work, apparently on account of pre-occupation with his own thoughts, he has announced that his health is being undermined by radioactive emanations from a hydrogen bomb, that he has a mission to save mankind but is prevented from carrying it out by Russian agents who interrupt his thoughts, disarrange his books and papers, and spy upon him in the street.

After taking a detailed history from the patient and his relatives, we find that he has been reasonably normal until a few weeks previously, though liable to religious doubts and slightly concerned as to the possibilities of war and its consequences, including those on his career. There have been no recent changes or stresses in his home environment or conditions of work.

On examination, we also find that he hears hallucinatory voices that criticise him and quote Biblical texts. But he is in clear consciousness, in touch with his surroundings though slower than usual, is not confused though somewhat bewildered by what he believes to be going on, and is without signs of physical disease.

How are we to construe such a case? Are we to say that this is a psychological reaction provoked by the cumulative load upon his mind of religious conflict and concern over future war? We reflect that many people have religious doubts, and many are afraid of a future war; but it is a long way from that to developing a mission to save mankind, to feeling already under the influence of the hydrogen bomb, hearing imaginary voices and being persecuted by Russian agents. We think that this youth has a severe mental illness, with disordered perception (hallucinations), false beliefs (delusions and misinterpretations), leading to a serious disturbance of function. The psychological factors of religious doubts and worry over war would seem inadequate as causes of a disorder of this severity and massiveness.

It is true that the more we study this youth, the more probably shall we discern some connection between the delusions and hallucinations on the one hand, and his own mental pre-occupations on the other. But that is not to say that the latter have *caused* the former. The mere understanding that there is some connection does not explain why he should have come to have these beliefs, to have accepted them as true, or why he should have hallucinations. We cannot consider this a mere psychological reaction without doing violence to the facts. It looks more as though we are dealing with some basic illness, to which the personal pre-occupations have lent an individual colouring as in the case of typhoid delirium that we have previously considered.

But this patient is not delirious and we can demonstrate no signs of physical disease. We are thus in the difficulty that the psychological factors seem inadequate to explain the whole, and that the physical factors, though we may suspect their existence since there is a disturbance of function, are not obvious. In this dilemma, rather than stretching the facts by attributing the state to psychological or physical causes, it seems most logical to invoke constitutional factors as the cause. This may be vague, non-committal and an admission of imperfect knowledge. But at least it is likely to prevent serious error, such as we might fall into if we adopted conclusions unwarranted by the available facts. In attributing the condition to constitutional causes, we are only saying that we believe there is something in the patient's make-up that has caused him to break down in this particular way, and that the environmental stresses do not seem to have been of prime importance. We shall be fortified in this conclusion if we find, as we often shall, a family history of the same sort of condition in the patient's own or preceding generation.

We may take much the same view in cases of long sustained and uncontrollable excitement, and in cases of long sustained and severe melancholia. There may have been precipitating factors in the first place, and initially the state may have appeared comprehensible as a reaction to them. But, as the reader may agree when he comes to read the description of these conditions in Chapter 9, there are few psychological factors that could justifiably be used to explain the long continuance of states of such severity, even though they may have acted as precipitating agents.

In general, we invoke constitutional factors when there is an absence of *adequate* and demonstrable physical or psychological factors, and when genetic factors can be demonstrated, as in schizophrenia and the major affective illnesses. It is true that the patient may react to these illnesses with anxiety or disturbance of mood; such might almost be considered a normal reaction to the abnormal experience of such illness. But such added reaction is secondary and is not causal.

It will be realised that in this aetiological exercise of assessing the relative importance of constitutional, physical and psychological factors, we are seeking a satisfactory quantitative relationship between the condition as we see it and the causes that we can find to account for it. Detailed knowledge of an individual patient may show us why the particular symptoms that he has take the form that they do (as when the delusions of an oft-convicted felon take the form of being persecuted by the police), but it does not necessarily explain why he has the symptoms in the first place, when he has not had them before. Further, the exercise becomes less difficult with increasing experience, because the more cases one sees the more does one realise that, as in Kraepelin's classification, there are groups of cases that have symptoms in common. By attending to the clinical picture one may then recognise it as belonging to a particular group. One may then know from experience what weight should in general be attached to the constitutional, physical and psychological factors in that particular group of illnesses. That is one should attend to the symptomatology of the condition and try to classify it, rather than seek to explain the individual symptoms essentially in terms of reaction.

The questions are: 'is the patient ill, if so in what way, and why?' If a woman seriously believes that the plants in her garden are repeatedly dug up by a busy neighbour and replaced very exactly by weeds, it may be concluded that she is ill, and that her illness takes the form of at least one delusion; it is not enough to say that she thinks as she does because she is a keen gardener and dislikes the neighbour; to conclude that that is the explanation of the illness is to mistake the pathogenesis of one particular manifestation with the aetiology of the whole.

The need for a multiple aetiological approach, taking all three groups of factors into account, can sometimes be seen in almost diagrammatic form. Thus, a man lost his job and became profoundly depressed. Previous loss of job had not had this effect. But on this occasion the loss occurred during an attack of influenza. Even with the cooperation of these physical and mental factors, the occurrence of severe depression is unusual. But here there was evidence of constitutional predisposition in that the patient's mother had committed suicide while in a mental hospital for melancholia. Few cases show their mixed aetiology quite so clearly, but all possess it, and in every case both the symptomatology and the relative importance of the various causes and their interaction have to be assessed.

Aetiological fallacies

Neglect of this basic principle of multiple causation by psychological, physical and constitutional factors, is responsible for two main aetiological fallacies and over-simplifications. First, the view is sometimes held, though less often than in the past, that mental illness must always have an essentially physical cause. The train of thought seems to be that if normal mental activity depends upon physical conditions, then any mental abnormality must be physically determined. In practice, this is sometimes but by no means always the case. The mental symptoms in intellectual deterioration or delirium may properly be attributed to the underlying physical disorder, as we have seen. But of course this is not necessarily so in other conditions. Psychological factors may be predominant, as in many cases of excessive anxiety, and there is no scientific basis for supposing that mental symptoms cannot arise as their more or less direct consequence. Constitutional factors may also be predominant, as in the cases of schizophrenia, mania and melancholia that we have considered. In fact, any of the three groups may be of prime aetiological importance, and to insist on the essentially physical as a cause is mistaken.

Even where the physical factors are aetiologically predominant, the psychological factors must necessarily make some contribution to the picture; as we have seen, the individual differences between one case and another depend upon them. That one patient sees snakes and another sees archbishops depends upon their personal preoccupations and experiences. That one patient's suspicions are directed towards the Catholics or Jews, and another's towards cyclists or Freemasons, depends on the prejudices and attitudes that the individual has developed.

More than this, although the physical factors may be aetiologically predominant, the whole pattern of the illness may be constitutionally determined, as in the case quoted above where a severe depressive illness was precipitated by influenza. Again we see that insistence on the purely physical as 'the cause' is fallacious.

The second main fallacy is the converse one that mental symptoms are entirely dependent on mental causes. This is equally erroneous. We have already considered some of the schizophrenic, manic and melancholic states in which no satisfactory physical pathology can be demonstrated, and how it may then seem logical and natural to turn to the psychological factors for the aetiological explanation. As we saw in the introductory chapter such attempts have often been made. Psycho-analysis in particular has sought explanations of these illnesses in purely psychological terms; Meyer's psycho-biology has sought to explain schizophrenia, in particular, as a gradual retreat from reality under the cumulative effects of a persistent failure of adaptation. More recently theories of schizophrenia have been put forward based entirely on abnormal relationships within the family, or on other social pressures; and some have even suggested that a schizophrenic breakdown can be seen as a useful adaptation to unbearable stress—a difficult view to hold for those who actually deal with these patients. The interplay of genetic and environmental factors in the development of schizophrenia and affective illnesses is considered in more detail in the relevant chapters (p. 133 and p. 164).

Very striking examples of the misunderstandings which can arise are found when a person with melancholia experiences feelings of guilt, which may happen as a symptom of that illness, and efforts are then made to explain both the guilt and the melancholia as arising from some trivial misdemeanour, perhaps committed years before and having been no source of concern meanwhile. As an extreme form of this illogicality, the case may be quoted of a severely melancholic patient who brooded persistently (as is common in melancholia) on the fact that she had once taken, uninvited, an extra piece of cake at a wedding twenty years before. She sought to explain her illness—as did the relatives—as arising from this amoral act and the worry that it had occasioned. But of course the illness was constitutionally determined; the brooding was a symptom, not a cause; the fact of having taken the cake merely lent direction to the sense of guilt which was part of the illness itself.

Again, a patient with general paralysis of the insane may have delusions of grandeur. It is reasonable to suppose that these represent his wishes, but it is not reasonable to suppose that his wishes caused the illness. On the contrary, they merely account for some of the symptoms he shows in it. In fact, although intimate knowledge of the patient may explain the particular form of some of the symptoms, it is not necessarily enough to explain the illness itself. Although psychological factors will always be present and will lend some individual colouring, their existence must not lead to the fallacy that a mental illness must have purely mental causes.

We will now consider these three groups of factors, constitutional, physical and psychological, in turn. We will consider them in that order, on the principle of dealing with the more constant and basic ones first. It will soon be further apparent how artificial is their separation, and how much they are interrelated and overlap.

Constitutional factors
It is generally recognised that the make-up of an individual at any given time is due both to nature and to nurture, to the hereditary equipment with which he started and to the influences upon him of what has happened subsequently.

Some genes, like those for eye colour and Huntington's chorea

(p. 115) exert their effect independent of any known environmental influences; but usually genes can be seen as setting limits to an individual's potentialities. This is seen very clearly with height, in which nutrition also plays an important rôle, although a food intake larger than optimal does not lead to increased height, but to obesity.

The importance of the genetic equipment in (a) setting a limit to potentialities, and (b) leading to very diverse manifestations mostly falling within the bounds of normal variation, has not, however, been so widely recognised for psychological as it has been for physical phenomena. This is partly because the greater complexity of the problem has hindered the development of precise knowledge, but no doubt partly also because of a natural reluctance to accept such a frustrating doctrine of personal limitations. None the less, there is evidence in its favour, and this is illustrated by the work of Kretschmer who has described different physical types which are associated to some extent with corresponding personality types. The chief of these are:

(1) *The 'asthenic' (lepto-somatic) type.*—This is characterised by narrow build, an angular profile, and a lean, dyspeptic, hungry look. Asthenics appear taller than they really are. The musculature is poor and gives a tendency to droop. The chest is long, narrow and flat, with a subcostal angle of less than 90 degrees. The skin is pale and the hands and feet tend to be cyanotic. There is some association between this build and an introverted personality whose emotions tend to be cold leading to aloofness, whose interests tend to be intellectual and abstract, with an inclination towards contemplative rather than active pursuits, in line with the fact that the reserves of energy are usually small. There is some affinity between this so-called schizoid personality and a liability to schizophrenic breakdown.

(2) *The 'pyknic' (pyknosomatic) type.*—Here the physique more resembles Humpty-Dumpty, Falstaff or John Bull. It is characterised by large body cavities, a short neck, and small but graceful extremities. Pyknics are liable to look shorter than they really are. The thorax and abdomen are wide and deep. The subcostal angle is greater than 90 degrees. The musculature is good unless, as is not uncommon, the person has run to fat. The skin is ruddy and the peripheral circulation good. There is some association between this build and a personality characterised by emotional warmth and sympathetic responsiveness, a tendency to extroverted activities and to maintaining the common touch, towards activity rather than contemplation, and a high endowment of energy. There is some affinity between this personality and cyclothymia (p. 164) and a liability to manic-depressive developments.

(3) *The 'athletic' (athleto-somatic) type* comes between the other two.

Fig. 2.1 Asthenic type

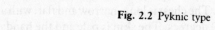

Fig. 2.2 Pyknic type

Fig. 2.3 Athletic type

It is characterised by broad shoulders, narrow hips, good proportions of trunk and limbs, large bones and a well-developed musculature, especially in the proximal muscle groups. Any associated
personality type is less well-defined than with the asthenic and
pyknic physique, but this physique is disproportionately common in
young criminal delinquents.

Kretschmer's work has been carried further by Sheldon and his
associates who have concluded, as a result of physical measurement,
photography and psychological study of normals, that in physique
there are three basic dimensions, endomorphy, ectomorphy and
mesomorphy, each of which makes an approximately equal contribution to the statistically average individual, while those other than
average are variants along one of these three dimensions. The
endomorphs (with large body cavities and massive digestive viscera)
are akin to Kretschmer's pyknic type with temperamental characteristics to match; the mesomorphs, with predominance of bone,
muscle and connective tissue, are the analogue of the athletic type;
the ectomorphs, in whom delicacy and angularity of appearance are
striking, with temperamental accompaniments of restraint and
inhibition, correspond to the asthenic type.

The associations between physique, personality and liability to
breakdown are of interest and sometimes have practical value in the
assessment of certain mixed psychiatric syndromes. But they are by
no means invariable and there are many exceptions; they exist,
therefore, only as general trends in a broad sense. To that extent,
however, their existence supports the view that genetic limitations
may be set to psychological potentialities.

More powerful evidence, perhaps, comes from the study of
intelligence. This, as measured by intelligence tests, appears quite
comparable to height in being largely determined by the hereditary
endowment [i.e. the genes] and in exhibiting a normal curve of
distribution in the population. That is to say, just as there are large
numbers of people of medium height, while the numbers become
smaller towards the extremes of tallness or dwarfism, so there are
large numbers with medium intelligence and the numbers become
smaller towards the extremes of intelligence, high or low. However,
the full genetically determined potentialities may not be realised if
the environment is markedly unfavourable at any stage of development. Among the factors identified as harmful or limiting have been
intrauterine ones such as heavy maternal smoking, toxins such as
lead, and infections; perinatal factors such as anoxia; early severe
malnutrition; and an upbringing with little intellectual, perceptual
or emotional stimulation and richness.

Although such personal characteristics as character and temperament are not as easily susceptible of measurement, there is no reason to suppose that all mankind starts life with equal potentialities in these respects. On the contrary, minor variations in every aspect or attribute of character can readily be observed, with extreme variations less common. That is, a normal curve of distribution exists, just as in intelligence and height.

Studies of identical twins brought up together and apart have shown that such fundamental attributes as degree of outgoingness, proneness to anxiety, and basic levels of drive (energy) seem to be largely determined genetically.

Constitutional factors, therefore, may contribute to mental breakdown through the limitations that they impose upon the individual as regards his physique, personality, intelligence and temperament. But they may do more than this by providing a predisposition to the development of mental disorder on a genetic basis.

Genetic influences
Broadly speaking, genes can be considered under two headings, those of minor and those of major effect. Variations in intelligence and character and in liability to minor 'nervous' symptoms are now attributed to the influence of many genes of small but additive effect. Whilst it is true that any individual may show nervous symptoms under sufficient provocation, there is evidence that all people are not *equally* liable to such developments. The liability to such a response varies from person to person, in contrast to the universal tendency to respond to infection with fever. The differences between individuals in this respect cannot be accounted for solely, or even mainly, on the ground of the environmental stresses that they have met, but are considered attributable, in part at least, to the influence of these genes of minor effect.

Such a genetic endowment does not necessarily result in breakdown, but it renders it possessors more susceptible to the effects of stress, as is shown particularly by studies of identical twins. It will be realised that, however little is known of the mechanisms of genetic influences, the tendencies that they confer make their appearance at different times of life. Thus, although the tendency to brown eyes and dark hair is innate, the appearance of some characteristics may be delayed, just as an innate tendency to baldness may not be manifest until later life. In the same way, the liability to breakdown may appear early if it is marked, or if it is mild may be delayed until the individual comes under considerable stress. The extent to which this occurs is complicated by the fact that a man may be normal or average in many respects, but an extreme variant or abnormal in one or in only a few. He may be abnormal, for example, only in extreme sensitiveness, conscientiousness or aggressiveness. That is, his liability to breakdown may be of a very specialised kind, which may be brought out only by particular environmental stresses, or by internal stresses arising from incompatibility of contrasting character traits provoked by special situations.

It is in the production of these minor abnormalities that the genes of minor effect have influence. The genes of major effect, by contrast and as their name implies, are responsible for the constitutional loading that contributes to the development of major abnormalities, of a more marked, more clearly cut and more specific kind. There are certain rare conditions in which this is plainly demonstrable, such as Huntington's chorea and phenylketonuria (phenylpyruvic amentia). The latter can be shown to arise from a single recessive gene. The former can be shown to arise from a single dominant gene; its onset in the potential victim is inevitable and certain, so that the only way that he can avoid the disease is to die of something else before he reaches the time of life at which it develops. In recent years phenylketonuria has become preventable by giving a diet free of phenylalanine, thus demonstrating that to identify a genetic cause for a disease does not mean the outlook is hopeless, although that is the attitude of most people. It is possible that similar results will be possible in other genetically determined diseases.

Mongolism has been shown to occur only in association with certain chromosomal abnormalities. Conditions in which the genetic relationships are so clear cut are few, but that they occur at all is of great significance as regards genetic influence in general. Such genetic influence can be discerned, though in a less obvious and plain form, in such other major psychiatric disorders as schizophrenia and manic-depressive psychosis. Just as the ordinary man is most unlikely to fall below an adult height of four feet, and it needs pathological dwarfism to produce that effect, so is he unlikely to sink into a really profound melancholia.

There is, of course, no reason why specific genes of large effect, resulting for example in a classical manic-depressive psychosis, should not be combined in the same individual with several genes of small but additive effect. In fact, this does appear to happen. If the genes of minor effect make for stability, the resultant is the occurrence of manic-depressive psychosis in an otherwise stable person; if they are unfavourable ones, the resultant is manic-depressive psychosis in someone already predisposed to minor abnormalities and neurotic reactions. In practice, manic-depressive psychosis can afflict both types of individual.

The above outline represents a convenient working hypothesis, which may help in the understanding both of individual cases and of the difficulty in obtaining more exact data concerning the heredity of mental illness in general.

Despite this difficulty the constitutional aspects of illness must not be ignored; even if, in a particular case, the environmental influences appear predominant, they are not its sole constituents, for the genetic endowment will have limned the patient's development in outline and may even have contributed to it in detail. Further, even when the heredity appears free from predisposition to mental illness, it cannot be legitimate to infer a total absence of constitutional factors on that ground alone. A snub nose does not necessarily cease to be part of the constitution because all the traceable ancestors had Roman ones; in such a case it should not be argued that the snub nose *must* be attributable to squashing in infancy, although this may have happened.

Environmental influences

Apart from these hereditary factors, a person may acquire patterns of reaction, either through being encouraged or through not being checked in their development, which, through repetition and long continuance, become characteristic and all but automatic. Those who have been encouraged to run for help in any difficulty may so continue until their dotage. Those, obstinate and of sterner stuff, who, though hopelessly lost, refuse either to ask the way or return to the starting point, may show a like intransigence as part of their normal approach to life. Such persistent and characteristic behaviour may be so integral a part of the personality as to justify its being called constitutional. In this sense there are thus both psychological as well as physical constitutional factors, as is only to be expected since 'physical' and 'mental' are but different aspects of the constitutional whole.

The upbringing is obviously of great importance in encouraging the development of behaviour patterns that are of a helpful kind. Life makes many demands on our powers of adaptation, and successful adaptation calls for flexibility. What is required is that a person should not be unduly rigid on the one hand, nor liable to panicky impulsive action on the other. To maintain the mean between these two requires steadiness of mind, and the best way of acquiring it is to be reared in a steady atmosphere.

Children are imitative by nature, and they should have steady people to emulate if they are to become steady themselves. Tradition and cultural influences are of great formative value. Repeated changes of background, living with different relatives or in different places with repeated changes of school, may make demands on the child which he is unable to meet and therefore have an unsettling effect. The child also needs affection and this should be of a steady kind on which he knows that he can rely. Where the parents are loving and over-protective at one moment but angry and threatening the next, in accord with their own caprices, the effect is to discourage steady attitudes. Likewise, the child requires discipline but this should be of a consistent kind that he is able to understand. If he is to learn to respect the rights of others, his own rights should be respected also; if the discipline is unduly repressive the naturally spirited child will rebel and the timid child will become cowed. The same may happen if there is invidious discrimination so that one child is deprived in favour of another. All children need moral support, but this should stop short of over-protection. Financial security is obviously helpful.

In summary, the home background should be emotionally and financially steady, with affection that can be relied upon and is properly distributed, with reasonable liberty but with reasonable and consistent discipline. Within this framework the normally constituted child should grow up normally enough.

Where there are marked departures from these requirements, the growing child may adopt attitudes unhelpful to his adaptation, and these may well persist not only into but throughout adult life. Poor management of the home situation in the early years may result in such persistent traits as jealousy, resentment, intolerance of frustration and authority, incapacity to show affection, undue dependence, inferiority feelings and inability to meet people on even terms. These may be a considerable handicap and hindrance, and may be so ingrained in the personality as to be habitual and therefore, as has been said, a part of the constitution.

However, while no one doubts that it is a good thing to have come from a happy home, it is perfectly possible to emerge from an unhappy one and yet have a good personality. The converse is also true. This illustrates how difficult it can be to evaluate genetic and environmental influences in any given case. The latter can probably be of paramount importance. If it should seem that undue emphasis has been laid on the genetic rather than the environmental influences in the foregoing discussion, this does not arise from any intention of minimising the importance of the environment, but from the necessity to draw the attention of the student to the possible importance in any given case of more recondite factors, of whose existence he should be aware.

Summary
In summary, hereditary factors are of prime importance in setting limitations to the development of physique and intelligence; they also

make a substantial contribution to the personality and temperament. There are certain broad trends in the association between certain types of physique and personality. There is evidence that many genes of minor but additive effect provide a predisposition to the development of minor mental abnormalities, and that specific genes of major effect are associated with the development of more marked mental abnormalities in the form of specific and major illnesses. In all these ways the constitutional factors will always have contributed to the patient's development, and their influence must not be ignored, whatever other apparent causes there may be of the condition that the patient presents. Nor does the apparent absence of hereditary predisposition mean that constitutional factors are absent. In addition, the importance of environmental as opposed to hereditary factors having influenced the development of the constitution must not be overlooked. These may have led to the development of attitudes of mind and habits or reaction that remain with the individual as a permanent part of himself. The genetic and environmental influences should be weighed in every case, or at least some attempt in this direction should be made. Where acquired attitudes of mind and habits of reaction have become so habitual as to be an integral part of the personality, they also may be considered constitutional. The more precise genetic data concerning particular psychiatric syndromes will be found in the appropriate chapters.

Physical factors
By physical factors are here meant the states of physical disorder or disease that are studied in general medicine, such as infections, intoxications, disorders of nutrition and circulation, metabolic, endocrine and degenerative disturbances. Now, the origin of these may be exogenous, as in infections, or constitutional, as in the degenerative disturbances, or both, as in the intoxications. We have already noted that one patient with typhoid fever may develop a delirium, whereas another equally ill may not. Likewise, a chronic alcoholic may develop delirium tremens, but another who drinks more under the same conditions may remain free from delirium. The inference is that their make-up is different, and that there must be constitutional factors involved, as well as the physical ones. This again emphasises the artificiality of the separation. Reminding ourselves, therefore, that the terms 'physical' and 'constitutional' are not mutually exclusive, we may consider the physical factors in mental illness under three headings:

1. Those that produce their effects through permanent changes in the physical structure,

2. Those that are associated with mental symptoms though in the absence of permanent changes in the physical structure; in these some transient but reversible structural change is to be inferred,

3. Those about which we may speculate but know nothing certain.

Factors producing permanent structural changes
In this first group are such degenerative conditions as the senile and presenile dementias; the late results of cerebrovascular disease including major strokes and diffuse arteriosclerotic dementia; the late results of head injury and sometimes of cerebral tumour; chronic alcoholism; occasional cases of poisoning with carbon monoxide or heavy metals; general paralysis of the insane due to tertiary syphilis; and numerous other rarer causes. The clinical pictures arising from these causes have enough in common to be recognisable as showing an 'organic type of mental reaction'. The cardinal features of these organically determined states are impairment of intellect and personality, often with emotional changes, and they are described in Chapter 6.

Factors producing transient structural changes
The second group, those associated with mental symptoms though in the absence of permanent changes in the physical structure, comprise a considerable variety. First, we may mention the variable and reversible physical changes that accompany emotion, and are an integral part of emotion as experienced in the mind. These are mediated by the autonomic system, and the commonest are palpitation, sweating, tremors, various symptoms arising from the alimentary tract, and frequency of micturition. In this connection it is noteworthy that thyrotoxicosis may be associated with psychological stress, and may present in the first place as an anxiety state, which can sometimes be successfully treated by psychological methods if it is not too far advanced. More dramatic and widespread in their effects than these physical accompaniments of emotion are toxic states of exogenous origin, i.e. the febrile and toxic deliria, which present the above symptoms of the 'organic mental reaction' with additional features of disorientation, clouding of consciousness, with misinterpretations of what goes on around them (amounting to fleeting delusions), and often with hallucinations. Such states can occur in any severely toxic condition, in uraemia, carbon monoxide

and metallic poisonings, and in the course of chronic alcoholism. Cases that die show degenerative changes in the nervous system to an extent that varies with the severity and chronicity of the poisoning. It is a reasonable inference that in those who survive there have been changes of such lesser degree as to be reversible. This view is strengthened by the discovery that cases of Korsakoff's psychosis, a form of deterioration that may occur as the end result of toxic states (usually alocholic ones) and previously considered irreversible, can be improved and even cured provided they are given sufficient doses of thiamin over a long enough time.

It was at one time thought, and the conception still persists in some quarters, that apart from such severe toxic effects as delirium, intoxications of lesser degree (arising from 'focal sepsis' and auto-intoxication from the bowel) might be responsible for much in the way of mental disorder. There is, however, no good evidence for this beyond the fact that the development of psychological illness may be facilitated in a non-specific way by anything that lowers the efficiency and well-being of the patient. As the man in the street rightly believes, 'worries get a hold' more easily on those who are physically run down from whatever cause.

Uncertain physical factors

It remains to consider the third group of physical factors, those about which we may speculate, but of which we have no certain knowledge. First, as to structure, although much work has been done, histological studies have not succeeded in establishing any definite connection between mental symptoms and cellular pathology except in such degenerative conditions as the dementias, in states where irreversible damage has been done by toxicity, and where there has been localised damage with resultant mental symptoms of organic type as may occur with cerebral tumour or after head injury, or following vascular accidents. That is to say, histology has been of help where there has been permanent and irreversible damage, but has otherwise told us little.

Many studies have claimed to demonstrate that patients with chronic schizophrenia have evidence of cerebral atrophy, dilatation of the third ventricle on lumbar air encephalography; and others have tried to demonstrate histopathological changes either at post mortem or by brain biopsy. None of these studies has been really convincing, however, although one must realise that the techniques are relatively crude. Computer assisted tomography is now being used in this field, and a recent study has shown cerebral atrophic changes in chronic schizophrenia, which strongly suggests some organic brain disease.

Electroencephalography has not yet lived up to earlier hopes in studies on schizophrenia and other mental illnesses, although it is so useful in neurological investigation and has helped to elucidate the nature of sleep. Patients with schizophrenia often do show abnormalities on their e.e.g., but there is no general agreement on the meaning of these, and it may be that the abnormalities are the result of the abnormal mental state rather than indicators of underlying causal disturbance.

Endocrine studies have in recent years been more productive, especially in manic-depressive illnesses and other affective disorders. We know that the autonomic and endocrine systems exert a profound influence on metabolism, and play an indispensable part in the integration of mind and body. There is no doubt of the importance of this, but there is little precise knowledge of their mechanisms. For example, it is known to every one that the sex glands influence the mind; it is the more striking that how they achieve their effects is known to no one. Again, we know that there is a specially high incidence of mental illness in adolescence and at the climacteric, i.e. in the early and late stages of the reproductive period; we know that menstruation may be accompanied by marked degrees of emotional disturbance; we know that amenorrhoea is a common accompaniment of major mental illnesses, as are alterations of libido and of production of sex hormones. These observations suggest an intimate connection between the mental state and the biochemical and endocrine systems. Further, the intimate connections between the hypothalamus and the pituitary gland, and between the cortex and the hypothalamus, both directly and via the thalamus, are such as to place the pituitary under the influence of the nervous system. The other endocrine glands can be influenced through the pituitary, and all in their turn can influence the function of the nervous system through their hormones. In general, we can see the possibilities but we do not know the details.

Summary
In summary, then, physical factors are of predominant importance in the production of degenerative, confusional and delirious states. They are also accompaniments of emotion and an integral part of emotional experience. In this respect they contribute to those emotional reactions precipitated mainly by psychological factors; but they usually play small part in their causation. It is probable that physical factors, in the form of obscure and subtle endocrine and metabolic disturbances, play a considerable role in the development of major mental illnesses such as schizophrenia and manic-depressive psychosis. Our knowledge, however, is at present so incomplete that

the attribution of major mental illnesses, other than degenerative conditions and deliria, to physical factors is at present no more than speculative.

Psychological factors
It has already been said that these may colour an individual illness in an individual way, and that by determining the particular form of a delusion or the particular pattern of a delirium, they help to account for the individual differences between one case and another. But psychological factors, though contributory in this way, do not cause delusional or delirious states. They may precipitate psychotic illnesses in those who are constitutionally predisposed, and so lead on to delusions and hallucinations. In general, psychological factors do not themselves cause distortions of mental content. They can be of prime importance, however, in causing conditions which, while they may be very disabling, are relatively minor in the sense that they do not lead to insanity. The development of such states depends essentially on emotion. They occur when emotions are aroused of such abnormal intensity and duration as to interfere with the patient's adjustment to life.

Individual emotional reactions
Such emotional reactions may occur as a result of changes either in the individual or in his environment, and they may happen suddenly or gradually, according to the nature of such changes. Such sudden changes are bereavements, injuries or illness, unexpected financial reverses, or the loss of a job. Gradual changes may occur as the result of ageing, with inability to accept the limitations imposed by increasing ill-health and frailty, or when it slowly becomes apparent that a long struggle towards some desired end is resulting in failure from which there seems no escape, or when a situation of early promise has ended in disappointment. Sexual difficulties and frustrations may also be important factors.

In general, the failure of adjustment that such emotional reactions represent results from a discrepancy between the demands made upon an individual and his ability to cope with them. It will be noted that such demands may be made upon the patient not only by the external situation but also by himself, through his ambitions and his social and ethical standards. Such reactions are, therefore, the product of the interplay between a particular situation and a particular personality, and their pattern depends on the nature of the emotional currents that the situation evokes. In conditions where the psychological factors are predominant, attention should therefore be focused upon these emotional currents. For example, overwork is often cited as a cause of nervous breakdown. But where the patient has in fact worked to an abnormal extent, what is important is not the overwork itself but the emotional strain under which it has been done or which drove the patient to undertake it. Indeed, it can almost be taken as an axiom that overwork is a euphemism for overworry. The key to understanding breakdowns in which psychological factors predominate lies, therefore, in the emotional response that results from the interplay between the provocative situation and the patient's personality.

More complex emotional reactions
Sometimes these may be easily intelligible, as when the stress is one which would shake anybody, such as a bereavement or being bombed. More often, however, the intensity of emotional responses and their time-relationship to stresses become intelligible only with knowledge of the patient's personality.

Where the time relationships are unexpected, this is usually because (1) worries and stresses tend to be cumulative in their effects, and the 'last straw' effect is often seen in precipitating depressive illnesses, (2) the initial symptoms may, through causing worry or through other reasons, have led to other symptoms, with the later development of further and secondary reactions, (3) people come to need the stimulations to which they are accustomed, and in the absence of such may feel disorganised and at a loss; thus, decrease of tension may be as emotionally upsetting as increase of tension, as may be seen in acute form in the normal experience of feeling worse after danger than during it, (4) there is an unexplained but common tendency for symptoms in both depressive and schizophrenic patients to follow about three weeks after some emotional turmoil or upheaval.

The intensity of the emotional response also may seem anomalous, if the situation has had some special significance for the patient that is not at first clear to the observer. This is especially liable to happen if the patient is subject to inner conflicts, which involve the higher emotions attached to values, standards, ideals and ambitions. The more subtle emotional responses thus involved are on the whole more important in producing breakdowns that are comparatively gross ones. This is partly because their very subtlety makes them more difficult for the patient to solve, but partly also because they may present to the patient difficulties of an intimate and distasteful kind the nature of which does not encourage him to deal with them in forthright fashion.

Mental mechanisms in neurotic states
The patient may prefer not to look at these difficulties mentioned above, or he may see only their less unpleasant aspects. But this does not do away with the emotional currents themselves; all that happens is that the patient finds himself in the grip of something that he does not understand. He finds his situation the more difficult to manage as a result. These points may be illustrated by simple examples. A soldier in the front line may fully realise that he is homesick and terrified; but with goodwill he may fully do his duty. On the other hand, although the stress was far less overtly severe, the conscientious secretary of a business man found herself unable to carry on owing to a functional dyspepsia. This was attributed to overwork, for which there was some evidence, and to dental sepsis, for which there was not. After dental extractions and a holiday had not resulted in improvement, in that she relapsed as soon as she returned to work, it emerged that the real cause of her trouble was that she had fallen in love with her employer. She had not admitted this to herself since she was a girl of strict standards and he was a married man. Her feelings had actually induced her to work long hours for him, and she had persuaded herself that her emotion was one of admiration only. After she had realised the true nature of her difficulties, she changed her job and did well.

It may be thought that the foregoing is an extreme example, but failure to understand the factors that induce our feelings and dictate our actions is to some extent present in everyone; and even if it is not always obvious in ourselves, it is plain enough in those around us. The average man is surprisingly deficient in introspective desire or capacity; his self-knowledge is often limited to a vague awareness that he finds difficult to put into words. This absence of clear formulation has an important bearing on the therapeutic results that can follow a diagnostic interview which obliges a patient to formulate for the first time and to express his feelings in words. Few psychiatrists have not had the experience of receiving thanks for 'putting things so clearly' after an interview during which they have scarcely opened their mouths. Nor is lack of self-knowledge confined to the simple or to the tongue-tied and inarticulate; the self-esteem of those with intelligence, introspective gifts and verbal facility, is often subtly self-satisfying rather than accurate. In fact, it is very difficult to make a just self-estimate.

The difficulty is much increased by the normal tendency to attend to those aspects of ourselves which give us satisfaction, with a relative disregard of our own less satisfactory aspects. The emphasis is naturally upon the former. It is easy to make mistakes in describing what is in and on our minds as it is to make mistakes in describing some outside event, especially one in which we have been unpleasantly involved. In each case, desires, prejudices and expectations will distort observation and falsify recollection, so that the real constituents of the scene will be ignored, wrongly described or emphasised, or a wrong attribution of their origin made. This is especially likely to be so if the results of more accurate introspection are disconcerting or damaging to the self-esteem, and thus calculated to arouse emotions of an unpleasant character. That is why, while many people do not mind complaining of their poor memory, so few complain of their poor intelligence and judgment, although the latter can scarcely be less frequent or serious in their effects. Again, a man will pride himself on his capacity for compromise where others will see only weakness; or upon his high standards and strict discipline, where others see only the reflection of an irritable and aggressive personality.

Memory, and therefore our conception of our past, is apt to be affected in the same way. Unpleasant facts tend to receive preferential treatment in the normal process of forgetting. Murderers tend to develop an amnesia for the murders they have committed. Less dramatically, patients tend to forget, when giving their work record, the jobs that they disliked or did badly. The authors themselves have been reminded by their friends of discreditable past episodes, though they have again forgotten them. More vividly, a sergeant of sensitive disposition was the only survivor of a group of men who all came from his own village; he forgot all details of the actual engagement, an amnesia facilitated by his having to break the news to his fellow-villagers. Again, another patient could recall a quarrel with his wife, but not that he had threatened suicide if she did not behave better. He was ashamed of it.

Thus lack of self-knowledge, both past and present, tends to keep us in ignorance of our true selves, largely through a shift of emphasis from what is unpalatable to what gives us satisfaction. This, as will be mentioned, is to some extent a merciful provision. But where a person has inner conflicts, this mental mechanism tends to operate more strongly, and by obscuring the issue makes the conflicts more difficult to resolve. As such conflicts give rise to unpleasant emotional responses, the patient is left under a greater or lesser handicap according to their severity.

It will thus be realised that in these conditions in which psychological factors are of prime aetiological importance, what happens is that particular circumstances lead to emotional repercussions in a particular personality; the causes may have to be sought more in that personality than in the circumstances; consequently, they may lie more in the past than in the present. The true nature of the emotional disturbance may be obscured from the patient by that lack of self-knowledge which is common to all of us, and by psychological mechanisms, shared to some extent by all of us, which prevent us from accurate assessment of ourselves and of our reactions to situations.

Advantageous use of the same mental mechanisms
These psychological mechanisms can be useful in promoting the adjustment of the individual, in that they may buffer him comfortably from the unpalatabilities of reality. They become handicaps only when the emotional repercussions aroused by conflict are too powerful for adjustment by such methods; they then become harmful to those whom they prevent from realising the true nature of their difficulties, which last do not cease to exist because they are not recognised, but which, if correctly recognised, it may be possible to face and solve. In ordinary life these mechanisms can be of value in adapting the picture of reality so that it becomes emotionally acceptable. It has been mentioned already that we are inclined to regard ourselves in a more favourable light than would the detached observer. We are enabled to do this in present time by shifting the emphasis from our less favourable to our more favourable characteristics, and in viewing our past lives we forget more easily what we do not wish to remember. Such a process is often referred to as *repression*. Repressed facts do not disappear completely; they remain potentially available, but are not recalled owing to emotional interference. The less tolerable they are to the conscious mind, the less easily are they recovered. Although it is often said that such facts are 'repressed into the unconscious', it will often be found that patients are in fact capable of remembering them, but prefer to keep them in some separate mental compartment, and so manage to disconnect them from the stream of consciousness rather than remove them altogether. Repression thus enables one to forget an invitation to lunch that one did not wish to accept, and to overlook, through its influence on perception and the registration of perception, what one does not wish to see. The extent to which it successfully does so without giving rise to symptoms depends on the extent of the emotional response to what is repressed; where the emotional response is great, this may continue to be troublesome. The other common devices that make for deceptive mental ease are *rationalisation* and *sublimation*. In

rationalisation one provides a reason for what one does that is not the true one, but one more palatable and sufficiently plausible to deceive oneself. In sublimation, one finds a personally and socially acceptable channel for the expression of primitive urges whose more naked appearance would conflict with personal ideals or social standards. These mechanisms may influence not only isolated acts but whole careers. A crude ostrich-like policy can sometimes be seen in a certain type of eternal student who rationalises his fear of the rough and tumble of the world as the search for truth in the life of learning, although there are many gradations between the British Museum library addict and the great scholar. Again, many rolling stones are not so much prompted by a love of adventure as by an inner uneasiness and dissatisfaction which they vainly hope to leave behind as they move on. As to sublimation, Sir Richard Burton perhaps rather overstated the case but was certainly in advance of his time in declaring 'All the passions are sisters . . . Seeing the host of women who find a morbid pleasure in attending the maimed and the dying, I must think that it is a tribute paid to sexuality by those who object to the ordinary means.' Perhaps the classic example of successful sublimation may be afforded by the man of homosexual tendencies and high ideals who emphasises the social value of such activities as that of schoolmaster, rather than the sensual element that may play a part in this choice of occupation; and who is thereby enabled to do most valuable work.

The extent to which such mechanisms are successful in maintaining adjustment over a long period of time is variable, and depends much on chance. The eternal student and his like may lead an existence free from care and nervous breakdown, but at the cost that he who seeks to save his life shall lose it. The rolling stones may see much and enjoy themselves though usually not without some anxious self-questioning; one of them said, 'A priest once said to me "You haven't got the guts to stay anywhere for long"—I wonder what he meant by that?' And they are apt to end by having achieved little, with their problems still unsolved, and without those commitments often resented by youth but which are found stabilising sources of gratification in later years. Sublimation tends to be the most satisfactory mechanism, and many who adopt it live happily and successfully, without indication that their mode of life has any but its *prima facie* value. It was pure ill-luck that moved an admirable schoolmaster of advanced years to reflect one day while playing bridge with his headmaster's wife: 'What a fine thing a boy's bottom is'. That he did so was the first sign of the cerebral tumour from which he soon afterwards died, and which disintegrated the psychological mechanisms by which he had held his feeling and actions in check so that they accorded with personal and social propriety.

The development of physical symptoms from emotional causes

The foregoing is an example of how physical factors may influence psychological ones. But it must never be forgotten that psychological factors can also set physical ones in train. Emotional upset, however caused, may produce symptoms of mental or bodily distress, or both combined. Such physical symptoms may be psychologically precipitated in two main ways. First, while the well-adjusted person feels at ease, the less well-adjusted feels less at ease; it is not such a great step from feeling not at ease to dis-ease, nor from not feeling well to feeling ill. That is to say, the patient feels something wrong; as we have seen he may be unaware of just what it is, and if it is something psychologically distasteful he may not wish to know. This in itself inclines him to incriminate his body rather than his mind. The part of his body on which his attention comes to be focused in expressing this feeling of ill-being will depend on his previous experience of illness, in himself or other people. Physical symptoms are then suggested to him by such experiences, and in his then receptive state of mind, he may come to experience them himself, such acceptance being facilitated often by genuine worry and apprehensiveness. Such physical symptoms are, however, only the expression in physical terms of some psychic disturbance.

The second main way in which emotional disturbances may induce physical symptoms is through the mediation of the autonomic system. Anatomically, this is achieved through connections between the cortex and hypothalamus, some direct and some via the thalamus, and thence from the autonomic hypothalamic centres through the sympathetic and parasympathetic systems. Thus, anxiety may lead to headache, both through vaso-constriction and through tension of the scalp muscles; it may lead to palpitations, to a sense of constriction in the chest, to the stomach 'turning over', to irritability of the gut and bladder, with consequent looseness of the stools and frequency of micturition; it leads also to sweating, and to increased tension of the muscles which becomes exaggerated into tremor. All or any of these symptoms may become alarming or a source of worry in themselves, leading to such suppositions as the presence of cerebral tumour, respiratory, cardiac, abdominal or neurological disease; indeed many psychiatric cases present with physical symptoms and not with mental symptoms at all.

Dissociation of physical symptoms from their emotional causes

Where physical symptoms are experienced in either of these main ways, or both, the patient may prefer to stress the physical rather than the psychological side of the complaint. This may be because he feels that the doctor expects physical symptoms; often it is so, and it is striking how the same patient's presenting complaints may vary with the particular hospital department that he attends. But it may be because he is unaware of the psychological aspects of his case, or if he is aware of them, that he does not see the connection between the psychological and physical aspects. Sometimes this is due to ignorance; but it may be that the patient is not so much unable as unwilling to see the connection, since physical illness is often considered more respectable, and it is pleasanter to attribute symptoms to a potent poison rather than to a poor personality.

Examples may help to clarify these points. An ignorant girl of sixteen, reared as an only child in an atmosphere of oppressive respectability, had had no instruction about the 'facts of life'. When kissed for the first time by an undergraduate, she later felt that she had trespassed against the laws of gentility. In a fit of self-reproach she even feared that she might have become pregnant. This threw her into some emotional perturbation; among her symptoms of anxiety she experienced sinking feelings in the stomach and mild alimentary discomfort. The fact that her mind was already focused on her abdomen no doubt magnified these, and the fact that the symptoms were abdominal confirmed her worst fears, which she dared not reveal. Consultation was sought with a surgeon who— presumably 'to be on the safe side'—advised and performed an appendicectomy. She made an uninterrupted recovery, but the symptoms returned some time later, when she was again kissed by the undergraduate on his next vacation. She was then admitted to another hospital with the diagnosis '? adhesions', but came under the care of a surgeon whose keen appreciation of the psychiatric aspects of his cases led him to refer her for specialist advice. The story was elicited, and after suitable explanation the symptoms disappeared. As to how far the result was really successful the reader may judge in the light of the fact that when last heard of, several years later, the patient was rowing in a women's eight. Again, a popular young curate of charm and ability began to develop religious doubts. Shortly afterwards these were followed by palpitations, sweating and a feeling of impending collapse, at first only when called upon to preach, but later at other times as well. After exhaustive physical investigations had proved negative, he was referred for psychiatric opinion. The above story rapidly emerged, and it was found that he had made no connection between his religious scruples and his symptoms in the pulpit. When discussion had obliged him to formulate his difficulties, however, he saw the connection at once and so was able to concentrate on the relevant aspects rather than upon the unjustified fears of physical disease that had previously been the presenting trouble to his mind.

Finally, it may be pointed out that the foregoing examples illustrate the intimate connection in mental illness between psychological and physical factors, and their actual inseparability in practice. In this connection it must be added that the development of physical symptoms from psychological causes is facilitated in those whose constitution is such as to respond readily to emotional disturbance. Thus, people with a naturally labile autonomic system readily respond to emotion with such autonomically mediated symptoms as tachycardia, fainting and dyspepsia. Further, a predisposition to particular physical effects often seems to run in families. These findings illustrate the importance of constitutional as well as physical factors even in those conditions in which psychological factors are predominant. In fact, they remind us again of the necessity for this triple approach.

Summary
In summary, we may say that psychological factors are always present in mental illness. Where they are not aetiologically predominant they will at least account to some extent for the differences between one individual clinical picture and another, as, for example, in the pattern of delirious states or the form taken by delusions. Where they are aetiologically predominant, the states to which they give rise are characterised by emotional disturbance rather than by distortions of the mental content, and in the sense that they do not lead to insanity are relatively minor conditions, though they may be markedly disabling. Such emotional disturbances arise from the effect of particular situations on the personality, and represent some degree of failure of that personality to adjust under stress: although often the stress may have been imposed by the personality itself rather than by the situation. For this reason, as well as because the same situation may evoke different emotional responses in different people, the key to states where the psychological factors are predominant usually lies more in the personality than in the situation. To understand the personality, it is necessary to know the past history and development as well as the present circumstances, for it may be the former that determine the faulty adaptation: and very often it is, though not always. Emotional disturbances of more or less subtle kinds arising

from inner conflicts are usually more potent causes of breakdown than are the more gross emotional disturbances arising from severe external stress. The comparative subtlety of the former makes the emotional difficulty harder for the patient to cope with, as do lack of self-knowledge, the normal tendency to obscure one's deficiencies from oneself, to rationalise one's actions and to fail to see what one does not wish to see. These tendencies, though present in all people and often useful in promoting adjustment, become handicaps when they prevent the clear formulation and understanding of emotional disturbances that have already led to breakdown. Such understanding may be the more difficult to gain because emotional disturbances often lead to physical symptoms, either indirectly through auto- and hetero-suggestion or directly through their effect on the autonomic system, with the result that they may dominate the clinical picture and obscure the real causes. The patient may fail to see the connection between the physical symptoms and the psychological state, either through ignorance or from choice. That psychological factors can lead to physical ones, and especially so in people of a particular constitution, serves to emphasise that all three groups of factors must always be taken into consideration.

3

Symptoms encountered in mental illness

It is essential that the student should know the more important symptoms encountered in mental disorder, and that he should be clear as to the meaning of the technical terms used to describe them. Contrary to popular belief, fewer technical terms are used in psychiatry than in other specialities. This has disadvantages, since it often leads to well-known terms being used in a special and technical sense that differs from their ordinary meaning. For example, 'hysteria' means something quite different to the psychiatrist from what it means to the layman.

Unconsciousness

An unconscious patient is neither aware of his environment nor capable of responding to stimuli in any well-directed way (*inaccessibility*). He is subsequently incapable of recalling any mental activity during the period in question. This is called anterograde as opposed to retrograde amnesia. States of unconsciousness are best observed after severe concussion, in deep anaesthesia and as a final stage of many intoxications. The duration of anterograde amnesia is good evidence of the severity of concussion, and a probable indication of the length of time that the patient will be off work (p. 94). Between unconsciousness and consciousness there are various types and degrees of disturbed consciousness.

Disturbances of consciousness

These are mainly due to physical causes, and the general characteristics are as follows:—

1. Deficient grasp.
2. Disturbances of attention and concentration.
3. Slowness of thinking.
4. Disturbances of memory (*retention*).
5. Lack of direction in thought and action.

Consequently the patient shows:—

Disorientation (i.e. he has lost his bearings as regards place, time and other people).

Confusion (by which is meant something simpler than may be normally experienced on being confronted with an income tax form or legal enactment. The patient is confused when he mistakes the use of a knife and fork, puts the right shoe on the left foot or cannot find his own bed).

Disconnected and often incomprehensible behaviour.

Subsequent amnesia.

Three intermediate states between consciousness and unconsciousness are often recognised:—

1. *Dimming or clouding of consciousness.* Less than normal rather than anything abnormal is experienced. All mental processes are slow. Association of ideas is scanty. Thinking is difficult or impossible. These patients are apathetic and bemused, show no initiative, are easily fatigued, and it is hard to attract or to hold their attention. They tend to pass into a dreamless sleep, stupor or coma. In *mild* cases the patients may answer and behave rationally under examination, but readily relapse when left to themselves. In cases of moderate severity, although out of touch with their surroundings, they may be roused to answer simple questions correctly. And in severe cases it may just be possible to get an occasional appropriate response by forcible questioning or commands.

2. *Delirious states.* The consciousness is clouded, and the continuity of mental processes is interrupted or shattered by abnormal experiences such as hallucinations. Restlessness is a most common feature.

3. *Twilight states.* There is rarely a peculiar alteration of consciousness and personality for certain periods of limited duration, with subsequent amnesia. Such are mainly encountered in epilepsy (p. 103) and also, uncommonly, in some hysterical states (p. 275).

Attention

This is the term used for describing the experience that certain objects are in the centre of consciousness, whilst others lie more towards the periphery. This distribution may be achieved either voluntarily or involuntarily. Attention may be disturbed in various ways:—

1. It may be difficult or impossible to *arouse* the attention of the patient. This generally occurs in organic states resulting in disturbed consciousness; but it may also occur in states of 'retardation', perplexity, or self-absorption due to depression or schizophrenia.

2. It may be difficult or impossible to *keep* the attention of the patient, (*a*) because the patient returns to predominant preoccupations (depression and schizophrenia); (*b*) because the attention of the patient is readily distracted by stimuli from the outside, this distractibility preventing concentration on any given subject for any length of time (manic and certain organic pictures); (*c*) because of variation in the level of consciousness where this is dimmed or clouded. Such variation should always arouse suspicion of organic intra-cranial cause.

Disturbances of volition, general activity, motor behaviour

Lack of initiative may be a life-long characteristic, especially in dullards and inadequate people. When it appears as a new symptom this is usually in states of debility after physical illness, neurasthenic states, and in depression and schizophrenic psychoses, but it is not uncommon with cerebral lesions, especially those involving the frontal lobes.

Retardation denotes a condition, not natural to the person but associated with illness, characterised objectively by slowness of speech and action, but in fact due to difficulty in execution. (It is rare for retarded patients to experience slow thoughts and empty minds.) It is most often seen in depressions and some schizophrenic states, and when of rare severity may result in stupor. Patients with organic mental conditions can also be slow in the uptake.

Stupor means complete suppression of speech, movement and action not accounted for by profound disturbances of consciousness. Though less common than formerly, it is produced by schizophrenic disturbances of will, but it may result from extreme retardation in melancholic patients. *Flexibilitas cerea* (a peculiar type of 'wax-like' rigidity of the muscles), *catalepsy* (the tendency to keep up postures which have been imposed), and *negativism* (automatic resistance to all outside stimuli) are symptoms sometimes found in schizophrenia and also in some conditions of organic cerebral disease.

Psychomotor overactivity, together with an increased speed of action, can be seen in all states of excitement, most commonly in manic conditions, in which it is sustained, and sometimes in organic confusional states in which it is less sustained and more variable. Impulses may follow one another so rapidly that none is carried out or completed. Psychomotor overactivity can also occur in certain abnormal personalities under the influence of alcohol.

In *Catatonic excitement*, which occurs in schizophrenia, the motor behaviour is generally more disintegrated, and features like *stereo-*

typy (monotonous repetition in speech and movements), mannerisms and grimacing are often observed and are highly characteristic.

Perseveration denotes a repetition of a phrase or movement, apparently due to inability to change to a new one, as when the patient asked to answer a question continues to give an answer previously given. It may be most marked in the field of speech and may be regarded as part of aphasia. It is common in all organic psychiatric conditions.

Suggestion means influence by processes other than reason; *suggestibility* is the capacity—varying in each individual—of yielding to such influences. This normal attribute is increased in states of disturbed consciousness. It is strikingly present in the hypnotic state. In schizophrenics it may reach the extreme degree of *automatic obedience*. *Echopraxia* and *echolalia*, i.e. the automatic repetition of actions which are seen, or of words which are heard, are particular examples of this.

Abnormal impulses, such as *kleptomania* (the impulse to steal) and *pyromania* (the impulse to set things on fire) do sometimes occur in obsessive-compulsive states, i.e. as impulses experienced against the will and under a subjective feeling of compulsion. Where thefts and arson have been committed, however, there is usually some much simpler explanation despite the pleas often put forward by those who are brought to justice.

Disturbances of thought
There is frequently confusion in the student's mind when considering thought disorder, of which '*schizophrenic thought disorder*' is one particular type, but which is so frequently mentioned that the existence of other forms is ignored.

By the term '*schizophrenic thought disorder*' we mean a complex disturbance of the grammatical use of language, both with the spoken and written word. There is a basic disturbance of the associations of sound or meaning, or both, which leads to a rambling vagueness, or to more severe disturbances. It is described in the chapter on schizophrenia (p. 140) in more detail.

Thought blocking and *neologisms*, both mentioned below, are also very characteristic of schizophrenia, but are not necessarily present even in the presence of severe thought disorder. Delusions, even if characteristically schizophrenic, do not come under the heading of 'schizophrenic thought disorder', which is essentially a disturbance of the way in which thoughts and feelings are expressed.

Retardation, encountered mainly in depressive states, is characterised by slowness or difficulty in thinking, often accompanied by a poverty of ideas of which the patients are clearly aware. Many depressive patients who are retarded do not, however, so much complain of slow thoughts or empty minds as of thoughts that go round and round but do not get on. An extreme poverty of association may lead to a form of perseveration very like that seen in organic conditions.

Circumstantiality means slow progression of thought because of a continual tendency to digress into detailed accounts of trivial matters—such as the exact date and time of some event many years ago. It is very characteristic of those with obsessional personalities; but also occurs in unintelligent or very self-centred people. As a new development it suggests schizophrenia or organic brain disease.

Flight of ideas is typical of mania. Manic patients think quickly and have a great wealth of association which prevents them from pursuing a purposive line of thought. Flight of ideas is an exaggeration of what Schopenhauer attributed to certain authors. 'They write as if they were playing dominoes. The incidental number of the last piece determines the next, and the following piece has no relation to the last but one.' An example of 'flight of ideas' is provided by a manic patient who said 'maternal, paternal, infernal, Dante'.

The term *Incoherence* is self-explanatory. It may occur in normal people who are emotionally upset. When persistent it should suggest either organic confusion or schizophrenia.

Blocking, or sudden interruption in the stream of thought, occurs in schizophrenia.

Neologisms are frequently invented by schizophrenics. A patient, for instance, described a drawing: 'Cordron. A theme of curved and fancy lines, stcollic st, from steeple word from the point on the top of the post collic (unexplainable) word matching the point; caller from the cordron and cross piece. Squirrel, wirrel from wearl; the curls in the lines which look like a wearl pool.'

Predominant ideas are convictions not based on reason but on an emotional foundation. They are not necessarily pathological, and every normal person tends to develop them in the fields of politics, religion, and love. They must be distinguished from obsessional ideas (p. 56).

A *delusion* is a false belief which cannot be corrected by an appeal to reason or logic, making due allowance for the individual's cultural and religious background. *Secondary delusions* are those which arise as explanations of, or understandably from, some other disturbance. For example, a depressed patient who feels very ill, has severe constipation and is losing weight, may believe with delusional intensity that he has cancer of the bowel. Another, plagued by guilt, may feel that the police are watching him.

A *primary (or autochthonous)* delusion has a different quality. This is a delusion which springs suddenly into the mind of the patient, often after a period of puzzled unease, in which the world seems full of some hidden meaning, threatening and vague (*delusional mood*). Suddenly, he sees, or less often hears, something—in itself ordinary—but perceives it in an extra-ordinary way. This is the '*delusional perception*', which introduces the primary delusion. For example, a young man, a student of German history, spent all night wandering around the City of London, in a world full of mystery and fear. At dawn he saw a traffic light change from red to yellow to green—and he 'knew' that this was a signal to him, and that it was now his task to complete Bismarck's work and re-unite Germany.

Delusional mood, delusional perception and primary delusions, are three of the so-called 'first rank' symptoms of schizophrenia discussed in Chapter 8.

Many delusions are secondary to hallucinations, but they can occasionally develop from a real event or experience as the result of systematic although emotionally biased reasoning.

Delusions are also classified as those of grandeur, of self-reproach, of poverty, of reference*, of persecution, or as hypochondriacal delusions, according to their content.

Quite often delusions can be understood rather simply, as can some auditory hallucinations. For example, someone usually troubled by marked feelings of inadequacy and failure may develop delusions of grandeur when psychotic; and someone troubled by fears that he is unattractive to women and has homosexual doubts or urges, is likely to hear voices commenting, unfavourably, on his sexuality if he develops schizophrenia.

The fact that the content can be understood in this way does *not* provide an adequate expanation for a delusion developing. This is the old problem of 'content and form'. In psychiatry the 'form' of a psychotic illness is usually more basic than the 'content'. This is demonstrated by the fact that in the nineteenth century patients had religious delusions and hallucinations, whereas now they are more likely to be about hypnosis and X-rays, although the underlying schizophrenic illness is the same.

---

* i.e. erroneous ideas that things happening have special reference to the patient.

The term *Paranoid* as used in psychiatry ranges from ideas of being done down and put upon, to a more fully developed resentful sense of hostile environment coupled with a tendency towards the formation of delusions of a systematised character to explain it. In this way its use may range from an attitude of mind not in itself at variance with reality, to definite delusions of persecution. It may, therefore, reasonably include a man who thinks his boss is doing him down, which may be more or less true, and a man who is patently mistaken in thinking himself persecuted. In deciding the truth of the matter, what is important is the evidence rather than the patient's belief; a man's wife may be unfaithful, but more evidence is required than a belief arising from a torn scrap found in the waste-paper basket.

Obsessional ideas (compulsive thoughts) must be distinguished from delusions and from predominant ideas. Compulsive thoughts are recognised as being abnormal and foreign to the personality, and are resented and resisted. The patient struggles against the obsessional idea, but may fight for his delusions. Predominant preoccupations are not obsessional in that they are fully accepted and should be distinguished from compulsive thoughts on that account; i.e. for a student to be preoccupied with examinations is not abnormal. In content, obsessional thoughts are often banal and pointless, but they are sometimes indecent, blasphemous or aggressive.

Passivity and related experiences

Passivity experiences are those in which the patient feels that some other power—human or non-human—is influencing, controlling or making his thoughts, feelings, utterances or movements. He may feel like a robot, or he may feel that the influence is only partial or that it is an attempt to control him which has not yet succeeded.

The related experiences of the title are in a way the opposite of passivity, in that instead of some force coming into the mind, there is the experience of thoughts or feelings leaving. Thus there is *thought broadcasting*, when the patient feels that what he is thinking or feeling is coming out into the open, as it were, so that others can pick it up, and perhaps record it. *Thought withdrawal* is rather more selective, so that only certain thoughts or ideas are being extracted; *thought insertion* is the exact opposite of thought withdrawal.

All of these are *experiences*, and not perceptual distortions or ideas, and they have in common a loss or disruption of the boundaries or limits of the self. They are disturbances of the ego-boundary, to use another term. They are absolutely characteristic of schizophrenia, and each of them counts as a first rank symptom in diagnostic importance. As with other such symptoms, they lose that importance if there is any organically determined clouding of consciousness.

Disturbances of affect

Affect means emotion or mood. Disturbances of affect may consist of variations in intensity or duration, or the emotional response may be abnormal because inappropriate to the particular situation. The term 'Affective Disorders' (p. 161) refers to sustained disorders of mood rather than to transient emotional reactions.

Intensity. Increased intensity of emotion is often complained of by hysterical and histrionic 'sensitive' patients. Of more significance as regards seriousness of illness is the converse, i.e. poverty and loss of emotion (*affective loss*). This is common in depression and in early schizophrenia.

Shallowness of affect. This may be a life-long feature of some people—(certain hysterical psychopaths and dullards). Where it appears as a new feature it is suggestive of schizophrenia or organic deterioration. Again, certain quite normal individuals are acutely aware of complete emotional detachment after a psychic shock, such as seeing an accident. This is usually a transient experience of no significance.

Incapacity to control the emotions and their expression is characteristic of organic syndromes (*emotional incontinence and lability*). Normal emotional experiences, such as elation, depression, irritability, anxiety, may become morbid by reason of their intensity and duration, but the extreme degrees of melancholy and panic are never experienced by the normal individual.

Irritability is increased in normal people by fatigue, overwork and hunger. It is liable to be marked after head injuries, in epileptics, and in patients whose emotional control has been reduced through organic changes.

Ecstasy may be described as a feeling of overwhelming bliss combined with an all-pervading sense of clearness of perception. It is often associated with a feeling of suspicion and fear, and not infrequently accompanied or followed by the appearance of autochthonous delusions. True ecstasy is probably beyond the experience or imagination of normal persons. States of ecstasy are chiefly seen in schizophrenia.

Incongruity of affect. This exists when the patient's emotional reaction is markedly different from that expected in the given situation. It is mainly used to describe schizophrenic patients, who often laugh or smile in an empty and fatuous way at inappropriate times. (This may not reflect their inner feelings, the normal expression of which is disturbed.)

In an unemotional psychopath incongruity of affect may be striking, e.g. when he acts without embarrassment or distress when caught in a major delinquency.

Ambivalence denotes the simultaneous existence of contradictory emotions. It is a part of normal experience, but in very exaggerated form is commonly seen in schizophrenia.

Anxiety may occur in any psychiatric syndrome. It sometimes appears in the special form of '*phobias*', which are specific fears (e.g. of sharp knives) that the patient recognises to be irrational. Fears of closed and open spaces (*claustrophobia, agoraphobia*) are fairly common. Phobias may arise on an obsessive-compulsive basis, or in course of a depressive illness or as part of a personality problem in, for example, neurotic women who may be rendered housebound.

Disturbances of memory

The function of remembering is generally divided into (1) Registration, (2) Retention, (3) Recall.

1. *Registration*. Registration of the material to be remembered may be disturbed by lack of concentration. Thus in manic states the distractibility prevents the patient from perceiving properly what is happening. The manic patient will therefore tend only to remember subsequently those things that by chance, or because of their special impressiveness, did not escape his attention. By contrast, registration may be prevented by intense pre-occupation with something else, as in the absent-minded professor. In states of unconsciousness nothing can be recorded, hence the subsequent amnesia. When consciousness is dimmed or clouded, only a partial or patchy recollection of what has taken place remains. This may even extend to a complete amnesia if registration was grossly deficient. Serious defects of registration usually arise from organic cause.

2. *Retention*. Disturbances of retention should only be assumed if it is certain that registration and recall are unaffected. Retention for short or longer periods of time (the latter being essential for learning) may be disturbed to a different degree. The capacity for retaining visual and auditory material may also differ markedly. In general, the capacity to retain material is better if associations are present with which it can easily be connected. Poverty and slowness of association may simulate a memory disturbance. Again, serious defects of retention usually arise from an organic cause.

3. *Recall*. Recall may be either automatic or voluntary. In morbid mental conditions automatic recall is often preserved whilst the

capacity for voluntary recall (i.e. involving conscious effort) is frequently impaired. These phenomena can often be observed in normal individuals who are fatigued, or in the aged, and the disturbance is most marked in trying to recall names. It is generally possible for a person to recognise something immediately which he could not recall on voluntary effort, or only to be able to recall facts when something associated with them is recollected. Voluntary effort quite often seems to interfere with recollection.

The ability to recall is facilitated by richness and rapidity of association; consequently poverty or slowness of association may make memory disturbances appear more severe than they really are. All disturbances of recall cannot, however, be explained as being due to loss of initiative or poverty of association. Nor should all memory disturbances be attributed to 'repression', although this may play an important part in determining which material is not recollected. Thus, although failure to recall may have an organic basis, emotional factors may play a larger part than is usual in failures of registration and retention.

When memory impairment is due to organic brain disease this is usually for recent events rather than for remote ones. The gaps of memory, or amnesia, consequent upon sudden damage to the brain (head injuries, epileptic fits, apoplexies) are often for a longer period than that of the actual unconsciousness. This is frequently seen in *retrograde amnesia* after injury to the brain, as when a person cannot remember the accident or the events for a variable length of time preceding it. The amnesia for the period of unconsciousness, or of disturbed consciousness, is due to lack of registration. *Anterograde amnesia* (that is, loss of memory for a period after consciousness has apparently been regained) is due to a state of altered consciousness during the period which the patients do not remember afterwards.

Total loss of memory over a long period, or over the whole of life, is generally a hysterical symptom, and inconsistencies between the knowledge which the patient shows and what he claims to have forgotten may show that this material is very near the surface of consciousness: in other words, if not deliberate deceit, self-deception plays an active part. The material is available if the patient cares to look, but he succeeds in keeping it out of sight and apart from the rest of his mental content (*dissociation*, p. 268). Such hysterical amnesias are also related to *fugues* (see p. 275). In these the patient wanders off in a dissociated state. The motive is usually to avoid some difficulty or situation which he feels incapable of facing.

A normal quality of remembering is that it tends to mould the past according to desire and to fill in defects in memory with facts which may have been in the past rather than with facts which are genuinely recollected; and the conviction that such false recollection carries is often very striking. When there is a pathological loss of memory the gap is often filled in with elaborate fabrications. Broadly speaking, the less critical the patient, and the more active his initiative, the more capable he becomes of producing such fabrications, and of changing them under cross-examination. This, called *confabulation*, is often striking in the Korsakoff psychosis (p. 112) and organic dementias.

The feeling of familiarity which is experienced on recognition may also, in certain abnormal conditions, be attached to facts or things that have not previously been known to the individual. This experience of *déjà vu* is known to many normal persons when fatigued or sleepy, and it may be a prominent feature in certain neurotic syndromes, and sometimes in disturbances of temporal lobe function.

In the Korsakoff psychosis patients not infrequently get the order of past events wrong, so that the disturbance does not so much involve correct fact as correct sequence.

Disturbances of intelligence
Variations in the amount and type of intelligence are very great. A poor native endowment is the main feature of *mental subnormality* (*amentia*, p. 229). An acquired impairment of intelligence that is irreversible is known as *dementia*. The mentally subnormal have never been intelligent; the demented may have been but have lost the faculty. The onset of dementia is gradual, except where it has followed some severe head injury or acute illness with destructive effect on the brain, such as meningitis or certain poisonings. In the progress of dementia, creative thinking suffers first, abstract reasoning next, until finally primitive tasks such as the definition of words or the findings of opposites or common qualities, become impossible. A moderate degree of dementia may show itself only in an ability to cope with new problems and situations, though ordinary activities and familiar tasks can still be managed. Severe degrees of dementia interfere with even the simplest activities, such as dressing, eating and care of toilet.

Apart from amentia and dementia, it will be realised that various factors of a more or less transient kind may interfere with a person's intellectual application, so that there may be a relative failure in performance without actual deterioration in the intelligence itself. In such cases, if there is uncertainty whether the condition is recoverable or not, it is preferable to use the general term *intellectual impairment* rather than dementia, since this last implies irreversibility.

In trying to assess intellectual impairment of whatever kind, it is always necessary to compare the patient's present performance with his past performance, as shown by the school career, occupational training and work record. In addition, special tests may be used. These mainly depend on the facts that the patient's vocabulary and general knowledge give a fair idea of his educational and intellectual level, and are relatively resistant to mental deterioration, so that if preservation of these faculties contrasts sharply with performance on other tests, the presumption is that deterioration has occurred. It will be realised that the lower the original intellectual level, the more difficult it is to estimate impairment. (See p. 89.)

Disturbances of sensation

Hallucinations. These may be defined as sensory perceptions (mental impressions of sensory vividness) without objective stimulus, e.g. seeing a pink elephant when no pink elephant was present. *Illusions* are real perceptions falsified, e.g. mistaking a dark stain on a pillow for a bed bug. These definitions may be accepted for practical purposes, but it should be borne in mind that normal sensory perception is far from being an objective picture of reality but is conditioned and modified by many personal factors, both sensory and extra-sensory. In other words there is always a personal contribution to a perceptual situation, but the amount of this personal contribution varies enormously. This holds true for illusions and hallucinations as well as for normal perceptions.

Some anomalies of sensation may be mentioned that should be separated from hallucinations and illusions in the stricter sense. Thus, distortions of visual impressions, owing to detachment of the retina, noises in the ear or labyrinthine sensations due to vascular disturbance, numbness or tingling in the extremities due to pressure on the peripheral nerves, all being disturbances of the apparatus of sensation, are better kept apart. The same applies to flashes of light, if produced by stimulation of the optic nerve, or the more complex subjective experiences produced by stimulation of the sensory areas of the cortex or cerebral pathways.

Visual hallucinations are most commonly found in states of impaired consciousness (delirium and twilight states), and should always suggest the predominance of an aetiological cause of an organic type. Some normal individuals, however, experience visual hallucinations just before they go off to sleep (*hypnagogic hallucinations*). Temporal lobe epilepsy may lead to very elaborate and complex visual hallucinations. Visual hallucinations in toxic and delirious reactions may range from kaleidoscopic patterns appearing when the eyes are shut, to the most complex visions of varying scenes, persons, animals and objects, either still or moving at various speeds. The impression may be vague, or very clear and detailed. The hallucinated objects may be projected in a real setting, i.e. a man may be seen sitting in a real chair, but may be transparent and uninfluenced by any physical happenings around him. Schizophrenics may experience symbolic visions, often possessing a quality of intense significance; but visual hallucinations in schizophrenic conditions are more usually in the nature of vivid mental pictures rather than experiences which are thought to be part and parcel of the external world, and, except in acute phases or episodes, are rare in our culture. There is evidence that they occur more often in schizophrenics from very different societies, e.g. in Saudi Arabia.

Auditory hallucinations. These are most common in schizophrenic states but also occur in toxic confusional conditions, and sometimes in involutional melancholia and senile dementias. They are usually localised in the head, but may appear to come from outside. Less frequently they are located in some part of the body; this is very typical of schizophrenia. They usually occur in the form of voices of varying distinctness, and even when the exact words are not clearly heard the general import is often felt to be plain. They may speak to him, or they may speak about him, commenting on his actions perhaps. This distinction of second person and third person is important. Voices speaking about the patient are characteristic of schizophrenia; as are the voices which echo, anticipate, or immediately follow his thinking—the '*echo de la pensée*' or *echoing thoughts*. Noises, such as creaking, shooting, ringing and so on, may also be heard. Auditory hallucinations often have an illusional foundation.

Tactile hallucinations. Tactile hallucinations are described by schizophrenic and delirious patients. The patient may feel he is being touched or blown upon, or may experience a drizzling sensation of sand or dust. The genital organs are often the seat of tactile hallucinations, which may be elaborated into a belief that the patient has been the victim of rape. Some schizophrenic patients feel that their body, or some part of it, has changed in size or weight. Statements about a change in the internal organs, such that the heart has become a stone, or that the bowels are blocked, may be metaphorical expressions, but are sometimes accepted later as statements of facts, and, in so far as this is the case, become delusions.

Olfactory hallucinations. Olfactory hallucinations, which always seem to have an unpleasant character, are frequently complained of by schizophrenics, less frequently by involutional melancholics, and occasionally by delirious patients.

Hallucinations have many points in common with sensory perceptions, but they also possess certain distinguishing qualities, quite apart from the absence of appropriate stimulus. Their perceptual character, or the conviction that they represent something of external origin, varies from case to case. Hallucinations appear to be more obtrusive in character than perceptions, and tend to occupy the foreground of the patient's mind and to absorb his attention: otherwise the fact that patients are unable to disregard voices and other sensations that are practically meaningless could not be explained.

The content of the hallucinations is determined to a varying extent by the past history of the patient concerned. Elementary hallucinations are more easily explained on a neurological level, but more complex hallucinations of visions and voices can often be traced, as regards content, to the previous experiences, attitudes, views and fantasies of the particular patient. It is sometimes possible to distinguish the physiological from the psychological element in their production. Thus, patients with delirium tremens usually see small and moving dots, as do patients with small scotomata. Elaboration of these into rats, mice, etc., depends upon extrasensory factors. Similarly the more complex hallucinations of cocaine addicts (cocaine bugs under the skin) are built around the nucleus of their tactile sensations. In other instances it is not easy to discover a sensory element in the development of hallucinatory experiences, nor any illusional basis.

Depersonalisation. This is 'a state in which the individual feels himself changed throughout in comparison with his former state. This change extends to both the patient and the outer world and leads to the individual not acknowledging himself as a personality. His actions seem to him automatic; he observes his own actions like a spectator. The outer world seems strange to him, and has lost its character and reality' (Paul Schilder).

The sense of the outer world being changed is sometimes known as *derealisation*, as opposed to the feeling that the patient is himself changed, which constitutes depersonalisation in the more strict sense. Depersonalised patients complain of loss of feeling, whereas observation of their behaviour shows natural emotional responses. There are, however, cases when the subjective poverty of emotions is followed by objective 'affective loss' (p. 173).

Depersonalisation and derealisation may be experienced in a

variety of psychiatric conditions, anxiety and obsessional states, depression, schizophrenia, disturbances of temporal lobe function, temperamental adolescent states and after electrical treatment. They are not necessarily of ominous significance.

The problem of *time perception* and its disturbances is still obscure. They may be observed chiefly in affective disorders, after head injuries and some cerebral operations, and in delirious or subdelirious states. The patients may complain that time moves too fast or too slowly, or in extreme cases that it seems to stand still or rushes on so fast that they cannot follow.

4

Classification of mental disorders

We have already mentioned (p. 8) that one of the main contributions of the nineteenth century to psychiatry was the establishment of a workable classification of mental illness. This followed the lines traditional in general medicine, and consisted of a series of more or less rigidly defined 'disease entities', each with an aetiology and pathology (presumed but in only a few instances demonstrable), symptomatology and course of its own. Later it came to be realised that many psychiatric conditions were not so much actual diseases in that sense as the individual reactions of particular personalities to situations that they found difficult or stressful. The old classification then had to be adjusted to include this concept, and mental illness thus came to be divided into two great groups: (1) *the psychoses*, and (2) *the neuroses*. The *psychoses* were the disease-entities, major illnesses, which in their full form involved insanity (e.g. schizophrenia, manic depressive psychosis); the psychotic patient experienced life in a distorted way, owing to delusions, hallucinations or misinterpretations, which were symptoms of an illness arising mainly from constitutional causes and probably of an obscure physical sort. The *neuroses* were minor illnesses in the sense that the patients experience only such mental symptoms as anxiety or tension not in themselves outside the realm of normal experience, which were unrelated to insanity and did not lead to it, but arose as a response to difficulty or stress, though experienced to an exaggerated degree.

The validity of the distinction between psychosis and neurosis has been disputed from time to time on the following grounds. First, it is sometimes objected that there is no sharp borderline between sanity and insanity, or therefore between neurosis and psychosis, so that certain cases cannot be assigned definitely to either group, and the difference between neurosis and psychosis then becomes one of degree rather than of kind. Second, it is sometimes objected that the supposed aetiological differences (as arising from attitudes of mind, on the one hand, and from presumed obscure physical causes, on the other) are in invalid distinction in that physical causes for the psychoses have not been satisfactorily established. Third, it is sometimes objected that neuroses cannot be distinguished from psychoses on grounds of severity of the illness, because a person who is mildly insane may be far less handicapped than an entirely sane person with a heavy load of neurotic symptoms.

We hold to the usefulness of the distinction, particularly for schizophrenia and bipolar manic-depressive illnesses. In these the rôle of genetic and constitutional factors is most clear; physical treatment is most useful and purely psychological treatment least effective; and the departure of the patient from normal modes of thought and experience is most striking. In unipolar depression (without manic upswings) the distinction is more blurred, but remains important.

In practice we must be able to offer correct treatment; and in order to do this schizophrenia, bipolar manic-depression, and unipolar depression—for each of which there is rather specific treatment—must be accurately distinguished from each other and from organic and neurotic conditions.

We submit the following classification of the psychoses:

1. *Organic psychoses.* The main features are disturbances of consciousness and of the intellectual functions of memory and grasp. They range from clouding of consciousness through delirium and, where the condition is more than transient, Korsakoff's syndrome, to dementia. Physical factors are predominantly important in their causation. The conditions will be discussed later.

2. *Functional psychoses.* These receive this non-committal name because their aetiology is not yet proved. They are two in number:

a. *Schizophrenia.* This is not so much a specific illness as a group of heterogeneous conditions which have features in common. The main features are progressive introversion with disintegration of thought, of emotional responses and of the personality. Constitutional factors are largely responsible.

b. *Affective illnesses.* It is now recognised that this group includes:

(i) *Bipolar manic-depressive illness,* in which there are sustained phases both of depressed and elevated mood; and

(ii) *Unipolar depressive illnesses* in which abnormally elevated mood does not occur.

Schizophrenic illnesses can be defined fairly clearly and do not merge with neurotic conditions, but depressive illnesses cover a very wide range, varying from minor and purely reactive states of depressive mood, to true psychoses with agitation, delusions and hallucinations.

Involutional melancholia is a special form of depressive illness that occurs for the first time in the involutional period of life and is characteristically accompanied by agitation and/or bizarre hypochondriasis.

All the foregoing conditions are liable to be major illnesses in the sense that they may lead to the patient viewing life in a distorted way owing to the occurrence of delusions or misinterpretations. For example, in the organic psychoses the failure of grasp leads to suspiciousness with delusional beliefs that sinister goings-on are afoot; the failure of memory leads to beliefs that things mislaid have been stolen, that people who are dead are alive, that people and things are other than what they are, and so forth. In schizophrenia there are invariably distortions of content (delusions, hallucinations, misinterpretations) at some stage and in some form. In manic-depressive psychosis the manic (i.e. excited) phase may lead to grandiose but false ideas, such as an engagement to Royalty or the possession of riches, in line with a mood of exaltation; and the depressive phases may lead to false beliefs of actual or impending ruin, death and destruction, in line with the pessimistic mood. In involutional melancholia the hypochondriacal ideas, whether of bowel-blocking, malignant disease or destruction of organs through deteriorative processes may be altogether delusional. This is not to say that every single psychotic case necessarily has distortions of content, but that the type of illness is one in which distortions of content *can* occur, as shown by clinical experience. Many patients with recurrent depressions of manic-depressive type may escape the development of delusions in fact, as may those with mild recurrent excitements; but the patterns of these illnesses are such that they belong to the manic-depressive group, in which it is known that distortions can occur, though they may happen not to do so in a particular individual case. After all, it is possible to have mild or severe attacks of bronchitis, without the severity affecting the diagnostic category to which it belongs. In the bipolar affective illnesses typical delusions might well develop in any subsequent breakdown, despite their absence before.

On the other hand, distortions of content do not occur in the neuroses, whether mild or severe, and, although they may be very disabling, these are benign illnesses in the sense that they are not associated with such grave developments. Traditionally, the neuroses are listed as follows:

1. *Anxiety and phobic anxiety neuroses*, characterised by the prominence of anxiety, which is undue, unduly easily provoked, and unduly persistent. Psychological and constitutional factors are both important in their causation.

2. *Neurotic (or reactive) depression*, characterised by a variably depressive mood (of different symptom-pattern from that of manic-depressive depression) occurring as a personal reaction to conflicts or situations of stress.

3. *Hysteria*, characterised by the patient developing and making use of some symptoms to serve some particular personal purpose, but without awareness or without full awareness of the motives for doing so.

4. *Obsessional neurosis*, characterised by the repeated and involuntary intrusion into the patient's mind of thoughts or impulses, of which he cannot rid himself by an act of will.

Traditionally, these are described as separate entities, as in early editions of this book. We have come to the conclusion, however, that it is more logical to consider them under the general heading of 'Personality Reactions'—except for obsessional neurosis which does have such special features of its own as to warrant its being considered separately. The manifestations of anxiety, reactive depression and hysteria are, after all, not so much those of illness in the formal sense, as of the patient reacting to the life situation with anxiety, with depression or hysterically; moreover, the patient may react in all three such ways at the same time, or with any of them at different times, i.e. with anxious, depressive or hysterical symptoms occurring in different degrees and combinations. Rather than trying to view such cases as suffering from *either* an anxiety neurosis, *or* neurotic depression, *or* hysteria, we have come long since to prefer a more elastic approach, thinking in terms of 'How much anxiety, how much depression, how much is hysterical?'

Our classification has therefore become, so far:

1. *The psychoses*
   a. Organic psychoses
   b. Functional psychoses
      (i) Schizophrenia
      (ii) Affective illnesses.
2. *Personality reactions* with anxiety and depressive symptoms, and hysterical features.
3. *Obsessional states.*

There remains a heterogeneous group of cases whose common

feature is a failure of normal development, whether in the field of personality, sex, or intelligence. Thus, the psychopathic personality, as described on pp. 224–228 shows failure to develop emotional maturity as a main feature; cases of sexual deviation represent a failure of normal development in a different sphere, as do those with anomalies of intelligence. These are essentially 'Disorders of development', which is an alternative title. They are grouped together here under the heading 'Disorders of personality and intelligence', although there is much overlap in practice with various abnormal reactions arising in those with 'Personality reactions'.

The classification thus becomes:

1. *The psychoses*
   a. Organic psychoses
   b. Functional psychoses
      (i) Schizophrenia
      (ii) Affective illnesses.
2. *Personality reactions* with special reference to anxiety and depressive symptoms and hysterical features. Sexual difficulties, psychopathic and other developmental disorders are often relevant.
3. *Obsessional states.*
4. *Disorders of personality and of intelligence (disorders of development).*

This classification is not exhaustive, and there is considerable overlap in practice, but it provides a scheme into which most patients can be conveniently fitted. The student may be helped by the following diagrams. Suppose that the organic conditions are represented by a circle (A), the schizophrenic conditions by another circle (B), and personality reactions by a third circle (C). These circles should not be considered as quite separate from one another as in Diagram I, but rather as overlapping as in Diagram II.

Individual cases can then be represented as at any point within the system of circles. For example, the area A1 would represent an organic condition in almost pure culture, A2 would be an organic condition with personality problem as well, and C2 would be a mixed picture with a schizophrenic and personality problem combined; and so on in various combinations and proportions. The same principle holds good for the various subdivisions within the main groups. Thus it is not uncommon to meet with cases that can most conveniently be described as obsessional states with depressive features and so on.

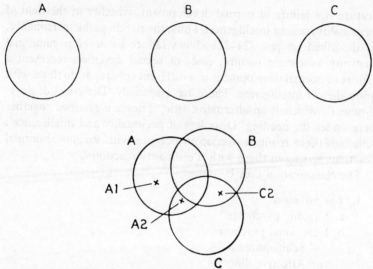

Fig. 4.1 Relationship of various syndromes.

Multi-dimensional diagnosis

Psychiatric diagnosis (or classification) is not, however, exhausted by describing a clinical picture in terms of its diagnostic category. The reader will have observed that in the foregoing discussion of classification, reference to aetiology was not entirely omitted. There is in fact a certain affinity between the nature of the cause and the type of condition that ensues. This relation is closest between organic causes and organic states; but hysterical states have a close relation to specific psychological factors and psychopathic reactions to a particular type of constitution.

When attempting to make a more complete psychiatric diagnosis, (1) the *aetiological* should be distinguished from (2) the *descriptive* aspect. The latter consists of the syndrome that is observed. The aetiological aspect comprises the assessment of the physical, psychological and constitutional factors and their relative importance in bringing about the condition in question. (3) No condition can be fully understood without taking into account personality reactions as seen in the light of the past history and environment. Therefore, a complete psychiatric diagnosis should include the essential characteristics of the patient's *previous personality*. (4) The practical value of any diagnosis lies in its therapeutic and prognostic implications. The symptoms as such may have little significance in assessing these. Therefore, in making the diagnosis, the expected course of the condition, assessed by clinical experience in the light of the clinical picture, aetiology and personality of the patient, should also be indicated.

An example of a diagnostic formulation that would satisfy all these criteria might be:

'Acute recoverable anxiety state, reactive to a terrifying accident, in an immature, ill-adjusted personality of low intelligence', or

'Acute delirium, due to chronic alcoholism and malnutrition, in a hypomanic personality of the *faux bon homme* type, with pre-existent organic deterioration.'

It is, of course, possible and may be desirable to go into more detail, in particular by weighing the various aetiological factors and assessing their importance in either bringing about the condition or in colouring it. For example, a case might be diagnosed as follows:

'A transient depressive reaction with anxiety and obsessional features in a dependent, sensitive, over-conscientious foreign youth following interrogation by the police over suspected customs irregularities', or

'Progressive pre-senile dementia coloured by alcoholism in a retired general with highly aggressive pre-morbid personality.'

Diagnosis of the above kind are sometimes called 'multi-dimensional'.

Classifications are inventions and not discoveries; and the student can save himself a good deal of puzzlement about individual cases if he realises that a psychiatric diagnosis is essentially a short-hand description.

5

Psychiatric case-taking

It is just as important in psychiatry as in general medicine to have a scheme of examination, for unless the examination is systematic, important aspects may be missed. The examination of the psychiatric patient differs from that of the general medical case mainly in (1) the attempt to cover a wider range, (2) the need for more informality, and (3) the greater need for corroborative information. These three main points may be briefly explained.

(1) *The wider range* is necessary because in psychiatry it is particularly important to assess, as will later be seen, how far the patient's present state differs from, or how much it is merely an extension of, what has gone before; this demands some knowledge of his previous personality and habits of reaction.

(2) *The greater informality* is desirable for much the same reason, namely that one aims to see the patient as he really is, and therefore unhampered by artificial constraints. Although there must be a scheme of examination, this should be reasonably elastic in application, since it is desirable that the patient should express himself freely, and he will be prevented from doing so if the examination is conducted in a rigid and formal fashion. What is required, therefore, is for the doctor to carry the necessary framework in his head so that he can mentally tick off the items as the patient produces the necessary information, which will be done both spontaneously and in answer to questions. As the scheme of examination is rather extensive, the student may find that he cannot carry it in his head all at once. He need not be dismayed if he has to keep the written scheme before him and follow it in detail with his first few cases. Indeed, he will be wise to do so. Although the scheme may seem rather formidable at first sight, it is logical enough to be memorised with no great difficulty, and with a little practice can then be quite easily applied from memory. Once it is held in mind, it will be found unnecessary (and is often undesirable) to pursue each item in the set order. Even so, the student will be wise to indulge in short cuts only when he has had some experience and practice; otherwise his short cut may be to the wrong shop.

(3) *The corroborative information* is necessary not so much from any lack of co-operation and unreliability among psychiatric patients (though these are sometimes found), as from the difficulty of seeing ourselves as we really are and therefore of giving an unbiased account of ourselves (p. 42), so that an objective description of the patient and his condition from relatives or friends is likely to be helpful and may be indispensable. Thus, to take two extreme and perhaps cynical examples, patients on a criminal charge and pleading their abnormal mental condition as a defence, tend to remember numerous neurotic traits in their past lives as well as a large number of mentally afflicted relatives; whereas applicants for pensions of the grounds of neurotic disability, tend to forget previous breakdowns and any psychopathic inheritance. The critical sifting of evidence obtained from outside sources as well as from the patient will not only make for greater accuracy but may also save much time in the end. The relatives or friends should, of course, be seen separately, and it is better to see them after the patient, to lessen the feeling that he is 'being talked about behind his back'.

The help of a trained psychiatric social worker in collecting the necessary data may be considerable; and naturally the general practitioner starts with a great initial advantage over the specialist since he is able to know the domestic and social situation at first hand.

EXAMINATION OF THE PATIENT

This consists of two parts, the *interview* and the *physical examination*. It is always desirable to perform a thorough physical examination, with special attention to the central nervous system; but unfortunately the pressures of hospital life often lead to this being omitted in out-patient departments. In fact a sizeable percentage of psychiatric patients have a significant physical illness, particularly those admitted to acute psychiatric wards.

The purpose of the psychiatric *interview* is threefold: to gain a picture of the patient's state of mind: to understand the setting, the personality and the development of the patient in which the state of mind has occurred: and to create or maintain a helpful relationship between the doctor and the patient.

The establishment of the right atmosphere must be kept in mind throughout. The first essential is to listen, and the second is to give enough time—at least an hour for a first interview and preferably more. The rapport between patient and doctor is based on the latter's interest in the patient's complaints. The patient should be encouraged to talk and should be diverted as little as possible. It always pays to spend time on the patient's description of his symptoms, in which he will incidentally reveal a good deal about himself. Throughout the diagnostic interview the doctor should play a secondary rôle. He should never seek to impress the patient, but should allow the latter to be himself. It is inevitable that the doctor will have to ask some questions, but these should be as few as possible. If questions have to be asked on intimate topics, they should be asked frankly and without diffidence, since diffidence is easily imparted. In fact, the interview should be conducted on level terms as between equals, but unnecessary trespass on the patient's feelings and private affairs should be avoided. Where the patient shows marked hesitation or defensiveness over some sensitive point, the issue should not be forced. Note of his attitude should be made and the matter may be reopened later as may be necessary.

The student will find practice of the greatest help. The two main mistakes which he must avoid are (1) asking leading questions, and (2) moralising. He may find this difficult at first. It is almost irresistible to put questions in such a way as to suggest the answer (e.g. 'you didn't?' 'it wasn't?') and this fault is often combined with an inflection or facial expression which leaves little doubt in the patient's mind not only as to what answer is expected, but as to what reception a different answer might receive. The reticent or allegedly uncooperative patient is usually the product of a poor examination technique, for most people like to talk about themselves; most patients are surprisingly willing to discuss even their intimate problems with small encouragement, and many are grateful for the opportunity. But any rapport that may have been established tends naturally to be broken by such a remark as: 'You don't mean to say that a great big chap like you is afraid of the dark?' Moreover, a poor technique of examination can easily result in inaccurate as well as inadequate information, and this is especially likely to be so if the questions asked are not geared to the patient's intelligence. Finally, it is permissible to laugh with a patient but never at him.

Scheme of examination
The following items are suggested as a frame of reference:

Particulars
Name. Age. Sex. Single, married, separated, divorced. Occupation. Religion. Address and telephone number. Addresses and telephone numbers of next-of-kin and private doctor.

Complaints
These should be noted in detail, if possible verbatim.

History of the present illness
Begin by establishing 'when did you last feel quite well?', and then take a careful chronological account of the development of symptoms both mental and physical, so that they can be related to important life events before and during the development of the illness. It is common to find that the more carefully this account is taken the further back the history extends, and the more clearly the relationship to life events appears.

Personal history
The importance of different epochs of life and development will, of course, vary considerably with the age of the patient; neurotic traits in childhood will obviously have less significance in a senile case than in an adolescent.

(1) *Early development.* Birth injuries. Whether brought up by parents or not. Dates of weaning, walking, talking. Home atmosphere: relationship to parents and others in the family; sleeping arrangements. Neurotic traits, e.g. morbid fears (of dark, etc.), thumb-sucking, stuttering, temper-tantrums, enuresis and other difficulties in toilet-training, sleep-walking, night-terrors, food fads.

(2) *School record.* Scholastic attainments; social adaptation as regards friendliness, participation in games and recreations, home-sickness, discipline and discipline difficulties.

(3) *Work record.* Jobs held, why taken on, how long held, reasons for leaving, financial returns.

(4) *Social record.* Attitudes towards relatives and friends, towards authority (including anti-social trends, lying, stealing, rebellion), towards religion and politics. Steady, or variable and moody? How spare time is spent. Hobbies, interests. Successes and disappointments. Ambitions. What makes life worth living?

(5) *Sex.* Development. Information, how acquired. Masturbation and attitudes towards it. Sex experiences and attitudes towards them. Menstruation. Marriage. Pregnancies, miscarriages, abortions. Contraceptive measures. Menopause. Difficulties in sex life. Happiness or otherwise of marital relations. (Do *not*, for example, ask an unmarried girl if she has *no* boy friends, but rather if she has any *special* boy friend.) Details of the sexual history may well not be forthcoming, particularly at a first interview with a reserved person. It is usually unwise to push the patient for more informa-

tion than he is willing to give, but you should let him know that it might be important.

Medical history

(1) Physical illnesses, and how readily recovered from. (2) 'Nervous' or 'mental' illnesses, and whether or not in circumscribed attacks, whether treated, and if so, where. (3) Attitudes towards health, bodily disturbance, and treatment; use and abuse of drugs.

Family history

Enquiry is often best delayed until the patient's confidence has been gained. Obtain the occupation of the father and, if possible, of other relatives as well, and where they lived. This is often a good indication of the social and cultural background, and of how far the patient has travelled, geographically and culturally. Determine the place of the patient in the family and the numbers of sibs (i.e. brothers and sisters). Do not begin by asking whether there is insanity or suicide in the family, but ask first after physical health, then after 'nervous' and 'highly strung' relatives with special reference to interference by these conditions with happiness and efficiency. Then ask about major mental illnesses (noting if admission to hospital was required), including epilepsy, alcoholism, drug addiction, criminality, suicide. Take case in each case to distinguish between the two sides of the family. Try to determine more of the home atmosphere, whether happy or not, and the 'health-consciousness', as regards how seriously minor ailments were taken and how far robust attitudes were encouraged. Apart from the possible genetic implications, the family history and background are of importance as indicators of the early environment. Note the ages at which the parents died, as depression in later life is associated with bereavement in childhood and around puberty.

Personality traits

Indications of these will already have been yielded by the facts elicited, and the life history will probably have brought the patient's outstanding personality traits to the examiner's attention. They will afford some guidance as to how far the patient is a positive and effective person, how far he is negative and inadequate, and how far his present state contrasts with his previous personality. The main indications will be afforded by whether the patient has tended to show *fight* by trying to overcome difficulty, or *flight* in trying to dodge or run away from it; *self-confidence* in social relations, as opposed to shyness or timidity; *courage* in physical danger, or cowardice; *initiative*, or lack of it; *self-reliance* in forming judgments and making plans, or dependence on others; *rigidity* so that he is hard to influence, or undue suggestibility; *adventurousness* or a tendency to caution and counting the cost; *enterprise* or preference for the old and familiar; *dominance*, leadership, or self-subordination; *candour*, or suspiciousness; *warm-heartedness*, or emotional coolness; *equability*, or moodiness; *conscientiousness*, or irresponsibility; and so on. The list might be extended indefinitely, but these are the sort of trends to be looked for. People are relatively seldom all of a piece and consistent; contradictory attributes may often be observed and should cause no surprise. When they occur, however, they may be valuable indications that the patient has problems within his own personality, as when a person shows obvious see-sawing between aggressiveness and submissiveness, and can achieve no harmonious integration of such contrasting traits. The more the personality traits are discrepant in relation to each other, the less stable is the personality likely to be. This may be both diagnostically and prognostically important. The assessment of the patient's stability is considered later (p. 80).

Having thus established the nature and development of the complaints, the setting in which they have occurred, the type of personality and its development, as judged by the heredity and facts of the life-history, it remains to complete the formal examination of the mental and physical state.

Mental status

(a) *Appearance and behaviour.* Tidy or unkempt? Easy or difficult to make contact with? Calm or agitated? Cheerful or depressed? Any noticeable oddities, such as mannerisms or grimaces? Behaviour appropriate or inappropriate?

(b) *Talk.* The form rather than the content is considered here. Does he talk readily or reluctantly? Abnormally fast or slowly? To the point or discursively? Are there any incoherences, strange words, puns? Any sudden stops or changes of topic? Does the form of talk vary much with the subject?

(c) *Orientation.* Does the patient know where he is, the time of day and the date, and recognise he is being examined by a doctor?

(d) *Mood.* Is this disturbed? In what way? Note the appearance, for this may give some indication. Non-committal questions should be asked: How do you feel in yourself? What is your mood? How are your spirits? Many varieties of mood may be present—not merely degrees of happiness or sadness, but irritability, fear, worry, restlessness, bewilderment, indifference, and others conveniently included under this heading. It should be noted particularly (i) how much the mood is constant; (ii) how much it varies with circumstances—can the patient 'snap out of it' to normality? (iii) what are the influences that change it; (iv) whether it is appropriate to the circumstances. Are suicidal ideas present (see p. 198)?

(e) *Thought content.* Are there any special worries or preoccupations.

(f) *Distortions of content.* (i) Are there any delusions or misinterpretations? Does the patient show abnormal attitudes towards people or things in his environment? Do people treat him all right, or in some special way? Ask the patient if he has self-conscious feelings that people are talking about him or looking at him. If yes, does he believe it or imagine it? In what way do they do so? Does he feel he is under some outside influence or control? Have things happened that have perplexed or puzzled him? Did they seem to have some special meaning? Does he read things in newspapers, see things in advertisements, hear things on the radio that refer specially to him, and, if so, kindly or unkindly? Does he depreciate himself, e.g. in morals, possessions, health, or does he appear to regard himself grandiosely?

(ii) Are there hallucinations or other disorders of perception? Auditory hallucinations are far the most common. Do the patient's thoughts turn to words in his head? Does he hear them spoken? Does he hear his name called when alone, hear himself talked about when alone? Does he experience peculiar body sensations, feelings of deadness or electricity? The frequency, vividness, and timing of such occurrences should be noted, and the patient's reaction to them and beliefs as to their origin.

(g) *Obsessive-compulsive phenomena.* Does the patient experience thoughts or impulses that repeatedly intrude against his will? Does he have to repeat actions unnecessarily, e.g. go back to make sure doors are locked or taps turned off? Does he have unreasonable fears? What is the relation of these symptoms to his emotional state, especially as regards anxiety and depression? Does he have insight into their illogicality?

(h) *Sensorial faculties.* (i) *Memory.* Good or bad? Better for recent or remote events? Evidence of deterioration? Test by comparing the life-history as given by himself and others, or by examining history for gaps and inconsistencies. Ask about recent events such as admission to hospital (or journey to consulting room) and subsequent happenings, what eaten at last two meals, what knowledge of current events. Does he know his way around the ward, the names of some staff members, and the name of the ward? Note any selective impairment of memory for recent or special incidents. Test further by giving series of digits to repeat, first forwards and then backwards (a normal person should be able to repeat at least seven forward and five backward); and by giving a name, address and three words, which he must repeat immediately, two minutes later and five minutes later.

(ii) *Concentration.* Ask the patient to subtract 7 serially from 100 (93, 86, 79, etc.) and note time taken and number of mistakes.

(iii) *Grasp.* How is the patient's general information? Tests must be geared to his educational level and interests. Suitable questions are: name of the Monarch and her immediate predecessors, Prime Minister, Chancellor of the Exchequer, six large cities in Britain, capitals of European countries, dates of beginning and end of last war.

(*i*) *Intelligence.* Standardised tests are discussed on page 238. The assessment of intellectual deterioration will be found on page 89. A fair estimate can be gained by going over the school and work record and discussion of the patient's jobs and hobbies. Simple rough tests are the definition of abstract words, e.g. 'envy' and 'surprise'; the explanation of proverbs, e.g. 'the early bird catches the worm', and differences, e.g. between a dwarf and a child, or idleness and laziness.

(*j*) *Insight.* Does the patient regard himself as ill? Does he understand the extent and nature of his abnormality? Does he think he can get well?

(*k*) In every patient details should be recorded of any disturbance of appetite and weight; and also of sleep, noting whether there is delay in getting to sleep, early morning wakening, or whether sleep is fitful and broken. Physical examination follows, with emphasis on the central nervous system.

ASSESSMENT OF THE CASE

When the complaint, its development, the setting and personality in which it has occurred, are considered in the light of the full history and results of mental and physical examination, it should be possible to arrive not only at a diagnosis but also at a prognosis and a provisional plan of treatment. The diagnosis and prognosis will depend also to some extent on the stability of the patient's previous personality. The assessment should be made on the *facts* as revealed by the life-history and examination. Reliance should not be placed on mere subjective impressions. The following are the main pointers.

The work record is important. Instability is indicated by frequent unemployment, frequent changes of job, and failure to increase earning capacity with age. This does not necessarily apply to adolescents, who often vary their jobs until they settle down. Suspicion should also be aroused where jobs are often changed on alleged health-grounds, through becoming easily fatigued or intolerant of noise, or in favour of open-air or lighter work. Where such changes are attributed to medical advice, it will often be found that the doctor was merely prevailed upon to endorse the patient's or relatives' own views.

Apart from work, the most valuable evidence of instability is the failure to *sustain* interests and personal relationships. There will be instability where there is no pertinacity in hobbies, and where there is no constancy in friendship or the love-life. Most unstable people show small output of physical energy and distaste for team games or activities where they can hurt themselves. Many lead sheltered and restricted lives because they regard themselves as highly strung or requiring protection from undue effort. Many also lack humour, and though capable of laughing at others, are prevented from laughing at themselves by their egocentricity.

Finally, the family example and tradition are often most important in setting the ethical and social standards as well as the 'health-consciousness' of the patient; knowledge of these is therefore desirable for understanding his reaction to life.

The main questions are as follows:

Is the present state foreign to the patient's previous personality? The answer depends on (*a*) how long it has been present; (*b*) how far the personality was previously stable; (*c*) whether, if anything similar was previously experienced, that was in circumscribed attacks; and (*d*) how far the personality was stable between such attacks. If the present state appears foreign to the previous personality and has not been experienced before (or experienced only in circumscribed attacks with normality between), we start to think in terms of (i) organic syndromes, especially when impairment of memory and grasp is prominent, or (ii) conditions belonging to the schizophrenic or affective groups. That is, we think in terms of specific illnesses. This is especially so where the state is not easily construed as a reaction to circumstances. Such a decision may be easy, but it may require judgment. For instance, profound gloom with hopelessness of recovery, guilt, and unworthiness occurring in an ordinarily stable person, even after a bereavement, would be taken as something more than a mere reaction to the event, *viz.* a true depressive illness.

Is the present state explicable as a reaction of the patient's personality to circumstances? The answer depends on: (*a*) the nature of the symptoms. We should expect anxiety, emotionalism, poor control, a variable degree of depression, and difficulty in getting to sleep. We should *not* expect intellectual impairment, distortions of content (delusions, misinterpretations, and hallucinations), or severe guilt; (*b*) whether the present symptoms are in line with previous instability; or (*c*) are such as the previous personality (as judged by the life-history) might reasonably be expected to show in the circumstances. If the symptoms are not foreign to the previous personality, but seem to arise from it, and to be reasonably construed as provoked by the circumstances, we start to think not in terms of specific illness but of attitudes of mind arising from an unstable personality.

Are we dealing with an unstable personality who, apart from symptoms arising from the instability, is also developing a specific illness? This question is more difficult to answer. It depends on (*a*) the extent and constancy of new symptoms; (*b*) their nature; (*c*) how far they conform to those found in the more specific illnesses. Such assessment may be far from easy. These are cases that may require some observation before a firm opinion can be given.

As regards treatment, the more the illness appears a specific one, whether organic, schizophrenic, or manic-depressive, the greater is the likelihood of some physical treatment being required. The more the condition seems to arise from attitudes of mind as part of a personality difficulty, the more will psychological management and psychotherapy be required.

6

Organic mental states

Certain principles determine many of the manifestations of impaired brain function from brain lesions of any type: trauma, ischaemia, degenerative conditions, infections and others. It is for these reasons that throughout this chapter the term 'brain damage' refers not only to the results of trauma, but also to any other cause of brain cell disease or death.

Rate of onset. The more acute the injury or damage the more likely is consciousness to be disturbed. Slowly progressive tumours or atrophy do not disturb consciousness until very late, whereas quite minor head injuries do so early.

Severity and extent of damage. Naturally the more severe and extensive the damage the greater the effects, although there is much individual variation, and site of damage is also very important in this. Overall, the larger the quantity of brain tissue damaged or dead the more severe the long term effects will be.

Site of damage. This is important because of the localisation of brain function, as with the differing effects of right and left hemisphere lesions, or frontal as opposed to parietal lesions.

The actual pathology is irrelevant, except in so far as it determines the rate of onset, site, and extent of damage. There is no final difference between the effects of a stroke and the surgical removal of a tumour, if similar areas of the brain are involved.

Mental changes

Although undoubted brain damage may occur with no detectable mental changes, most patients with neurological signs of cerebral hemisphere damage will have some psychological deficit; and mental changes may persist when the physical signs have cleared up. This chapter is therefore also concerned with those many thousands of patients with strokes and head injuries, not very often seen by psychiatrists, in whom mental changes may be more important than their physical disability. Not only is an understanding of their psychological deficits and difficulties helpful in management, but these patients are quite often significantly depressed; and many of them can be helped by antidepressants or electrical treatment (q.v.). Too often however, depression is ignored, or is considered as an inevitable result of the stroke, so that no treatment is offered.

In non-progressive brain damage, spontaneous improvement after a single insult—such as a stroke or head injury—continues for some time. Young children may go on improving for a decade or more; young adults for three or four years; the elderly for only six to twelve months. In all cases however, the rate of change is greatest in the early stages, and the position at twelve months is a fair guide to the future. In older people a fairly accurate prognosis is possible at six months.

Interview with the patient alone may be misleading, as another informant may clearly describe personality changes not detected at interview. In fact, if organic personality deterioration is obvious at interview it must be fairly severe.

It is important to realise that dementia is not an 'all or nothing' affair, but that there is a continuum ranging from mild forgetfulness to gross dementia; and that in many patients with progressive brain disease, specific defects—for example receptive dysphasia, visuospatial agnosia, or personality change—may dominate · the clinical picture for some time before more generalised changes appear. The level of function may also vary from day to day.

Brain damage *alters the capacity to respond adaptively*. Patients are less able to cope with tasks of various types; less able to tolerate emotional stress; and are subject to new stresses arising from their disabilities. When stressed beyond their capacity they become increasingly anxious, and this sometimes becomes so severe that the patient ends up trembling, mute, unable to respond adaptively to the situation, at times even becoming incontinent; and is afterwards confused and exhausted. This is called *catastrophic anxiety*. A typical situation in which it develops is that of the partly paralysed stroke patient trying to cross the road before the lights change, who stops in the middle of the road trembling, unable to move either way. Lesser degrees of anxiety accompany many activities, depending on the patient's particular physical or mental disabilities and his previous personality. In many cases the result is a progressive reduction of activity, particularly after a bout of catastrophic anxiety, so that the patient withdraws from danger as it were, and his life becomes more and more limited.

The long term effects of any brain damage, including the ability of the patient to cope with life and the way he feels about it, can be seen as the result of the interaction of two main sets of factors—organic and personal: the organic factors depending on the extent and site of damage as mentioned earlier. The subdivisions used here are of course to some extent arbitrary and overlapping.

Organic factors	Personal factors
Perceptual impairment	Premorbid personality and con-
Intellectual impairment	stitution
Personality change	Life situation
(Physical disability, including	(Rehabilitation and treatment)
epilepsy and endocrine changes)	

\   /

Psychiatric symptoms

ORGANIC FACTORS

Perceptual impairment

The importance of this is often missed, because the disabilities do not arise from straightforward impairment or blunting of the sense of light touch and pinprick, to which neurological examination is too often confined by the non-specialist. The most striking disabilities arise in patients in whom parietal damage has led to visual inattention in one half field ('sensory extinction') who cannot perceive stimuli arising simultaneously in both half fields, although they can see them adequately if presented separately. This is not just an academic neurological curiosity, because every time the patient stands on the kerb with traffic moving in both directions he may be *functionally* blind in the affected half field. The anxiety generated by his mistakes in assessing traffic etc. may lead him to stay at home; and he cannot easily explain his problem to others, nor comprehend it himself, because he can see adequately most of the time, as for example when talking to the doctor.

Other important sensory disabilities, associated again with parietal damage, arise from severe impairment of visuo-spatial perception and memory. The patient may no longer be able to assess the size or shape of a room or a space to cross, he cannot remember right from left, he gets lost, bewildered, and frightened. Again, mounting anxiety in the face of the inexplicable leads to a progressive reduction of activity, and at times to withdrawal to the safety of one or two rooms only. Some of these patients may be misdiagnosed as having a neurotic phobic condition, or as 'not really trying'. Although there is no treatment for the perceptual loss, great benefit can follow simple explanation to the patient and relatives, particularly if the latter have felt he only needed to 'pull himself together'.

Intellectual impairment
This is itself a vast subject, and a great deal of work has been done, mainly by psychologists, in studying the effect of cerebral lesions on intellectual performance. Only a few of the main clinical aspects are mentioned here.

Rigidity. A common early sign of impairment is difficulty in 'switching set', that is in turning attention from one subject to another. For example, if watching television intently the patient may seem unable to hear a question asked by his wife, so that she may say he is going deaf. He may be unable to follow a conversation in which several people are taking part, because he cannot switch from one aspect to another easily, although he can discuss matters intelligently with one other person.

There is a narrowing of interest, and even without any memory difficulties in the usual sense of the word there is a lessened ability to take in new ideas. These changes are very familiar with increasing age.

Concentration. When there is clouding of consciousness this is always disturbed, but it is also impaired in many alert patients with chronic brain lesions. An early manifestation is of a paradoxical change from very intense concentration (as mentioned under 'rigidity') to a state in which the attention wanders and flickers from one subject to another. The 'set' of concentration having been broken, it may take some time before it can be re-established. Later in the course of progressive brain disease it is permanently impaired.

Concrete thinking. As impairment progresses there is a lessened ability to grasp abstract concepts, and thinking becomes more elementary and 'concrete', as shown in the well-known proverb tests. For example, people of average intelligence and education when asked a proverb such as 'People who live in glass houses should not throw stones', will explain it in terms of human relationships. The brain injured, even if of previously high intelligence, may respond with 'the stones would break the glass'.

Memory. This is a complex activity, including immediate recall, retention of new information for short and longer periods of time, the ability to recollect, and the ability to recognise. All of these may be disturbed to varying degrees. Memory for words and for visual material are often impaired selectively; the former more by dominant and the latter by non-dominant hemisphere lesions.

Clinically the most common early manifestation is *forgetfulness*, in which everyday recent information and recent activities are not remembered. Even with quite severe brain damage, memory for the distant past may be well preserved, and family informants have been known to say that the patient's memory is improving because he dwells on his childhood with such loving detail. As the lesion progresses, all memory functions break down.

The *Korsakoff state* is a particular type of memory loss, first described by Korsakoff in alcoholics. It is dealt with on page 112.

Comprehension. The ability to understand the meaning of words and of events etc., is disturbed when consciousness is clouded, as are all intellectual functions, and it deteriorates with generalised brain damage. In patients with receptive dysphasia, verbal comprehension is specifically disturbed, and the patient may be severely disabled by quite small localised lesions in the dominant temperoparietal regions. At interview this disability may be mistakenly diagnosed as a global dementia, although the patient may be able to function quite well in some situations—as in caring for himself, or even reading. An opposite situation is seen when a patient has relative sparing of the dominant hemisphere, and his well preserved verbal abilities give a false impression of his intelligence and ability to cope. This may lead to difficulty if he therefore takes on tasks beyond his competence.

PERSONALITY CHANGES

These fall into three main groups, which may overlap clinically, especially if the brain damage is diffuse or multifocal.

Apathy, irritability, anxiety. These are perhaps the commonest early changes. Characteristically the patient tends to withdraw, to be apathetic and uninterested compared to his previous self; and to respond to any form of outside stimulus or interference—such as being asked to do some chore—by a little explosion of anger, or by becoming tremulous and anxious. This can be seen as a protective mechanism in a way, as it has the effect of lessening the demands made on the patient by others, and lessens the chance of him being stressed beyond his capacity, when real catastrophic anxiety might ensue.

Exaggeration of premorbid personality traits. This is common. For example: the introverted suspicious character may become more difficult and paranoid; the friendly extrovert excessively jolly and tactlessly interfering; the obsessional, careful with his money, frankly miserly; and so on.

Frontal lobe syndrome. This occurs in patients with frontal lobe damage, in whom intellectual functions are relatively little disturbed, but who show disinhibition and alterations in drive and activity. Sexual and aggressive impulses, normally controlled, are expressed openly and without shame. In eating habits, manners, dress, cleanliness, and other conventionally determined things, the patient becomes slipshod and careless. He may be casually incontinent. Conscience loses its force, worries and anxieties are no longer troublesome, and some patients ·with only mild changes may feel a good deal happier and more carefree. Most patients become relatively apathetic and less active, but a few become restlessly overactive, and, when this is combined with disinhibition of sexual and aggressive impulses, great social problems may develop.

It.is in the family circle that the main impact of these personality changes is felt. When a man becomes aggressive, irritable, and sexually disinhibited after a head injury, the lives of his wife and children may become absolutely intolerable; although he may return to work, and seem to his work mates merely a bit odd and unpredictable. Recently, the introduction of a drug called Benperidol which lessens libido without feminisation has proved useful in some sexually uninhibited patients of this type.

With more severe damage patients often become fatuous seeming, and emotionally dependent and labile. Marked emotional incontinence, with sudden changes from empty laughter to tears and an expression of agonised grief, occurs mainly in those with bilateral damage to the pyramidal tracts at any level. Such patients may be unresponsive to a verbal approach, but tricyclic antidepressants (q.v.) often seem to make them calmer and happier seeming. In the late states of progressive brain disease there is an obliteration of all personality characteristics, as the patient ceases to communicate and respond in the final stages of dementia.

PERSONAL FACTORS

Premorbid personality and genetic factors, and the patient's environment and life situation, largely determine his reaction to the organically based deficits. Anxious vulnerable people, who have found life difficult to cope with at the best of times, may be overwhelmed, and regress into complete invalidism and despair. Even someone of previously stable temperament, who struggles hard against a disability, may be unable to cope if he is hard up and confined to a fifth floor flat in a wheelchair; or if his wife is suddenly taken ill or leaves him. An accountant suffers much more from a minor impairment of concentration or from dyscalculia than does a railway porter; and so on. In every case these personal factors must be considered.

There are some particularly difficult situations which crop up again and again. One of these is common in all branches of medicine; that which develops when a person of hysterical and manipulative personality develops a disability which leads to the family rallying around, perhaps even ending a period of estrangement. The secondary gain of increased attention often outweighs the gain from physical improvement, and the illness becomes hysterically prolonged. Driving and perfectionistic people, who cannot tolerate anything less than the best, are often overwhelmed by the effects of a stroke. They start off working very hard at their exercises, but suddenly despair at their lack of progress, and may become quite deeply depressed and even suicidal.

In families in which there has been a struggle for dominance between husband and wife, or in which one spouse has resented their dependent and submissive rôle, an illness like a stroke can profoundly disturb the relationship between them, sometimes with tragic effect. For men especially, to find that they are no longer turned to as head of the family by the children, can be humiliating and distressing. For nearly all a loss of self-respect, a loss of purpose and meaning in life, results from these illnesses which not only lead to physical impairment, but to a real loss of intellect and personality.

PSYCHIATRIC SYMPTOMS

The increased tendency to anxiety has been mentioned earlier; but many brain damaged patients also become depressed—at times very severely—more commonly in those with a family or personal history of depression. It is worth remembering that brain damage is no contraindication to antidepressant drugs or even e.c.t.; and if patients have symptoms of depressive illness, with sleep disturbance, anorexia, diurnal variation, feelings of unworthiness etc., they should certainly be offered treatment. In others the depressive mood is fluctuating and shallow seeming, part of the personality change. In these patients treatment is rarely successful, but in doubtful cases it should be tried. Side effects from tricyclic drugs are more common in the brain damaged, who easily become ataxic; so that the dosage should be small at first and cautiously increased. The new tetracyclic antidepressant mianserin is relatively free from atropine-like side effects, and is well tolerated by the brain damaged. It does lead to postural hypotension at times, so the dose should be built up gradually from 10 mgm to a maximum of 60 mgm daily.

A few brain damaged patients develop obsessional symptoms, and, particularly if the temporal lobes are involved, may develop schizophrenia-like symptoms, which are described in the section on temporal lobe epilepsy.

Organic syndromes may show much variation in their course, as the intensity and severity of the interference with cerebral function fluctuates, and as the patient's reactions change. The principal syndromes to be described, which may thus overlap considerably at times, are: (1) *Organic neurasthenia*, characterised by emotionalism, oversensitiveness and debility, in relation to any physical illness, not necessarily involving the brain; (2) psychiatric aspects of *head injury*; and (3) psychiatric aspects of *epilepsy*; (4) *post-encephalitic states*; (5) *organic psychoses*: with delirious and subdelirious states characterised by clouding of consciousness; dysmnesic syndromes (characterised by difficulty in remembering and confabulation); and dementias.

Assessment of intellectual impairment
This can be done clinically and by using standard psychological tests.

Clinical assessment
The account given by the patient and his relatives may be sufficient, if definite change in the ability to do his previous work, marked forgetfulness, inability to follow a previously enjoyed T.V. show etc. has developed. Simple tests may also be helpful: Repeating a name and address immediately and two minutes later, repeating three simple words after three minutes, subtracting 7 serially from 100, doing mental arithmetic, explaining well known proverbs, giving an account of recent world news, the names of members of the Royal family, etc. These time honoured methods, although unstandardised, do give some indication, so long as the doctor has used the tests often enough to know how people may be expected to react. With inpatients in hospital their knowledge of the name of the ward and ward sister, the geography of the ward, the times of meals etc. can all be asked about; and at interview the patient's recollection of previous interviews can be informative.

Psychological tests
If after clinical examination there is still doubt about the presence of organic impairment, psychological tests, usually given by a clinical psychologist, can be used. Unfortunately it is in those borderline cases where the clinician is uncertain that the test results are also ambiguous. Naturally the patient should not be sedated at the time

of testing, and the tests are unreliable in those who are markedly depressed or otherwise disturbed.

Intelligence tests

On the standard tests used for IQ assessment, such as the Wechsler Adult Intelligence Scale, brain damaged patients tend to perform relatively better on the verbal scales, which measure vocabulary, than they do on the performance scales, which measure the ability to solve problems and do mental arithmetic etc. There is therefore a discrepancy between the two scales, so that for example, the verbal IQ may be 126, but the performance IQ only 84. A gap as wide as this almost certainly indicates organic brain damage. However, if the discrepancy is between say, verbal IQ 110 and performance IQ 90, the difference of 20 points is found at times in the general population, with a certain known frequency, and the position remains uncertain. These equivocal tests are still extremely useful however, if later testing is done, because in progressive brain disease the scores will worsen; and if the patient is recovering they will improve.

Learning tests

These are, in our opinion, more generally useful than the intelligence tests, in that they are more sensitive to minor impairment.

Verbal learning. These test the ability of the patient to learn new words and their meaning, that is to extend their vocabulary; or they test the ability to learn pairs of words which have no logical connection in meaning. Examples are the Walton Black and the Inglis paired associate test.

Visuo-spatial tests. These test the ability to retain and reproduce diagrams which are shown to the patient for a standard time. The Benton Visual Retention Test and the Graham-Kendall Test are perhaps the best known in this country.

These two groups of tests can be said, to a limited extent, to test the two cerebral hemispheres separately, in that there is a tendency for visuo-spatial impairment to be commoner with nondominant, and verbal impairment to be commoner with dominant hemisphere lesions.

As with any test equivocal results are common, and again it can be most useful to do the tests serially to assess change. For details of these tests and the many others available, psychological texts should be consulted.

Organic neurasthenia

This can occur as a complication of debilitating physical illnesses, usually in their later stages or during convalescence, but it can occur also in the early stages of, or in convalescence from, the more severe organic mental syndromes about to be described. It is characterised by over-sensitiveness, emotionalism with lability and fatigue, often coupled with querulous irritability, headache, hypochondriacal attitudes, insomnia and subjective complaints of memory disturbance and difficulty in concentration. The course is variable but is apt to be prolonged in those with feeble personalities who become readily demoralised. Treatment consists in improving the physical condition, protecting the patient from stress, allaying his anxieties as far as possible, and judicious rehabilitation. A similar clinical picture is sometimes seen in certain vulnerable personalities of asthenic physique who show the condition in a modified and fluctuating form as a life pattern, characterised by tendencies to complain rather than enjoy, to seek protection rather than run risks, and to show invalid reactions on small provocation.

PSYCHIATRIC ASPECTS OF HEAD INJURY

Mental symptoms are often produced by injury to the head. In the majority of cases, however, these mental symptoms are of secondary importance, the surgical aspect of the case needing and receiving primary attention. Moreover, such mental symptoms as are shown usually disappear as the patient recovers from his injuries, so that most cases of head injury are scarcely regarded as psychiatric problems at all. However, modern care is leading to an ever increasing number of survivors of severe head injuries, who in the past would have died. Most of those who have been unconscious for several weeks are left with permanent mental changes, often very severe; and less severe injuries may also leave permanent damage.

Concussion

Concussion is in more severe cases a state of unconsciousness, or in milder cases a state of disturbed (clouded) consciousness, produced by a mechanical injury to the skull. In some cases there is no disturbance of consciousness, but only diplopia or vertigo. Certain types of injury are more liable to produce concussion than are others. It is most readily caused by injuries when the head is free to move at impact, presumably because of the 'swirling' motion of the brain within the cranium. It is less frequently observed when the skull is fractured with displacement of bone, and it is comparatively rare in cases of penetrating injury from high-velocity missiles or stabbing wounds.

Pathology
The brain has a porridge-like consistency, and sudden deceleration leads to a fluid-like swirling of the contents of the skull, with shearing stresses in the brain tissue which lead to damage to both neurones and to small blood vessels. These are the principal changes in, for example, motorists and motor cyclists who come to post mortem; although there are also more localised areas of damage with cerebral contusion in the frontal and temporal regions. It is not know what, if any, microscopic changes take place in those who have relatively minor head injuries and develop the 'post-concussional syndrome' described later.

Mental symptoms
The mental symptoms differ in the mild, the moderate, and the severe cases.

In a *mild* case the patient is only unconscious for a period lasting from a few seconds to about an hour. He wakes up just as he would from a deep sleep. He asks where he is and what has happened to him. He understands and accepts explanations and can correlate them with his own recollections. He does not remember the accident and is aware of his amnesia. Questions often disclose a short retrograde amnesia, i.e. a loss of memory before the accident. Though the patient may complain of some headache—about half of them do—or feel sleepy and slow, no objective evidence of impaired mental function can be found a few hours after consciousness has been regained.

In cases of *moderate* severity the patient is unconscious for a longer period—perhaps a few hours. He does not wake up so quickly, but passes through a state of clouded consciousness (p. 51) during which he may be restless and irritable. After consciousness has been fully regained, these patients show a retrograde amnesia similar to the mild cases; but their post-traumatic amnesia is longer, and covers not only the unconscious period, but also the time during which consciousness was clouded, although islands of memory for this latter period may remain.

In *severe* cases the patient passes through the same stages as those of moderate severity; but the unconsciousness lasts longer still——days or weeks—and during this time the patient may be very restless and resistive to nursing care. Instead of returning to normality on emerging from the state of clouded consciousness, he continues to show an abnormal mental condition which is dominated by a severe disturbance of memory. At this stage he is not drowsy, although he may be inactive and apathetic; he is capable of grasping questions and of answering sensibly and may even be quite witty in his replies; but he fails in situations or problems which test his capacity for remembering. His spontaneous retention is more affected than his capacity for remembering as the result of deliberate effort. This disturbance of retentivity results in disorientation. Memory for recent events is worse than for remote ones, recall is often erratic and the temporal sequence of events is frequently muddled. Consequently these patients often picture themselves at some earlier point in their lives. Confabulation is a most striking but always a secondary symptom at this stage. The more these patients are pressed for facts which their memory does not supply, the more false recollections will be produced. Even normal memory tends to oblige in this way. The amount and content of the confabulation are mainly dependent upon the previous personality and past experience of the individual concerned, but the cerebral damage sustained also plays its part. Thus a patient whose initiative is much reduced as the result of organic causes may produce very little, while another whose judgment and insight are grossly disturbed may confabulate to a prodigious extent.

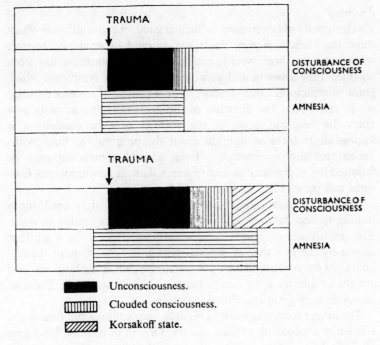

Fig. 6.1 Disturbance of consciousness and amnesia in moderate (top) and severe (bottom) concussion.

This syndrome—disturbed retentivity and confabulation—constitutes the post-traumatic *Korsakoff state*, for which the patient is subsequently amnesic, although sometimes a patchy recollection of a few lucid intervals may be present.

Post-traumatic delirium. The gradual recovery of consciousness is occasionally interrupted by delirious episodes. This rather unusual type of reaction after concussion is often due to accessory physical factors such as wound infection, severe loss of blood or embarrassment of the circulation. Chronic alcoholism causes a general predisposition for delirious reactions and this should always be suspected when no other cause can be found. A constitutional predisposition not associated with alcoholism is sometimes responsible.

Post-traumatic twilight states are rare. But it occasionally happens that a patient after a head injury, which has resulted only in a very short period of unconsciousness, or none at all, finds himself at some strange place, with no recollection of the accident or how he got there. He may during this time have behaved quite normally to all outward appearances.

Prognosis

The prognosis of concussion as such is good. Almost all cases which show the clinical picture described as mild or moderate recover within one to three weeks, unless after consciousness has been regained they show neurological signs or mental symptoms which point to structural brain damage. The duration of unconsciousness or, in retrospect, the duration of the post-traumatic amnesia provides the best indication of the severity of a concussion; it is impossible to form an opinion about the prognosis so long as the patient remains unconscious. Even a mild concussion may be followed by symptoms of severe brain damage in compound fractures and penetrating injuries.

Overall, in large series of unselected patients after head injury leading to hopsital care, only about 1 per cent are unable to work. The importance of post-traumatic amnesia (P.T.A.) as a guide is shown by the fact that of patients with a P.T.A. of more than 24 hours, 10 per cent are likely to be unemployable in the long run, and about one quarter must accept work of a lower standard. There is, however, very great individual variation.

The longer term prognosis as regards restoration of full fitness and efficiency depends on various factors. One is, of course, the degree of *cerebral damage*, but others of great importance, and which at first sight may seem surprising to the student, are the patient's *previous personality* and the presence or absence of *environmental factors* conducive to recovery. It is the co-existence of these three factors that mainly determines whether or not the patient develops the so-called 'post-concussional syndrome' which is about to be described.

The danger of post-traumatic epilepsy in cases of closed injury is comparatively small, from 1 to 3 per cent; but in penetrating injuries the incidence may rise as high as 50 per cent.

Treatment

It is no longer regarded as necessary to keep a patient suffering from a concussion flat on his back in bed for several weeks as older textbooks of surgery recommended. This procedure often gave the patient an exaggerated idea of the seriousness of his condition. As soon as a patient is capable of understanding advice, he should be encouraged to move his head, to sit up and to occupy himself. Nor is there any point in keeping patients with memory disturbances in bed unless surgical complications demand it. Nearly everybody tends to feel, not unnaturally, that a concussion is something much more important and dangerous than an injury to any other part of the body. The awareness of the amnesia, which is frequently interpreted as a 'mental' symptom of very ominous significance, often enhances this anxiety and is another potent factor in the production of post-traumatic neuroses. Fears and doubts about these matters should therefore be discussed with the patient before he leaves hospital.

The incidence of postural dizziness can be reduced if graduated physical exercises are started at an early stage and the same remedy should be applied at a later stage if this symptom persists.

Occupation is a therapeutic and prophylactic agent of cardinal importance in all cases who have to stay in hospital for any length of time, whether because their disturbance of consciousness and of memory is slow in clearing up, or because they need treatment for injuries to the other parts of the body. On discharge from hospital the patient, and perhaps above all his relations, must be convinced that what is needed is not rest but exercise, occupation and work.

Long term effects of cerebral injury

These can only be assessed some weeks or months after the injury, and depend on the extent and severity of the damage and on the patient's personality and life situation, rather than on the nature of the pathology, as was explained in the introduction to this chapter. Head injuries from road traffic accidents, which far outweigh all others in frequency and severity, lead to diffuse damage, almost always involving the frontal lobes and anterior temporal lobes. The patients tend to resemble each other greatly, because they frequently have a generalised spasticity, which affects the face and tongue as well as the limbs; they are often euphoric and disinhibited, prone to sudden brief depression or to bursts of irritability and sometimes frightening anger; and are intellectually impaired and often insightless. In others the prevailing mood is of sullen depression, anxiety, and irritability, with a greater insight into their own deterioration. Many are listless and apathetic, and their emotional responses are shallow and ill sustained. Loss of libido and potency are common, especially after mid brain injury, although in some, sexual appetite is increased at the same time as social inhibitions are lessened.

These changes in the sphere of emotion, will, and instinctual drives occur in various mixtures, but three common combinations are generally recognised: the euphoric—talkative—disinhibited type; the sullen—morose—irritable—explosive type; and the apathetic—slow—inactive type. All may occur with much or with little intellectual impairment, which can be assessed by the methods set out earlier in this chapter (p. 89).

These personality changes make many patients extremely difficult to live with, and great emotional stress often develops in the families. Sadly, the greatest incidence of head injury is in the impulsive and poorly controlled young men who contribute so much to the road accident statistics, especially with motor cycle accidents. People of somewhat psychopathic temperament are more likely to have accidents, and less likely to wear seat belts in cars, and show even more disturbances of behaviour after their head injuries than do people of previously more stable temperament.

Prognosis

It is best to avoid an opinion as to the final outcome until about six months after the injury. As mentioned earlier the factors which determine recovery include: (1) the severity of the injury, as shown by the degree of impairment; (2) age, as the younger the patient the longer will improvement continue; (3) previous personality and life situation. The less satisfactory the previous personality, and more stressful the family life and work situation, the greater is the risk of recovery being delayed or prevented by the development of a post concussional syndrome or symptoms of anxiety or depression.

Treatment

Rehabilitation, with physiotherapy, remedial gymnastics, graded occupational therapy, and job retraining, in an enthusiastic atmosphere, is the most effective way of preventing invalidism and rebuilding confidence. Job placement, using the D.R.O. (Disabled Resettlement Officer) and Labour Exchange facilities if necessary, helping the patient to find work with which he can cope without strain, is the next step. Discussion of his difficulties, practical help from social workers, encouragement and emotional support, explanations to the relatives, antidepressants or tranquillising drugs as necessary, and one or two years of anticonvulsants as prophylaxis against post-traumatic epilepsy, are all part of the treatment. Patients should be pushed towards such facilities as are available, but the number of special centres designed to cope is all too few.

Post-concussional syndrome
This condition differs from the foregoing in that it occurs in the absence of obvious intellectual impairment or personality deterioration, and without evidence of persistent organic damage. But it can be tiresome and disabling and is a frequent cause of delayed return to work.

Aetiology
Emphasis used to be laid on trying to distinguish between a *'true'* post-concussional syndrome, on the one hand, and a post-traumatic *'neurosis'*, on the other. Such a distinction is unreal and unnecessary. The fact is that in post-concussional syndrome, physical, psychological and constitutional factors all play a part. In assessing the individual case, the emphasis should not lie on whether it is *either* 'organic' *or* 'neurotic', but on the extent to which these various factors contribute to the whole picture. In some cases physical factors may be predominant, in others psychological or constitutional ones. Thus, over any large range of cases, there is a lack of correlation between the severity of the head injury and the development of a post-concussional syndrome, which suggests the importance of factors other than the purely physical.

As to the organic factors, there may be several. Nothing certain is established. Headache is, with dizziness, the central symptom, but nothing is known about its pathogenesis in organic terms. Tension and anxiety are more probable causes of the headache than is anything else; and the longer the duration of the headache (which may last for years) the more prominent are the emotional factors. The dizziness which is another prominent feature has been attributed to vestibular damage by some and there is evidence of positional nystagmus in many of those in whom dizziness is the main complaint. The fact that these symptoms, especially headache, are uncommon after severe head injury with obvious physical disability is against any straightforward 'organic' explanation.

The psychological and constitutional factors will, of course, be various. It is natural for people to attach importance to their heads, and to some an insult to the head may represent a threat to life. This may lead to anxiety if the patient is a predisposed person, and the surroundings of a neuro-surgical ward may then add their quota, especially if the patient is constitutionally suggestible, leading to an introspective scrutiny with the development of various fears, of blood clots, paralysis, intellectual damage, etc. This will lead to the development of an emotional climate unhelpful to recovery, and conducive to the continuance of symptoms. Psychological factors of an environmental sort will also have their rôle; domestic friction will encourage irritability and discourage the return of well-being; the nature of the work situation to which the patient is expected to return may also have its encouraging or discouraging effect. The patient's reaction to these, for better or for worse, will be influenced by his constitution. The possibility of compensation for the injury is a frequent complication, and prolongs the syndrome in many people, as described on a later page.

Symptoms and signs
The symptomatology is monotonous. The main complaints are of headache and dizziness, with subjective disturbances of memory and difficulty in concentration, and varying irritability. Intolerance to alcohol and heat are also characteristic.

Classically, the *headaches* are severe and persistent, interfere with the patient's life and activities and are made worse by anything tending to increase the intracranial pressure, e.g. stooping, coughing, sneezing, straining; that is, they are what is often called 'postural' in type. *Dizziness* is classically also postural, occurring on standing after stooping, or sitting after lying down. *Memory disturbance* is shown most classically by difficulty in remembering names, dates and where things have been put. In addition to the foregoing fundamental features, some cases may show affective symptoms of depression and anxiety, and a small proportion may complain of other symptoms that may be seen in neurotic states, such as transient feelings of unreality, obsessions and compulsions. Occasionally, fugues and hysterical amnesias occur, and these are discussed on pages 275 to 278.

The clinical picture may vary considerably from case to case, often owing to the extent of the psychological contributions. The constitutionally querulous patient is likely to complain more, and of more symptoms, than is the constitutionally robust one, as are those with previously unstable personalities and predisposition to neurotic symptoms. Thus, some patients may complain of headaches, dizziness, and difficulties in remembering and concentrating, but in a more vague and less specific way than that outlined above. The headaches may not be affected so much by posture or changes of intracranial pressure as by emotion or worry; they do not then usually interfere so much with the patient's life or activities, and if they do, it will probably be in a selective way so that he is less deterred from pleasant activities than unpleasant ones. The dizziness, too, may be far less distinctly postural and may tend to be continuous rather than transient, when it is probably an expression in physical terms of what is really a psychic insecurity, and prolonged on that basis. The memory difficulty also may be more vague and less specific without the production of definite examples, and the difficulty in concentration attributable more to preoccupation with self, symptoms and the future, than to any other cause.

Assessment

The following points may be useful. Where there has been a severe injury (as judged by the post-traumatic amnesia), to a previously stable person, who describes his symptoms soberly and consistently, finds them little influenced by surroundings and circumstances, is reasonably free from contemporary stresses and without good motive for being ill, the high probability is that the physical factors are predominantly important. On the other hand, where there has been a relatively trivial injury to a previously unstable person, who describes his symptoms over-dramatically and inconsistently, finds them much influenced by surroundings and circumstances, is subject to current social stresses, and can be absolved by illness from doing things which he would like to avoid, the high probability is that psychological factors are predominantly important, or in course of time have become so; nor does this necessarily mean that the patient is consciously or deliberately exploiting the symptoms. An intermediate range will lie between these extreme cases.

Course and prognosis

Taking cases of head injury as a whole, most follow-up studies have relied on the period of disablement from work (which is straightforwardly measurable) as the indicator of how long symptoms last. Even so, estimates vary greatly. It seems that of those who return to their normal work, the majority will do so within the first four weeks after injury. The average loss of working time for those who eventually return to some employment is variously estimated as between eight and eighteen weeks. Between 3 and 20 per cent may not return to their normal work. There seems, however, general agreement that prolonged disability after minor head injury is related to the post-concussional syndrome. Even so, return to work does not necessarily mean that the patient has recovered clinically; it may only mean that some patients are more willing than others to tolerate symptoms and prefer to work in spite of them. Studies of symptomatic recovery are fewer. They indicate that between 8 and 25 per cent of cases may still have symptoms after a year, but that there seems to be a general tendency towards recovery in from two to twenty-four months. The figures on the whole suggest that the prognosis as regards working and social efficiency depends more on the personality of the patient than upon the injury itself. A bad family history, any personality disorder, long-standing hypochon-driasis, low intelligence and a history of previous breakdowns, especially if precipitated by small stress, are all prognostically unfavourable, as are the presence of domestic or personal conflicts or of difficulties and dangers in the work situation, and concern over compensation—often a major factor.

After severe head injury varying degrees of dementia and of organically determined personality change render many patients incapable of truly independent life, but these patients rarely com-plain of headache or of the other main symptoms of the post-concussional syndrome.

Treatment

There is no better method of encouraging the development of a post-concussional syndrome than to ask the patient repeatedly about headache, or to advise him to keep as quiet as possible lest he gets one, or to tell him to report such a development as soon as it occurs. During the convalescence from head injury, the patients may be in a highly suggestible condition which encourages hypochondriasis and invalidism. There can be little doubt that much more harm can be done by advising them to go slow rather than by trying to make them go too fast. Occupation and graded physical exercises should be instituted as soon as possible, and there is no better way of convincing a patient that he can do more than he thought than by a practical demonstration of this kind. Group activities may be of value in this connection. In the established post-concussional syn-drome, however, the paramount necessity is an assessment and understanding of the individual case, with a corresponding attention to the psychological and environmental as well as to the physical factors. Depression associated with this may be helped by anti-depressant drugs (see page 399).

Compensation problems

The hope of financial gain, in the form of pension or compensation, is often over-emphasised as an aetiological factor in the production of post-traumatic disabilities. When such an intention is fully conscious, the case is one of malingering, but this is probably rare. When the intention is not fully conscious its psychological significance varies considerably; but assessing the inner motives and degree of insight in such cases is extremely difficult.

In some cases the intention seems to be to punish the guilty or to receive just consolation for an innocently suffered wrong. In other cases the money enables the patient to succumb to or keep up a neurosis which has its real origin in conflicts not necessarily connected with the accident at all. In yet another group of cases the accident acts as a psychological trauma; the experience of a serious threat to life or limb releases anxieties with which the patient is unable to cope, and leads to a neurotic reaction. Each case must be considered individually in the light of the patient's personality and life-history, and these do not reveal clear evidence of neurosis or psychopathy in every instance. All that can be expected and is usually found are character traits which render the individual liable to break down under particular stress, but which may not previously have given rise to serious maladjustment or to the formation of symptoms. Even so, there is a higher incidence of post-traumatic diability after industrial than after sporting accidents, in the insured as opposed to the uninsured, and in soldiers as opposed to civilians. Compensation factors are often very important, and when the head injury has been trivial many cases seem to recover when the compensation case is settled.

Mental symptoms in encephalitis lethargica

Though now rare, sporadic cases seem to occur. In the acute phase the mental symptoms show nothing specially characteristic. In recovery, there is inertia and sloth with restlessness, irritability, moodiness and hypochondriasis. Subsequently, Parkinsonism may develop, with ptyalism, oculogyric crises, 'coordinated tics' (compulsions to make purposive but unnecessary movements, such as straightening or smoothing) and other obsessive-compulsive symptoms. Later developments may be depressive, schizophrenic or paranoid. The Parkinsonian slowing may give an erroneous impression of dementia, whereas the reduction in intellectual function is really only slight, arising from slowness and lack of initiative.

Encephalitis lethargica in childhood may produce gross personality change with hyperkinesis, aggression and loss of all moral sense leading to stealing, lying, cruelty, sexual aberrations and indiscipline. Follow up studies have shown, however, that about one third of cases regain social adaptation and that another third develop Parkinsonism.

Psychiatric aspects of epilepsy

Epilepsy is a very common condition, and although few epileptic patients present psychiatric syndromes, there are important psychological problems for almost every epileptic. In childhood and adolescence, the fits are especially frightening, not only to the child but also to his parents and siblings, his schoolfellows and even the teachers. He becomes the focus of attention, must be specially treated, may be forbidden to ride a bicycle, to go swimming and many other things, and has his future career choice restricted. Everyone treats him as 'different', and parents can very easily become seriously over-protective.

If the child is lucky enough to have the fits fully controlled these features tend to fade away, but for the others life is certainly made more difficult. Within the limits of the fit type and frequency, children should be encouraged to live as actively and normally as possible, and a lot can be done by careful and repeated counselling of all those involved.

In addition to the natural anxiety and despondency caused in many patients, some epileptics are prone to spells of surliness and irritability, often accompanied by spontaneous mood changes. These spells may be ended by a fit. Phenobarbitone also causes depression, sometimes quite serious, in a certain number of epileptics.

Epilepsy itself does not lead to intellectual or personality deterioration, but a progressive lesion causing the epilepsy may do so, of course. High levels of medication, repeated head injuries and cerebral anoxia in the unfortunate few who are poorly controlled are other factors. Persistent focal discharges in the dominant hemisphere, even without fits, lead to difficulties in learning and impair verbal skills generally. In a few patients a picture amounting to 'dementia' can be produced by continuous abnormal electrical discharge without actual fits.

In adults emotional disturbances and the major epileptic syndromes are commoner in patients with a focus in the temporal lobe than in others.

'Epileptic personality'. A few epileptics of longstanding, poorly

controlled and usually institutionalised, become slow, narrow, bigoted, religiose, pedantic, suspicious and irritable. They can be extremely difficult to contend with in a ward, and become very unpopular with others. Most mental hospitals have a few such patients. The factors mentioned earlier which lead to personality deterioration are usually present, combined with the effects of chronic institutionalisation.

In a number of epileptics, it seems that temporal lobe disturbances at certain critical periods of life prevent normal personality development, which cannot be recouped, even if the fits are later stopped. The development of transvestism (q.v.), for example, has been linked to this in some people.

Aggressiveness. This is undoubtedly a characteristic of some epileptics, especially those with temporal lobe lesions acting as the focus.

Epileptic psychoses

Confusional states and twilight states. These are uncommon, and are clinically indistinguishable from other confusional states, although the history gives a clue. They may follow a fit, or seem to occur instead of a fit, as an ictal phenomenon, especially in temporal lobe epilepsy. Rarely patients in these states are seriously violent, but mainly they present as 'blank', perplexed, tense, failing to grasp their environment or what is said. They may wander about in the street, urinate in public, or do other things of which society disapproves. The term 'twilight state' is often used when the patient is also obviously hallucinated, and shows marked disturbance. There is complete amnesia afterwards for all these states. They can be stopped by intravenous diazepam, if it can be given; intramuscular diazepam must be used if intravenous injection is impracticable.

Temporal lobe epilepsy is sometimes encountered in psychiatric departments, usually because the peculiar subjective experiences involved have led to an erroneous diagnosis of anxiety, hysteria or psychosis. It can be understood as focal epilepsy, with the focus in the temporal lobe, the complex functions of which are intermittently disturbed. It is characterised by periodic disturbances of consciousness with entry into a transient dream-like state, with or without loss of touch with reality and with more or less confusion.

In the milder forms, the patient remains correctly orientated but may feel in a dream or as if something is happening that has happened before. Simultaneously he may experience altered affect often in the form of intense panic, sometimes with feelings of loathing or revulsion. At the same time his perceptions may be distorted so that familiar things, though recognisable, assume an altered appearance often tinged with unpleasantness or horror, and he may experience inexplicable tastes or smells. His thoughts may become disordered or inappropriate, so that he may find himself struggling to remember something without knowing what it is he has to remember, or may find nonsensical phrases recurring to his mind in a way he cannot control. There may be accompanying autonomic disturbances, such as sinking feelings in the abdomen, dryness of the mouth or palpitation. In the motor sphere, the patient may perform stereotyped but inappropriate automatic acts, such as chewing, spitting or aimlessly moving things from one place to another. In fact, there may be a disturbance at all levels of nervous function, autonomic, sensorimotor and psychic, of varying complexity in each.

The attack may be ushered in by an aura, of a simple epigastric kind as in more ordinary forms of epilepsy, or of a complicated and highly organised kind such as suddenly seeing the appearance of some figure or pattern; a sense of there being some body or object, uncertainly glimpsed and only partially apprehended, behind one or other shoulder is specially characteristic. Usually the attack lasts but a few seconds or a minute or so. On recovery, the patient may have an almost complete or only a vague and partial recollection of the incident, but is usually left anxious or frightened by such an unexpected trip into the unknown.

More severe attacks can last for longer periods of time, during which all contact with reality is lost so that the patient can only remember the very beginning of the attack. He may then 'come to', and find himself somewhere unexpected, or inexplicably wet, or without some possession he should have had.

The main diagnostic points are as follows. The longer attacks are rare and must be distinguished from states of hysterical dissociation (p. 268). In this, the main guides will be the personality of the patient, the essentially episodic nature of the condition, the genuineness of the disturbance of consciousness, the purposelessness of the behaviour, and the ready resumpton of normal conduct on recovery. The shorter attacks are commoner than may be realised, and their essence is their suddenness and transience, coupled with an eerie, nightmare quality which the patient will emphasise but may find difficult to describe. Where anxiety is a component, this is usually of a supernatural intensity, different from anything the patient has normally experienced and different from the anxiety he feels lest the experience should recur. A sober account of a sudden, transient, queer disturbance, with astonishment that it should have happened and uneasiness lest it should happen again, will suggest the diagnosis, especially if the patient is of previously stable personality and there is no evidence of motive or secondary gain.

The treatment of temporal lobe epilepsy is principally by anticonvulsants, which are better described in a neurological text. Phenothiazines may also be useful in the control of psychotic symptoms so long as the patient is already on anticonvulsants. As for any other type of epilepsy, onset after adolescence should lead to investigations to exclude a cerebral tumour or other lesion. If the attacks cannot be controlled by drugs, or there is behavioural deterioration between attacks, temporal lobectomy may be necessary. This can only be done if the contralateral temporal lobe is perfectly intact, as very severe memory disturbances of Korsakoff type (q.v.) may develop with bilateral damage to or removal of the medial temporal lobe structures.

Transient psychoses. In addition to the chronic schizophrenic-like psychoses of epilepsy described later, epileptics occasionally suffer from brief, acute psychotic illnesses, resembling both schizophrenia and affective illnesses, or mixed schizo-affective illnesses. They usually last only a few days, although sometimes many weeks, and may be typical of a functional psychosis or have a more or less marked admixture of confusional symptoms.

The schizophrenia-like psychoses of epilepsy

A certain proportion of patients with long standing epilepsy, mainly of temporal lobe origin, develop an illness closely resembling chronic paranoid schizophrenia with delusions and hallucinations, but with relatively well preserved affect. The development of schizophrenia-like symptoms is commoner when the lesion is tumour or hamartoma, rather than when it is mesial temporal sclerosis, and is particularly common in left handed females.

In our experience of such patients organic impairment of memory and other intellectual function is also marked. Both anticonvulsants and phenothiazines are useful in treatment, but the symptoms are difficult to control completely.

The occurrence of epilepsy must not necessarily be regarded as a bar to higher education or to academic training, as the follow-up of epileptics has demonstrated. Another encouraging point is that, contrary to previous medical belief, a normally intelligent person who develops idiopathic epilepsy is much less likely to deteriorate mentally than one who develops symptomatic epilepsy. Just as there are societies for sufferers from conditions such as diabetes and poliomyelitis, the British Epilepsy Association (at present at 3 Alfred Place, London, W.C.1) sets out to help epileptics, and may offer guidance over problems of employment and social contacts. Finally, the greater efficacy of the various anticonvulsant drugs that have been developed over the last twenty years renders control of the seizures less difficult than it used to be, and in only a few cases does serious deterioration develop.

ORGANIC PSYCHOSES

These can be divided into three main groups:

1. Acute states of clouded consciousness, including delirium and sub-delirium; also called 'acute brain syndromes';
2. the dysmnesic syndromes (Korsakoff states) in which recent memory is mainly affected; and
3. the dementias, which are characterised by irreversible impairment of intellect and personality; also called 'chronic brain syndromes'.

In common usage in medicine the term 'organic psychosis' is often restricted to the first group, but really all belong conveniently under the same heading.

Delirium and sub-delirium

These terms are used to describe states of clouded consciousness in which there are symptoms such as hallucinations, delusions, depression, excitement and fear, as well as clouding with its attendant confusion and disorientation. Sub-delirium is used to describe the less florid cases, but is not exactly defined.

The characteristic acute organic mental symptoms, the presence of which must *always* arouse suspicion of organic disease, are:

1. Disturbances of consciousness;
2. Disorientation for time and place;
3. Failure of grasp of the environment and of what is occurring; and
4. Objective impairment of memory.

These are the features of confusional states in general, which are extremely common in medical and surgical wards, especially in the elderly, while florid delirium is quite rare. Most confused patients are old and frail, suffering from heart failure or chest infections, and with some degree of pre-existing senile or arteriopathic cerebral disease. They often call out in a confused and frightened way, and may be noisy and disturbing to others, especially at night—

when they cannot see clearly enough to keep their flickering sense of orientation. They are not often more disturbed than that.

Aetiology of delirium
In addition to the age associated factors mentioned above, constitutional factors are important in that some people become clouded and delirious more easily than others, for unknown reasons. Children are also particularly prone to delirium, which may accompany high fever with common childhood fevers, especially those viral illnesses such as measles and mumps, in which some degree of encephalitis is common.

Psychological factors are only secondary, in that they determine the content of the fears, hallucinations, and so on. Genetic factors also influence the content, as someone with a family history of schizophrenia is more likely to develop schizophrenia-like symptoms in a delirium than someone else. If an individual has successive delirious illnesses, even from different physical causes, the mental symptoms will be almost identical in each.

As was emphasised at the beginning of this chapter, the disturbances due to organic factors do not tell us anything specific about the underlying pathology. They tell us only that organic disease is present and interfering with the function of the brain. We must then make a *medical* diagnosis. As an example, the mental disturbances due to hypo- and hyper-glycaemia in the same patient in successive weeks, might be identical. The history and physical findings, supplemented by blood sugar estimations, distinguish one from the other.

The physical factors which can cause clouding of consciousness, and thus lead on to sub-delirious and delirious states, are very numerous. Anoxia, as with congestive heart failure or extensive lung disease, is a common cause; as are various infections, including meningitis, encephalitis, pneumonia and typhoid. Some severe infections, however, rarely lead to clouded consciousness: for example, cholera and bacillary dysentery.

Any drug which can lead to unconsciousness in overdosage will cause clouding in an intermediate dose: alcohol and barbiturates are perhaps the commonest, but tricyclic antidepressants, bromides, amphetamines and many others can be responsible. Alcohol and barbiturates can lead to states of clouded consciousness either directly or by sudden withdrawal in the physiologically dependent. Metals such as lead and manganese, and very many complex industrial poisons may be responsible also.

Electrolyte and metabolic disturbances are quite common precipitants, particularly potassium depletion following diuretics. Prolonged vomiting as in hyperemesis gravidarum and pyloric stenosis; and self induced vomiting in anorexia nervosa, can disturb electrolyte balances enough to affect the mental state, as can severe diarrhoea. Hypo- and hyper-glycaemia can both cause states of clouded consciousness.

Prolonged malnutrition, with vitamin deficiencies, predisposes to clouded consciousness, as in Pellagra (Riboflavine and Nicotinic acid especially), and vitamin B_{12} deficiency can do the same. Prolonged shortage of these vitamins leads to dementia.

Finally, head injuries, cerebrovascular accidents, and many other acute cerebral disorders, are quite commonly responsible.

The e.e.g. is always disturbed in confusional states, which may occasionally be helpful in diagnosis. Characteristically, there are slow waves of very high voltage.

Symptoms and signs

Specific illnesses do not give rise to specific kinds of delirium. The clinical picture tends to be much the same whatever physical agents are involved. The only exception to this is that the more prostrating the underlying physical condition, the more torpid is the patient likely to be.

(a) Physical. Where the condition is of any severity, it is common to find a sluggish reaction of the pupils, nystagmus, diplopia and slurred speech, together with other evidence of incoordination that may be brought out by attempted movements. Control of the bladder and even rectum may be defective, leading to incontinence.

(b) Mental. The essential features are (i) clouding of consciousness, leading to (ii) disorientation, (iii) impairment of memory, and therefore (iv) difficulty in grasp. With these are associated (v) restlessness and (vi) increased suggestibility and responsiveness leading to confabulation. The difficulty in grasp and the increased suggestibility are coupled with (vii) an anxious or fearful affective state. The patient is perplexed. The combination of these leads to (viii) misinterpretations which, owing to the emotional condition, are usually of a paranoid sort. Apart from the foregoing there are commonly (ix) hallucinations, especially visual ones; these are often of a frightening kind and enhance the paranoid condition. Finally, unless the patient is so toxic as to be stuporose, the delirious state is characterised by (x) a remarkable variability in all the symptoms from one time to another.

Thus, the extent to which consciousness is clouded will vary from moment to moment, but the attention is at all times poorly sustained, so that the patient's concentration is very bad and his thinking laboured and even disconnected. The patient tries readily, and though he may be transiently roused from his confusion will soon sink back into it, so that, though momentarily accessible, he will soon become inaccessible again. This may prevent him from grasping the simplest thing, even his whereabouts, and he may not even be able to give his name, so that he is disorientated for time, place, and person.

The restlessness depends largely on the degree of physical debility; a spry alcoholic in delirium tremens may show highly purposive and coordinated movements, whereas the patient who is physically prostrated will merely toss, turn and flop. In the more active patients investigatory and occupational activities are highly characteristic; for example, they may drive imaginary cars, enact telephone conversations or tell imaginary rosaries. These last are motor or acted confabulations, as opposed to the type of confabulation into which the patient can be suggested by persuading him to read messages from blank sheets of paper or to give circumstantial accounts, which are entirely untrue, of what he has just been doing or where he had just been. Such confabulations are in part an expression of the heightened suggestibility and responsiveness, as are the various misinterpretations. These last often arise on an illusional basis, as when a shadow on the wall is mistaken for a figure that is later seen to have stolen silently away.

Visual hallucinations are very common in the more acute intoxications, and when so real as to be accepted by the patient as part of the external world they are almost pathognomonic. Auditory hallucinations, though less pathognomonic, are about as common; they may persist for some time after evidence of gross confusion has disappeared.

The marked variability of the state is shown also in the paranoid attitudes and delusional ideas, which are typically transient, shifting and ill-systematised. Where there is a variable difficulty in grasp coupled with anxiety and fearfulness, it is inevitable that doubt and suspicion should arise; again, the heightened suggestibility and responsiveness encourage the development of misinterpretations. These form the starting point for the formation of delusions, but the latter are not sustained owing to the poor memory, confusion and impaired grasp, although in the course of any delirium the patient will feel himself at some time and to some extent the subject of persecution and annoyance. Such feelings will lead to various degrees of disturbed behaviour, ranging from querulousness with the expression of ideas of reference, to more crystallised notions of plots, of being poisoned, kidnapped or tortured, or being involved in gang warfare or revolutions.

In mild cases the patient may behave normally enough in the day, later to become restless and confused as night falls.

In summary, delirium is a clouded, confused, restless but essentially variable state, with a striking frequency of visual hallucinations and paranoid features, accompanied by a labile (variable) mood that is predominantly anxious, fearful, depressed and irritable. Its vividness is increased by the heightened suggestibility and responsiveness, but will be decreased *pari passu* with the extent to which the patient is physically prostrated. The whole picture is strikingly coloured by the personality and previous experiences of the individual sufferer—this being shown in its simplest form when aggressive people become even more aggressive when drunk.

The essential *organic mental symptoms* are the clouding of consciousness, the confusion, the impaired grasp and memory, and the variation in the level of consciousness from one time to another.

Differential diagnosis

This depends on the occurrence of organic mental symptoms in association with some physical condition that may adequately explain their development. These symptoms are readily missed if certain others, such as anxiety or depression, are particularly marked. Special attention must therefore be paid to the examination of the patient's sensorium, in order to elicit evidence of clouding, and of impairment of grasp and memory. The difficulty of differentiation from manic or schizophrenic excitement may sometimes be very great—even for a time impossible. In the doubtful case, the characteristic variability of delirious symptoms may be a crucial diagnostic point. Visual hallucinations make it almost certain that the diagnosis is of an organic state, except in patients from much less developed societies in which visual hallucinations occur in schizophrenia sometimes.

Course and prognosis

This depends on the severity of the underlying physical illness and on the physical condition of the patient. Thus, the development of acute confusion in the elderly, and even in the young when debilitated by a long physical illness, is quite often a prelude to death. In other cases, restlessness and excitement may lead, through the physical prostration that they cause, to a fatal outcome that would not otherwise have been expected. Wild and impulsive deliria of that sort are prone to occur in unstable and psychopathic cases, in the young and in the mentally subnormal; their prognosis is accordingly less good. Another risk, which may be quite real in depressed patients, is that of suicide; a history of a previous suicidal attempt should be an indication for special precautions.

Apart from the foregoing reservations, the prognosis for the mental state is usually excellent, and recovery rapid and complete, where the underlying physical condition is itself essentially a recoverable one. Even so, there are certain exceptions, as follows: (1) when the delirium is superimposed on another and pre-existing psychosis; this is common enough as the result of excessive alcohol, barbiturates, or bromide. After the delirium thus induced has cleared, the underlying and original psychosis will remain. (2) Delirium may precipitate or usher in an ominous psychosis. Certain schizophrenic and paranoid psychoses start in this way. The prognosis for mental recovery should therefore be more guarded when the previous personality gives ground for concern over such developments, especially when schizophrenic features occur in course of the illness. (3) Delirium superimposed on organic brain disease may lead to the development or increase of dementia.

Treatment

The first essential is to make a medical diagnosis of the underlying cause. Extensive investigation may be necessary, although an accurate history from an informed person, and a thorough physical examination will usually provide the answer.

It is also essential to ensure adequate nourishment and fluid intake, if necessary by nasal feeding or intravenous infusion. Since avitaminosis can be a factor, vitamin medication should be given if there are suggestive indications. This can be done by the intramuscular or intravenous route, as well as by mouth. A suitable preparation for the former is Parentrovite as described later.

If possible the patient must be helped to rest, without excessive sedation. Barbiturates should be avoided, because as the effect wears off they can increase the confusion. The phenothiazines, in a dosage which produces tranquillisation without deep sedation, are probably best. Chlorpromazine can be given by intramuscular injection, in doses of 25–100 mg every three to six hours, as required.

Skilled nursing remains extremely important. It is best in a quiet room, preferably with a very limited number of nurses, so that the patient can more easily become familiar with them. Everyone in contact with a delirious patient should remember how easily misinterpretations and excitement develop, and should repeatedly tell him that he is in hospital and who the speaker is. The room should be well lit to avoid spooky shadows, and whispering about him in earshot should be avoided.

There remain some obscure and intractable cases who remain delirious even after the causative illness has apparently been effectively treated. In these cases, electrical treatment (p. 405) can be rapidly successful, two or three treatments quietening the patient, relieving confusion and stabilising the emotional state.

In *alcoholic delirium tremens*, all the foregoing principles of treatment apply, but special claims have been made for (1) the substitution of other tranquillisers for chlorpromazine in order to minimise further liver damage. Chlormethiazole (Heminevrin) is very useful in this situation, using a reducing dose schedule from 1.5G four times daily, for one day, then 1G four times daily, and so gradually tailing off the dose.

Diazepam is also very useful as a tranquilliser, and can be given by mouth or by intramuscular or intravenous injection. As epileptic fits often occur in association with delirium tremens, as another manifestation of alcohol withdrawal, the anticonvulsant action of diazepam is helpful.

The intensive vitamin therapy needed is most conveniently given by intravenous high potency Parenterovite for a few days, switching to the intramuscular preparation for a further week, before giving oral vitamin B complex in a high dose for several months.

Many alcoholics in this state have significant infections or fractures, and electrolyte disturbances are common. They all need careful investigation.

See also the section on delirium tremens on p. 322.

KORSAKOFF'S PSYCHOSIS

(Dysmnesic syndrome)
In this condition the memory disturbance is the most striking feature, not the difficulty in grasp or clouding of consciousness. In the full blown state the patient is unable to hold new verbal memories for more than about 90 seconds, so that he is unable to remember what he was talking about before then, and he tends to confabulate, that is to fill the gap by making something up.

Aetiology
The Korsakoff state develops whenever the tracts which run from the hippocampus through the fornix to the mammillary bodies are interrupted bilaterally. In alcoholics thiamin deficiency may lead to

degenerative changes in the mammillary bodies, and a Korsakoff state may follow Wernickes' encephalopathy in which there are other mid brain disturbances, or delirium. In alcoholics peripheral neuritis is usually present as well. The term Korsakoff's 'psychosis' should properly be reserved for this picture in alcoholics. A Korsakoff 'state', in non-alcoholic patients, may follow head injury, coal gas poisoning, destruction of the relevant areas by tumour or surgery, or cerebrovascular accidents. It is not uncommon therefore, in an incomplete form, in arteriosclerotic dementia.

Symptoms and signs
At first sight the patients may present no overt abnormality. They may even appear to be abnormally quick in the uptake, and they often speak with great fluency and plausibility. But examination reveals gross defects in memory. These are most obvious in the appreciation of time relationships, especially for recent events, and may be so marked as to cause gross disorientation in time. As if to compensate for these defects of memory, the patients are specially liable to *confabulate* in course of which they often show a striking suggestibility. At first their confabulations may seem plausible, but on longer acquaintance it will be realised that their tales are quite untrue, even though they are embroidered with extraordinary detail, and that with a little suggestion and encouragement they will tell of adventures that are preposterous, fantastic and beyond any hope of credulity.

Apart from the disturbance of memory and confabulation, the patients are usually markedly cheerful, almost euphoric, but in a silly and fatuous way. This cheerfulness is usually punctuated, however, by marked irritability. In addition, they are usually indolent, with abnormally little initiative, and there is some impairment of intellectual grasp.

Course and prognosis
In alcoholics great improvement may result from massive thiamin dosage, given intravenously as Parenterovite as described. Improvement can continue slowly for up to eighteen months or more once it has started. If there is no improvement after one month the outlook is bad.

It is a matter of urgency to begin treatment with thiamin in large doses if Wernicke's encephalopathy or Korsakoff's psychosis is suspected. Blood can be taken to assess serum pyruvate for reference later, but treatment should not be delayed. We have seen permanent memory loss follow delays while elaborate tests were performed.

For the non-alcoholic Korsakoff states no treatment is usually possible, although, as with all forms of brain damage, there may be spontaneous improvement.

THE DEMENTIAS

Dementia is an irreversible impairment of intellect and personality, due to organic damage or disease affecting the brain. The term is mainly used for the progressive dementias, several of which are described in this book, but it also applies to non-progressive damage such as that due to head injury, encephalitis, anoxia, or any one of many other insults to the brain. The term 'chronic brain syndrome' has the same meaning.

The two most important dementing illnesses are senile and arteriopathic (arteriosclerotic) dementia. They are not described in this section, where they might be expected, but in the chapter on Psychiatry in the Aged, because of the many practical problems which they cause in old people and their families. The main clinical features of progressive dementia will therefore be found on page 126, which should be read in conjunction with this section. Apart from the ages, and those aspects of life which largely depend on age, such as increasing frailty, the clinical descriptions apply overall.

There are a few illnesses, such as hypothyroidism and vitamin B_{12} deficiency, which lead to permanent dementia if untreated but which remain reversible for quite a long time after onset. If untreated for too long, they too lead to irreversible damage. Their detection is essential, and is considered later in this section on page 116.

PRE-SENILE DEMENTIAS

A pre-senile dementia is one which comes on before the age of 65, by arbitrary definition.

Alzheimer's disease

The essential feature is the early onset. But this condition can often be distinguished from the other pre-senile dementias by the exceptional preservation of the patient's social behaviour and emotional responses by comparison with the severity of the dementia that such preservation covers. In this respect Alzheimer's disease resembles arteriosclerotic dementia. Symptoms of aphasia, agnosia, etc., are frequent, but less well defined than when they result from focal lesions of vascular origin. As the condition progresses, stereotyped movements and speech are usual, and the latter finally deteriorates into repetitive utterances that are intelligible but meaningless. The histopathology is indistinguishable from senile dementia, so that some neurologists refer to 'Alzheimers disease of senile onset' depending on the patient's age.

Pick's disease
This is similar in that it gives rise to a profound dementia, but the deterioration is more general so that social preservation is lacking. Gross restlessness is a rather frequent finding. The underlying pathology differs from Alzheimer's disease in that the latter condition is found to be diffuse at post-mortem, whereas cases of Pick's disease show only circumscribed areas of cerebral atrophy, in the frontal or temporal lobes or both. Microscopically the degenerating neurones form 'balloon cells', and there are also neurofibrillary tangles and plagues as in Alzheimer's disease. Death usually occurs after six to twelve years from the onset.

Huntington's chorea
This condition is of special interest in that it is hereditary and transmitted by a single dominant gene. It affects therefore half the offspring of any sufferer on average. It usually occurs at middle-life or soon after, but there is often a pre-morbid history of eccentricity. The symptoms and signs do not develop in any set order. The choreic movements may be the first developments, and, if they are, curious smacking of the lips may be the earliest one, later to be followed by spasmodic sudden jerkings which may be of a generalised kind. In other cases, the choreic movements may be preceded by changes in character, of which irritability is specially common, and may later lead to ungovernable rage, while lack of prudence and impaired judgement are usual. These changes in character may or may not precede the dementia, which, in its turn, may or may not precede the chorea. The dementia itself has no special features. The course is essentially downhill, the prognosis is hopeless, and there is no treatment, except that thiopropazate (Dartalan) often lessens the severity of the movements. The family history will be of special aid in the early diagnosis of this melancholy condition, and may also be some prognostic guide. The average survival from onset to death is about 12 years.

Jakob-Creutzfeldt disease

This extremely rare disease is included because of the interesting developments in understanding its cause. There is rapidly progressive dementia with marked motor and sensory impairment leading to multiple neurological signs, because of widespread cortical atrophy. The cause is apparently a slow virus, and passage through animals has been demonstrated. It is probably identical with the illness 'Kuru' affecting certain Pacific peoples who eat the brains of enemies.

Other pre-senile dementias

Many pre-senile dementias do not fit pathologically into any of the named illnesses above, and are often called 'simple' or 'non-specific' dementias. They lead to cerebral atrophy as do the others, and the clinical picture is no different.

General Paralysis of the Insane (GPI)

General Paralysis (or Paresis) is an inflammatory disease of the brain due to syphilis, coming on 10–20 years after the primary infection usually, and leading, if untreated, to spastic paralysis with profound dementia and death. It is commoner in men than in women, and only affects a small percentage of syphilitic patients.

In most patients mental changes precede physical disabilities, although Argyll-Robertson, or other abnormal pupil signs, are found quite early.

It is now a rare disease in the Western world, presumably because of the more efficient treatment of early syphilis. Nevertheless, a serological test for syphilis is essential in every patient being investigated for dementia. There are no particular mental symptoms which distinguish it from other dementias.

The cerebrospinal fluid shows characteristic changes in the Lange (colloidal gold) curve, and in the follow up after treatment the CSF should be studied at six months and one year, to confirm that the disease is inactive. Details of diagnosis and treatment should be sought in a neurological text.

The prognosis for mental recovery depends on the stage at which treatment is begun, as penicillin, or other appropriate antibiotics, will arrest the disease, and a fair amount of functional recovery will occur.

'Treatable dementia'

This somewhat paradoxical heading is to remind the reader that there are some conditions which lead to progressive dementia if untreated, but can be effectively treated if diagnosed early enough. If untreated the damage is permanent. It is therefore very important indeed to bear them in mind whenever confronted by a dementing patient, and to exclude them by careful investigation.

The conditions concerned include the following:

1. *Deficiency and metabolic disorders.* Hypothyroidism, deficiency of vitamin B_{12} and folic acid (and very rarely of other vitamins of the B complex), hyperparathyroidism, spontaneous hypoglycaemia if repeated, and uraemia.

2. *Space occupying lesions.* Primary and secondary tumours, sub-dural haematomata, and very rare conditions such as cysts or giant aneurysms.

3. *Others.* Syphilis and rare inflammations; normal pressure hydrocephalus; and alcoholism, which may be unrecognised. Very rarely chronic poisoning, for example, by lead or manganese might be responsible.

Remember that drug abuse, especially with benzodiazepines and barbiturates, can cause apparent dementia; and in the elderly severe retarded depression can produce a pseudodementia, as described in the chapter on Psychiatry in the Aged.

Differential diagnosis of dementia
It was emphasised at the beginning of this chapter that the mental effects of damage to brain tissue depend on the site and extent of the damage, and the rate of onset, and not on the pathology, except for the ways in which the pathology determines those factors. Clinically then, one can only diagnose 'dementia', and after that medical and neurological investigation is necessary to exclude a treatable cause. This is exactly parallel to the acute confusional states.

In an old and frail person, with a considerable degree of impairment, especially if there is a history of repeated small strokes, elaborate investigation is inappropriate. In younger people the opposite is true, and every effort must be made. The difficulty comes with the patients in between, 65–75 years of age, in deciding whether or not to investigate fully. The investigations are expensive, but not dangerous, now that Computer Assisted Tomography has replaced air encephalography and angiography for screening purposes. Thyroid function and a full blood count to exclude megaloblastic anaemia, are worth doing even in the very old, along with routine studies of the urine and a chest X-ray. Occult infection makes many mildly demented patients much worse.

Brain biopsy is very rarely justified on clinical grounds, as there is a considerable morbidity.

Special investigations

It has been emphasised that the features of the mental state in organic brain damage are of little help in establishing the cause of the deterioration. 'Dementia' may be confidently diagnosed on clinical grounds, but in many cases further investigation is needed. In the old, or when a history of cerebrovascular accident or head injury is obtained, it may be considered unnecessary to subject the patient to extensive investigation, but even in these cases a subdural haematoma may be suspected, and investigation may become desirable.

The methods are those used in neurology and neurosurgery; and they are capable of demonstrating the presence of tumours or other space occupying lesions, vascular malformations, and cerebral atrophy. They are always preceded by a full neurological examination, blood serology, skull X-rays, and often by a lumbar puncture.

Electroencephalography
Berger, a German psychiatrist, was the first to record the cerebral bioelectric potentials using a string galvanometer, in 1927. With developments in electronics, multichannel scalp recordings on moving strips of paper have now become a standard laboratory facility in many centres. Patterns of electrical activity in terms of frequency and amplitude vary with age, level of awareness and metabolic state, as well as with local cerebral disease. In general the electroencephalograph (e.e.g.) has little diagnostic specificity and early hopes for its especial application to psychiatry have not been fulfilled. No clinically useful correlations with emotion or thought processes have been discovered, though interesting research trends are appearing with more subtle recording techniques.

A single normal record does not exclude organic cerebral disease. On the other hand the finding of a grossly abnormal record in a psychiatric patient should make one hesitate to accept a condition as purely functional. Records taken from psychiatric patients show a higher overall incidence of mild and nonspecific abnormalities than are found in the population at large. More marked abnormalities are often seen in the records of psychopathic patients; these resemble the under-developed records of children and it has been postulated that these patients suffer from a failure of maturation of the brain. Severe and often unilateral abnormalities in the records of aggressive patients reflect possible structural disease of the temporal lobe and are sometimes associated with temporal lobe epilepsy. Some paroxysmal disorders of perception may also have a basis in temporal lobe epilepsy. A special technique using sphenoidal electrodes for recording activity from the underside of the temporal lobe may be useful in these cases to provide evidence of pathology in a surgically accessible area.

The e.e.g. now has an established place in the investigation of those cases in whom intellectual loss or clouding of consciousness suggest an organic pathology. It may provide valuable help in distinguishing primary from secondary dementia and in excluding the pseudo-dementia of the retarded depressive. In confusional states with paranoid ideas, a diffusely slowed e.e.g. weighs the diagnosis in favour of an organic condition rather than schizophrenia.

In barbiturate takers and barbiturate coma the e.e.g. shows a characteristic fast rhythm induced by these drugs. During the withdrawal phase from barbiturates, the increased tendency to develop fits is indicated by a lowered threshold for the appearance of epileptic activity during photic stimulation.

Finally occasional hysterical conversion states may be recognised with the e.e.g. A dominant rhythm responsive to light excludes blindness, and the appearance in the record of an arousal response following auditory stimulation excludes deafness. A patient in a hysterical coma has a normal waking record. Adapted to record muscle electrical activity, the e.e.g. machine can be applied to the investigation of functional disorders of movement.

E.E.G. recording is simple and painless. With its limitations borne in mind it can be a valuable diagnostic aid in psychiatry.

Echoencephalography

This is a comparatively simple procedure when facilities are available, and is painfree and rapid. A beam of pulsed ultra-sound (very high frequency sound) is directed through the head from one temporo-parietal region, and reflections or echoes are obtained —mainly from the midline structures. The main value is in detecting shifts of the midline laterally, but in many cases the size of the lateral ventricles, and even of the third ventricle, can also be measured.

Radioactive isotope scan

This method is also painless, but the patient must lie still for up to one hour, and it is therefore unsuitable for restless patients.

Radioactive tagged elements (e.g. mercury) are injected into the blood stream and the pattern of take-up in the brain recorded by means of a scintillation counter. Characteristic patterns or 'maps' of take-up are shown by different types of tumour, etc., and very clear demarcations of normal and abnormal tissue may be obtained.

Lumbar air encephalography (L.A.E.G.)

Air is injected in small amounts via a lumbar puncture, as C.S.F. is withdrawn, with the patient sitting upright. X-rays taken as the air fills the ventricular system may show distortions, or obstructions due to space occupying lesions etc., or may show the ventricular dilatation of cerebral atrophy. The air may also demonstrate the pattern of the sulci on the brain surface, indicating cortical atrophy.

This investigation is dangerous in the presence of raised intracranial pressure.

Ventriculography

This is used when L.A.E.G. is contraindicated because of raised intra-cranial pressure. Air is introduced into the lateral ventricles via burr holes in the parieto-occipital regions. It provides similar information to the L.A.E.G., although the lower parts of the ventricular system are not so clearly demonstrated.

Cerebral angiography

Radio-opaque materials are injected into the internal carotid, or less frequently the vertebral arteries. Serial X-rays taken with careful timing can then demonstrate various arterial and venous phases of the cerebral circulation. In addition to its value in the identification and localisation of tumours and vascular malformations, atheromatous and stenotic disease of the arteries may be demonstrated.

Brain biopsy

Needle biopsy of the brain may be performed through burrholes, and the material obtained examined microscopically. Tumour cells or the changes characteristic of various dementias may be identified.

Computer assisted X-ray tomography (E.M.I. Scanner)

This method has proved of very great value. The head is scanned by a beam of X-rays in a series of slices a few mm apart, and the relative density of tissue measured. A computer is used to print the data as a picture which is inspected by the radiologist. There is no discomfort or morbidity, but the patient must be able to lie still for about one hour.

Caution

Of these investigations L.A.E.G., ventriculography, angiography, and brain biopsy all involve discomfort and a small serious morbidity of 1 or 2 per cent. The decision as to which methods should be used will be made by the neurosurgeon or neurologist consulted. Air encephalography and angiography are now needed infrequently.

7

Psychiatry in the aged

A separate chapter on this subject is justified by the special problems posed by the elderly, and by the vast numbers of patients concerned.

Old age begins officially at 65 years, for purposes of retirement for example, but at that age many people are still bright and lively, with active minds and bodies. Enforced retirement may have harmful effects, especially in those with few interests outside work. It leads to depression, and often to an apparent increased rate of ageing.

The earliest mental features of ageing are increasing forgetfulness for recent events, and especially for recently spoken words, with easy fatigue, lessened ability to sustain concentration, and an increasing 'rigidity' of mental processes. This is not just a rigidity of opinion and attitudes, but an inability to switch attention easily from one aspect to another and back again. Comprehension of complex matters and sound judgement may be preserved for a long time, but these also, along with other intellectual abilities, do decline as death of neurones proceeds. Ageing merges imperceptibly into senile dementia in those people in whom neuronal death progresses more rapidly.

Other psychological developments, as age increases, are intertwined with physical and social events. Bodily strength declines, degenerative arthritis, poor eyesight, deafness, shortness of breath, and other disabilities advance; the ageing person finds life increasingly difficult, and is increasingly confronted by mortality as friends and neighbours die. Most serious is the death of a spouse, and it is now firmly established that there is a major rise in morbidity and mortality, especially from heart disease, in the first six months after a spouse dies. Social isolation increases as time passes, intensified by the limits imposed by frailty, and often by relative poverty. In many the diet also becomes more limited and vitamin deficiencies become quite common, especially in elderly widowers living alone.

Social isolation is not only due to the factors outlined above. Much depends on personality. The eccentric woman hater, always relatively isolated, becomes more so; and as senile changes progress he is more likely than others to become paranoid and disturbed, and thus to come early to the attention of the social or medical services. Those of warm and outgoing personality, and especially those who have kept on good terms with their now grown up children, are more likely to be visited, or taken to live with the family when appropriate. The awkward, demanding and over-critical are more likely to be isolated.

Others who become isolated easily are the shy and reserved, the unmarried for any reason—for example those who stayed at home to look after mother years ago. Those who have such close relationships with their spouse that the rest of the world has been excluded, in a kind of childlike dependence, also do badly after bereavement.

When people live alone, without any social 'feedback', abnormalities of personality become more and more marked, a development intensified by senile cerebral changes. There is often increasing egocentricity and hypochondriacal self-concern. Functional psychiatric illness is more common in those with abnormal personalities of all kinds, and is increased by social isolation and physical disease. Suicide, for example, is common in lonely old people with chronic painful diseases. Organic brain disease is equally common in people of all types, but in those with abnormal personality it is much more likely to lead to florid behavioural disturbances.

The social structure in which the person lives is also relevant to all this. Small cohesive groups offer more support to the bereaved and ill than do disparate individuals recently rehoused in tower blocks of flats. Small cohesive groups can, however, be very rejecting of the eccentric individual who has never fitted in.

Psychiatric morbidity in the elderly

There is a large and increasing proportion of old people in Britain and the other countries of the Western world. The 1971 census of England and Wales showed almost 6 400 000 over 65 years, of which almost 2 250 000 were over 75 years. The number over 65 years is increasing by about 15 per cent per decade, which means an increase of almost one third between 1971 and 2000. There will, with recent birth rate trends, be relatively few younger people to support the elderly, services for which are already grossly inadequate. No adequate plans to cope with this problem have yet been put forward within the National Health Service.

The best estimates we have of morbidity suggest the following: In those over 65 years about ten per cent have some significant dementia, half of them quite serious; 31 per cent have significant anxiety or depressive symptoms—in some of long standing, but in many of recent onset—of whom few are receiving any treatment other than benzodiazepines (q.v.). Many of these elderly people have multiple pathology, with psychiatric disorders co-existing with cardiovascular, gastrointestinal, and other diseases. Those over 75 years have still higher morbidity, and are less likely to have a living spouse.

Depression in the elderly

This section should be read in conjunction with the chapter on Affective Disorders, in which the aetiology, clinical features, and treatment are described in detail.

Depression is very common in the elderly, but is often unrecognised and untreated, as for example, in those who have had strokes, many of whom are seriously depressed. Doctors tend to feel 'I would be depressed too, if I were like that', and therefore do nothing about it, although such patients can often be helped by antidepressants.

Too many elderly depressives are given benzodiazepines or other minor tranquillisers (p. 397) which help associated tension and anxiety, but may make the depression worse, and often cause confusion and unsteadiness.

Serious depressive illnesses, with retardation or agitation, produce a picture easily mistaken for dementia (so called depressive pseudo-dementia). The distinction is extremely important as spontaneous remission in serious depression in the elderly is rather uncommon, whereas treatment is often very successful. This history must be obtained from another person. Dementing illnesses usually develop over months and years, whereas depression deepens over weeks and months. It is only in the final stages of depression that psychomotor agitation or retardation and withdrawal are so marked that they interfere with communication and cause mis-diagnosis.

In the demented, depressive mood is less sustained; and incontinence, deterioration of personal habits, and behavioural disturbances of all kinds are much more common. More serious and sustained depression can occur at times in early dementia, and well being can be improved with antidepressant treatment.

Treatment

The forgetfulness of the elderly is a big problem with drug treatment, and makes the use of monoamine oxidase inhibitors unwise in someone who lives alone and has memory difficulties. Electrical treatment (e.c.t.) tends to cause more memory disturbance in the elderly than in others, but may still be very useful, and so may tricyclic antidepressants. The elderly are prone to many disabling side effects with tricyclic drugs generally, including confusion, glaucoma, constipation (which can even develop into paralytic ileus), retention of urine, cardiac arrhythmias, and postural hypotension. If they are prescribed, small doses, such as amitriptyline 10 mg three times daily, should be used to begin, and the dose increased as side effects allow.

A recently introduced tetracyclic drug, mianserin, is free of these side effects, is equally effective, and is in our opinion preferable. Dosage should start with 10 mg, and build up slowly to 40 or 60 mg daily.

Paranoid psychosis in the elderly

This section should be read in conjunction with the chapter on schizophrenia, especially pages 146 to 153. Paranoid psychoses in the elderly are common, particularly in those of suspicious and reserved temperament, and social isolation, especially that related to deafness, is often a factor. In some, there are classical 'first rank' symptoms of schizophrenia, but in others there are only persecutory delusions. Personality is usually well preserved, and the term 'paraphrenia' is often used for these states. There is no general agreement on terminology, unfortunately, but we suggest 'schizophrenia of late onset' when truly schizophrenic symptoms are present, and 'paranoid psychosis' when they are not. Treatment is as for schizophrenia, but the delusions are sometimes very resistant to treatment.

In some patients persecutory delusions are the first sign of a dementing illness; and paranoid features are common in confusional states and depressive illnesses.

Confusional states in the elderly

The most important diagnostic point here is to distinguish transient confusion from dementia, remembering that confusion is an integral part of advanced dementia (Ch. 6 on 'Organic States' should be consulted for the account of confusional states). The problem presents in those for whom no history is available, perhaps because they live alone, so the doctor cannot easily tell how long the patient has been disorientated and confused.

Confusion arises in those with and without some degree of pre-existent dementia, more easily in the latter. It can be due to any infection, especially urinary, to electrolyte imbalance from diuretics, head injury (elderly people are prone to fall), and numerous other causes; and very commonly with chest infections and heart failure. Careful physical examination and investigation is necessary.

A common cause of confusion in the elderly is drug intoxication. Normal doses of tricyclic antidepressants or benzodiazepines can lead to it; and too many patients have a large variety of drugs prescribed, often at different outpatient clinics. The bathroom cupboard may easily contain psychotropic drugs, diuretics, anti-inflammatory drugs for rheumatism, and painkillers. If the patient is already forgetful, mis-dosage is common, and confusion with added falls may develop.

Another cause of transient confusion, especially in those already slightly demented, is a major emotional upheaval—such as bereavement or a sudden enforced change of house, or admission to hospital. The death of a spouse may 'uncover' dementia, as mentioned later, but quite often upheavals and turmoil lead to confusion which settles down in a few days.

DEMENTIA

This section should be read in conjunction with the chapter on organic states (Ch. 6). The possibility of depressive pseudo-dementia, and of deterioration due to treatable causes, must always be remembered.

Senile dementia

Senile dementia is the commonest of all dementias, affecting about 5 per cent of those over 65 and considerably more of those over 75 years. There is a marked hereditary element. Pathologically, senile dementia and Alzheimer's disease are indistinguishable, and they should be regarded as the same illness: the age 65 years being an entirely arbitrary division. Most cases start after 70 years. Microscopically neurones disappear, senile plaques and neurofibrillary tangles appear, and cerebral atrophy develops, with dilatation of the ventricles and broadening of the sulci. The frontal lobes are affected early in many cases, with consequent early personality deterioration.

Major emotional upheavals, such as the death of a spouse, often seem to precipitate the illness, but this is probably more a matter of 'exposing weakness' in that the patient is less able to cope with the stress, and therefore suddenly deteriorates.

The clinical picture is one of progressive deterioration of intellect and personality, in which memory disturbances are very prominent, but which affects all aspects of mental life sooner or later. These clinical features also apply to the pre-senile dementias.

The onset is typically gradual. Memory fails for recent events, the patient becomes slower, vitality diminishes, interests narrow, comprehension begins to lessen, emotional blunting occurs with increased egocentricity. There may also be emotional lability with unexpectedly easy tears or empty laughter. Irritability is common in short lived bursts, and any mental or physical task—even a call to join in a conversation—may lead to anxiety with tremor and restlessness, if the patient is unable to cope with it; and catastrophic anxiety (p. 83) may also develop in similar but more demanding situations. As the deterioration progresses it becomes less and less possible for the patient to get involved in any task, and therefore these distress signals of failure to cope diminish.

Sleep becomes disturbed, and the normal rhythm reversed, often leading to restless pottering all night. Very frequently, confusion increases at night to such a degree that the patient loses touch completely with time and place, and goes out for some imaginary appointment or to visit a long dead mother miles away. Such nocturnal wandering is dangerous, especially on cold winter nights, and is very worrying to relatives and neighbours. It is perhaps the single most common reason for referral for psychiatric care.

Personal standards and habits deteriorate. Early on there may be an unexpected and out of character sexual offence, such as exhibitionism or sexual interference with a child, as social inhibitions decline; and clumsy shoplifting or other theft might occur. Incontinence always develops at some stage, at first seemingly because the demented patient ceases to care where she empties her bladder, later because she cannot anyway find the way to the w.c., and later still, because all sphincter control is impaired. Habits of eating, personal hygiene, standards of dress, all deteriorate.

Memory loss leads to mislaid articles and misunderstandings, and persecutory delusions of a transient and poorly organised type are very common, more so in those of previously suspicious temperament.

There are usually focal disturbances at some stages, such as dysphasias and dyspraxias, but not so markedly as with arteriopathic dementia, and focal neurological signs do not occur. Visual, and less commonly, auditory hallucinations, and misinterpretations are common.

In some the illness advances very rapidly, so that within a few months there has been a total change of personality, and great physical weakness, and death follows soon. Others may endure for several years, especially if well cared for, although towards the end the patient may seem devoid of any mental life at all; hunched up, incontinent and inaccessible.

Arteriopathic dementia (Arteriosclerotic dementia)

This is the other type of common dementia in the old, although it can develop in younger people, especially if hypertensive. Clinically it may be indistinguishable from senile dementia, and in many there is microscopic evidence of both pathologies. Certainly in the later stages the clinical description given for senile dementia applies here too.

In the classical form the most marked feature is that the illness has a sudden onset, with a 'little stroke' causing transient dysphasia, confusion, or weakness and unsteadiness, depending on the site of the lesion. The patient then improves quite quickly, although rarely returning completely to normal. Recurrent attacks, with lesions in different parts of the brain, lead to the step-wise deterioration classically described. There is a tendency for personality to be preserved more than in senile dementia, for any given degree of intellectual impairment. Focal neurological signs and specific psychological deficits due to local brain damage are almost invariable at some stage.

The pathology is not now regarded as primarily due to thrombosis in sclerotic arterioles in the brain. One cause increasingly recognised is micro-embolism due to clumps of platelets formed on the surface of atheromatous plaques in the major vessels of the neck or aortic arch. Aspirin lessens platelet 'stickiness', and is under trial as a long term treatment. A neurologist's advice should be sought before starting this regime. Peptic ulceration is a contra-indication.

Another cause of patchy infarcts in the brain, causing dementia, is failure of perfusion through seriously narrowed major arteries. Any episode of hypotension, as from a myocardial infarct, haemorrhage during an operation, a prolonged anaesthetic while sitting up in the dentist's chair, and so on, can lead to permanent brain damage and dementia. Great care must be taken in anaesthesia for the elderly for this reason.

Hypertensive encephalopathy, commoner in middle-aged people, can also lead to some degree of non-progressive dementia if prolonged.

Treatment of dementia

There is no drug treatment known to arrest the progress of these dementing illnesses, although aspirin may help in some cases of micro-embolism, as mentioned. Cyclandelate 400 mg three or four times daily is claimed to improve cerebral blood flow, and improve mental functions. Although there is no convincing evidence, in such grim conditions it is perhaps worth trying these drugs, so long as side effects are not troublesome.

Antidepressants (q.v.) can be very useful in relieving depressive states even in the demented who cannot describe their feelings verbally. A changed demeanour, improved sleep and appetite, and the disappearance of weeping, indicate that treatment has been helpful.

Paranoid disturbances can be helped by phenothiazines and thioxanthines as used in schizophrenia, but in smaller doses. Depot injections prevent accidental overdosage by the forgetful. Thus, 10 mg of flupenthixol or 12.5 mg of fluphenazine decanoate intramuscularly every two or three weeks may lessen suspicion and paranoid outbursts, and make the patient calmer and happier-seeming. Sometimes a paranoid old lady at home can in this way at least accept a home help or meals on wheels which she has been refusing.

Extrapyramidal disturbances develop easily in the elderly with brain damage, and the drugs should be stopped if they occur. Anti-parkinsonian drugs tend to cause their own side effects, and the correct amount is unlikely to be taken by a forgetful person, and so their use is not recommended except for occasional small intramuscular injections.

Care and management

Except in the more severely demented, who pass beyond response before they die, every attempt should be made to keep the demented person active, physically and mentally. Company, trips out, occupational therapy, music and simple games, are all helpful when pitched at the correct level. Those who can be cared for in the family are obviously most fortunate, and whatever chores they can cope with should be given to them.

A well balanced diet may need careful supervision. Bowel function is most important, as constipation is a frequent cause of mental disturbance and nocturnal restlessness in the demented, as well as leading to faecal incontinence from overflow. Both bowel and urinary incontinence can be helped by regular 'habit training' in hospital. Chiropody is another helpful adjunct, as feet become painfully neglected often.

Doctors must realise that one of the most useful functions they have in caring for these patients is in maintaining the morale of the family or staff who do most of the necessary work. If doctors do not show interest the level of care deteriorates, especially in large hospitals with heavy case loads.

For the patient at home, attendance at a day centre or day hospital, or 'holiday' admission for a few weeks as an inpatient, relieves the burden on the family, and can help a family to keep their demented relative at home. These services are considered in the next section.

In the terminal stages of dementing illness life can be preserved by vigorous treatment of infections and so on, but in our opinion this should not be done. In hospital the situation should be discussed with the nurses and the family, and an agreement reached that the patient should be allowed to die peacefully. (Pain and discomfort should always be relieved if possible). The feelings of the nursing staff must be considered seriously here. Those who spend their working life in psychogeriatric wards caring for old people cannot just 'switch off' their attentions, and it may seem to them that this is what a decision to abandon certain forms of treatment implies. In Britain many nurses have entirely different cultural backgrounds to those of the medical staff, and they should not be expected to share attitudes which may seem to others self evident.

Services for the elderly mentally ill

Two parallel sets of services exist, those of the health and the social services, which should be harmoniously integrated.

The medical services start with the general practitioner, who can call on services from health visitors and district nurses, and can refer to, or ask for, a domiciliary visit by a psychiatrist, geriatrician, or other appropriate specialist. The patient can attend a day hospital, or become an inpatient. Community psychiatric nurses have an important role; they may be attached to the family doctor or to the psychiatric team.

The local authority Department of Social Services provides social workers and assistants, home helps, domiciliary occupational therapy, meals on wheels, attendance at social or luncheon clubs or at occupational day centres. Finally, they provide residential old people's homes (so-called Part III accommodation), some of which may also have a day centre function. Local authority homes vary a great deal in the amount of confusion and disturbance with which they can cope, whereas hospitals of course have to cope with the most disordered.

All the services mentioned above, which are aimed largely at keeping the old person more happily at home, are very seriously overstretched at present in the U.K. There are many demented old people still at home who would be better off in hospital or a home, and whose families would also be much relieved.

8

Schizophrenia

The word schizophrenia, literally 'split mind', describes a range of mental disorders, and many students find the concept a baffling one, as such varying clinical pictures are given the same name. It does *not* mean the split personalities of Jekyll and Hyde type, who are usually psychopathic or hysterical, and a better analogy is of a widespread splintering or fragmentation of the mind.

The concept is perhaps best understood historically. Until German psychiatrists began their careful clinical studies with long term follow up in the nineteenth century, most of the mentally ill were lumped together as 'insane'. Many died of such illnesses as syphilitic General Paresis or because of lack of care or from concurrent infection; a great many deteriorated; and some recovered. By the end of the nineteenth century, building on the work of many others, Kraepelin had firmly established two major groups among those who did not die of organic brain disease—Manic Depressive illnesses and Dementia Praecox. They were distinguished essentially by the finding that the manic-depressives recovered, although they often relapsed; while those with Dementia Praecox did not, ending up in a characteristic end-state (the 'precocious dementia') despite rather widely varying patterns of early illness. The essential difference was therefore prognostic. Later Bleuler suggested the name 'the schizo-phrenias', and broadened the concept, leading the way to include patients who did not necessarily end up 'demented', but who share some of the characteristic signs and symptoms at the onset. We no longer use the plural, not all psychiatrists are in favour of the broader concept, and some have broadened it beyond useful limits.

It is important to realize that many psychiatrists abroad, particularly in the U.S.A. and U.S.S.R., would not share the views put forward here, and this should be remembered when reading foreign articles or books. That does not mean that our view is necessarily more correct—although we may think it so—but that conclusions about aetiology and treatment, for example, cannot be applied if the diagnostic criteria are different. In the U.S.A., for example, patients are diagnosed as schizophrenic in some centres, especially those with a psycho-analytic orientation, who in Britain and continental Europe would be regarded as suffering from depression in a setting of personality disorder. The use of psychotherapy as the main treatment for schizophrenia (p. 379) is understandable in that diagnostic context, but not when patients are diagnosed by the criteria used here.

These mental illnesses are grouped together because they show similar disorders of thinking, emotional reaction, will power and motility. They are characterised by a marked tendency to drift out of contact with reality into an inner subjective world dominated by fantasy and delusion. Thinking becomes unrealistic and distorted and emotional reactions shallow and inappropriate. During the early stages the clinical picture may vary considerably from patient to patient. Frequently a gradual change of personality in the direction of increasing ineffectiveness, oddness or eccentricity is observed, often accompanied by non-specific symptoms that are apparently neurotic; but the onset may be sudden and the symptoms florid. Should the disease progress, individual differences become less marked. In severe cases, the end result is a characteristic form of profound mental deterioration, the patients living in a world of their own, unoccupied, inaccessible, and apathetic, but without that clouding of consciousness or true intellectual impairment which are seen in organic psychoses (p. 106). For example, a patient who had been mute and inaccessible for many years, suddenly wrote fifteen letters in one day, all clear and coherent and correctly addressed.

Schizophrenia should not be thought of as a single 'disease' with varying manifestations, but as a group of related syndromes which have important things in common. It may well be that varying causes for the syndromes will one day be clear, or that they represent different reactions, determined by constitution, to some common causative factors.

Epidemiology

Schizophrenia is a very common illness, affecting about 0.8 per cent of the population between the ages of 15 and 45 at some time in their lives. In 75 per cent of cases the onset is between 17 and 25 years of age, but there is a smaller wave of increased incidence between 40 and 50. There are about 150 000 people with some disabling form of schizophrenia in the United Kingdom now. It is rather more common in men than in women.

Until fairly recently approximately one quarter of all hospital beds in Britain were for schizophrenics, but modern treatment and changes in discharge policy have reduced this considerably. It is most often found in areas of social disintegration, poverty, and rootlessness, such as characterise urban centres, and particularly areas with many lodging houses such as are found near large railway stations. It is commoner in people working in semiskilled or unskilled occupations (social classes IV and V on the Registrar General's classification). However, these findings are due to the downward social drift of those who are developing schizophrenia, or who are already ill: the social class of the families of origin is distributed normally, and they have usually moved into the decayed urban area shortly before being admitted to hospital—the way they enter the official statistics. The illness affects people of all grades of intelligence. It occurs throughout the world, and has been found in all types of society which have been adequately studied.

Aetiology and pathology

Genetic aspects
Ideas about the relative importance of genetic and environmental influences in the development of schizophrenia have been changing recently. Older studies suggested concordance rates in identical twins as high as 90 per cent if they had been brought up and living together, falling to 78 per cent if they had been separated for 5 years. These figures were probably artificially raised because they were based on hospital statistics only, and overall it seems that the concordance rate in identical twins is about 45 per cent. In non-identical twins it is about 10 per cent, and is higher if they are of the same sex. The identical twin who develops schizophrenia seems often to have been smaller, weaker and less dominant from birth than his mentally healthier co-twin. Where one parent is schizophrenic, the chances of the illness developing in the children are 10 to 14 per cent, rising to about 40 per cent if both parents are schizophrenic. If a grandparent was schizophrenic, but the parent healthy, the risk to a child is only about 3 per cent compared to the general population risk of about 1 per cent. The risk for full siblings is 14 per cent, and for half siblings about 7 per cent.

These figures show the very great importance of hereditary factors, but leave much room for environmental influences, including, of course, the intrauterine environment.

Environmental stresses alone do not seem to lead to schizophrenia unless the basic genetic predisposition exists. This has been shown in long term follow-up studies of babies separated at birth from their mothers, who were mental hospital inpatients, and brought up in

134   PSYCHOLOGICAL MEDICINE

foster homes and orphanages. Only the children of schizophrenic mothers developed schizophrenia themselves, with a frequency of about 12 per cent, a rate similar to that for children brought up in the home with a schizophrenic parent. Similar results have come from studying children who have been fostered from early infancy by other families. The fostered children of schizophrenic parents develop schizophrenia in about 10 per cent of cases, whereas other fostered children do not, and nor do the biological children of the foster parents.

A schizophrenic hereditary loading is associated not only with an increased risk of schizophrenia, but also of character disorders and neurotic states, and there is some evidence of an increased incidence of people with artistic interests and talents among the relatives. The facts of schizophrenic heredity do not fit any simple genetic pattern of dominant or recessive genes, and there are probably several genes involved. In some people, the hereditary loading is so marked that they are almost certain to develop schizophrenia, however favourable the environment might be, but in most cases they inherit a character or personality vulnerability, which predisposes to schizophrenia in an unfavourable environment.

Environmental aspects
Genetic factors, although necessary, are insufficient to explain the development of the illness, as appears from the 40 per cent concordance in identical twins. There is still uncertainty about the environmental stresses involved, although a good deal is known about the stresses which can lead to relapse in known schizophrenic patients. It seems reasonable to assume that similar factors affect the patient in his first illness, as in subsequent breakdowns, and clinical impressions support this idea.

Factors leading to relapse

Life events
Relapse in known schizophrenics often follows a few weeks after a build up of 'life events', as described on page 166 for affective illnesses. Life events are defined in various ways in different research schedules, but essentially they include such matters as births or deaths in a family, loss of jobs, car accidents, a brother's marriage, jilting by a girl friend, move of house, and very many more. Known schizophrenic patients tend to be very vulnerable to such events, which seem to set going inner changes—presumably neurochemical and psychophysiological in nature—which then

develop their own momentum, and lead on to a breakdown and the development of psychotic symptoms. In assessing the importance of precipitating life events, one must be careful to identify those which are the consequence of early schizophrenic deterioration, rather than a causal factor. For example, a young man might lose a job and a girl friend over the space of a few weeks *because* he is becoming ill, rather than become ill as a reaction to those stresses.

'*Expressed emotion*'. Another important factor known to lead to relapse, and almost certainly involved in the precipitation of first illnesses as well, is the nature of the family interaction. In families where much open criticism and hostility is expressed about the patient, relapse rates are higher. This is particularly true where the patient spends many hours of each week in close contact with family members. These factors explain, at least in part, why patients often do better in a hostel, or somewhere else less emotionally intense, and also show that the marked withdrawal from family life, and in fact from all emotional involvement, which is so characteristic of schizophrenia, may be serving a useful purpose.

Schizophrenic people on the whole do not cope well with emotional intensity of any type, and seem to live most contentedly within a rather narrow range of emotional and other environmental stimulation. What to many are the very things which make life worth living—love, responsibility, variety, a challenge—are to the schizophrenic an intolerable stress. They also tend to cope badly with too little stimulation, and the apathy and lack of willpower which so many chronic schizophrenics show, and which is such a problem in rehabilitation, is part of this. They tend to lack self-generated drive, and unless stimulated do very little.

There have been many claims that specific patterns of family relationship or mother-child interactions are related to the development of schizophrenia, but it is more likely that the effects are non-specific, in that any intense family conflict or disturbance is experienced as stressful, and those with a constitutional predisposition to schizophrenia become more liable to breakdown. Other children or family members might react differently, depending on temperament: some developing neurotic or depressive symptoms perhaps, but others coping more actively, for example by leaving home. Clinically, it is often apparent that the family life of a schizophrenic is difficult and full of resentment and tension, and the patient may do much better when he leaves home and enters the relatively neutral atmosphere of a hostel. The parents' reaction to an eccentric and later mentally ill child often leads to deterioration in the family relationships, and one or both of the parents may have personality abnormalities related to the schizophrenic heredity, if they are not themselves actually psychotic. In other cases one sees families where the parental reaction is excessively tolerant and protective, and the patient may regress and become more dependent and childlike than he might otherwise.

It is our clinical experience that first attacks of schizophrenia, in those with a clear cut onset, often follow life events which, in others, would lead to feelings of depression: for instance, the loss of a girl friend or of a job, as mentioned earlier. In a good many of these patients, treatment with phenothiazines alone leads to the emergence of depressive mood after thought disorder and delusional ideas have settled down.

Although there is evidence that first attacks of schizophrenia are precipitated by such stresses as leaving home to join the army or go to college, it is important to note that there is no increase in schizophrenia among combatant troops, nor in prisoner of war camps. The environmental stresses should be seen as precipitants of illness in vulnerable people, rather than the cause. By the time soldiers have gone through their initial training period, most of those predisposed to major mental illness will in fact have been weeded out. The guiding principles generally adopted in connecting the development of schizophrenia with traumatic events, e.g., in awarding war pensions, are (1) that the stress should have been demonstrably severe, and (2) that the symptoms should have followed shortly after the stress without a long latent interval.

Schizophrenia is commoner in the long term prison population, but this is due to the repeated offences of some schizophrenics, rather than to the psychic trauma of prison.

Psychophysiological aspects
There is a good deal of evidence that in schizophrenia there are raised levels of activity in some central and autonomic nervous system activities, especially in the ascending reticular activating system, producing quantitative or qualitative changes in 'arousal'. It is not just that arousal is generally raised, thus affecting all functions, but that some systems and functions are differentially affected, and the delicate balance of activating and inhibitory feed back systems disturbed. Skin conductance, heart rate, electromyography, finger pulse volume, and other measures have been used, and all show changes in schizophrenia.

Skin conductance can be shown to rise in the presence of a relative who is critical or hostile, and to fall with one who is more neutral emotionally. It is not only in acutely disturbed patients, where one would expect it, that high arousal is found, but also in chronically ill and withdrawn patients. Abnormalities of the galvanic skin responses have been shown to be present years before psychiatric breakdown in studies of the children of schizophrenics, who have been followed up after the testing. Children who did not break down later, but were otherwise well matched, did not show the same abnormalities. In this last study it was demonstrated that various perinatal complications seemed to be related to later schizophrenic breakdown, in these children with a schizophrenic heredity. This is a reminder that environmental influences begin very early in life––immediately after conception.

Studies of the *electroencephalogram* (e.e.g.) in schizophrenia have so far been disappointing. Although there is general agreement that abnormalities of various types are present these might be reflections of the abnormal mental state rather than directly related to underlying causes of the illness. There has been a revival of interest in the subject recently with studies of cortical evoked potentials, the use of computerised techniques, and more careful clinical correlation with e.e.g. findings. A recent study suggests that different schizophrenic subgroups have different e.e.g. abnormalities.

Neuropathological studies in schizophrenia used to be very popular, but for several decades little work has been done in this field. Of the many claims made of histopathological changes in schizophrenia, none has been substantiated. However, cerebral tumours, especially those involving the limbic lobe, can produce illnesses indistinguishable from schizophrenia.

Biochemical studies in schizophrenia have waxed as neuropathological studies have waned. The findings that substances like mescaline and LSD (lysergic acid di-ethylamide) could produce states somewhat resembling acute schizophrenia without clouding of consciousness (unlike any other drugs known before), and that these substances had molecules related to those of adrenaline, was a powerful stimulus to research.

Currently much research centres on dopamine and dopaminergic pathways, largely because all neuroleptic drugs useful in schizophrenia have dopaminergic-blocking effects which are proportional to their potency against schizophrenic symptoms. It is thought that the meso-limbic dopaminergic pathway is that relevant to schizophrenia, and that effects on the nigro-striatal pathway, also dopaminergic, are responsible for the extra-pyramidal side effects of these drugs. Supporting evidence comes from the fact that dopamine-releasing and dopamine-mimicking substances and amphetamines can cause a schizophrenia-like paranoid psychosis.

Against the theory are the lack of schizophrenic symptoms after laevodopa, the fact that Parkinson's disease, with low dopamine levels, can co-exist with schizophrenia, and various other inconsistent findings. There are at least two different types of dopamine receptors known at present, and there may well be more, which complicates matters.

Premorbid personality. Children who later develop schizophrenia are not only characterised by abnormal psychophysiological test findings. They tend to be nervous, conforming, quiet children, who work hard at school but achieve less than might be expected from their diligence. They also tend to be friendless and withdrawn, and they often gradually develop the so-called 'schizoid' personality which almost 50 per cent of schizophrenics show before breakdown. (The schizoid personality is described on p. 220). In those patients in whom the schizophrenic illness develops gradually from a schizoid type of personality, so that one can hardly say when deterioration began, the prognosis is bad.

In other people the premorbid personality is not schizoid, but wayward and impulsive, unpredictable in reactions, easily anxious and upset, and generally vulnerable seeming. Yet others have normal seeming personalities, and in them the illness is usually of later onset and the prognosis is better. It is a general rule in psychiatry, certainly applicable in schizophrenia, that the more abnormal the premorbid personality the worse the prognosis.

In older people, especially those who develop paranoid schizophrenia or other paranoid states, the personality is often paranoid. By this is meant over-sensitivity, looking for slights, tending to blame others when things go wrong, and generally seeing the world as a hostile place, full of individuals and institutions who are out to do one down.

Although, as indicated above, environmental factors play a part in causation, no means of preventing the illness are known. In particular, there is no evidence that the development of child psychiatry in Child Guidance Clinics or individual psychoanalysis have any prophylactic value, although such evidence would be very hard to collect.

Parents should not be given the impression that they are to blame for the illnesses of their children, although it is helpful to try and lessen the family tensions and hostile criticism by discussion in many cases. On the other hand, as regards eugenics, many relatives of schizophrenics are haunted by fears for themselves and their children to an extent that is quite unjustified actuarially.

Schizophrenia seems sometimes to be precipitated by febrile

illnesses, childbirth, and occasionally by head injury. It is difficult to know how far these events may be causal or coincidental. For example, although schizophrenia seems to occur far more often after childbirth than during pregnancy, the actual incidence of puerperal schizophrenia* is much less than the incidence of schizophrenia unrelated to childbirth in women of child-bearing age. Further, an attack of puerperal schizophrenia may have been preceded and may be followed by confinements without psychiatric incident.

As far as head injury is concerned large scale studies show no more schizophrenia in the brain injured than in the normal population, except in those in whom there is temporal lobe damage. Temporal lobe epilepsy may produce illnesses very like schizophrenia, (see p. 103) and there is an overlap of the two illnesses in some way.

As the result of a careful study of the biography and background of individual cases, some understanding can be reached of the meaning of the symptoms to the patient. The understanding of a patient can be of great help in his management and treatment. This is true, of course, of all disease. But in our view psychological theories fail to account for the actual origin of schizophrenic symptoms, whatever light they may throw on the form that these may take.

Symptoms and signs

It has already been said that the schizophrenic disorders are a group of illnesses that have certain signs and symptoms in common, although not all of these are present at any one time in each patient, and some of them may never appear. The different forms are liable to have different modes of onset and to run different courses, as will later be described. We are here concerned with the essential characteristics of the disease as it occurs in full form. These may be considered under the headings of signs and symptoms, as in general medicine, distinguishing those features which we observe, and of which the patient may be unaware, from those features of which he complains or which he describes.

Signs in schizophrenia

The principal objective signs come under the headings of thought

---

* The student will sometimes come across references to 'puerperal schizophrenia', 'puerperal mania' and 'puerperal depression'. Sometimes these are referred to collectively as 'puerperal psychoses'. Puerperal psychoses are not special entities of their own. All that is meant is that the patient has had an attack of schizophrenia, or of mania, or of depression that happens to have been related to childbirth. See also page 168.

disorder; emotional disturbance; disturbances of will and volition; disturbances of motility; and withdrawal.

(1) *Thought disorder*

A poverty of ideas and associations may be all that is noticeable at first, but a sense of sudden interruption or blocking in the stream of thought is more typical. Some patients experience countless non-identifiable thoughts rushing through their mind.

The most important characteristic of schizophrenic thought disorder is seen in the abnormal association of ideas, nicely described as the 'knight's move in thought'. In well-advanced cases this becomes evident in the spontaneous utterances, which sound incoherent or entirely incomprehensible, but in milder cases it may come to light only if the patient is given a set problem, such as to explain the meaning of a proverb.

There are many varieties of schizophrenic thought disorder, the results of which differ from the product of mere stupidity to which, however, they may bear superficially a close resemblance. In many instances a sort of stilted or pontifical woolliness in expression is the most prominent feature, which has a certain affinity to what is occasionally observed in religious or demagogic exhortation or exposition, but not occurring in a setting that would make it justifiable. The consulting-room is not, for example, a normal or appropriate place for manifestations of the kind that might pass muster in the pulpit or on the public platform. Thus an early schizophrenic wrote: 'Poor people are entitled not only to the benefit of "Education", because some of them don't need it, but also to compensation. I don't mean money they have lost, or not made the best of, but moral compensation as well—to reimburse them for what they have failed to obtain.' In other instances the meaning is obscured by the use of symbolic or metaphorical expressions not readily comprehensible to others. Thus, another early schizophrenic, when asked for his complaint, replied: 'I have feared the numinous from an early age and still do. The stage of trouble from which I am now suffering is such that I do not believe that my fate is governed by the factors that should govern one's fate . . . The spirit of fear is to some extent a safeguard from normal trouble, since I am governed by the spiritual fear and not reason.'

The development of a gnawing anxiety that something may have gone wrong with one's mind because of an inability to understand what the patient is getting at, possesses some diagnostic value in schizophrenic thought disorder, particularly when it is coupled with a history of impairment in social efficiency or in social relationships and evidence that the method of expression exhibited has not been a lifelong characteristic. Conversation with schizophrenics is apt to continue without any progress being made and without the elicitation of definite facts, owing both to the patient's obscurity of expression and tendency to reply in vague, evasive generalities of the 'sometime', 'may be', 'yes and no', 'perhaps' variety. Schizophrenics tend not only to be woolly and vague, but woolly in an odd way, whilst occasional remarks demonstrate they are very much in touch.

Again, in certain instances the utterances of schizophrenics may appear not only bizarre but comic as well, yet what may sound like a joke was not meant to be one. This arises from an inability on the part of the patient to separate the abstract from the conrete and to distinguish clearly between metaphors and facts. For example, a schizophrenic girl, when asked why she was turning round in a circle, replied that she felt she was in a knot and was trying to unravel herself: and a schizophrenic sailor seriously maintained that in his opinion, or rather experience, the brain was divided into three parts, second sight for'ard, understanding amidships and memory aft, adding that the top of the mind should be kept empty in order to have a place to air one's views.

This aspect of schizophrenia doubtless plays some part in exposing psychiatric patients to that ridicule which adds to their misfortunes. The victims of cancer or blindness are not similarly treated with facetiousness and contempt.

The schizophrenic thought disturbance may result in 'double orientation'. Thus, a patient may believe he is God or the King, but at the same time may act and speak as an inmate of a mental hospital and will argue with the doctor and complain about the other patients.

These two lines of thought may be kept up in spite of all contradiction; or they may be interwoven. There is no logic, or the logic is peculiar.

From the subjective point of view, schizophrenic patients may, in the early stages, complain of difficulty in concentration. Many such patients turn their attention to subjects that lend themselves to vague speculations, such as mysticism and spiritualism, and so-called philosophy and psychology; and this is often interpreted as an over-compensation for their vaguely felt incapacity. But when the thought disorder becomes worse, the patients usually lose insight gradually. The thought disorder colours the various delusional systems, and contributes to the misleading appearance of dementia.

The elements of language may be well preserved, but various mutilations of individual words may occur, so that the verbal production of these patients may resemble that of an aphasic. In the most severe stages, language is disintegrated into a sequence of incomprehensible syllables and neologisms ('word salad').

Early cases often show an inclination for highbrow, odd or artificial expressions (mannerisms of speech), and the newly coined words or neologisms that appear later usually result from the patient's urge to describe his experiences, for which purpose an ordinary vocabulary is inadequate. The neologisms invented can be ingenious, e.g. 'teleognosis'.

It is quite common for patients to be able to converse sensibly on some neutral topic, and yet to become thought disordered as soon as important personal matters are touched on. It is not as though the patient deliberately screens himself from distress, but more as though a rise in inner tension (or 'arousal') alters cerebral function so that thought disorder appears. When drug treatment controls thought disorder in acute schizophrenia, depression and anxiety are often revealed.

(2) Emotional disturbance

Emotional reactions tend to be inadequate or inappropriate or both. A schizophrenic illness often starts with unspecific, vague, emotional disturbances. The patient becomes irritable, over-sensitive or depressed, sometimes in reaction to an upsetting experience, sometimes without any demonstrable external cause. Relatives often say that he has become 'more difficult'. In other instances, or at a later stage, it becomes apparent that his emotional responses, in particular wherein higher feelings are concerned, are less intense, less warm, shallower; he is less considerate, less polite, less loving. He loses interest in his work, in his hobbies, in his friends and relations; he becomes casual, sometimes flippant, often unpredictable in his responses. He may become rude, aggressive, suspicious. He may show a callous brutality and even commit brutal crimes, showing no emotional concern when caught. A mixture of hyper-sensitivity and detachment may be a very striking feature. The loss of emotional rapport may often be felt by friends and relations before it becomes clearly manifest in the patient's behaviour, and even good observers may find it extremely difficult to describe it in terms of specific illustrations or actual happenings. Even after a psychiatric interview nothing more tangible may be left than the feeling of a glass wall between the patient and the interviewer.

In other instances the patient may be able and willing to give an introspective account of his change and may be pathetically aware of the gradual loss of his emotions. In some cases the change is experienced as a loss of feeling in the perception of the outside world: the sunshine has become less bright, the flowers less colourful, people's faces less lively; in psychiatric terms, the syndrome of depersonalisation and derealisation may occur at that stage. In other early cases, and more often in advanced cases, the loss of normal emotional response is disguised by a silly, cheerful indifference, and an empty giggling is one of the most often seen affective disturbances. This indifference or fatuousness is often the first demonstrable sign of the typical incongruity and inadequacy of affect (p. 57), of the fully developed case. This emotional disturbance may be shown by the behaviour, e.g. if a patient laughs when talking about serious topics, gets violent on trivial provocation, gets dirty, neglects his clothing and fails to be ashamed when his attention is drawn to it; or if he exposes himself, or masturbates in public, as deteriorated cases do.

But in other cases the disturbance is much more subtle, and, in assessing it, one is up against the patient's (and his relatives') tendency to rationalise it, and one has to consider very carefully what emotional reaction would be appropriate in the light of the patient's normal (i.e. pre-morbid) personality. As with many other symptoms, it is the change of his reaction, as seen against his past, that is of real significance.

In those patients who do badly, emotional shallowness, progressive apathy, and loss of interest are associated with the patient's increasing withdrawal from contact with the outer world, so that he becomes more and more solitary, self-absorbed and frequently hypochondriacal, until finally he appears to live entirely in a world of his own.

Particularly in early cases disturbances of emotional expression are perhaps more important than disturbances of emotion itself––although obviously we usually judge the latter by the former. In many patients quite marked anxiety and depression may be hidden under an expressionless or even incongruous facade. Patients find it difficult to express their feelings verbally, but if given a symptom questionnaire will often indicate quite severe levels of depression and anxiety. Later in the illness there seems to be a real and permanent loss of depth of feeling, and very many schizophrenics do show some permanent flattening of affect even if they have otherwise recovered well from the illness.

(3) *Disturbances of will and volition*
'Lack of energy' is a frequent complaint in the early stages of the illness. Friends and relatives may describe the patient's poverty of

initiative, loss of drive, lack of decision and determination. More often such disturbances must be inferred from the description of the patient's behaviour and mode of life. His work history is often the best indicator. A psychopath may frequently change his job because he quarrels with his superiors or workmates, but an early schizophrenic can give no adequate reason for such changes or, if he does, his reasons are illogical or coloured by his abnormal emotional condition. More characteristic still is a gradual downward trend in the type of work the patient is given by his employers. There is often no gross negligence or misconduct, just a very slow falling off of that initiative and spontaneity required in independent and responsible work. This deterioration may be so gradual that nobody can date its onset; it may go on for years until such a patient, without ever having shown more dramatic symptoms, is found sitting about the house doing nothing or ends up as a tramp, drifting about the world without aim or purpose.

When the loss of initiative and spontaneity becomes more profound, and when it affects more primitive biological functions, it leads to those chronic conditions once a feature of mental hospitals—immobile figures sitting or standing about the wards. These states are now much less often seen, because patients are not left without occupation or stimulation as they used to be.

Ambivalence is the term used for another characteristic schizophrenic feature: contradictory impulses are present simultaneously, or arise in rapid succession. They may give rise to actions followed by counteractions so that the behaviour has no positive result, or they may contribute to the inertia. The effect of ambivalence may sometimes be obvious in the behaviour and is occasionally demonstrable, for example, when such patients are asked to shake hands. Thus, the patient may begin to hold out his hand and then withdraw it; the examiner then withdraws his hand; whereupon the patient holds his hand out again, only to withdraw it once more when the examiner makes a response. When a request or suggestion is immediately followed by counter-impulses the disturbance is called *negativism*.

(4) *Disturbances of motility (catatonic disturbance)*

There are several different types of motor disturbance, but they can be put under the two main headings of acute and chronic. They are all generally much less frequent and severe than they used to be because of earlier and more appropriate and effective treatment, although older patients with chronic catatonic disturbances are still common in mental hospitals, having had less effective treatment on admission decades before.

The common forms of acute catatonic disturbance are either extremes of overactivity (catatonic excitement) or of underactivity (stupor). Both are associated with very high levels of autonomic arousal, and can be precipitated by some form of rough handling, such as can happen when a patient is taken compulsorily by the police to hospital. The patient is in fact usually terrified, often by the strange mental experiences he is undergoing, such as hallucinations or passivity feelings (see below), in combination with the situation in which he finds himself. A state of stupor can switch to one of excitement suddenly and patients may become destructive, noisy, or aggressive without apparent motive. These sudden outbursts of activity are sometimes carried out in obedience to hallucinatory voices, but in other instances patients who are able and willing to provide information can give no reason for them. As one girl said: 'It's just as much of a surprise to me as it is to you', and she adhered to this even after recovery.

The patients may adopt strange attitudes, or peculiar positions, apparently expressive of such states as terror or ecstasy, or they perform wild and apparently purposeless, incomprehensible, movements. The movements themselves are often not performed with the normal degree of precision and coordination.

The chronic catatonic states do not have the same emotional disturbances behind them. They are mainly stereotyped repetitions of curious movements, such as knocking, rubbing or rocking, but may be more complex, and sometimes seem to hold in themselves the distorted reflection of some old purposive activity.

There are often disturbances of muscular tone, and a stiffness or awkwardness or lack of normal gracefulness is present; and with tic-like additions and distortions bizarre mannerisms develop. There is often also facial grimacing, commonly including a marked pursing and pushing forward of the lips. Some awkwardness and mannerisms may persist even after otherwise good recovery.

In other instances there may be a sustained increase of tone so that fixed postures are maintained for long periods, and, if these are deliberately altered by someone else, the patient will retain a new position. This state is known as *flexibilitas cerea*. If flexibilitas cerea is combined with stupor the result is *catalepsy*.

As with the disturbances of volition, these disturbances of motility are sometimes projected and rationalised, in that they may be attributed to the effect of outside influences and sometimes to that of hallucinatory voices.

(5) *Withdrawal and introversion*

These go together almost always, and are an important aspect of schizophrenia, present in nearly all patients at some stage. They are especially prominent in slowly developing illnesses of poor prognosis, and, combined with the characteristic apathy, lead to patients just sitting on their own, often lost in a dream world of fantasy. The degree of withdrawal shown is often extreme, as with two patients who had been in the same ward, with adjoining beds, for over ten years, but did not know each other's names.

Symptoms in schizophrenia

The symptoms of schizophrenia can be put under the main headings of *delusions*; *hallucinations* and other perceptual disturbances; and *passivity experiences* and related phenomena.

(1) *Delusions* occur in other psychotic conditions. They have relatively little diagnostic value in schizophrenia unless they are *primary or 'autochthonous'*.

The essence of primary delusions is that they appear suddenly, fully developed with an unshakable quality of conviction, without any logical connection with the immediate environment or circumstances at the time. They are often preceded by a strange feeling that the world is full of some hidden secret or mystery, or that things are charged with hidden meaning (delusional atmosphere). A chance observation or remark is immediately realised to have an intense personal significance or meaning. The traffic lights turn green in succession—this can only mean he is a Royal Personage; a piece of paper torn up—this means the unsuccessful destruction of a letter from the husband's mistress, and so on. The term 'delusional perception' is used for that moment in which some apparently natural event is misinterpreted or perceived strangely by the schizophrenic.

So called *secondary delusions* are also common. They are delusional misinterpretations of something experienced, and they explain the experience. For instance a nasty taste in the tea means that it has been poisoned; abdominal pain and constipation indicate that the bowels have been blocked by a piece of plastic inserted by the doctor overnight. Secondary delusions can also occur in severe depression, or with organic states.

The degree of systematisation and elaboration of the schizophrenic delusions depends to a large extent on the severity of the co-existing thought disorder. Delusions of persecution, often by political or religious bodies, are the commonest, followed by hypochondriacal delusions, typically with a bizarre quality, and delusions of jealousy, grandeur or self accusation. Favourite themes are the erotic, the philosophical, the religious, the mystical, the political and the hypochrondriacal, frequently strangely combined often with a paranoid or grandiose colouring and backed up by misinterpretations of the most varied kinds, involving pictures or advertisements in the newspapers or what is heard on the radio.

The patient's attitude to his delusions is typical in that he does not usually react appropriately and thus will go to his doctor when it would have been more logical to have gone to the police.

(2) *Hallucinations* of any of the senses may be found; but auditory hallucinations are the most frequent and characteristic (p. 61). Their clarity varies. Some patients are able to describe the character of the voices in great detail and the impression may be so vivid that the patient answers hallucinatory questions and discusses the statements of his supposed interlocutors. Other patients, although they are immediately aware of what the voices say, cannot repeat the exact words or otherwise describe the sensory character of their experience. The voices are generally disagreeable, threatening, aggressive, and abusive, and frequently make allusions to sexual matters. Sometimes the voices give orders that are often carried out to the letter, and hence it is always important to determine what hallucinatory commands are received.

The most characteristic voices are those which talk about him, argue about him, or comment on his actions in the third person. These are only found in schizophrenia, whereas voices talking *to* the patient may occur in severe depression and in some organic states.

Another characteristic type of schizophrenic hallucination occurs when the patient hears his own thoughts, either immediately before he has conceived them (they are 'dictated to him'), or simultaneously with the process of thinking, or immediately afterwards ('echo of thoughts'). In later stages the voices become more incoherent and incomprehensible, and neologisms often appear. Voices sometimes develop from obsessional thoughts; these increase in vividness, 'as if they were heard, and finally they are being heard 'inside the head' (pseudo-hallucinations) until they are finally experienced as coming from outside.

Visual hallucinations in the strict sense of the word are rare, at least in Western cultures. Disturbances of visual sensation and perception are not so uncommon in the early stages of the illness. The vividness of visual perception increases or decreases; faces or objects change shape, appear distorted. True visual hallucinations in acute stages of the illness are sometimes described as small images or pictures, often distorted or bizarre, flashing through the visual field. In rare cases of religious-ecstatic excitement the beginning is sometimes marked by one overwhelming vision of Christ or God in His Glory.

Complex and organised visual hallucinations, such as of living figures or identifiable objects, strongly suggest an organic state, like delirium tremens, and not schizophrenia.

'Pareidolic' illusions are not uncommon in the last stages of the illness when the patient, withdrawn and autistic, allows his phantasy freer play, and sees faces, people, and monsters in the clouds, wall-surfaces, etc.

Hallucinations of taste, smell and touch are often woven into the delusional system or are quoted to confirm it. Bodily sensations such as tinglings and 'shooting' feelings are quite common, and genital hallucinations occur, which the patient may interpret as meaning that sexual intercourse has taken place. Hypochondriacal delusions of a bizarre nature are often combined with hallucinatory and passivity experiences.

(3) *Passivity experiences and related phenomena.* These are very common in early schizophrenia, and are found only in that illness, so they have great diagnostic value. In chronically ill patients they may not be described.

True passivity experiences are those in which the patient is aware of some outside power or force, human or non-human, influencing his own thoughts, feelings, reactions or bodily activities. It is a direct experience, not an 'as if' feeling. There are no words which can easily describe these experiences, so analogies are used: 'it's like telepathy' or 'hypnosis', or 'cosmic rays affecting the brain' or 'it's like being a robot'. It is not surprising that secondary delusions grow up around these strange and frightening feelings.

Related experiences are those in which the patient's own thoughts and feelings seem to leave his mind so that they can be 'picked up' or 'read' by others (thought broadcasting); or taken away from his mind (thought withdrawal); and the experience of having some other thought or idea slipped into the mind from outside (thought insertion). Very often nowadays schizophrenic patients believe that their thoughts are being electronically recorded somewhere, an idea which, like many others, clearly shows the influence of a changing culture on the content of delusions.

Clinical forms of schizophrenia

The well known classification of schizophrenia into Simple, Hebephrenic, Catatonic, and Paranoid schizophrenia has been largely abandoned, because of the marked overlap between the sub-types, and because at different stages the same patient might fall into different sub-types. A brief outline of them is, however, given here because they have some historical interest, and because the term paranoid schizophrenia and the related terms paraphrenic and paranoia are still used, sometimes loosely.

(1) *Simple schizophrenia (schizophrenia simplex)*. This term is used to describe those patients in whom there is a very gradual onset of personal deterioration, eccentricity, loss of affect and of drive. They do not have the characteristic symptoms, only some of the signs, of schizophrenia. Bleuler, who popularised the concept (and introduced the word schizophrenia), included in it the eccentric and 'schizoid' relatives of schizophrenics; and many vagrants and 'drop-outs' were thought of as belonging to this group. Prognosis is very poor.

(2) *Hebephrenic schizophrenia*. This is characterised by onset at about puberty, with affective flattening and incongruity, with marked thought disorder, and a poor prognosis. Some cases begin suddenly, with marked depression or anxiety, but hebephrenic deterioration sets in later.

(3) *Catatonic schizophrenia*. In this group catatonic disturbances are prominent, onset is later than in hebephrenia, usually with an acute onset of stupor or excitement, or of perplexity; and impulsive acts, often violent, are common. As mentioned earlier, catatonic motor disturbances are usually associated with great fear or terror, and frightening hallucinations and delusions are common. There may be difficulty in distinguishing catatonic excitement from mania at times. Prognosis is uncertain, some patients doing very well.

(4) *Paranoid group*. These psychoses are the latest in onset, the majority of them starting in the fourth or even fifth decade. They begin with paranoid ideas, and the development of hallucinations completes the picture. The delusions are not generally systematised, and various delusions often co-exist without being related or combined. The discrepancy between the grotesque delusions, the terrifying hallucinations and the poor emotional response which they evoke, is often very striking, and this may enable the patient to have some insight into his condition. Thus, he may complain: 'I am suffering from ideas of persecution'; and a German paranoid schizophrenic wrote to his physician during the war: 'I have been given the Iron Cross. The schizophrenic indifference is appreciated in the front line.'

The name *paraphrenic* has been given to those sufferers from paranoid psychoses who, in spite of more or less systematised delusional ideas and in spite of hallucinations, yet retain their personality in a relatively intact state. Thus, the patient may show few symptoms of withdrawal or thought disorder, and the emotional rapport may remain strikingly good. Paraphrenic psychoses begin later in life than the other paranoid psychoses, often at the time of the climacteric or the beginning of the involutional period. The preservation of the personality may be due either to the fact that the pre-psychotic personality was resistant to the development of the illness, or to the late onset, or due to both reasons. Apart from actual paraphrenia with its tendency to systematised delusions, more loosely organised paranoid states of a more variable kind appear quite commonly in the old age groups and may yield to treatment.

The term *paranoia* was used by Kraepelin to denote those cases whose personalities were essentially preserved, and whose delusional systems developed insidiously and by logical steps in an essentially systematised way, such development being unaccompanied by hallucinations. Paranoia, in this sense, is no longer regarded as a special clinical entity, but rather as an incompletely developed form of paraphrenia. The delusions of these patients are commonly grandiose as well as persecutory, so that they may believe themselves descended from royalty or other exalted personages, or believe that they are prevented from holding titles or high office through the machinations of eminent persecutors. Thus, though the term *paranoid* essentially implies hostility and resentment, the term *paranoiac* connotes megalomania and grandiosity with which hostility and resentment are usually combined.

Some paranoiacs live at liberty as queer inventors, founders of eccentric sects, or as apostles of peculiar social reforms; many are ultimately admitted to mental hospitals because of some friction with society. Owing to the preservation of the personality, the firm belief in their own delusions, and the logic of their well-systematised reasoning, paranoiacs are often capable of persuading others of the righteousness of their cause. This is specially likely to arise when the paranoiac lives alone in secluded circumstances with a submissive partner; the latter may then come to share the delusions, a condition known as *folie á deux*. The number of people who share the delusions is, of course, not necessarily restricted to two, but depends upon the circumstances. When such a state of affairs comes to light, with resultant separation of the parties concerned, the secondary sufferers from the condition readily recover through the corrective effect of mingling with more normal people, although the real sufferer from the disease does not.

Schizo-affective psychosis. This term was introduced to describe an illness of sudden onset, in which florid schizophrenic symptoms are accompanied by marked depression or elation, arising in a young person of good previous personality, often with a family history of affective illness and clearly precipitated by some recognisable emotional stress. Other sub-types of schizophrenia have been described under such names as '*schizophreniform*' and '*cycloid*' psychoses, but it seems they are essentially the same. The clinical features are all recognised as indicating a good prognosis in schizophrenia, as mentioned later. Whether or not we should consider these psychoses as separate illnesses is unclear. The authors' attitude is that they are best regarded as being at one end of a continuum of schizophrenic syndromes, those at the other end being characterised by the worst prognostic features, with cases of intermediate prognosis in between. However, recent genetic studies suggest that they should be separated more definitely from the great body of the schizophrenic illnesses. If this is done it amounts to a return to the early views of Kraepelin.

Pseudo-neurotic schizophrenia. This is a term mainly used in the United States, to describe patients with severe personality problems, difficulties with and anxieties about nearly all aspects of life, with rigid and insightless views, and not responding appropriately to psychotherapy. As described it does not really fit into European ideas about schizophrenia.

Diagnosis and differential diagnosis
The introduction of modern physical methods of treatment makes early recognition of cardinal importance, since the best results are obtained in recent cases.

A distinction must be made between schizophrenic *symptoms*, which may occur in numerous psychiatric conditions, and schizophrenic *illnesses*. The mere presence of symptoms, often rather loosely called schizophrenic, such as paranoid delusional misinterpretations and catatonic phenomena, does not necessarily mean that the patient is suffering from schizophrenia; the former can occur in depressions and the latter in organic disease. Again, there are many paranoid personalities, suspicious, touchy, ready to take offence, who feel unwanted and that the world is against them, who are not suffering from schizophrenia.

One serious difficulty is that several of the most important features of schizophrenia are often difficult to identify with confidence in the early stages, particularly thought disorder and affective and volitional loss. For example, a girl who giggles as she gives a muddled account of some physical disorder to her doctor may be showing incongruous affect and thought disorder; or she may be a nervous and shy girl, too embarrassed to speak about the problems she intended to discuss with him. An adolescent boy who moons about the house all day, who avoids his old friends, plays records for hours at a time, and keeps promising to get a job but never makes the effort, may be developing the withdrawal and volitional loss of schizophrenia. He may instead be suffering from depression, or may be taking drugs, or there may be serious problems in the family to which he is reacting.

There are however a number of very clear cut 'first rank' symptoms on which a diagnosis of schizophrenia can be made with fair confidence in the early stages, so long as there is no clouding of consciousness of organic type, and so long as no psychotomimetic drugs such as LSD have been taken. These first rank symptoms (a term introduced by Kurt Schneider) are not indicators of outcome, nor are they important in the life of the patient and his family in the way in which, for example, loss of affect is important. The term 'first rank' refers only to their usefulness in diagnosis, and they include: primary delusions; hallucinatory voices in the third person talking about him or commenting on his actions; echoing thoughts; all passivity experiences; and thought broadcasting and thought insertion. Useful though these first rank symptoms are, they are not the only important diagnostic features, and in chronic patients may not be elicited.

Another important diagnostic point is the lack of insight many patients show into the abnormality of their behaviour, which is neither explained nor excused by the schizophrenic as similar behaviour would be by neurotics or psychopaths or those suffering from personality disorders.

In taking the history, careful enquiries should be made as regards increasing introversion and emotional indifference or shallowness. Has the patient done less and less? Has he seemed increasingly vague and dreamy? Has it seemed difficult to get at what he is driving at? In order to establish the diagnosis of a progressive schizophrenia, it is necessary to discover whether the personality of the patient has changed in a schizophrenic way that cannot be accounted for by environmental or developmental factors. The more extroverted the previous personality, the more noticeable will be a change towards introversion, seclusion and emotional shallowness and detachment. The greatest difficulties arise in sensitive, shy, shut-in personalities, and in such the nature of the disease is seldom recognised except in retrospect, unless the unrealistic or bizarre quality in the complaints or behaviour betrays their schizophrenic origin at the time of their occurrence. Here again the lack of insight, as shown by lack of explanation, of excuse, or of realisation of the need for these, possesses diagnostic value.

The early presenting symptoms may be of a non-specific kind and resemble those of a state of anxiety or depression; and the true diagnosis may be only permitted or suggested through the development of additional symptoms, especially passivity feelings, hallucinations or primary delusions. Sudden inexplicable behaviour, antisocial or not, that seems senseless or startling should always suggest schizophrenia, so long as it is not obviously gainful.

Amphetamines may produce illnesses very like paranoid schizophrenia, and so may psychomimetic drugs like LSD (see p. 339). Rarely, schizophrenia-like pictures may develop in physical illnesses with some confusion (in the organic sense), or clouding of consciousness, for example in encephalitis. The only clue in the history may be from the nursing staff who report that the patient becomes muddled and confused at night. Also rare are schizophrenia-like illnesses with tumours in the limbic system or elsewhere. Diagnosis is of really vital importance, because these very rare conditions are usually potentially fatal.

Real clouding of consciousness only occurs rarely and transiently in the most acute forms of schizophrenia. The differential diagnosis from other acute psychoses is of less immediate importance since most psychotic patients need hospital care. In the differential diagnosis from hysteria, a fair rule is that where there is reasonable ground for doubt, the case is one of schizophrenia.

Course and prognosis

Schizophrenia is a grave illness. It used to be said that its course could be crudely compared with that of a switchback downhill, but that the gradient was difficult to predict since the downhill course might stop or spontaneous remissions occur. About one third of the cases recovered or showed considerable improvement after the first attack, while the other two thirds failed to do so, and if followed up after ten years were either in mental hospitals or had died. The chances of a spontaneous remission were greatest within two years and were negligible after five years from the onset. It had been worked out that if a patient had remitted for three years, he was probably safe for another seven, but recovery from a third attack was improbable. But this state of affairs has been considerably altered by the introduction of the phenothiazines and later drugs, and other improvements in care. It is still advisable to start treatment early but more can be expected than formerly, even for the more chronic type of case.

One major difficulty in discussing prognosis will be a surprise to the medical student, used to assessing degree of recovery by the patient's symptoms, signs and level of function. Most patients on adequate doses of neuroleptic drugs have no symptoms, anyway, although there may be marked signs in the sense of lack of drive or emotional flattening. (Excessive drug dosage increases apathy and flattening, and must be carefully monitored). Discharge from hospital and gainful employment are unfortunately unreliable indicators. The former depends on public and medical attitudes as much as on well-being, and the latter is greatly affected by local and national unemployment levels, legislation to help the disabled, and other non-clinical factors. This makes it very difficult to compare recovery rates now with those of some years ago, and with those of other countries and varying rehabilitation methods. Although very many chronic schizophrenic patients have been discharged from hospital in the past thirty years, it is difficult to know how much they have gained as a result of this, or how much their relatives have suffered. The idea that discharge from hospital is necessarily a good thing is too naive a view. Discharge should be to a better life than hospital can provide, but unfortunately it has not always been so.

Despite the disclaimers above there is no doubt that prognosis has greatly improved for patients admitted to hospital in the past twenty-five years and treated from the beginning with phenothiazines or other neuroleptics; and without doubt the most important single cause of relapse and re-admission to hospital is stopping drug treatment. This applies to many who are symptom free, working and living successfully and happily in the community, as well as to those in a more precarious balance.

The prognosis in any individual case remains difficult. The old rules still hold good; that the more acute the onset the more favourable is the outlook, so that acute catatonic cases, though much rarer now, do best; that an affective admixture whether of excitement or depression is a favourable feature; that hopeful prognostic points are a good previous personality, a sudden onset, obvious precipitating factors whether physical or mental, a manic-depressive rather than a schizophrenic heredity, a pyknic (endomorphic) physique, a well-preserved emotional response within the psychosis, and, curiously enough, a good intelligence.

By contrast, an insidious onset may still be ominous. A schizoid pre-psychotic personality, emotional flattening, early introversion, a family history of deteriorating schizophrenic illness, low intelligence and the absence of precipitating factors, are still unfavourable signs.

By *schizophrenic defect* we mean the characteristic picture, compounded of emotional blunting and lack of drive, often with some degree of vagueness or woolliness of thinking, which tends to follow symptomatic recovery from a schizophrenic illness—both the first breakdown and subsequent relapses. In many patients each relapse leads to further step-wise deterioration, so that even patients who seemed at first to have a good prognosis, judged from the criteria just given, can end up doing badly. It is for this reason that it is important to prevent relapses—each can do permanent harm.

Treatment

There are three principal methods of treatment, all applicable to nearly every patient: the use of phenothiazines and other anti-psychotic drugs; environmental changes; and rehabilitation. In many patients there are also other aspects to be considered, which are mentioned later. In all psychiatric illnesses, as in all other illnesses, a relationship of trust and confidence between the patient and those treating him is of the greatest importance.

Drug treatment

The phenothiazines remain the mainstay of drug treatment in schizophrenia, although other groups such as butyrophenones and thioxanthenes also have a place, and are preferred by many psychiatrists. It is striking that all the drugs useful in the control of schizophrenic symptoms are liable to produce extra-pyramidal disturbances, although their efficacy is not proportional to those side-effects as was once suggested. Drugs used for the relief of depression and anxiety do not cause similar side effects. This clinical fact supports the current theories that abnormalities in dopaminergic neurotransmission are important in schizophrenia.

In clinical use the drugs available can be considered under three simple headings: more sedative; less sedative; and depot injections. Details of the use of the drugs are given in the chapter on treatment, which should be read in conjunction with this section.

The more sedative drugs such as chlorpromazine and thioridazine are most useful when the patient is very tense or disturbed, frightened perhaps by hallucinatory voices and other symptoms, or potentially violent. After the florid disturbances have settled many patients are too sedated by these drugs, and they benefit from a change to something less sedative, such as trifluperazine. If a patient is not markedly disturbed he can be started on one of the less sedative drugs. Thought disorder, and perplexity with passivity feelings, often seem to respond best to trifluperazine.

The great benefit of the depot injections is that patients cannot so easily stop taking their medication, which is the most common single cause for relapse and readmission to hospital. Some just forget to continue because they feel well; many others stop because they feel so much better that the drugs seem no longer necessary; some object to side effects; and others very naturally object to the idea of having to remain on drugs indefinitely. It is obviously important to explain to the patient and his family the reason for the prolonged drug therapy and also to concentrate on minimising side effects. A lower dose may be necessary, and antiparkinsonian agents are often very helpful. A change of drug, for example from fluphenazine (a phenothiazine) to flupenthixol (a thioxanthene), may be the best course of action. The depot injections are on the whole less sedative, but overdosage with resultant apathy and slowness can develop insidiously, and the patients often benefit from missing one of the monthly or fortnightly injections and re-starting on a smaller dose.

All schizophrenic patients should be given phenothiazines or one of the antipsychotic drugs in the early stages of the illness, and the majority should continue to take them either continuously or intermittently. There are many chronic schizophrenic people in long stay hospital wards who receive bigger doses than they need, almost as a matter of therapeutic habit. In fact, while living in the sheltered atmosphere of a hospital they may seem to need no drugs at all. It is different outside hospital however. Many schizophrenics are liable to relapse in the face of quite minor stress, or even when confronted by changes of routine. The antipsychotic drugs lessen this overreaction. Even in well run and harmonious long-stay wards patients are not certain to avoid all relevant stresses; for example, relapse can follow the departure of a nurse to whom the patient is attached, or an upheaval such as redecoration of the ward.

The side effects of these drugs, and ways to combat them, are described in more detail on page 392. Some other drugs, such as pimozide, which have more limited uses, are also discussed.

Environmental change
In the early stages of a schizophrenic illness the patient is nearly always better treated in hospital. A day hospital can be as good as an in-patient stay, if the home situation is suitable and the patient not too disturbed. Hospital care allows drug treatment to be supervised more closely, many patients feel much safer and the family situation, which is often extremely disturbed and tense by the time the patient first presents, can then simmer down. In hospital the patient can be observed in much more detail. The way in which he relates to other people and the degree of withdrawal, suspicion, anxiety and depression can all be assessed; and as he improves, his concentration, interests and abilities at work, and his level of drive or apathy can also be studied. The reports of nursing staff and occupational

therapists on these matters can be almost as important at times as the actual care which they give the patient.

During the patient's stay in hospital, contact should be made with the family, both by direct interview and if possible by a social worker who can visit the home. (At the time of writing unfortunately the social services are very hard pressed, and social worker services are hard to obtain.) Through these contacts with the family a better idea of any relevant stresses within the family can be obtained. The family can often be helped to come to terms with the problems generated by the patient and his illness, and there may well be problems which have contributed to the breakdown for which help can be offered. When the family atmosphere is full of emotional tension and conflict many patients do better not to return home, but to go and live in a hostel or some other more neutral environment. In some homes there is too little tension, and the patient is allowed to sink back into an overprotected invalid's life, with almost no demands being made upon him.

It is easy to criticise, from a distance, the way in which parents react to a schizophrenic son or daughter, but the abnormality of the reactions of the patient must be remembered; one or both of the parents may well have character abnormalities of their own related to schizophrenia (as described earlier); and the experience of living with a schizophrenic for a long time can have very distorting effects on all concerned. In recent years it has become fashionable in some circles to consider schizophrenia as the direct outcome of family disturbances for which the parents are to blame, almost as though they had been deliberately and maliciously harmful to their child. This is both untrue and unfair, and by introducing a note of hostility and condemnation of the parents serves only to increase the guilt and sense of failure which they naturally feel. If there are extreme tensions and unhappiness in the home of the schizophrenic it is better not to concentrate on who is to blame, but to make sure that the treatment the patient receives is as effective as possible, to try and lessen tension by discussion and by practical advice and often to help the patient to find somewhere else to live.

Rehabilitation

In those patients who were generally well integrated personally and socially, and who have made a good recovery from a brief illness, no rehabilitation may be needed. In very many cases however, the patient was poorly integrated before, and has had a long illness. He may need to learn to work steadily, to keep regular hours, to look after himself in terms of personal hygiene, money, clothing, and even diet; and he needs to be motivated to do all these things. Forces acting against him will include the apathy and loss of will power so characteristic of schizophrenia, unhappy experiences of failure, illness, and rejection in previous work and living situations, and the social isolation experienced by nearly all chronic schizophrenics.

Rehabilitation is usually centred around work, but many other factors need to be tackled. A regular programme of industrial type work, with regular pay and productivity agreements (all very small in hospital settings) is the mainstay of rehabilitation in most mental hospitals, which is obviously most suited to those who previously did similar jobs. It is much more difficult to devise rehabilitation programmes for other types of work, although clerical skills such as filing, shorthand and typing can be taught easily in hospitals. Many men can be interested in woodwork, which has a creative quality and domestic work and cooking is valuable for many, including men who are leaving hospital to live on their own. Some patients need practice in such matters as making telephone calls and how to deal with interviews for jobs. Occupational therapists can also provide help in general socialisation, for example by conducting quizzes, encouraging patients to take part in running a hospital magazine, and to take responsibility for some activity or for some other patient.

It can be very helpful to transfer the patient to a special rehabilitation ward after he has settled down in the admission ward, when his symptoms have responded to drug therapy and the change of environment. The emphasis then should switch to self help, as opposed to nursing care, to a regular day of work in occupational therapy, and to social rehabilitation. Social workers can help with family problems, work prospects and with accommodation, and psychologists can offer training in social skills and other personal help.

The atmosphere of the ward is extremely important. Nurses must be continually aware of the need to encourage self reliance, social interaction with other patients and the staff, regular hours and regular attendance at the occupational therapy department, and good personal hygiene in those who have deteriorated in that way. The more unnecessary restrictions, arbitrary authority, and lack of individual care and concern, the more likely are patients to slip into withdrawal and apathy. It must be clearly understood, however, that it is in the very nature of schizophrenia for such changes to occur, and the most perfect environment, although it can mitigate the tendencies, cannot prevent them.

Towards the end of the stay in hospital the problems of overriding importance are of work and accommodation. Many can go back to doing the job they were doing before, but most patients with schizophrenia find it difficult to function at their previous level, and need some help from social agencies such as the Disabled Resettlement Officer (DRO) who is based at the local labour exchange; and from various industrial training schemes run by government agencies. Some can be employed in sheltered workshops such as those run by Remploy. Obviously, the level of employment and the state of the national economy can make a huge difference to the prospects for a discharged patient.

Suitable accommodation is often a bigger problem than finding a suitable job. Many patients have no home at all if they have spent long in mental hospitals, or may have been rejected by their families. Others have homes which are too full of emotional tension to be comfortable or healthy, and the patient might do better in a hostel or other form of 'half-way house'. A great deal has been said about the necessity to provide suitable accommodation, and many promises have been made, but over the country as a whole little has been done. As more active treatment and rehabilitation methods have developed, and the staff of psychiatric hospitals have aimed at early discharge of the patient to 'community care', more and more patients with chronic schizophrenic illnesses have left hospital but found themselves no better off outside. Many fail to cope with the rigours of life and are repeatedly readmitted to hospital, only to be discharged again. Others end in prison because of petty offences; some live in common lodging houses or doss houses; and others live rough. As the policy of vigorous treatment and early discharge from hospital developed, it became apparent almost twenty years ago that many fewer mental hospital beds would be necessary, and plans to phase out many mental hospitals were made. Unfortunately it seems now that the long term needs were not correctly assessed, and many psychiatrists, and others involved in the care of the chronic schizophrenic, think that there will always be a sizeable minority who would be better off in hospital. If more hostels are not provided, there may be even a majority who would be happier and healthier in hospital, than fending incompetently for themselves in the community.

Subsidiary treatment

We have said that the three main pillars of treatment are antipsychotic drugs, environmental change and rehabilitation. In a good many patients other specific treatment is needed.

Depression and anxiety. These are often present, especially in the acute stages, although they may be overshadowed by the symptoms and signs of schizophrenia. As mentioned before, the control by drug therapy of delusional ideas or of hallucinations may uncover quite marked depression, which may benefit from antidepressant drugs or electrical treatment. When using antidepressants in schizophrenia, especially those of the MAOI group, it is important that adequate doses of a phenothiazine or other antipsychotic drug are given. Otherwise the schizophrenic symptoms may be made worse.

It is unwise to offer any formal psychotherapy for depression or anxiety in an acute schizophrenic, even if the depression seems related to conflicts and problems in an understandable way. Discussion of the problems and emotional support are always indicated, and sometimes practical or social help is needed. Explanatory or insight-directed psychotherapy, particularly of psychoanalytic type, unfortunately tends to make schizophrenic patients worse, as they often cannot deal with the emotional problems and conflicts brought to the surface in the course of psychotherapy, and become more disturbed in consequence. In North America psychotherapy is often used in acute schizophrenia, but nearly always in conjunction with phenothiazines. There is, however, no evidence that those who get the psychotherapy do better than those who get drug treatment without psychotherapy.

Electrical treatment is not only helpful in the treatment of depressive symptoms, but it is dramatically and rapidly successful in catatonic stupor; in the states of acute perplexity and bewilderment which some patients develop; and in states of turmoil and tension which in some patients renders them almost inaccessible. Although electrical treatment is often helpful symptomatically, and can make the patient feel much better, it seems to have no effect on the long term results of treatment, in terms of remission and relapse rates.

Psychosurgery. This was extensively used, in the form of pre-frontal leucotomy, before the phenothiazines were introduced. It has some place in the treatment of severe and intractable tension where all other methods have failed to produce relief, but that is rare.

Insulin coma therapy (deep insulin treatment). This is no longer used, but a brief account is given in the chapter on treatment (Chapter 15). It remains of historical interest because it was the first treatment to produce good results in schizophrenia, and it sparked off new hope and interest in therapeutic possibilities.

Helpful organisations. Both patients and their families, and other interested people might find helpful some of the leaflets and information put out by the National Association for Mental Health, 39 Queen Anne Street, London, W.1. and by the National Schizophrenia Fellowship, 29 Victoria Road, Surbiton, Surrey KT6 4JT.

9

Affective disorders

INTRODUCTION AND CLASSIFICATION

The affective disorders are the commonest of all seen by psychiatrists, the term including those abnormal states in which disturbances of mood and emotion are the prime features. (The Latin word 'affectus' means emotion or mood.) They include various types of depression and the manic-depressive illnesses, and range in severity from mild and transient reactions to severe psychoses.

Later in this chapter the clinical pictures of *endogenous* and *reactive* patterns of depression are described in their classical forms, but in fact there are major disagreements among psychiatrists about this classification. Many regard the two forms as qualitatively distinct conditions, which at times overlap to produce mixed clinical pictures (often called the bimodal hypothesis); yet others see them as shading one into the other, as part of a continuum of depressive disorders with mixtures of endogenous and reactive features in most patients, and with the classical forms representing the extremes of the continuum (the unimodal hypothesis, as illustrated). The writers favour the latter. It is not necessary to take sides in the argument, but it is worth stressing that the more the clinical picture resembles the classical endogenous pattern, the more likely is physical treatment with antidepressants or electrical treatment to be helpful.

Bipolar manic-depressive illnesses do clearly form a group on their own, and have a fairly clear cut tendency to breed true. Nevertheless they overlap with the others, in that the clinical picture in the depressed phase of a manic depressive illness is identical with that of classical endogenous depression. In fact, until fairly recently, the terms 'manic-depressive' and 'endogenous' were often used interchangeably to describe a depressive illness, and only modern genetic studies have separated the two, so that it is now useful to use the term 'bipolar' manic-depressive in order to make the distinction clear, and indicate that mood swings up and down have both occurred.

Another important introductory point is that in deciding which pattern of depression a patient shows, in order to determine treatment, it is the pattern of symptoms which is important. It does not matter very much whether or not the depression has been precipitated by emotional trauma or not, as many depressions of endogenous pattern, and also many bipolar manic depressive illnesses, are triggered off by emotional factors, despite the fact that the word 'endogenous' means 'arising from within'.

In this book we do not use the terms 'psychotic' and 'neurotic' depression, but a brief note might be useful, as the terms are widely used, more or less as the equivalents of 'endogenous' and 'reactive' respectively. 'Psychotic' depression means that the patient has such a severe illness that he has lost contact with reality, and developed delusions or hallucinations; or, and rather confusingly, that he has the type of depression in which those psychotic symptoms might develop if the illness became more severe. 'Psychotic' depression does correspond with 'endogenous' depression. 'Neurotic' depression implies that the symptoms are neurotic in quality, that the patients are neurotic in personality, and that their depressive state is a neurotic syndrome, which is naturally classified with the other neuroses. In fact reactive depression is classed as a neurosis by those who regard it as qualitatively distinct from others.

The term 'neurotic' depression is unsatisfactory, in our view, because there are patients who develop depression as an understandable reaction to very severe emotional stress, who are not at all neurotic in personality. The term 'reactive' includes these people comfortably.

It is clear that the classification is less than perfect, but this is inherent in the subject. The purpose of classification is to aid in treatment and prognosis, and until some other criteria, perhaps biochemical or neurophysiological, are discovered, this one seems as efficient as any other. It has the benefit that it does not require each patient to be put into a single category of endogenous or reactive depression. It also includes without difficult those patients in whom the clinical picture changes with time.

The classification of the affective disorders offered here is therefore: (a) bipolar manic-depressive illnesses, in which the patient has sustained periods of both depression and excitement at different times and (b) depressive illnesses, the range of which can be illustrated as in Figure 9.1, although no truly mathematical relationships should be read into the diagram.

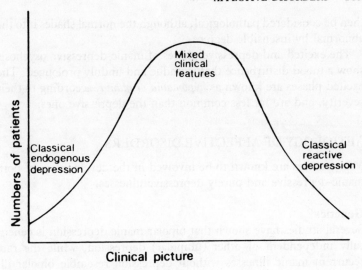

Fig. 9.1 The range of depressive disorders

When a patient is said to suffer from swings of mood, people sometimes say 'Don't we all?' Of course we do, and they may be normal, but they may also be pathological. Thus, *elation*, which is the opposite of depression, may follow some successful achievement; it is transient, natural, and normal enough; unless it is associated with other psychiatric symptoms there is nothing pathological about it. So seldom, if ever, does it call for medical care that elation, unlike depression and excitement, may be said never to constitute an affective disorder on its own.

Excitement also may transiently follow some sequence of events that has caused a person to become 'strung up'. It may be observed, for example, after motor accidents or committee meetings that have caused frustration or annoyance. If it is transient, it is normal enough. But if excitement occurs as a main feature in a person's behaviour, in the absence of outside cause, and is sustained over a considerable period of time, it may be considered pathological. This occurs in manic-depressive psychosis.

Depression likewise may follow such reverses as failure in examinations or in securing a coveted job, of which it may be regarded as a normal and natural consequence, and is usually transient. More severe and less brief episodes may follow bereavements, major financial reverses or being jilted. These may not be abnormal in view of the precipitating causes. But, as with excitement, depression can occur as a main feature in a person's behaviour and be in duration and severity out of proportion to any apparent outside cause. It may then be considered pathological, although the normal shades into the abnormal by insensible degrees.

The excited and depressive phases of manic-depressive psychosis show a mood disturbance that is undue and unduly prolonged. The excited phases are known as *hypomania or mania*, according to their severity, and are far less common than the depressive ones.

AETIOLOGY OF AFFECTIVE DISORDERS

Many factors are known to be involved in the development of both manic-depressive and purely depressive illnesses.

Genetics
Several studies have shown that bipolar manic depression is genetically independent of other (unipolar) depression, while the rare recurrent manic illnesses without depression resemble bipolar illnesses genetically. In other studies no clear cut genetic differences emerge between depression of endogenous, involutional, and reactive patterns, which is one of the reasons why they are not considered as qualitatively different in this book. It can be taken that the genes involved are not recessive, as in that case affected siblings would be more common than affected parents or children, whereas the risk is, in fact, much the same in all first degree relatives; nor are the genes sex linked. It seems that the method of transmission is polygenic and complex, and that what is inherited is an increased tendency to develop depression, which may never show unless the right environmental factors are present at the right time. In some people, as with schizophrenia, the genetic loading seems so pronounced that they become repeatedly depressed without much environmental stress. Recently it has been claimed that a good deal of alcoholism is genetically related to depression, and one certainly sees many alcoholics who drink, or who begin drinking, to relieve depressive feelings. Genetic factors also show in the response to treatment, as relatives tend to respond well to the same drugs.

Personality and constitution
Remarkably little is known about the personalities of those most likely to develop depression, perhaps because people of nearly all types of personality can be affected.

Bipolar manic depression is distinctly more common in those of *cyclothymic* personality, that is to say people in whom there are sustained mood swings above and below average, not amounting to illness. Relatives of manic depressives also often show this personality characteristic. Many of these people seem to be set at a higher level of drive and activity than are ordinary mortals, may be extremely productive and successful people, sociable and extroverted, and 'the very last person you would expect to be depressed', as is so often said.

There are several common personality traits in those prone to recurrent depression. A good many are anxious, emotionally labile, chronically pessimistic people, easily upset and worried. Others are outwardly calm for most of their lives, but always troubled by feelings of inadequacy and inferiority. Yet others are chronically melancholic and brooding, never seeming happy in any circumstances; and there is a large group with very varied neurotic problems and conflicts. There are no personality traits which distinguish reliably between those who do and those who do not develop affective illnesses.

Physical make-up shows some correlation with affective disorders, in that bipolar manic depressives, and those of cyclothymic personality, are rather more likely to have a pyknic (endomorphic) body build (see p. 29).

The effect on personality of early life experiences has been the particular study of psychoanalysts (p. 368) and naturally there have been many attempts to relate character development and later depressive illness to infantile experiences. There is no single and generally accepted psychoanalytic theory of depression at present, but there is a general consensus that the child gains secure self esteem by developing good relationships with the parents or their substitutes; and that in later life depression, with loss of self esteem, is associated with disturbances in this area. This view is quite compatible with what we observe in many patients, but by no means all.

There is also evidence that the death of a parent in childhood, especially in early puberty, predisposes to depression, and that this is more marked when the parent of opposite sex is the one to die. It is as if the child is sensitised to grief and mourning at this stage, feelings which are rekindled in later life, especially by 'loss' as described later.

Emotional precipitants of affective disorders

As mentioned earlier, the bipolar manic depressive illnesses are the most likely to develop without any obvious precipitant, but in many of them some factors can be discerned. A prolonged period of angry frustration in which the patient feels he is making great effort but getting nowhere, is quite a common background to a manic upswing. Both upward and downward swings can be precipitated by events which would in most people cause anxiety or sorrow. A good example was that of the doctor who unexpectedly received a haematological report on his son which indicated leukaemia, and within a few hours was hypomanic.

In all other depressives, there are many types of situations which can call forth depression. Perhaps the commonest is the 'last straw' sequence, in which there has been a long period of cumulative stress, including perhaps money worries, marital disharmony, problems at work or with the children, and during which the patient has felt progressively more troubled and strained, until there is some further episode or problem, not intrinsically very important, and the patient becomes truly depressed. Other depressive illnesses, however, follow some single major blow, of which the commonest is some important loss—or threatened loss. The loss of a spouse is perhaps the commonest single major event of this type, but of course much depends on the importance to the individual of such situations. The death of a child or parent; the loss of a child through marriage or emigration; loss of work, of prestige, of self respect, of health, of a limb, or even of a much loved home or pet; all these at times can precipitate depression.

When the death of some loved or important person precipitates depression there are often complicating individual factors. Particularly when a parent has died for whom there have been marked hostile feelings, the death may produce troublesome feelings of guilt, centred around the anger and agression which the survivor may have felt for the deceased. Depression also seems more common, after bereavement, in those who have felt unable to mourn in a natural way, either because of personal inhibition or because of some special social situation at the time.

In recent years the importance of both loss and of 'last straw' sequences has been demonstrated statistically by the use of 'life-events schedules', in which a systematic enquiry is made about all kinds of events which disturb the pattern of life. These range from the apparently trivial to the obviously important, cover both joyful and distressing events, and include such things as change of job, marriage of a sibling, move of house, death of a relative, and many more. Patients with depression show more life events, as defined in these schedules, particularly of the type in which some important person leaves the circle of the patient, by death or in some other way. Life events schedules of this type also show similar patterns in schizophrenic relapses, and in some physical illnesses. All these precipitating events have a rather extraordinary tendency to be followed by illness in about three weeks, as though in some way a chain of events is triggered off in the individual which takes three weeks to come to fruition.

Physical factors in the development of depression

Quite severe depressive illnesses can be triggered off by physical illness, influenza being the most frequently responsible. Glandular fever (infectious mononucleosis) is also quite often followed by depression, much more commonly in females. Quite minor head injuries, which lead to no significant organic cerebral damage, are another well known trigger.

Prolonged states of depression occur in any illness in which there is organic cerebral impairment, as after strokes, serious head injuries, cerebral tumours, and the dementias due to degenerative changes. In all these conditions the patient is usually very aware of his impairment, as described in Chapter 6, and depression is a very natural seeming reaction. It is very important not to view the depression as inevitable and untreatable because the circumstances are so grim for the sufferer. Relief from the worst of the depression, even if not cure, can often be achieved by treatment.

The rôle of the menopause in depressive illnesses is well known but obscure. There is no doubt that for a period of several years around the menopause, women are more likely to become depressed, and the symptoms often include 'hot flushes' and sudden drenching sweats which are known to be due to oestrogen deficiencies. Some people regard all menopausal mood disturbances as due to hormonal imbalance, and suggest that oestrogens are needed rather than antidepressants. Of the patients whose depression is severe enough to lead to psychiatric referral this is certainly not true, and the use of oestrogens, including the non-synthetic ones, often has little effect on the depression, even if it relieves the flushes and sweats.

Hormonal factors are of course not the only important ones in the menopause. Even though a woman may be glad to be relieved of the nuisance of menstruation, the menopause means the end of an era. Options which were previously open are now closed; she may well feel inherently less attractive sexually because the biological purpose of sex has gone; and her husband may react to her differently for the same reason, even if he is not fully conscious of it. At more or less the same time her children are becoming grown up, and she is that much less needed, while probably having fewer interests outside the family than her husband. He is at his prime, probably, as far his work is concerned, unless his job is strictly manual; and in the professional and managerial occupations work is often increasingly demanding at this time.

The menopause is therefore a period of great change, personally and socially, and in the depression which is so common at this time these factors often play a part. Similar problems of personal and social readjustment are at their greatest for men when they retire from work, at which time they become more prone to depression. By then their wives have made the necessary adjustments, but the retiring man is twenty years older and that much less flexible, and does not even have the organization of the home to fall back on as a useful daily task. The loss of prestige, interest, occupation, and companionship which follows retirement, are often more serious blows than the loss of income.

The puerperium is another time of major upheaval in both hormonal and psychological terms, during which depression is more common than at other times. To some people any depression occurring within twelve months of childbirth is 'puerperal', but this seems too extended a period to us, and three months seems to be more suitable. In the typical puerperal depression the mother is well for a period of about three to seven days after the birth, and the depression comes on very suddenly and at times with great severity; so that unexpected suicide is sometimes the first manifestation. Very many women go through a period of 'the blues' after childbirth; in most it does not need specific treatment, but it may develop into a true depressive illness.

In addition to the major hormonal changes and other physical changes as the body reverts to its non-pregnant state, the physical fatigue often caused by the care of a new baby, such factors as blood loss and infection (much less common now in the Western world), there may be very important psychological difficulties. Not every baby is whole-heartedly wanted, and there is quite often underlying hostility and jealousy, about which the mother feels deeply guilty. The reaction of the husband and of the other children, and the effect of the baby on the whole pattern of life, may well be difficult to cope with. There is definitely more puerperal depression in women with neurotic personality problems, and with illegitimate births.

Although these personal and social factors as just outlined can be very important, there are many puerperal depressions in which hormonal changes, or perhaps some biochemical changes at present not appreciated, seem to be of overriding importance, which alter the mother's state of mind in some profound way. The term 'puerperal psychosis' is often used to cover both depressive and schizophrenic illnesses in the puerperium, as there is an increase in the latter at this time as well. In less developed countries, as in Britain a few decades ago, toxic confusional states are common in the puerperium, largely because of infection and blood loss. In a fair number of puerperal mental illnesses it is difficult to make a diagnosis, as affective and schizophrenic features may be very mixed.

Biochemistry and depression
The very 'physiological' or 'biological' disturbances of the endogenous depressive pattern, the hereditary background of much depression, the part played by endocrine and other physical factors in causation, and the response of patients to physical treatment, had long suggested that some biochemical disturbances underlay depression. This attitude was strengthened by the introduction of antidepressants and of lithium in treatment, and an enormous amount of research has been done in this field, which we will not attempt to review in this book, where we comment on only what seems to be of most importance.

The amine hypothesis. This hypothesis states that certain monoamines (e.g. serotonin, nor-adrenaline) have an important rôle as cerebral transmitters in those brain structures which are important in the control of mood. (The structures concerned are thought to be mainly if not entirely in the limbic lobe and especially in the hypothalamus.) When the concentration of these monoamines at important sites falls, depression results; and when the concentration increases the depression is relieved. Alternatively, decreased sensitivity of the post-synaptic receptors may be present. Similarly, manic disturbances are thought to be associated with increased concentrations of monoamines. It is known that reserpine, for example, decreases cell concentrations of serotonin, and also causes depression. The two main groups of antidepressants, monoamine oxidase inhibitors and tricyclic drugs, increase the concentration of monoamines. It is thought that the former do this by inhibiting the breakdown of the monoamines centrally; the latter by inhibiting uptake peripherally. Whether or not this hypothesis will attain the dignity of accepted theory is uncertain, but it has been the centre of much very useful and interesting research.

Electrolytes. Alterations in electrolyte metabolism occur in severe depression, with an increase in intracellular sodium possibly related to changes in cell membranes. The finding that lithium is useful in the treatment and prevention of affective illnesses is presumably related to the fact that lithium is chemically related to both sodium and potassium, and consequently may interfere with their functions.

Very rarely depression is caused by abnormalities of calcium metabolism, as in hyperparathyroidism.

Hormones. Changes in steroid hormones are known to be related to affective illnesses, although the relationships are uncertain. Examples are in the development of depression in Cushing's syndrome, the very striking mood changes of the premenstrual period and the effect on mood of oral contraceptives, which in some people lead to depression and in others relieve it (depending not only on the person but on the constituents of the contraceptive). Cortisol production is increased in patients with agitated depression but not in those who are retarded and apathetic, and the increase is probably due to the overactivity and arousal rather than the depression.

Deficiencies of thyroid hormone can lead to depression, and overt myxoedema is often preceded and accompanied by depressive mood, sometimes to the extent of a true depressive illness, and hypothyroidism should be considered in patients who fail to respond to treatment. Hypothyroidism also causes intellectual impairment, which can be permanent if treatment is begun too late.

Vitamin deficiencies. Lack of vitamin B_{12} can lead to prolonged depressive states which respond poorly to treatment, and also causes intellectual impairment amounting to dementia at times. It is important to realise that these mental changes can long precede any anaemia or neurological signs. Similar states occasionally occur with folic acid deficiency. Estimation of the blood level of these two vitamins is a standard part of the investigation of presenile dementia, and is worth considering in depression when the patient fails to respond to treatment.

DEPRESSION

We have already said, at the beginning of this chapter, that we preferred to view the range of depressive disorders as a continuum, with the endogenous and reactive patterns at the ends of the spectrum, and many mixed pictures in between. We now give descriptions of those two classical patterns, and the reader must understand that they are given as illustrations, and not from inconsistency of purpose.

Symptoms and signs of the endogenous pattern

The essential symptoms are so simple that they may be easily overlooked; indeed, failure to diagnose depression used to be the commonest psychiatric mistake. Nowadays, for various possible reasons, such as the introduction of the anti-depressants with its attendant publicity, the feeling that it is more 'respectable' for a patient to have a true depressive illness rather than a complicated neurotic personality problem, coupled with the fact that the former is easier to treat than the latter, depression is more often diagnosed, and perhaps over diagnosed. Another interesting change is that less severe forms of the illness are now seen, with less florid symptoms, presumably because of more efficient and earlier treatment. The symptoms and signs can be considered for convenience under two headings (1) physical and (2) mental.

The *biological symptoms* are, firstly, a persistent lowering of energy with consequently lowered drive and increased fatiguability. There is thus a reduction of activity. This is almost always accompanied by loss of sexual appetite, and by a characteristic sleep disturbance which consists in frequent and early waking. The patients can often get to sleep well enough, but this is interrupted after an hour or two, and they finally wake at three, four or five in the morning, after which they cannot get to sleep again, though some may doze fitfully and restlessly. Usually, but less invariably, there is constipation, loss of weight, and loss of appetite not only for food but for life in general. Amenorrhoea is not uncommon.

The *mental symptoms* run parallel. The reduction of activity is accompanied in the mental sphere by a feeling of being unable to cope as well as usual, coupled with a disinclination to do as much as usual. These almost necessarily involve a loss of interest, concentration, confidence and decisiveness, and lead to procrastination. The patient feels less than what he was, may feel inferior on that account, may thus become withdrawn, and anxious to avoid the company of others, except for those whom he knows well and from whose presence he may draw comfort and support. With the loss of interest the patient can neither experience enjoyment in the usual way nor 'get away from himself', and so remains to a greater or lesser extent self-absorbed and preoccupied with his own symptoms. He then tends to think repetitively 'Why am I like this?' 'What has happened to me?' 'How am I going to get out of it?' 'Why has this happened *to me?*' In fact, the picture resembles that of general debility with the keynotes of generally reduced vitality and animation, with worry. As an indication of this reduced vitality, it may be mentioned that, according to Kraepelin, there is a reduction of the rate of growth of the hair and finger-nails. Many patients feel just generally 'ill', and do not emphasise the lowering of their spirits and mood particularly, until asked about them.

The condition is persistent and steady, showing little variation from one day to another, though most patients feel worse when unoccupied, and show a spontaneous rhythm, independent of outside events, of feeling lowest in the morning and a little less low towards evening—in a fashion somewhat reminiscent of the normal temperature chart. This so-called 'diurnal' or morning-evening variation is not invariably present though it is usual; very occasionally it is reversed. It will be noted that the picture is one of depression in a general sense, like a 'depressed area', the depression is not confined nor specifically related to the mood, but affects the interest, activity and total function of the patient, the so called 'vital depression'.

The diagnosis is reached by (1) exclusion of recognisable organic disease which might account for the loss of vitality, (2) careful comparison of the patient's state when he is seen, with his state when he is well. For a proper evaluation of this, of course, it is desirable (and may be essential) to interview the relatives or friends. It will then be found that, though the patient may show some degree of response to congenial company and other pleasant diversions, this is temporary and incomplete, and that in general he never reaches his normal level of animation or enjoyment. This comparison between the patient's state when well and when ill is often rendered easier by the fact that many of these patients are of good personality. The change from a normal state characterised by energy, interest, extraversion, enjoyment, confidence, decisiveness and gregariousness, to one characterised by relative anergia, disinterest, self-absorption, joylessness, with lack of confidence, indecisiveness and withdrawal from company, may then be very striking, *provided that the comparison is sought*. The keynote is *reduction*, as opposed to the expansiveness of the contrasting manic or hypomanic phase.

The more severe cases are easier to diagnose. The reduction in activity may become very marked, leading to that generalised slowness called *retardation*, of which the indecisiveness already referred to is the first subjective experience. The indecisiveness may amount to gross vacillation, and may cause the depressed patient to raise hydra-headed objections to any course of action that may be suggested. The indecisiveness coupled with the retardation may result in *perplexity*. Depression of mood may now be the presenting symptom, and the patient may show a diffuse pessimism with hopelessness of recovery and suicidal preoccupation. By this stage the loss of interest may have increased so that the patient cannot experience normal emotion, is untouched by events of emotional significance (except perhaps by those that are sad and distressing), is unable to respond to a joke though intellectually he sees the point, cannot feel normal affection for others, gets no joy where he got it before, whether from music, from sights or from good company. In fact, there is an *affective loss*, which may be described in striking ways. 'I feel that I'm different from other people, and I usedn't to feel it, that they've got something that I haven't; I'm different from what I used to be, and I've lost something that I once had.' Another said, 'My heart feels as if it had been eclipsed'. A depressed Chinese scientist remarked, 'I have lost the function of my centre of happiness and my fighting spirit'. Another said, 'I feel that I have died inwardly'.

Self-absorption may become extreme, and the productivity of these patients, even in simple speech or letter-writing, may be negligible or non-existent, for they have little initiative or spontaneity. But this does not mean that their minds are empty. On the contrary, their thoughts tend to chase each other round, 'like', as one patient said, 'a squirrel in a cage'. The thinking continues, but in a restricted way and to no end, as though the mind were continually revolving in neutral without ever getting into gear.

Even the mildly depressed patient may be self-depreciatory; the markedly depressed patient almost always is. The self-absorption then encourages a brooding self-criticism with self-blame and preoccupation with past failures, real or imaginary, leading to the familiar 'If only I had acted differently', and 'If only I hadn't done that'. The remarks are given a self-reproachful twist; 'My heart feels as if it had been eclipsed' becomes 'I feel hard-hearted', and 'If only I had acted differently' becomes 'If only I'd had more will-power'. The patient supposes others to share his depreciatory feelings about himself, and may then feel unwanted and shunned. In this setting *ideas of reference* easily develop and lead to feelings of being critically spoken of, and of being able to discern disapproval or contempt in the innocent actions of others.

These feelings of self-reproach may be exaggerated into actual *delusions* of guilt or unworthiness, as the patients look into their past and find there causes for regret and self-blame. The line of thought generally follows the popular idea of moral and medical causation, so that the illness becomes attributed to masturbation by older patients, or to lack of consideration or failure to show affection or some other sin, real or imaginary. Whenever feelings of guilt are experienced in the absence of powerful justification, depression should be suspected. Delusions of punishment, present or impending, are a not unnatural consequence of the guilt-feelings. Other common ones, always in line with the melancholic mood, are those of impoverishment or ruin. Patients may thus refuse to eat, not only from anorexia, but because they feel they are unworthy or that they cannot afford the food. In many other patients there is increasing preoccupation with bodily health, with fear of cancer, and not infrequently delusional beliefs about this and other illnesses. These hypochrondriacal delusions are most common in the elderly, but can occur at any age.

Hallucinations do not often occur in depressive states in Europeans, but are commoner in less sophisticated immigrants from less developed cultures. When they do occur in Europeans it is mainly in older people with the syndrome of involutional melancholia described later, and they are almost always of voices talking to the patient, saying critical or hopeless things, or advising suicide. Their occurrence in other depressives should suggest a toxic cause, or a schizophrenic element.

These states will be coloured by the previous personality. Touchy and over-sensitive patients will show paranoid trends, believing others to be against them in a way they may feel wholly or only partly justifiable, but such paranoid ideas will be consistent with the mood, and comprehensible in the light of it. Easily agitable patients will become agitated and importunate, and this may mask the real reduction of physical and mental activity. Obsessional personalities are likely to show exaggeration of their obsessional traits. These extraneous developments make it the more necessary to attend to the basic symptoms of the depressive state itself, if an accurate diagnosis is to be made.

As regards *signs*, these are few but variable. The patient can usually be observed to be less active and more easily fatigued than is normal. Retardation both of thought and movement (psychomotor retardation) may be obvious in the more severe case. Rarely, it may be great enough to lead to stupor, though in young people this should raise suspicion of schizophrenic admixture. The severely depressed patient will look sad, with what has been described as a 'frozen mask of misery'. Agitation may be obvious, with wringing of the hands. Sighing is frequent. The complexion is usually sallow, the pores of the skin may be more prominent, and the hair may lose its lustre. The patient may appear to have aged and loss of weight may be evident. There are no other physical signs except that the blood pressure is often raised above normal in those who are agitated and tense. In the milder or even moderately depressed case, the patient may be able to retain an appearance which can be most misleading.

Some patients start to drink heavily or to use other drugs, in order to relieve their distress, so that they present a very misleading picture. It is essential to recognise and treat the underlying depression in such cases, and not just concentrate on the drink or drug problem.

Finally, this whole state is steady and persistent, varying little from one day to another except in the stages of recovery, and little from one time of day to another except for the morning-evening variation. This syndrome is experienced in attacks, with periods of normality between, so that there may be a history of a previous attack often with a family history of the same thing. The clinical picture will vary with the severity of the attack, with the personality of the patient, and with the addition of anxiety, hysterical or involutional features. The milder attacks will show no distortions of content. But, underlying them all, the basic syndrome as described is virtually constant, and will be found so on enquiry.

The clinical picture of depression just described is that of the fully developed *endogenous pattern*. The most important features of it can be summed up as follows: a general and pervasive depressive mood and lowering of spirits (rather than being depressed 'about something'); disturbances of a biological type including sleep, appetite, weight, bowel function and diurnal variation; psychomotor retardation or agitation; and self reproachful ideas, at times amounting to delusions. Psychomotor retardation and agitation, and severe self reproach are relatively infrequent, but the others are all very common. The more of these features are present, the more likely is the patient to respond to treatment with antidepressants or electrical treatment, and in fact if depressive delusions are present it is best to use electrical treatment immediately. Patients with this type of depression will not benefit from psychotherapy, but need effective physical treatment soon, not only to relieve their distress, but because of the risk of suicide. Most serious of all are those rare cases with such intense self reproach that the patient feels that he has ruined the lives of his whole family, and that they too would be better off dead. Such feelings lead occasionally to the murder of the children and attempted suicide.

A subtype of depression, considered by many to be almost a separate illness because of its clear cut clinical features, is *Involutional Melancholia*. This term indicates a severe depression coming on for the first time in later life, in which marked agitation and the development of delusions and of a bizarre hypochondriasis are prominent. It affects principally, but not solely, people of rather rigid, narrow and obsessional character.

Psychologically the illness usually develops against a background of disappointed late middle age. The patient has realised his assets, no new and interesting possibilities open up before him, life has set into a hard mould, and the hopes of earlier life are unfulfilled. At a time of some serious personal strife or loss the patient views the past with remorse and the future with dismay. The immediate precipitant is often a death, perhaps that of a parent, or the threat of ill health, or the emptiness and loss of self-respect that follows retirement for many people.

The onset is often gradual, and the earliest symptoms are of some physical complaint—most often of constipation—without apparent depression. Gradually depression develops, with the full range of endogenous depressive symptoms described earlier; and hypochondriasis and increasingly severe agitation become more and more prominent. The most characteristic picture then is of a deeply depressed man or woman, pacing or shuffling restlessly up and down, wringing the hands, and complaining of blockage of the bowels, of brains decaying, of cancer spreading through the body, or some other similar complaint. Delusions of poverty or of the imminent collapse of the family home, or of the family business, and similar concerns, are also common. Delusions of guilt, and even nihilistic delusions such as of being already dead may be present; and auditory and occasionally other hallucinations occur.

This florid type of depressive psychosis is much less often seen now, but before electrical treatment was introduced such illnesses often lasted many years, ending in death from self neglect or suicide; or in misery unrelieved by sedatives. The success of electrical treatment in these illnesses, which had previously been totally resistant to therapy, explains the impact on psychiatry which electrical treatment made after its introduction in the 1930s.

A strange and largely unexplained manifestation of depression in middle-aged women is *shoplifting*. It is not that most middle-aged shoplifters are depressed, but that a certain number are. They often steal goods for which they have no conceivable use, and may do it very obviously, as though hoping to be caught. In some cases it is clear that there are marked guilt feelings, and that they hope to be punished, but in others this is not obvious. Most magistrates are aware of this syndrome, and it is not uncommon for them to make the patient seek psychiatric help as part of the sentence—usually in the form of a probation order.

The reactive pattern of depression
At the other end of the depressive spectrum lies the pure *reactive depression*. Anyone may of course react to adversity with depressive mood, and everyone has a breaking point somewhere, but some people are much more vulnerable than others, and develop depres-

sion rapidly and repeatedly in reaction to life stresses which others might shrug off, or to which they might react in some other way. The most transient of these, lasting only hours or days, and in response to minor life stresses are not considered in this chapter, and are characteristic of those with vulnerable and inadequate personalities as described elsewhere (p. 223).

It is a mistake to think of depressive illnesses of endogenous pattern as being somehow more genuine and severe, and of reactive depressions as necessary milder; or to view reactive depression as always indicating a vulnerable or feeble personality. Some purely reactive depressive states are very severe, cause great suffering, and lead to suicide; they may follow such prolonged and severe emotional stress that on hearing the patient's account one recognises that almost anyone would have been similarly affected. In many depressions of any length and severity, as has already been stressed, symptoms of the endogenous pattern slowly develop, and the clinical picture shifts towards the middle of the spectrum, but the pure reactive picture is described here.

Reactive depressions are common in adolescence, when the marked temperamental variations that so readily occur in children first begin to assume a greater length, especially among those who are prone to be passionate or love-lorn. In adolescents, however, such reactions do not usually last long, though their duration tends to increase with age.

The psychological factors are any that may be traumatic to the personality of the particular patient. Often they are sudden, such as an unexpected failure with serious consequences, an unexpected bereavement, or any other loss that cannot be compensated for. Being jilted, or reaching an impasse in a love affair that cannot have a successful ending, are not uncommon causes. Perhaps commonest of all are those difficulties in relationships with other people which arise from neurotic personality problems. Marital conflicts, sexual problems, unresolved problems with parents or children, recurring clashes and temperamental difficulties with friends or colleagues, are all commonly found in the background.

Sometimes the psychological factors may be prolonged and of cumulative effect, as, for example, in people who lead unstimulating lives in uncongenial climates, cut off from home associations and from the sort of company that they would ordinarily choose. Such people may conscientiously struggle on though increasingly bogged in a slough of despond from which, in the end, they have not enough spirit to raise themselves. Those who are obliged to toil at exacting work for which they do not care, under exacting superiors who offer no hope of promotion, and have to devote meagre earnings to the support of ungrateful relatives for whom they feel responsible, may likewise slide into a depressive state in reaction to their circumstances.

On the other hand, the development of depression may depend more on the individual qualities of the patient; an unintelligent housewife with few resources of her own and small capacity for satisfactory relationships may become worn down into depression through her anxieties over bringing up what for her become too many children, and through her inability to do things to her own or her husband's satisfaction through muddle-headedness which, through imprudent expenditure, prevents her from ever having anything to spare for such amusements as might otherwise be beguiling.

Physical factors may also contribute, not only in such dramatic form as mutilating accidents, but through the lowering effects of chronic pain or weakness, the restrictive effect of conditions such as arthritis, especially when combined with failing mental powers into the development of which the patient has insight.

In general, the psychological stress may have been severe; if it has not been, the patient will have a marked constitutional liability to depressive reactions, or one that has been exacerbated by physical causes. Where the stress has been prolonged and cumulative, the patient will often be found to have a good personality, without which he would have given up the struggle before the depression had become established.

Symptoms and signs of the reactive pattern

The main symptom of the reactive depressive pattern is of depressive mood, recognised and described as such by the patient, and usually attributed to something in a straightforward way. Irritability, anxiety and tiredness are often present as well, but the loss of drive and of various mental functions, so characteristic of the endogenous pattern, are not prominent.

The degree of depression may be severe, with suicidal thoughts and even suicidal attempts. The patient will be pre-occupied with his state, and more so with the precipitating factors that have led to it. He will relate the two to each other, and in a way that carries conviction to the examiner. He will repeatedly mill over his affairs in his mind, and the more so if his circumstances are such as to call for some decision, over reaching which he may have some conflict leading to further anxiety. It is likely, however, that he will see the correct decision, quite clearly, though he may have difficulty in implementing it. His pre-occupations will interfere with his concentration to some extent, and may impair his work. But it is usually possible to distract the patient from his preoccupations, even if not for very long periods of time, and it will then be found that his mood improves and that he is responsive to other stimuli: that he is bogged down in his depression only to the extent to which he is pre-occupied with it, and it lightens with the provision of other distractions.

Physically, although there may be complaints of tiredness, this may not be much apparent; there may be some reduction of appetite; sleep is usually disturbed and the difficulty is usually in getting off; sexual activity tends not to be much interfered with, unless there is real tiredness or unless the precipitating factors are closely involved with the sex life. As regards signs, there may be none, beyond an appearance of gloom and some loss of weight, and those of anxiety where it is additionally present.

Elaborations of the basic condition may occur, either in the form of neurotic concern over the physical state, or of hysterical developments designed to exact sympathy and attention or to enforce some revision of the circumstances that have led to the depression.

Other presentations of depression

(a) *Physical symptoms*. Many patients present with physical symptoms of various kinds, especially pain. These may be headache, pain in the chest, in the back, abdomen, or elsewhere. Others may have prominent somatic anxiety symptoms, with palpitations, dyspnoea and so on, as described in the section on Anxiety states (p. 246). Anxiety is a prominent feature of many depressive illnesses, and in some people somatic symptoms are so marked that they swamp the depressive symptoms themselves. Fears of cancer or of heart disease are very common, and these fears may reach delusional intensity. Constipation with cancerphobia is one of the most frequent of these presentations; and a fear of throat cancer, occurring mainly when anxiety has led to swallowing difficulties, is another. Many of these patients have extensive and repeated investigations before the depression is recognised.

It is a good practice for every doctor to ask all patients about their mood and spirits, unless the diagnosis is quite straightforward. The questions 'How are your spirits?' or 'How do you feel in yourself—in your mood?' do not take long to ask, and could save much suffering.

On the whole this 'somatisation' of depression is commoner in older people, in the less sophisticated and less verbal, and especially in those from underdeveloped countries and cultures. Where a sophisticated Londoner will complain of 'depression', and relate his malaise to difficulties in his marriage or at work (not always correctly), an Indian immigrant is more likely to complain of pain, weakness, premature ejaculation, or some other bodily symptom.

In most of these patients there will be some of the biological disturbances that are typical of depression, especially anorexia and weight loss, sleep disturbance, and diurnal variation in mood. It can be difficult to persuade the patient to view his illness as a manifestation of depression, and many are angry at the idea. It is often best just to use antidepressants, as described later, for a trial period, explaining your reasoning but not trying too hard to persuade the patient to share your views.

(b) *Anxiety states.* We have just described how one or more of the somatic symptoms of anxiety can be so prominent that they come to form the presenting symptom, and may then mask the underlying depression. The same is true of mental symptoms of subjective anxiety and tension, accompanied by the usual somatic symptoms, which can be very marked, and lead to a depressive illness being misdiagnosed as an anxiety state. This is a common and rather serious error, because only too often the doctor responds to an anxiety state by the automatic prescription of a benzodiazepine, or of a small dose of a neuroleptic such as haloperidol. Drugs of this kind do relieve anxiety, but often make depression worse.

It is a sound rule not to diagnose an anxiety state, in a previously non-anxious middle-aged person especially, until you have excluded both a depressive illness and the possibility of organic cerebral impairment, as pre-senile dementias often cause anxiety in the early stages. Unrecognised alcoholism is another hazard in diagnosis here. If a patient has a low anxiety threshold, and has had previous anxiety states as a response to external stress or internal conflict, one of which is seen to be present on this occasion, the diagnosis of anxiety state is a safer ground.

(c) *Hysterical disturbances.* These are less common as presentations of depression than are anxiety states, but in people of hysterical personality they are not uncommon, as depression seems to lower their 'hysterical threshold', as it were. There may be multiple complaints made in a very histrionic manner, obvious manipulation of the family and apparent secondary gain, but underneath there may be distinct depressive mood. Effective treatment can lead to what seems like a change in personality as the hysterical elements fade away. As with anxiety states, one must be careful to exclude underlying depression and organic deterioration when a patient first presents hysterical symptoms in middle life or later.

(d) *Obsessive-compulsive symptoms.* As with anxiety and hysterical states, obsessive-compulsive symptoms may appear in a setting of depression, and be so prominent that a diagnosis of 'obsessive compulsive neurosis' may be made. Depressive symptoms must be carefully sought, as these illnesses will only respond to antidepressant treatment, not to the behaviour therapy which can be so helpful in the chronic obsessive compulsive states in which depression plays no major part.

(e) *Alcoholism*. This deserves a separate heading as a serious problem, although it has been mentioned already. A significant number of people seem to be unable to tolerate depression without alcohol, even though they may be able to cope with other problems in a more stoical and mature way. In these patients no progress can be made unless the depression is treated at the same time that alcohol is withdrawn.

Course and prognosis of depression
Apart from those cases that end in suicide, depressive illnesses are usually benign in that most recover. In the more reactive patterns of depression a major change of circumstances can be curative, if for example an apparently dying child were to recover, or an alcoholic husband stop drinking. On the whole, however, although depression is often precipitated by such events, once the illness has developed it tends to run its course independent of external factors of that type. Really chronic depression, as a form of serious unhappiness, and with little or no endogenous element, occurs at times in people locked in very unhappy marriages, or other intense family situations, from which they are unable to free themselves, perhaps because of loyalty, religious beliefs, or for the sake of children. At times nothing can be done to help in such situations, other than to offer sympathy. In only a few patients without obvious major conflicts or external problems does serious depression persist despite treatment, and it is for this small group that psychosurgery may be necessary (see Ch. 15).

Untreated severe depression is rarely seen now, but before any modern treatments were instituted the average in-patient stay in a mental hospital for depression was over twelve months, and some stayed much longer. As they did not enter hospital easily in those days, the whole course was very long. At present depression severe enough to need in-patient treatment is usually relieved within three or four weeks, and the patient discharged within six weeks. Patients treated effectively with antidepressants as out-patients are usually very much better within four to six weeks, but those who do not respond to the first antidepressant given may be depressed for many months. (The details of antidepressant drugs and of electrical treatment for depression are given in Chapter 15.)

In patients in whom reactive factors are predominant, and the endogenous features slight, antidepressants may not be indicated. If the depression has arisen from serious neurotic conflicts then some form of psychotherapy may be advisable. This can be given to the individual alone, or in a group; and if family conflicts are the centre of the problem, in so-called joint marital or family therapy. In our experience psychotherapy is not helpful in those who are still seriously and continuously depressed, and it is better for them to have been relieved of the worst of their symptoms by antidepressants or electrical treatment before starting psychotherapy, otherwise they may be too depressed to cope with the problems appearing in the psychotherapeutic discussions, and end up in a worse state.

In many depressive states, especially in middle life, and especially in women in the years surrounding the menopause, it seems that the patient is prone to relapse repeatedly for periods of up to several years. During that time he or she may respond well to treatment, but relapse each time it is stopped, and never be completely well. At the end of this phase of uncertain duration there is a spontaneous change to a higher level of well being, and antidepressants can then be stopped and the patient remains well. In menopausal women it may be that endocrine changes are responsible, but on the whole it seems that this period represents the natural period of the depression, and that during that time antidepressants have suppressed the symptoms with greater or lesser success. In some of these patients lithium therapy is helpful in preventing relapses during the period of vulnerability.

Some patients show a tendency to relapse at fairly regular intervals throughout long periods of their lives; and in some the relapses tend to be at the same season of the year.

It is common to see patients in whom there is a history of a fairly serious depression years ago, perhaps untreated in the days before antidepressants were introduced (1950s), in whom some neurotic symptoms have persisted. Chronic agoraphobia (p. 262) lingering after puerperal depression is perhaps the commonest; but other anxiety, phobic, hysterical or obsessional symptoms may also follow this pattern. These patients can respond to antidepressants by losing their long standing neurotic symptoms, even if apparently there is no significant depression left, and a thorough trial of antidepressants is well worth while before beginning other therapy in long standing neurotic states with this type of background.

Excluding those with a predominantly reactive picture, only a few patients show no useful response at all to antidepressants and electrical treatment, although in a good many there are early relapses, often but not always due to adverse circumstances, and not always associated with obvious vulnerability and feebleness of temperament. These patients can be most difficult to help, and linger in everyone's minds as treatment failures. However, a good many of those who do repeatedly relapse can be helped by very careful drug control, the use of lithium salts, and personal and social support such as that provided by group therapy, and a day hospital or day centre. Some of these non-responders are elderly people living alone, who are lonely but unwilling to give up their independence; or whose temperament is so seclusive or suspicious that they are unable to make use of the kind of social help offered by society.

It is important to consider three main possibilities when confronted by a depressed patient who fails to respond to treatment as expected.

Firstly, there is a sizeable group of people in whom there is a biochemical abnormality. In descending order of frequency these abnormalities are thyroid, vitamin B_{12} and folic acid deficiency; and much more rarely there may be disorders of calcium metabolism or other electrolytes. It is simple to exclude these, so long as the possibility is considered.

Secondly, there may be unsuspected organic brain disease or, much less often, some systemic disease such as carcinoma or tuberculosis. Slowly developing degenerative brain disease and cerebral tumours are particularly likely to be missed in younger people. In older people arteriosclerotic and senile changes are usually thought of, but may be missed.

Thirdly, there may be clinical features in the depression which have missed or wrongly assessed, or which the patient has suppressed. In some patients in whom the symptoms are of endogenous type, drugs or electrical treatment may repeatedly fail to help because of some major conflict or problem which has not come to light. Conversely, patients in whom neurotic problems and conflicts are obvious may spend a very long time, often years, in psychotherapy of one type or another, because the importance of the endogenous depressive element is not recognised, so that they do not receive the drug therapy they need. Unfortunately there are many people who adhere rigidly to dogmatic theories of causation and treatment, and who persist indefinitely with inappropriate therapy despite the obvious failure of the method.

An illustration of the complexities which may exist was provided by a middle aged lady, living alone, who developed moderately severe rheumatoid arthritis and then depression with an endogenous pattern. She only responded slightly to antidepressants. The problem was reviewed and she was found to be hypothyroid, but although thyroxine helped her to feel better and to be more active, she remained depressed. Several months later she suddenly admitted that she did not live alone, but with another woman, to whom she was deeply attached, but who had become addicted to amphetamines and consequently was almost impossible to live with. Shame and loyalty had prevented her from telling the truth, but after the confession she improved and recovered completely when her companion went into hospital for treatment herself.

Depressive mood and the other symptoms of depression may be relieved fairly soon by treatment, but there are often consequences in the patient's family and social life which take longer to recover. Family tensions may be a factor in leading to depression, but they are also often much intensified by depression. Inability to work and consequent lack of money, irritability or emotional withdrawal, failure to cope with household tasks or as a mother, loss of sexual libido and the recriminations which follow, and many other accompaniments of depression can all seriously harm relationships in the family. The seriously depressed mother of a young child may be unable to respond to her young baby, and thus lead to both physical and emotional deprivation, with long term ill effects at times. The patient's withdrawal from normal social life during a long depressive illness may permanently damage friendships and lead to relative social isolation even after recovery. It can often help a great deal to discuss all these and similar problems with the family, and to try and get them to recognise the patient's unacceptable behaviour as part of an illness, and therefore something for which she should not be blamed, and which can therefore be better tolerated.

Diagnosis and differential diagnosis
The first step is to establish that depression is present. The second is to exclude organic disease. The third is to assess the balance of endogenous and reactive factors. It is mostly in the milder cases where the depression is not so obvious, that the difficulties arise. The first is *denial of depression*. This is commoner than might be supposed. Quite a number of patients, unable to understand why they should be depressed in the absence of outside cause and feeling it a weakness in themselves that they should be, will refuse to admit to depression even though it is there. They will mostly complain of feeling vaguely 'off-colour', or of not being quite themselves, perhaps admitting to doing less than usual and to having less

inclination to do things, in a way suggestive of the depression that they continue to deny. 'I'm not one to let myself be depressed', 'I don't let things get me down', 'I'm always a one to look on the bright side', are the sort of phrases that they use, and these may put the examiner on his guard. With patience, and getting a comparison between the patient's present state and his normal one, together with a description from the relatives, the diagnosis may be established. Then there are patients who, admitting to some degree of depression, persistently *obscure the issue* by harping on *physical symptoms* that incidentally happen to be present, such as headache, dyspepsia, fatiguability or constipation. Others, since it is human to look for a cause, will ascribe their unwellness to some event which, on careful enquiry, may either seem inadequate or to have occurred at a time rendering it unlikely to be causal. Again, psychological symptoms such as anxiety, hypochondriasis or hysterical features may be more prominent than the depression itself, and may divert the examiner's attention from what is more basic and important, as already described.

Having established that depression is present, the next step is to exclude recognisable organic disease. Elaborate investigations are not necessarily required. What is needed is to bear in mind the possibility of organic disease and to make an adequate examination. This needs to be emphasised because the symptoms of mild depression closely resemble that debility which results from lingering illnesses not always obvious in themselves, such as malignant conditions, pulmonary tuberculosis, Hodgkin's disease, leukaemia, etc.

Next, it is necessary to consider whether there are any other symptoms associated with the depression. This is because depression can occur as a part of other syndromes, such as some organic senile states, Parkinsonism, and finally schizophrenia. Here, it must be borne in mind that a spurious appearance of organic intellectual failure can occur in old people when they are depressed.

In some patients a previous history or a family history of a manic disturbance will make it clear that the illness is bipolar manic-depression in a depressed phase. This is also suggested if the premorbid personality is markedly cyclothymic, that is, prone to sustained mood swings up and down.

The next step is to consider how far there are adequate causes in the environment or within the patient's personality for the present condition to be accounted for in terms of reaction. This should be a common-sense evaluation which should not do violence to the facts; and should include the type of 'life events' described earlier in this chapter.

Treatment

As stated earlier, the more clearly the depressive illness shows the endogenous pattern, with the symptoms and signs just described, the more likely it is to respond to physical methods of treatment. These consist mainly of the various antidepressant drugs and electrical treatment (e.c.t.)

The details of treatment are given in Chapter 15, but the basic principles are simple: antidepressant drugs should show some useful results within four weeks of full dosage being taken regularly, and should be stopped if no benefit appears. In serious depression with a suicide risk or self neglect, hospital admission is necessary as may be electrical treatment (e.c.t.). Patients with depressive delusions nearly always need e.c.t. If the patient fails to respond to treatment, such as a tricyclic drug or e.c.t., the diagnosis should be reconsidered, and in particular there should be a search for physical illness and for major life stresses that may have been overlooked, and which may be prolonging the illness. If no such factors are discovered, an alternative treatment should be given.

When a patient has responded to antidepressants, it is important not to stop them too soon. Many patients stop the drugs as soon as they feel better, only to relapse three or four weeks later. Very often the sequence is not seen as cause and effect, because it takes three or four weeks for the drugs to work, and a similar period to lose their effects. Drugs like tranylcypromine, which act within a week, lose their effect more quickly, too. It is wise to continue antidepressants for a minimum of four months after loss of symptoms, and the longer the depression has persisted before remission the longer the period of treatment necessary. Twelve months or more on a tricyclic or tetracyclic antidepressant is often necessary. When the drug is withdrawn, it is best to do this very gradually, taking three or four weeks over each single minor dose reduction—e.g., 25 mgm at a time, using amitriptyline and similar tricyclics. This means that if the patient still needs the antidepressant there is no sudden and severe relapse, and the dose can be raised for two or three more months before reducing it gradually again.

Amphetamine-like drugs should be avoided because of the dangers of dependence, and benzodiazepines should not be regarded as antidepressants, although they can sometimes be given with antidepressants to relieve anxiety and tension. It is also best to avoid major tranquillisers such as haloperidol, which can make depression worse. Flupenthixol, however, is a useful antidepressant as well as being effective in schizophrenia.

Apart from the antidepressants, tranquillisers and hypnotics may be useful in the treatment of depressive illnesses. Sleep disturbance is a prominent symptom and is often helped by giving 100–150 mg of trimipramine or amitriptyline at night, or by nitrazepam 5–20 mg or dichloralphenazone 650–1300 mg. In agitated patients chlorpromazine 25–100 mg is often useful. In patients with marked early waking nitrazepam is most suitable to be taken in the early hours of the morning, as it has little hangover effect. In the relief of agitation and tension by day barbiturates are best avoided, because of the serious results of overdosage and the tendency for habituation to develop, although they are effective. Instead a sedative tricyclic drug such as amitriptyline may be helpful, and chlorpromazine or a benzodiazepine (see Ch. 15) can be added.

If the patient is able to work, it is better that he should continue to do so, though being kept under observation, and offered reassurance and encouragement meanwhile. Patients who do not normally work should be encouraged to pursue some routine, and should have definite activities prescribed for them where possible. In this the help of relatives may be necessary owing to the patient's indecisiveness and lack of initiative. At the same time the work or other activities prescribed should be well within the patient's limitations; he will not be able to cope with new things or strange people, and will be able to do less than his normal. It is a good rule that he should be encouraged to do what he normally finds pleasant, but should avoid what, however willingly undertaken, he would find irksome when well.

Where the depression is sufficiently severe to prevent the patient from working, and where there seems any serious likelihood of suicide, special measures are required. In mild depression a holiday may help, but in more serious states, especially with an endogenous pattern, the patient usually requires more support and protection, and holidays rarely help. Admission to hospital is preferable when patient or family feel they can no longer cope. If suicide seems a serious risk compulsory admission may be necessary.

Electrical treatment
This, also known as e.c.t. for electroconvulsive therapy, revolutionised the treatment of severe depression. It is described in detail in Chapter 15, along with the indications for its use and the relatively trivial unwelcome side effects.

Psychological treatment
It must not be supposed that the treatment of depression is a routine matter of prescribing drugs and electrical treatment, even if the symptom pattern is purely endogenous. There is more to it than that.

Account must, of course, be taken of the patient as a whole, and the various contributory factors, both external and within the personality of the patient, must be evaluated and dealt with as far as possible. Unsatisfactory conditions of work or of life at home, where contributory, will call for adjustments. Conflicts must be resolved as far as may be possible by psychotherapy. It is best not to undertake this, however, until a considerable measure of improvement has first been gained in any severely depressed case. Severely depressed patients are incapable of the intellectual effort involved, and much harm may in fact be done by obliging them to mill over their problems when they are in no condition to grapple with them. Confidence and trust in the doctor, other staff, and the treatment used are essential; and the very act of 'handing over the problem' by seeking help is part of treatment.

When improvement is occurring, it is important not to yield to the temptations of (1) pushing the patient beyond his limitations, (2) discharging him or yielding to his requests to be discharged from hospital too soon. These amount to much the same thing. Stimulation of the improving patient should be gentle and gradual, for to encourage him to take on too much is to invite relapse.

BIPOLAR MANIC DEPRESSIVE ILLNESSES

These illnesses are much less common than depression, but are worth considering separately from the other affective disorders, because of their clinical features, genetic differences, and different treatment needs. The genetic aspect is considered in the section on aetiology and treatment is considered both in this section and in Chapter 15.

Clinical features

There is little to be said here about the depressive phase of manic depressive illness, because it is clinically identical with the classical endogenous pattern of depression described earlier. Agitation is rare but psychomotor retardation is common; the onset is often curiously abrupt; and both physical and emotional precipitants may be obvious, although often absent. Of all types of depression these are the most likely to come genuinely out of the blue, unrelated to circumstances or to inner conflicts, and not infrequently following some regular rhythm both in time and in relation to hypomanic upswings. It is in these illnesses that the importance of genetic and constitutional factors is most obvious; in which hormonal and biochemical changes are most clear cut; and in which psychotherapeutic treatment is relatively least important. In those patients in whom depressive or manic episodes are precipitated by neurotic or other personal conflicts, then psychotherapy can be very valuable when the patient has settled down to normal mood, and it can help to reduce the frequency of attacks.

The earlier in life a manic depressive illness appears, the more frequent is a family history of the same illness, and the more likely is the patient to have frequent recurrences. Although the personal sufferings of a patient with severe depression are very great, there is no doubt that it is the upswings which in the long run do the greatest damage, both to the patient's own life and to his family. To live with a manic depressive is for many to live in dread, because of the personal insults or violence which may suddenly develop; and because of the insecurity generated by unwise spending or investment, often enough leading to bankruptcy; or because of any one of a number of vitally important matters about which some unwise decision may suddenly be made, including, for example, suddenly giving up a good job, selling the house, or changing the children's school.

The manic phase
The onset is usually gradual, unless it follows a depressive phase, when the change can be very sudden. Many manic attacks seem more or less unrelated to outside events, but they are sometimes precipitated by external factors, of which the commonest are situations in which the patient has been subjected to considerable and continued frustration which he feels to be unwarranted and unjustifiable. In some cases an attack can be precipitated by an event which one would expect to lead to depression, and perhaps at some other time of the patient's life would have done so.

The term 'mania' is best reserved for illnesses so severe that the patient needs physical restraint, and 'hypomania' for all other degrees of severity.

Symptoms and signs
If there have been previous attacks, the development can often be recognised by the relatives before it is apparent to those who do not know the patient well. The patient may make gestures, stand in particular positions, or start to talk upon themes not in themselves remarkable, but which are peculiar to his manic phase. One of the commonest heralding signs is decorating the house, or doing other similar tasks, in the middle of the night. This may be happening for some days or even a week or so before there is any overt abnormality. This is usually followed by an increase in talkativeness, often with self-assertiveness, which is paralleled by an increase in activity. At first this may be well-directed, the patient still being able to do his

work efficiently, though there is often some lack of restraint, so that he is less scrupulous about what he says and to whom he says it; he may confide family secrets and intimacies to people who are surprised to receive them, and he may be unduly familiar with acquaintances and strangers. At the same time he may be extravagant, and if of a bonhomous disposition, may be overgenerous with gifts and in buying drinks for himself and others. In these ways he is almost always without insight into the fact that his behaviour is abnormal, and will insist that he has never felt better.

Just as the behaviour of the depressive is comprehensible in the light of his mood, so the behaviour of the hypomanic is also. And if called to account for his conduct, he will be able to produce plausible reasons for it which are hard indeed to refute—except perhaps on economic grounds, which he will disregard. It may thus be very difficult to control the situation when, though by no means 'certifiable', he is spending beyond his means.

It will be noted that whereas the depressive phase is characterised by restriction and loss, the manic phase is characterised by expansion and self-assertiveness. The expansion, however, is more apparent than real. The themes upon which the manic or hypomanic patient talks are commonly the same themes, though they may preoccupy him only in the hypomanic phase, and they tend to be repetitive in conception and expression; the expansiveness lies more in a distractibility, and a tendency for the periphery of his mind to be caught by passing fancies.

If the patient passes beyond the hypomanic phase the total activity increases and becomes altogether out of hand. The patient gets up early, rouses the household with noisy bustle, goes out to gather spring flowers or to have a bathe, clears out lumber rooms, and may have performed before breakfast time innumerable activities to which he is normally quite unaccustomed. He then may plan unnecessary expeditions, may get in touch with people whom he has not seen for years, much to their surprise, make unnecessary telephone calls and send unnecessary telegrams. He may organise supper parties with boxes at the opera, to which he will take taxis but will arrive late owing to various things that have distracted him on the way, and there will be some confusion because the number of people he has asked will probably have increased since he made the arrangements which will probably have been in any event incomplete. These inconveniences will be brushed aside in a flurry of further activity as he takes an inquisitive and extraverted, but superficial interest in all sorts of people and things, such as waiters, commissionaires, people encountered by chance at the bar, and so forth. Meanwhile, his plans for the evening may be undergoing many and rapid changes, as he may take up with people whom he meets, get fresh ideas from them, and may end up bringing strangers home for drinks in the small hours of the morning. The lack of restraint, the prodigal expenditure and the interest, though fleeting, in other people makes the patient a good target for parasites, hangers-on, and tellers of hard luck stories.

The patient may then retire for a few hours of uneasy sleep, after which the whole round of activity may begin again. His conversation similarly will be all but incessant, and one thought may so rapidly suggest another as to cause innumerable digressions without return to the main theme. The same distractibility characterises his actions, so that plans for effecting new improvements about the house will be broken off in favour of suddenly writing unnecessary letters, untidy with many afterthoughts and postscripts, which show the writer to be under characteristic pressure. One task after another is taken up but none completed.

At the same time, the patient usually feels possessed of marked clarity of thought, so that hesitations and doubts are cast aside, boldness is his policy and the decisions seem obvious, though his flurry of activity itself prevents him from implementing them. He may, however, offer advice freely, often in a way that carries conviction.

The pressure to which the patient is subject causes him to be intolerant of frustration, which, coupled with his over-confidence, makes him irritable and even markedly aggressive if unable to gain his ends. This is especially so if the customary lack of restraint has encouraged excessive drinking. Quarrels and even brawls are then quite liable to occur, and the more so when other people resent the inquisitive interference that such patients often show.

In such a state the patients' attention may be hard to hold, and their interest in what they are saying and seeing, coupled with their distractibility, may make it difficult to gain knowledge of their inner feelings. Such patients will often admit that their thoughts proceed at an unusual rate and follow each other with abnormal rapidity, but they will regard this as a satisfactory state of affairs and will not in the least concern themselves with its abnormality at the time. The mood is usually said to be 'elated' and the patient often described as showing an 'infectious gaiety'. Although this may occur, and the patient may laugh unduly often and loudly, it is by no means always the case. Many patients will say after the phase is over that, contrary to appearances, they experienced no real enjoyment, and an appreciable number will show a depressive content (occasionally even with suicidal ideas) even though their phase be a manic one. Excitement is thus a better term than elation, especially in view of the aggressive irritability that is so often seen.

As hypomania progresses further towards frank mania (and most cases do not progress as far) the tempo increases. The patient may shout, sing and dance, his conversation may become incoherent through pressure of talk which may be accompanied by gales of laughter, while the whole day is spent in a chaos of activity which seems purposeless owing to the rapidity with which one intention succeeds another. Violence often occurs. It is now that associations of ideas suggested by the sound of words will cause the patient to make rhymes and puns, and to show on the basis of such chance association, the so-called 'flight of ideas'. Lack of sexual restraint, which will previously have been noticeable in the ready introduction of *risqué* jokes, a tendency to philandering with erotic advances, may now amount to complete sexual shamelessness, with exhibitionism, overtly erotic behaviour and masturbation regardless of the circumstances.

In this state, the distractibility may cause the patient to be heedless of the passage of time, but he will otherwise be orientated. He may keep in remarkably good touch, and such patients often show a clear memory for everything that has happened, which is an indication for special care that nothing unsuitable should be said on the supposition that the patient is too distractible to notice it. Distortions of content (delusions and ideas of reference) may occur, but will be in line with the mood, so that the exalted patient may write cheques for a million, claim titles and confer them on others, boast of his physique and abilities and in general show grandiose behaviour; the patient who is excited and irritable may show marked paranoid trends, especially if previously he was a touchy person. Hallucinations, however, do not classically occur, and their presence should suggest the probability of intoxication or schizophrenic admixture. Judgement is impaired according to the extent of the grandiosity or paranoid trends, and the pressure under which the patient is acting.

Physically, the patient usually appears bright-eyed and with ruddy complexion. The voice is often hoarse through overuse. Loss of weight may become apparent as food is neglected in the general flurry of activity with which the patient increasingly exhausts himself. Sleep is disturbed both as regards getting off, and frequent and early waking, on which there is a tendency to resume activities immediately. Sexual restraint is diminished, leading to immodest or shameless behaviour.

The contrast between the two phases of manic-depressive psychosis may be illustrated by the following table:—

Depressive phase	*Manic phase*
Reduced animation.	Excitement.
Loss of confidence with feelings of inferiority and withdrawnness.	Over-confidence with lack of diffidence, with gregariousness and tendency to interfere.
Motor retardation up to stupor.	Over-activity.
Restriction and retardation of thought.	Acceleration of thought; flight of ideas; often restriction of main themes of thought but peripheral expansion.
Delusions of self-reproach, depersonalisation and hypochondriasis.	Delusions of grandeur, mental and physical.
Introversion.	Extraversion.
Suicidal ideas.	Irritability and aggressiveness.
Loss of sexual desire.	Increase of sexual interest and diminished restraint.
Sallow complexion.	Ruddy complexion.

Course and prognosis

In general, the manic phase, like the depressive one, may be regarded as benign since there is a tendency to spontaneous recovery. This is usually gradual. Often the first features of recovery are a diminution of irritability and aggressiveness, together with some return of restraint, as the pressure gradually subsides. The activity and talkativeness then become less. At this stage the patient may again be easily stimulated by having opportunity for excitement or for doing too much, but gradually he will return again to normal, if indeed he does not sink into a depressive phase. As with the latter there is great variation between one person and another in the length of attack; but manic attacks tend to be shorter than depressive ones. Three to six weeks is a fairly usual duration. Where, however, such a phase occurs for the first time in a patient over forty years of age it is liable to be prolonged and the prognosis should be guarded accordingly. Since the introduction of lithium and haloperidol in treatment chronic mania no longer occurs, although relapses cannot always be prevented.

Differential diagnosis

More attention may have to be paid to the evidence of relatives than to that of the patient. Although the latter may have little insight he may be astute enough so far to restrain himself as to put up a deceptively normal performance at interview. Allowance may have to be made for this in gauging the severity of the state, as well as for the fact that to live with an over-active and over-talkative hypomanic day in and day out is quite a different proposition from seeing him only for an hour in conversation. In some people with natural high spirits and a high endowment of energy, their normal state may be something approaching hypomania. The same is true of the cyclothymic when the swing of his mood is in an upward direction. But where a patient shows hypomanic behaviour for the first time, the diagnosis must be made by exclusion.

Many psychiatric conditions, like others in general medicine, are not clear cut, and it is not uncommon for schizophrenia to show manic-depressive admixture and for manic-depressive psychosis to show schizophrenic features. For this reason, what is really a schizophrenic psychosis may be ushered in by behaviour of hypomanic or manic type. The previous personality and history of the patient may offer some guide; the less there have been schizoid features, the more normal the personality seems to have been, and the more there is a history of anything resembling cyclothymia, the more probable does the diagnosis of manic-depressive illness become in such a case. More important are the presence of such features as the first rank symptoms of Schneider, a bizarre emotional quality, and stuporose episodes, which all make a diagnosis of schizophrenia likely. In general the conduct of the manic or hypomanic patient should be congruous and in harmony with the mood. The family history is less helpful in the differential diagnosis owing to the tendency for mixed forms to occur.

Apart from the foregoing, there are only two main pitfalls. The first is when the patient is referred as a dipsomaniac, i.e. a periodic drinker to excess. The possibility must then be borne in mind that such drinking may be symptomatic of the increased bonhomie, lack of restraint and over-activity that commonly accompany the hypomanic state. This is much less common than excessive drinking as a response to depression.

The second main pitfall is when the patient is referred as a hypomanic, but may actually be suffering from some organic cerebral disease affecting particularly the frontal lobes. That now rare condition, syphilitic GPI in its expansive form, was particularly difficult to distinguish. Physical examination, intellectual deficits, and positive serology should be enough to make the diagnosis certain, but more detailed neurological investigation may be necessary.

Certain very rare lesions, such as tumours, in the neighbourhood of the third ventricle have been known to produce manic-like pictures, but where such uncommon conditions happen to be encountered, the condition is likely to be inconsistent, prolonged rather than episodic, with associated symptoms of headache, and with signs that, if not initially present, will develop as the lesion expands.

In summary, the difficulties in diagnosing hypomania or mania should not be great. Awareness of the existence of such a condition will put the student on his guard against dismissing as mere boorishness or foolish conduct, behaviour of a hypomanic or manic kind in a person not normally subject to it. The history of previous phases, or of depressive ones, will be a guide. The main differential diagnosis is from the excited forms of schizophrenia and from frontal lobe lesions of various types.

Treatment of the depressive phase

The treatment of the depressive phase is almost identical with that of other depression, using the antidepressant drugs and electrical treatment in the same way. The only important practical differences arise from the fact that as the mood starts to improve with treatment, there is a very real danger that the patient will become hypomanic. It is wise therefore to start lithium therapy (described in detail later) quite early in the course of treatment, to lessen the chances of this happening. It may also be wise to lessen the dose of antidepressants early, especially if MAOI drugs are being used; and to interrupt a course of electrical treatment before the patient has completely recovered, as a marked upward mood swing of the patient often seems to develop after only a few treatments, and to continue the treatment may encourage hypomania.

Treatment of the manic phase

The mildest cases will not seek advice at all. The less mild ones will be brought, more or less reluctantly, by relatives who are concerned about them, and more particularly about their extravagance. Where there is undue expenditure, any serious risk of social embarrassment or of losing a job through the behaviour, or where the relatives find him intolerably tiring to live with, the patient will best be treated in hospital. This is far more easily said than done. The patient is unlikely to agree. All the arts of persuasion and bargaining may be called for, and in persuasion use should be made of any physical symptoms or lesions that he may happen to have.

If the patient still refuses, as is likely, attempts may be made to reduce the over-activity by drug treatment, preferably doled out by the relatives and taken under supervision. It may be possible to arrange some holiday or change of scene, essentially of a quiet and unstimulating kind, on which the patient can take plenty of physical exercise, and indulge in some innocuous pleasure such as bathing, or pursue some innocuous hobby such as fishing. Instructions may have to be given to tradespeople, etc., with a view to preventing the running up of large credit accounts. Attempts should be made tactfully to control the intake of alcohol where this tends to be excessive.

The attack may then gradually subside, or the patient may become worse to the extent that compulsory detention is possible. Where there is extravagance leading to serious financial hardship, or where other social embarrassments are occurring, compulsory detention should not be too long delayed, but can only be undertaken as a rule where the behaviour is creating a real social nuisance.

Drug treatment

The drug of choice at present is haloperidol (Serenace, Haldol) a butyrophenone derivative. It can be given by mouth in doses from 1.5 mg t.d.s. to as high as 80 mg daily, although 15 to 30 mg daily is enough for most patients. It can also be given in large doses intravenously or intramuscularly. More sedative drugs such as chlorpromazine 300 to 600 mg daily can be added. These drugs control the patient's excitement and over activity partly because of the Parkinsonian side effects they produce. Antiparkinsonian agents, such as orphenadrine 50 mg t.d.s., are necessary in nearly all cases, but, curiously, side effects seem less common when very large doses are used. This is probably because of the anticholinergic effects of the drug itself, which have an antiparkinsonian effect if in large doses, say 40 mg daily. The same paradoxical loss of extrapyramidal symptoms with very high dosage occurs with phenothiazines. Haloperidol often causes rapid lowering of mood, and seems to lead to an earlier depressive down-swing than would otherwise occur. It is our practice to lessen the dose progressively as soon as the patient's excitement and elevated mood settle to near normal.

Lithium Carbonate. The actions and toxic side effects of this simple salt are described in Chapter 15. It is of most use in preventing recurrences of hypomanic upswings, but in many patients it helps to control the acute attack, and also contributes to more rapid recovery in the depressive phase. Side effects are more common if large doses are given at the start, and it seems better to give 400 mg of the delayed release preparation Priadel daily for a few days before increasing the dose to 800 mg or 1200 mg, which in most people is enough to maintain the serum lithium between 0.8 and 1.4 millimols per litre, the most suitable range. Regular estimations are essential as the drug is dangerously toxic if the level exceeds 2.0 millimols, and usually ineffective if the level is below about 0.6 millimols.

Treatment in hospital

In hospital, the aim should be to allow the patient just enough occupation and activity to enable him to work off something of the inner pressure that he feels, while at the same time preventing him from becoming further stimulated. This is not easy to achieve. The drugs mentioned above will be found useful, and if necessary can be combined with minor tranquillisers such as diazepam, up to 30 or 40 mg daily in divided doses. Attention must be paid to the intake of food and intake and output of fluids owing to the danger of intoxication. It is usually wise to cut down contacts with the outer world, such as visitors and the receipt of letters, at first and until the patient shows signs of settling down.

Electrical treatment

It may seem paradoxical that this should be applied to both the phases of manic-depressive psychosis, in view of their somewhat contrasting nature; but it is effective in each to some extent. It has, however, been largely replaced by the use of drugs in the treatment of hypomania.

General management

It is characteristic of the manic or hypomanic patient to dislike the restraints imposed upon him. He will constantly wish to be extending the range of his activities, and must be dissuaded from this as far as possible. This almost always leads to bargaining, often of a more or less irritable kind. The best policy is to make concessions but only on the unimportant points. Often, the patient's humour may be exploited with advantage, and great use can be made of the distractibility by diverting the patient's attention from the main issues at hand. Occupational therapy and ward work can be useful as affording harmless channels for the output of hypomanic energy, but supervision will of course be required and care should be taken that the patient is stimulated as little as possible.

It is always a good rule to explain the state of affairs carefully to the relatives, not only with a view to securing their co-operation, but because the lack of insight of manic and hypomanic patients leads them frequently to complain and sometimes to be litigious, as to which the family may be accordingly forewarned.

Psychological treatment
As with the depressive phase, it is necessary to evaluate the factors that may have contributed to the hypomanic or manic development (e.g. frustrations, conflicts, unsatisfactory conditions at home or at work), and adjustments should be attempted as far as possible. The patient will be far too distractible for such considerations in the early stages, and attempts to deal with them are likely only to stimulate him into further excitement. They should be delayed until reasonable tranquillity has been gained.

Despite the use of lithium, which is of tremendous benefit to many sufferers from manic depressive illnesses, in some patients recurrences cannot be prevented. It is then worth trying to achieve a higher level in the blood than usually considered safe, so long as it is done with careful supervision, as in some people this is successful.

Suicide
A few general facts may be given before considering the individual case. Although more women attempt suicide than men, effective suicide is rather more common in men than in women. The commonest time of year is the spring and early summer. As regards age, the commonest in most countries for men is in the seventies, and for women it is about ten years earlier. There is a marked association with physical disease, and an even more marked one with alcoholism. Suicide is commoner in urban than in rural areas, among single people than among married, among the childless than among parents, among the socially isolated than among the gregarious, among those who have become improverished than among those who have always been poor, among the unemployed than among the employed, among the rootless than among those who have attachments, and among Protestants or irreligious than among Roman Catholics. By these criteria, a single, childless, socially isolated, drifting, impoverished, unemployed, irreligious, seventy-year-old townsman with intractable organic disease may be a candidate, especially if liable to depressive illness or personality reaction, with a history of a previous attempt.

The suicide rate in the United Kingdom has continued to fall slowly. In England and Wales for example it fell from 12 per 100 000 of population in 1963 to 8 per 100 000 in 1977. This is in contrast to rising, and usually higher, rates in most developed countries. This relatively low rate is difficult to explain. The Samaritan organisation may be partly responsible, as may more efficient treatment, the change to less toxic natural gas for cooking, and less prescribing of barbiturates.

Many patients go to their doctors in the days immediately before they commit suicide, but fail to reveal how they feel. In many of these cases their families have been at least partly aware of the severity of the depression, and may have encouraged them to make the visit. Unfortunately, because of diffidence and awkwardness, or because of the lack of time or the doctor's manner, they do not manage to communicate properly and get the help they need, but come away with a prescription—for indigestion mixture or an analgesic, as like as not. As has been mentioned elsewhere in this book, a question like 'How are your spirits?' should be a very common one.

Every patient with more than a mild depressive illness must be regarded as a possible suicidal risk.

At large, the most popular methods for suicide are by taking overdoses of drugs; but swallowing other poisons, hanging, cutting the throat or blood vessels, and jumping under trains are not uncommon. With the increasing spread of North Sea gas, in the United Kingdom, the use of the gas oven is less significant. Car exhaust gas is a not uncommon method. In hospital, suicidal attempts are most often made by jumping out of windows, hanging, self-strangulation, obtaining some sharp instrument with which to sever a blood-vessel, or hoarding sedatives until a store has been obtained. Measures should be taken accordingly.

Suicidal talk should never be taken lightly, and this is especially so with depressive cases. A popular notion that 'those who talk about suicide don't do it' is entirely fallacious, though it is also true that the most determined patients of all may dissimulate their intentions.

The assessment of suicidal risk

This may be very difficult, but every doctor in clinical practice should understand how to do it, just as he should be able to examine the cardiovascular system. Students sometimes hesitate to explore the question, out of misplaced delicacy, or a fear that they might put the idea into the patient's mind, but in everyone who is suffering from depression some assessment of suicidal intent should be made, and recorded in the notes.

With the patient who has not made any suicidal act or threats, it takes only a few words to establish the facts. After an account of the patient's feelings, symptoms, social and personal problems has been taken, and a rapport established, suicidal ideas should be asked about openly and frankly. One can ask 'How is the depression at its worst? . . .' 'Do you ever feel that you would rather be dead than put up with it indefinitely?' . . . and, depending on the answer to that question: 'Do you ever feel like ending your own life?' If the answer is 'Yes', then a more detailed assessment is needed. Very many depressives do feel that they could not tolerate such a state indefinitely, but they hope and expect relief from their suffering. Patients, with few exceptions, will tell the truth, and if they are evasive it should be taken as indicating strong suicidal thoughts.

A chapter on affective illnesses is the natural place to consider suicide, but not everyone who commits suicide is suffering from a depressive illness, and nor are all those who make more or less serious attempts. In assessing the likelihood of a suicide attempt, we may have to consider the following:

1. The seriousness of any attempt made recently
2. What the patient says about his feelings and intentions
3. The diagnosis
4. The method used or threatened
5. The immediate circumstances of the act
6. The social setting of the patient
7. Various sociological factors.

If someone has survived a suicidal act, then the likelihood of further attempts must be assessed, partly by how seriously ill he made himself, as well as by the factors given below. Remember, however, that people can make serious mistakes, both by under and over-estimating the potency of drugs, and the dangers of gas, electricity and so on. Quite a lot of those who survive serious attempts are quickly glad to be alive after all, but there are plenty who are not.

The patients' own statements of intent are the most important evidence of all, and an approach to the patient who is not known to be suicidal has already been outlined. After an attempt at, or threats of, suicide, the questioning must go further—for example:

'What did you hope would happen when you did this?' 'Can we feel confident that you will not try again?' and so on.

In addition to direct statements about suicidal intent, there must be an assessment of mood, of the degree of anger directed at others and himself (both very commonly found in suicidal patients), and of his determination. Any manipulative element in the suicidal threat or behaviour should also be assessed.

Diagnosis is sometimes very important. For example, suicide is very common in schizophrenia, especially in the early stages, when depression is a common symptom, and insight, with its attendant fear of future deterioration, is better preserved. Schizophrenics almost never make suicidal gestures, nor do they seek sympathy and attention by threatening suicide. They tend to violent and bloody acts, without warning. Because of the nature of their illness, it is more difficult to assess their mood and intentions, and great care must be taken.

Patients with psychotic depressive states, that is, with delusions or hallucinations, are also very much at risk, especially as they begin to improve from states of retardation which have inhibited any action. There is also a danger of murder, especially of children, by the deluded depressive who feels that she can bring only suffering to her family, and kills to spare them. If a patient expresses such delusional guilty ideas, full precautions must be taken.

Puerperal depression is another state in which very sudden suicidal attempts occur, usually within the first ten days after the birth, as when some woman jumps out of a window, perhaps carrying her baby. Doctors and nurses become so accustomed to mild puerperal depression that it seems almost normal, which it is not. They may then ignore the danger signals of increasing restlessness, sleep disturbance, anorexia and developing fears and bizarre ideas about the baby and themselves. If a woman has had a previous severe puerperal depression (p. 168), of sudden onset especially, she should be carefully watched after delivery, and if necessary given prophylactic antidepressants.

Suicide is very much more common in alcoholics and drug abusers than in other people. Assessment can be very difficult because, unlike most other patients whom we are considering, they are less honest—both with themselves and others. Unfortunately, they tend to generate dislike and consequent rejection by both doctors and nurses, and staff must guard against this.

Many people who commit suicide have no true psychiatric illness, but are in chronic pain, lonely, see no hope of improvement, and decide that on balance they might as well be dead.

The method used is important, because some of them are nearly always associated with serious intent to die, and rarely with attention seeking or other non-serious attempts. These are: fire arms, hanging, drowning, jumping from heights, swallowing caustics or acids and, especially recently, the use of paraquat and similar weed killers.

The immediate circumstances are relevant in that they usually indicate the likelihood of discovery before death; and also how much the act was planned or impulsive, how much a reaction to immediate conflict, and so on. Careful preparations, such as making a will or

202 PSYCHOLOGICAL MEDICINE

sending the family away on holiday, are also important, as are some suicide letters, depending on their content.

By the social setting of the patient, we mean his family and the degree of happiness and support it may provide; and his work, friendships, interests, future prospects, and much that gives life meaning and depth. We can ask: 'What is there in life worth living for if he were well?' and seek for an answer along these lines. The more lonely, sad and empty the life before depression began, the worse the outlook.

Various sociological factors have been mentioned already, such as religion and marital state, and others are mentioned below in considering 'self-poisoning'. These factors are of great interest and importance statistically, but should not be relied on in assessing the individual patient.

Suicide precautions

If after careful assessment suicidal attempts seem likely, the patient should be admitted to hospital, if necessary under a compulsory section, as described in Chapter 16. Very occasionally, skilled home nursing, by professional psychiatric nurses, may be adequate. Few can afford this.

In hospital every nurse and other member of the staff should be aware of the risk, and, after careful and sympathetic explanation to the patient, there should be a search for tablets, razors, or other potentially lethal articles, and, when given tablets as treatment, care must be taken that they are truly swallowed. If there is any doubt, liquid medicines or injections should be given. It is wise to keep the patient in bed, or at least in pyjamas and dressing gown, and he should be accompanied to the bathroom, as one can drown in a bath with time and determination. The lavatories should not have projections from which people can hang themselves with pyjama cords, which should in any case be replaced by buttons. Sedation or tranquillisation is usually helpful.

Such stringent precautions are rarely necessary for long, as tranquillisation and antidepressant treatment usually have fairly rapid effects.

Self-poisoning

In the last few years there has been an enormous increase in the number of 'suicidal gestures' by taking overdoses of drugs, often trivial. In many cases there is no suicidal intent at all, and they are perhaps better called 'self poisonings'. The patient is usually a young woman or adolescent girl, of hysterical personality, and the overdose is an expression of despair, anger and frustration, or an attempt to change family attitudes or manipulate the situation. These patients have become a major problem in casualty departments and medical wards. There are so many of them in some urban hospitals that they seriously affect the work load, and if all were referred to psychiatrists––as is often recommended—the psychiatrists would have little time for their other patients. There is now little sense of shame or guilt attached to such self poisoning, and the massive increase is partly a matter of fashion in what is acceptable behaviour. Nevertheless a number of the patients are seriously distressed and some will go on to commit suicide effectively, and it requires care and skill to distinguish those who need treatment from those who do not. The background of many of the 'self poisoners' is of social disorganisation, poverty, and personal inadequacy. They tend to come from unskilled working class families in which prison sentences, unemployment, children in care or on probation, are all much commoner than average, but they occur quite frequently at all social levels. There is rarely any evidence of psychiatric illness.

We know that careful assessment and appropriate treatment lower the chance of later death by suicide, and every case must be properly investigated. This initial assessment need not be done by a psychiatrist, as the skills can, and should, be learnt by every doctor who is dealing with these patients, who can then refer for psychiatric help the more disturbed and potentially suicidal. The essential factors in the assessment include interest, time and thoroughness.

Hypochondriasis

This word is used in various ways, but is best kept for clinical states in which the patient complains of various physical symptoms and disorders—for which no physical cause can be found—over long periods of time, usually with great intensity of feeling, and in which the symptoms are not simply part of some other recognisable mental illness such as depression.

The most typical patient is more often a woman, over 55 years, of obsessional personality, being meticulous, rigid, tense, ruminative and usually over concerned with bowel function throughout life; unhappily married or single, and poorly occupied. The patient's thoughts can seem almost totally dominated by concern about the symptoms. Bowel disturbances are perhaps the commonest problem, but any part of the body may provide the focus of concern. The main symptom may be pain, often described in extreme terms, although the patient does not look as though she is in agony, but may be less clear cut, and involve any system. The patient often goes to doctor after doctor, and hospital case records about her get thicker and thicker, while she collects an increasing number of reports and X-rays which she may take with her to consultations with new doctors. There may be some depressive mood, but these hypochondriacal states are distinct from depressive illnesses in which hypochondriasis is a symptom of a depressive illness, and is relieved by successful antidepressant treatment. Rather bizarre hypochondriacal states occur in schizophrenia also.

Patients with these chronic hypochondriacal states, often lasting many years, are very difficult to help. It may seem that their sufferings become their main interest in life, so that without them life would be more dull, and the interest of the whole family may indeed be focussed on the patient's health. The symptoms, when not of pain, are commonly of 'throbbing' somewhere, or 'movement' in the abdomen, and it often seems that the patient is too aware of normal visceral or vascular activity which in most people does not reach consciousness. The patient is then 'listening in' with heightened awareness and a sense of distress to aortic pulsation, peristalsis, or some other normal body activity.

It is worth trying antidepressant drugs, as some of the states may be the residuum of incompletely resolved depression, but social distraction and useful occupation, giving the patient something else to take an interest in, is the most generally helpful treatment in an almost untreatable condition.

10

Disorders of personality and intelligence (disorders of development)

This chapter should be read in conjunction with that following, and considers those disorders of personality and intelligence which can be regarded as constitutional; in other words, related to the basic nature of the person, and which we understand as the result of a life-long interaction of genetic and environmental factors. In clinical psychiatry it is mainly personality which is considered, although intelligence is often relevant, and even physical make-up may be important too. In the study of mental subnormality intelligence is naturally more important.

Personality is difficult to define, and no generally accepted theory of personality exists, nor is there any generally accepted way in which it may be described and assessed.

We use the word 'personality' here to sum up those enduring characteristics of a person which determine how he or she will react, in both behaviour and feeling, to the life situation and to changes in it. Many formal methods of describing personality have been put forward, but in practice there are three main approaches to the problem which are relevant here: (a) psychoanalytic, (b) quantitative and factorial and (c) clinical description of traits or types. An extensive literature exists about all of these and details of the first two in particular should be sought elsewhere, as only the merest sketch of them is given here. There are of course more ways of thinking about personality and its development, but these are the main ways in which it is described in practice.

(a) Psychoanalytic descriptions of personality arise naturally from psychoanalytic theories of personality development, in which people are viewed as passing through various stages in infancy and childhood, and in which great importance is given to the role of unconscious processes. During the early stages of development libidinal drives are focussed on oral, anal and genital functions in sequence, and are gradually turned from concentration on the self outwards to other people. Thus descriptions such as 'an anal character', 'oral dependency needs', or 'narcissistic' are frequently used, and have fairly clear cut meanings in theoretical terms. To the non-psychoanalytic clinician they are often misleading, they are often used too loosely and sweepingly and they carry theoretical implications which may well not be justified in what should be a description rather than a speculative interpretation (see p. 368).

(b) Quantitative and factorial methods of personality description have mainly been developed by psychologists. They use questionnaires to obtain answers to questions relevant to personality, and by careful sifting and statistical analysis end by excluding all but the most useful and discriminating questions.

One of the best known is the Eysenck Personality Inventory (E.P.I.); the answers to which define an individual's place on two independent dimensions, firstly one of extraversion-intraversion and secondly one of neuroticism. The first is a measure of how reserved or outgoing the person is; the second measures emotional lability, largely in terms of symptoms which arise from overactivity of the autonomic nervous system. Eysenck's work is based theoretically on ideas derived from Pavlov; that is, that people who develop conditioned responses very easily are more likely to develop excessive and maladaptive responses, and thus to be neurotic. In our opinion this idea is indeed very relevant to many patients, including most of those with anxiety states and simple phobias, and also to those people who never consult a psychiatrist but who throughout their lives are 'anxiety prone' and habitually over-react to trivial stimuli. However, the Eysenckian concept of 'neuroticism' is much too narrow to include people with neurotic character disorders (pp. 244–245); nor does it fit in convincingly with the nature of obsessional compulsive states (p. 301) or hysterical conversion (p. 273). At a theoretical level there are also serious doubts as to whether there is indeed a general factor of conditionability. The main use of the E.P.I. is in research studies involving large numbers of people. It is rarely of use in clinical situations.

The Cattell 16 P.F. (sixteen personality factor) Questionnaire provides a much more elaborate description of people than the two dimensional system of Eysenck, as it places people on sixteen different dimensions, and some of these can be combined to produce 'second order' factors. As with the E.P.I. the main use of the Cattell 16 P.F. test must be in research, as it has little clinical relevance.

A very different type of personality assessment is provided by the Kelly Repertory Grid, based on Kelly's theory of personal constructs. In essence the subject expresses his subjective feelings about people or things ('elements') in terms of 'constructs', which are chosen for their relevance to the person and problem being studied, but which may include for example 'kindness', 'aggressiveness' or 'motherliness'. After elaborate analysis, usually by computer, a picture of some of the subject's feelings and the way in which they are ordered and interrelated is obtained. In clinical work these so called 'grids' can be very illuminating, giving new insights into a patient's feelings and problems, and they are useful in assessing change, as for example in psychotherapy. They are, however, very time consuming to produce.

There are also questionnaires which are based more on clinical psychiatric concepts and ask about symptoms as well as putting questions related to underlying enduring personality characteristics. Two of these are the Minnesota Multiphasic Personality Inventory (M.M.P.I.) and the Middlesex Hospital Questionnaire (M.H.Q.). The M.M.P.I. is mainly used in North America, and contains about 550 questions, all originally chosen as usefully discriminating between patients already definitely diagnosed as psychiatrically ill. The M.H.Q. is much briefer and rates the patient on six scales, covering usefully the ordinary range of neurotic symptoms. Although the M.M.P.I. is used in clinical work in North America it is rarely used in Britain, and the M.H.Q. is used principally in research in this country.

In addition to the methods mentioned above there are also the so-called 'projective tests'. The best known of these is the Rorschach test, in which the subject is shown a standard series of ink blot designs and asked to describe what he sees. His answers are rated in a standardised way and his personality assessed accordingly. The rationale is very plausible—that he is expressing his fantasies and inner reactions—but the test has never been well validated (that is, objectively compared to other accepted measures and methods), and the results depend a great deal on the person doing the testing. The other well known projective test is Murray's Thematic Apperception Test (T.A.T.) in which a series of pictures capable of varying interpretations are shown to the subject, who has to tell a story about each one. Similar criticisms are levelled at this test, and neither of them is used extensively in Britain. Perhaps their greatest use is to identify particular conflicts or important emotional problems as a preliminary screening before psychotherapy, but they certainly do not give an overall view of the personality.

To the clinician, any system of personality description which is based purely on answers to a questionnaire must have serious shortcomings, for various reasons. For example, there is really no place in a questionnaire for objective assessments of such important matters as the person's capacity for effort or 'drive'; his ability to stick at things despite stress or difficulty; whether he becomes physically violent at times; his ability to form enduring relationships (as opposed to the ease or difficulty of meeting strangers which a questionnaire can well assess); or his 'likeableness'. All of these are of very great importance in the life of everyone, but several of them can only be well assessed from the reports of others or from the assessor's own responses. The benefits of questionnaires are obvious, in that they are not subjective, and they are reproducible; but in clinical psychiatry they are at best inadequate by themselves, and too often irrelevant.

(c) Whatever theory of personality development is accepted, and whatever formal tests are used as adjuncts, in our view personality is best assessed by a combination of personal interview with the patient and with other people who know him well. Often certain features of the initial history which the patient gives will have more value in assessing his personality and predicting his future behaviour than anything else he says. For example, if a man has had twenty jobs in two years, and says he left each one because he was 'fed up' or 'didn't like being pushed around', then he is not likely to stick to any treatment régime and will very probably fail to keep his appointments. He is also likely to show other features of a psychopathic personality (q.v.). Conversely, a man who has spent thirty years in the same clerical job, and whose hobby is stamp collecting, is likely to be cautious, reliable, and a perfectionist. It is usually most natural and convenient to interview the patient's spouse, but other relatives or close friends, or even employers or work mates may at times be helpful. Naturally the patient's approval should always be sought for this. Another benefit of seeing the spouse or whoever lives with the patient, is that the home is often where conflicts and troubles are most intense, and light will probably be thrown on these as well as on the patient's personality and well being.

Although scientific exactitude is not possible when assessing personality by clinical interview, an attempt at rough 'measurement' of character traits should be made. In the same way that intelligence is distributed throughout the population on a normal curve of distribution, with a few people very much above and a few very much below average, and most cluster around the mean, while intermediate numbers lie between; so can we conceive of any personality characteristic. We should try to rate each patient roughly in this way for traits such as proneness to anxiety, outgoingness or reserve, obsessional features, capacity for sustained effort and interest, proneness to depressive mood and to irritability, sensitivity, suspiciousness and tendencies to blame others (paranoid traits), aggressiveness, attention-seeking, impulsiveness, and tendencies to avoid reality by denying problems or escaping from situations into day-dreaming or drink. All of these are often relevant clinically, and may be brought out during detailed history taking and interviews with others. A good estimate of the patient's intelligence can also be made by considering the educational background, work, interests, and of course by what is said and the way in which it is said. For each trait the patient is roughly rated as being average, above or below average, or perhaps very far from average in one direction or the other. There is a very wide range of normality, and it is important to remember that personality characteristics— —although regarded as enduring features—are not independent of situation. For example, aggressiveness may be directed only at certain sorts of people in certain types of situations; perfectionism may be present in some activities and not in others; or irritability may be absent at work and severe at home. Nevertheless, on the whole these tendencies are mainly stable in given situations, and the way in which someone has behaved in certain circumstances in the past is usually a better guide to future behaviour than what he says he intends to do.

In keeping notes and when describing a patient's personality only the outstanding features will be mentioned, the unspoken implication being that any personality trait not mentioned is regarded as being near average in degree, or irrelevant. A patient might then be described simply as 'obsessional' or 'paranoid'; or as 'vulnerable' if throughout life he has reacted to stress by anxiety or depression, or by failure to cope in some way. In a more thorough description someone might be described as 'anxious, reserved and markedly obsessional' or as 'attention-seeking, lacking in drive and irritable'.

Accepting that there is a wide range of personality, and with the idea of a normal curve of distribution in mind, we can use the term 'abnormal personality' or 'personality disorder' when someone shows any extreme variation. The term is therefore essentially used statistically. In Germany and other Continental countries the word 'psychopathic' is used in this sense, to mean any personality disorder from which either the individual or society suffers ('pathos' being the Greek word for suffering), so that someone might be described as 'a depressive psychopath', meaning that his habitual mood is markedly depressive and pessimistic. In Anglo-American usage the word psychopathic carries the meaning of antisocial (p. 224), and the terms 'personality disorder', 'personality problem' or 'abnormal personality' are preferred; although even with these some flavour of antisocial features seems to have crept in, perhaps because some psychiatrists and others find the term 'psychopathic' too uncompromisingly critical, and they prefer not to use it.

It is clear that this method of personality description carries no theoretical implications, which is a benefit when the theoretical foundations of personality development are so uncertain. An elastic approach is required which recognises that certain instincts or drives provide the motive forces underlying human life and that, much modified and even distorted by genetic and environmental factors, these drives are always to be reckoned with. Psychological theories differ in the number of different drives they are prepared to recognise, but sexual drives, hunger, thirst and avoidance of pain are undoubted; to which many would add the drives to form personal and social bonds. Serious and persistent anomalies are most common in the fields of sex and of personal and social bond formation.

SEXUAL ANOMALIES

Anomalies in this sphere are certainly frequent, but the student should be aware of the very wide variations in practices, beliefs, attitudes, and feelings which exist within our own culture and in the world at large.

Homosexuality
Homosexuality means having a sexual propensity for members of one's own sex. Both the strength and the expression of this propensity vary in different individuals, and can also vary in the same individual during different epochs in life. For example, a homosexual phase is quite common in adolescence and should not cause undue alarm or concern.

Homosexuality is not an 'all or none' condition, and all gradations exist between apparently exclusive life-long 100 per cent homosexuality without any conscious capacity for arousal by heterosexual stimuli, and apparently exclusive heterosexuality without any conscious capacity for arousal by homosexual stimuli.

Kinsey has proposed a seven-point rating scale for the homosexual/heterosexual continuum, with a maximum of 6 points for exclusively homosexual arousals and activity, 0 for exclusive heterosexuality, 3 for arousals and acts equally with either sex, and intermediate scores accordingly.

The prevalence of homosexuality is a matter of definition. Thus, according to the psychoanalytic school a homosexual component (sometimes conscious but often not), exists in everybody and, if this is correct, homosexuality in this sense is universal. But even if the criterion for homosexuality is confined to overt homosexual activities, the prevalence that is claimed comes to many as a surprise, and Kinsey's findings that 37 per cent of the total male population have had at least some overt homosexual experiences to the point of orgasm between adolescence and old age provoked indignant scepticism. The lowest figure given in evidence to the Wolfenden Committee suggests that 1 per cent of all males are exclusively homosexual and that another 4 per cent have both homosexual and heterosexual impulses, and the Swedish authorities who provided these figures considered them too low.

Much more has been written about homosexuality in males than in females, and neither the law nor public opinion has been so concerned about the latter. According to Kinsey 4 per cent of adult single women are exclusively homosexual (lesbian), but one informed British estimate is of less than 2 per cent.

The main point to bear in mind is that a homosexual act or series of acts does not necessarily imply that the individual is the possessor of a predominantly homosexual make-up with a Kinsey rating of, say, 5 or 6.

Causation

No physical pathology has as yet been demonstrated, and nearly all biochemical and chromosomal investigations have been negative or inconclusive. Animal experiments show that the injection of male or female hormones into the pregnant female at certain critical periods of foetal development can produce homosexual behaviour in the offspring without any apparent physical deviation. On the whole individuals fit well into the 'gender role' in which they have been brought up, even when they have sexual ambiguities such as hermaphroditism. In some cases however, where the underlying endocrine sexuality has been in opposition to the apparent sex, there has been a breakthrough of the opposing biological sexual features at puberty. Another factor indicating the importance of biological factors is the genetic evidence from identical and non-identical twins, although the concordance is not as high as earlier work suggested.

Environmental factors which seem to be of importance have been demonstrated in several independent studies, but they do not apply to all cases. An absent or weak and passive father, with the development of a very close and intimate relationship with the mother, is associated with an increased incidence of homosexuality in males, especially in youngest sons. There is less agreement about the family situation with lesbians. It is probably best to view homosexuality as a kind of 'final common pathway' with several possible causes. Homosexual behaviour occurs in all human societies, and in nearly all mammalian species so the potential is probably present in everyone. Once homosexual patterns are established they may be kept going and reinforced more by social factors than by purely sexual ones, particularly in those many homosexual men in whom fear of women and a profound lack of confidence in their own masculinity leads to avoidance of heterosexual contact. Whatever the causes in the individual, the main features of psychosexual development have been laid down by puberty, and it is at this age that many individuals suddenly realise their sexual direction. The role of homosexual seduction is of little importance, and parents can be reassured on this point. Their own anxieties may well do more harm than the seduction itself.

Activities
The most frequent homosexual activity is masturbation with homosexual phantasies, and the proportion of homosexual, as opposed to heterosexual, phantasies in masturbation, both in the past and in the present, is a valuable indication of the Kinsey rating. Other common homosexual activities include mutual masturbation, bodily contact with ejaculation inter femora, oral-genital relations (fellatio) and anal intercourse (buggery or sodomy). Individuals have their preferences or antipathies, but the majority of practising homosexuals indulge at some time or other in all types of homosexual activity both actively and passively.

Classification
What actually takes place physically or in phantasy is far less important than the preferred age of the sexual partner. Homosexuals can be divided rather sharply into those who are attracted by prepubertal boys (paedophiliacs, or child molesters as the Americans call them), and those who are not. The overlap between these two groups is small, in the order, perhaps, of 3 per cent, and many of this overlap group are obviously unstable psychopathic individuals. Further, only a very small minority of the total homosexual population are paedophiliacs, and the popular concept of a sort of Rake's Progress, according to which those who indulge in homosexual activities with young men or youths are likely to end up by buggering little boys, has no foundation in fact. This main

division between those homosexuals who are attracted by children and those who are not is a far more fundamental one than whether homosexuals are active or passive, which may vary according to circumstances.

Personality types and associated psychiatric abnormalities

The majority of homosexuals do not differ in any obvious way from the rest of the population, and exhibitionistic feminine pansies form a small minority. We believe, however, that it is, on the whole, true that homosexuals tend to view people and problems from a personal angle. This is especially so in questions involving feelings, artistic appreciation and emotional nuances, and, whilst it can make for great consideration and understanding, it can also lead to touchiness and cattiness. Again, whilst it is true that homosexuals are not usually effete or depraved, it is not true that homosexuality is necessarily associated with any special talent, nor is homosexuality confined to the intelligentsia. Quite a number of homosexuals are just dull oafs.

It must be borne in mind that psychiatrists see highly selected homosexuals. Now that the law allows homosexual acts between consenting adults, and as public attitudes have become more tolerant, the homosexual is under less severe stress and it is our impression that many fewer homosexuals are seeking medical help. Anxiety and depression were very frequently seen in men, to whom a fear of exposure was often terrifying. Perhaps because of the more tolerant attitudes to female homosexuality, few lesbians ever presented to doctors. Those homosexuals who do seek help are those unable to accept their own deviance, often guilty and ashamed; and those in whom homosexual attraction or acts threatens the stability of their marriage. Paedophiliacs still seek help, often under legal duress, and there has been no increase in tolerance towards them.

Promiscuity is a striking characteristic of many homosexuals, and there is some evidence that the more promiscuous tend to be less stable. It is also our impression that homosexuals as a group tend to be more persistently preoccupied with sexual thoughts than are heterosexually orientated individuals.

The assessment of homosexuality

Homosexual arousals and homosexual acts may have a totally different significance, both as regards prognosis and treatment, in different individuals. For example, the same homosexual act (and it must be remembered that so far as males are concerned all homosexual acts at a genital level committed with others, whether private or public, were until 1968 criminal offences), may be committed as a piece of adolescent experimentation, or it may be the result of temporary or permanent mental or physical disorder or disease, or it may be part of the individual's life style.

The following headings may be found convenient when confronted with a homosexual problem:

1. Transitional homosexuality. As already mentioned, homosexual arousals that may lead to homosexual acts are quite common in adolescence, and they are often best regarded as merely manifestations of sex without special significance.

2. What might be called the true homosexual with a Kinsey rating of 5 or 6, who only seeks other men as partners.

3. The bisexual individual who may have made some kind of heterosexual adjustment, perhaps a very satisfying one, but who still seeks or desires homosexual relations.

4. The facultative homosexual, who is predominantly heterosexual, but who takes part in some form of homosexual activity on rare occasions or in exceptional circumstances, e.g. on board ship or in the Services, and

5. The psychopath who may indulge in any kind of sexual activity as the opportunity arises.

Treatment
The object of treatment can be arbitrarily divided under four main headings:

1. Change in the direction of the sexual urge.
2. Greater continence.
3. Greater discretion, and
4. A better adaptation to the sexual problem and to life in general.

Broadly speaking, established homosexuality, when there is good reason to suppose the patient should reasonably be regarded as a Kinsey 5 or 6, is a condition which seldom, if ever, undergoes spontaneous resolution. Psychoanalysis, which has made the study of sexuality its special province, has not on the whole offered special hope or expectation of cure. Recently, however, American analysts have made claims of quite high success rates in helping homosexuals to become more heterosexual. Endocrine treatment has no effect in changing any sexual orientation. But in certain cases where male homosexuals fear to sin or to incur social disapproval through lack of control, their urges may be reduced or abolished by hormone treatment. Female hormones or analogues such as ethinyl oestradiol 0.05 mg once daily or more often can be given, but these have the disadvantage of producing feminisation. Benperidol, a butyrophenone sometimes lessens or abolishes libido by some central action on brain stem structures without feminisation or other hormonal effects. The main use of these methods is in the paedophiliac. In some countries castration is used at times.

Another method, in line with the 'aversion treatment' of alcoholism (see p. 325) and the 'deconditioning treatment' of other conditions, is the attempt to 'avert' patients from and 'decondition' them to homosexuality on the supposition that the latter is a 'learned' reaction which it is possible for them to 'unlearn'. Accordingly, and after mutual discussion as to the type of stimulus most likely to cause arousal, experiments are designed in which patients are exposed to such stimuli (photographs, vocal recordings, personal appearances), and are subjected to unpleasant concomitant stimuli such as electric shocks, which may cause them to associate with displeasure what was previously considered to be pleasurable. Ingenuity may be needed in the design. These behavioural methods now have an established value in treating highly motivated patients, and naturally succeed best in those people who have sizeable heterosexual interests already (p. 210).

Discussion in order to explain the transitional nature of the difficulty can be of value in the transitional group of homosexuals, and it is perhaps wise to hold out hope of a change in sexual orientation even in those who seem predominantly homosexual who are under the age of twenty-five, and to suggest, for example, they should seek opportunities for heterosexual arousal. For those with a definitely high Kinsey rating, in practice the doctor usually has to be content with trying to make the patient better adjusted to his handicap. Discussion of the problem may much ease the patient's mind. The avoidance of special situations and environments provacative of sexual feelings is to be encouraged. Where satisfaction cannot be gained from the sex life it must be sought in other directions, in the development of special hobbies and interests, in suitable social contacts, as well as in the working life. With the recent upsurge of homosexual societies and clubs, and amid the well publicised demands for 'gay liberation', it is much easier for the homosexual, in big cities at least, to feel at home in at least some part of society. Those who are unable to profit personally from these changes are mainly those with other neurotic or personality difficulties who would find life difficult even if they were heterosexual.

OTHER SEXUAL ANOMALIES

It is not possible to describe all these. They are commoner than might be supposed but usually come to the notice of the physician only when they have led to some social embarrassment, or have caused concern by becoming actual *perversions*, i.e. have come to dominate the sexual life instead of being merely a part of it. Perversions are curiously rare in women and in psychotic patients.

The commonest are exhibitionism, sadism and masochism. But there are also the trans-sexualists, i.e. men who wish to become women and, less commonly, women who wish to become men.

Exhibitionism. This is most often committed by a man of reserved nature, with marked inferiority feelings, who is usually either impotent or has no experience of even attempting intercourse. The act is usually one of suddenly opening a raincoat to expose the erect penis to some girl or woman in a quiet public place, but sometimes it may be done standing at a bedroom window. The man concerned seeks to shock and frighten, rather than to lead on to a sexual encounter. To be met with unconcern or even by laughter from some sophisticated person is felt as deeply wounding. The exhibitionistic act is a primitive and infantile way of reassuring the man about his manhood and potency. Treatment is essentially by psychotherapy, and aims at stopping the exhibitionism and helping the patient both to gain his self-esteem and to cope with his inferiority feelings in a different way. It is rarely very helpful.

In *sadism*, sexual pleasure is gained or enhanced by the exhibition of physical cruelty. This may occur during love play or intercourse, or apart from them. It may even occur without any basis in reality, as in sadistic phantasy (a main interest of the Marquis de Sade, after whom the condition is named). In masochism sexual pleasure is gained or enhanced by the subjective experience of pain, which may range from a mild infliction to severe flagellation. This, again, may or may not accompany other sexual activity, may occur only in phantasy, or may be self-inflicted by the subject when alone, then usually as a prelude to masturbation. Allied to masochism are such abnormalities as deriving sexual pleasure from being handcuffed or tied up. The condition is named after Sacher-Masoch who described his own state in his novels.

Combinations of sadism and masochism are particularly common, but as a rule several perversions will be observed in the same person, and the exhibition of only one is unusual. It is rare for sadists or masochists to seek psychiatric help for the sexual deviation, and when they do it is almost always at the instigation of the spouse, who threatens to leave.

In *Fetishism* sexual interest is diverted from normal intercourse onto objects which become sexually rewarding and satisfying in themselves when used in masturbation. The commonest articles are of women's underwear, but there is a curious and unexplained frequency of interest in shiny black leather and rubber clothing (testified to in the advertisement columns of newspapers). Other common fetish objects are shoes or slippers and silky objects. A considerable interest in all of these things, except black rubber or leather, is very common in normal sexual relationships, but it becomes a perversion when the fetish object becomes the main interest. There is commonly present a markedly obsessional element, and the impulses may be struggled against. However, the deviant sexual feelings are not seen as somehow silly or inappropriate as classical obsessional symptoms are.

Transvestism is also quite common and can be considered as of two almost distinct types, although in both men dress up in women's clothing. In the first type the women's clothing is clearly an elaborate fetish object, is associated with sexual excitement, and the man concerned either masturbates or has intercourse while so dressed. Such people may seek psychiatric help at the instigation of the spouse. It is important to note that this is not associated with homosexuality or transexualism (q.v.) or any desire to live as a woman. The second type does show some overlap with the first, but the essential difference is that the man does not seek excitement so much as a feeling of peace and contentment, and is often at his happiest sitting reading or watching television while dressed like this. These people however, are still heterosexual in their main drives, see themselves as men, and are not transexual, although obviously rather nearer to that position.

The *causes* of these abnormalities are complicated. In general, perversions can be regarded as gross exaggerations of sexual features that are not in themselves abnormal. Thus, a degree of self-display is not abnormal in sexual intimacy; in exhibitionism it is exaggerated until it becomes a substitute. Aggressiveness and submissiveness, and combinations of both, are involved in all personal relationships; where the relationship is close and emotional, they may become associated with and an integral part of love itself. Underlying a state of sexual excitement there may normally be an aggressive quality which is the accompaniment of a man wishing to wreak his will. The man who is 'a slave to his lover' may feel an erotic pleasure in submissiveness. These may be exaggerated into a sexual assaultiveness and an amorous self-abasement. Such developments are presumably facilitated by the close association, from whatever cause, between sexual excitement and pain. The assaultiveness and self-abasement, each with its painful association, may then become an integral part of the sexual excitement—in perversion, its most important part.

The predilections for special materials seem to arise partly from a visual and tactile appreciation which adds an aesthetic element to sexual feeling, and partly from association of ideas that may be peculiar to the person and may have its roots deep in his history. An example was of a man with a fetish of high heeled shoes. He had been brought up principally by servants and had longed for more contact with his mother. He recalled how he had spied on her as she dressed to go out in the evening, but through the keyhole his field of vision was restricted to her legs, feet and high heeled slippers.

The development of these tendencies into actual perversions seems to be in line with the constitutional trends. The sadist, although his sadistic qualities may be circumscribed, may have qualities of aggressiveness and waspishness with an emotional appreciation of situations that involve others in distress. The masochist, although his masochistic tendencies may be circumscribed, may tend to play a passive and submissive role in his general life, and to take pleasure in acts that come near to self-punishment. The exhibitionist tends to be a showman in various ways. The lover of mackintosh, leather and silk tends to lead a rich sensory life, with attention to shapes, colours, scents, and the tactile and textural qualities of objects.

Circumstances themselves, as well as the constitutional trends, may aid these developments which are often assisted by lack of more normal sexual satisfaction, and so are more likely to arise where the circumstances impose frustration.

Prognostically, what is important is not the queerness of the abnormality itself, but the extent to which it interferes with the patient's actual performance. It may be a dominant feature to the extent that it worries the patient, but it is not prognostically ominous unless it shows signs of itself becoming a preferred substitute to more normal sexual activity, instead of an accompaniment. The more that it is confined to phantasy, and at the same time the less that it interferes with performance, the better is the prognosis.

Treatment is, for the most part, unsatisfactory. Exhibitionists are exceedingly difficult to treat on all counts. Psychotherapy hardly ever, if ever, succeeds, and we have no evidence that the results of psychoanalysis are any better. Even repeated imprisonment seems to have little deterrent effect. Sadism and masochism, if tendencies rather than established perversions, may show improvement if the patient succeeds in checking his indulgence in these directions and then achieves a satisfactory marital relationship. As with homosexuality, discussion may reduce the patient's concern, and he may then be less dominated by and therefore more master of such trends through seeing them in better perspective and with less in the way of associated emotionalism. Once the trends have become established perversions, the therapeutic opportunities are small, especially since they have a pleasurable quality which the patient will not wish to lose. Aversion therapy (p. 325) can be very helpful in the fetishistic disorders, when the subject is highly motivated to change.

Trans-sexualists
These patients, though rare, seem to be increasing in number and may present grave problems. They are usually men without chromosomal abnormality who wish to become women and often have been living as such; much less commonly, they are women who wish to become men. They complain that they are spiritually imprisoned in a body of the wrong sex and of severe frustration as regards expressing and fulfilling themselves. For those who come for consultation, the mere adoption of the opposite sexual role is not enough, and they may not be satisfied by anything short of an actual physical change. At first sight one supposes them to be crazed, probably schizophrenic. One hopes that the plastic surgeons, who have developed techniques for dealing with these patients but who are alert to the psychiatric aspects, have failed to notice treatable psychotic features. Sometimes the latter exist, in which event surgical intervention is probably inadvisable owing to the unpredictability of the outcome. Far more often, though they tend to be unstable and exhibitionistic, these patients are not psychotic at all. With increasing experience one realises that most of them are desperate and desperately sincere, often with a history of suicidal attempts, and the resolution with which they pursue their intention can be very striking. One of our patients, with some surgical knowledge, performed a bilateral orchidectomy on himself in two stages, and finally achieved a physical 'sex change' through further plastic surgery after years of unremitting effort, for which it appears that 'she' is much the happier after an apparently successful marriage to another man. We could tell of others just as determined. We have heard of patients having subsequent regrets but have seen several who have undoubtedly benefited. There are difficulties both as regards psychiatric recommendation and surgical technique.

Before surgery is performed the man should have oestrogens to increase breast size and diminish facial hair; and should live for at least a year as a woman in every possible way. Before and after surgery a great deal of counselling and other help may be needed.

DISORDERS OF PERSONALITY

A study of the personality of a patient is always of psychiatric importance, for no abnormal mental state can be properly understood without taking the personality into account. Such study may be essential in deciding whether the mental state constitutes, so to say, an illness in its own right, as being different from anything that has gone before, or is explicable, on the other hand, as the reaction of the particular personality to the experiences that have been undergone. Different approaches to the assessment and description of personality are outlined at the beginning of this chapter.

There is general agreement that many abnormal and unusual people exist who, though not suffering from any of the more formally recognised forms of mental disorder, may yet constitute psychiatric problems. Their recognition and classification has great social and psychiatric importance. Unfortunately, there is not the same agreement as to how such abnormal and unusual people should be classified, nor as to the terms that should be used for this purpose. One difficulty lies in the lack of agreed definitions, as for instance the different uses of the term 'psychopathic'. Although several different types are described in this section the limitations of personality assessment should be borne in mind.

The schizoid personality

This is not a uniform type, but personalities described under this heading show a combination of the characteristics commonly found among the families of schizophrenics (which is the original meaning of the term schizoid). In general, the personality tends to be introverted, with emotions that are cold, leading to aloofness and seclusiveness, with interests of an intellectual and abstract sort, often nature-loving, and with an inclination towards contemplation rather than activity, in line with the fact that the reserves of energy are usually small. To that extent there tends to be fair uniformity, but in addition schizoid personalities may be ruthless, as part of their emotional coldness, or passive and withdrawing from competition when opposition is offered. To many also may be added qualities of queerness, eccentricity and oddness, and to others paranoid features of either aggressive or passive kind. Thus, the dreamy, bearded, sandalled denizen of Bloomsbury or Montmartre is often a schizoid personality, just as much as is the wild-eyed, fanatical adherent of some political or religious sect. There is some correlation between the schizoid personality and an asthenic physique (see p. 29), and a tendency towards schizophrenic breakdown.

The cyclothymic (cycloid) personality

These frequently occur in the families of manic-depressives. They tend to be extraverted, good-natured, with emotional warmth and sympathetic responsiveness, sociable and adaptable, energetic and preferring activity to contemplation, practical and well in touch. There is some correlation between the cycloid personality and the pyknic build ('the 16-in neck in the 14-in collar') and with a tendency to cyclothymia (see p. 29).

But as Nature is never tidy, not all who are liable to mood-swings have these engaging characteristics. Those whose moods veer mainly downwards are often normally 'half a bottle below par'. Those whose moods veer mainly upwards are often unable to brook opposition and readily pass into an excited paranoid pet. The behaviour of certain surgeons when vexed by difficulties in the operating theatre is often of this type.

The hysterical personality

This is the type that is liable to show hysterical symptoms *par excellence*, but it must be remembered that very many patients who show hysterical symptoms are not hysterical personalities (see p. 268). A cardinal feature is the patient's desire to appear more than he (or more usually she) really is, with which is coupled a striking skill in self-deception. Hysterics are fond of picturing themselves in dramatic and romantic roles, and their emotions are vivid but shallow. They are easily influenced by people or ideas that appeal to them: they have a remarkable capacity for identifying themselves with, and imitating, others, and for dedicating themselves to various transient ideals. But these enthusiasms change readily. They are sentimental rather than realistic, often histrionic, and when confronted with difficulties tend to dodge them by taking flight into emotionalism rather than adopting effective action. They are immature in their thinking and emotional reactions, often sexually frigid and frequently incapable of long-term affection or sustained sexual relationships, though they are good short-term flirts and know how to dally with the other sex to satisfy their vanity. The instability of their emotions, vivid phantasy, and lack of solid qualities make hysterical personalities untruthful and unreliable, although they believe themselves to be candid. In fact, they deceive themselves more successfully than others. Hysterical conversion symptoms often provide the means by which they try to dominate their surroundings, with varying degrees of success.

The obsessional (anancastic) personality

This is not always traceable in the history of patients with obsessional neurosis, nor do obsessional personalities necessarily break down with obsessional symptoms by any means. The characteristics are tendencies to excessive neatness and meticulousness, undue caution and over-conscientiousness. In making decisions such people weigh each *pro* and *con*, repeatedly considering the matter from every aspect. They give their history with much detail and care, not so much from egocentricity as from anxiety not to mislead; they subsequently worry lest they have made omissions, and may either return to make a correction or send a letter to make some unnecessary addition. They tend repeatedly to make sure, and check and re-check their work, live by routine, and have 'a place for everything and everything in its place'. They are irked by things being out of place, cannot tolerate crooked pictures or things left undone, and do not adapt well to sudden changes. They are thus rigid and worrying. They show persistent unsatisfiable ways of thinking in an attempt to reach order and perfection—'attempting to unscrew the inscrutable' as one patient put it. Their attitude to health is similar; they tend to be more irked and pre-occupied by symptoms than the ordinary person. They commonly have qualities of considerable endurance, however, and the obsessional personality as such seldom calls for psychiatric aid.

It may be added that it is not justifiable to label as obsessional those people who are merely conscientious.

The paranoid personality

These are people who are persistently touchy, ready to feel aggrieved and put upon, prone to hold grievances and to be suspicious of the motives of those around them. On this account they often do not adjust well to society, and they are then liable to blame others for that maladjustment. Certain personality characteristics encourage the development of paranoid trends. Thus, rigid people have more difficulty in adjustment than do adaptable people, and are apt to be more put out by such difficulty. Aggressive people are more likely to feel aggrieved than are submissive people. Conceited people are more likely to feel slighted than are people characterised by humility. Over-sensitive people are more likely to be upset by, and see significance in, a casual attitude or unfriendliness shown to them by others. Dullards and the subnormal are more likely to be put upon than the normally bright and their attitudes may be coloured by this or the fear of it. When these characteristics of rigidity, aggressiveness, conceit, over-sensitiveness and low intelligence are combined, even in varying proportions, in one personality, paranoid developments are far more likely to occur than in someone who is adaptable, modest and ready to take the rough with the smooth.

Circumstances may also encourage the development of the paranoid personality, such as restriction of freedom, continued frustration in whatever sphere, and prolonged failure.

Physical disturbances may aid paranoid developments through increasing the irritability and over-sensitiveness of the personality, as when a patient is subjected to prolonged and nagging discomfort from physical symptoms, or from a menopausal upset, or is prevented from normal activity or social intercourse by physical handicap. Deafness is of special consequence in this connection and so is chronic alcoholism. The former cuts the patient off severely from society, leaves him uncertain of what is happening or being said, and so provides a good soil for suspiciousness to flourish in. Chronic alcoholism encourages the failure from which paranoid developments often stem, and destroys those inhibitory faculties that make for reasonableness and well-balanced judgments, so that the latter became increasingly impaired as deterioration occurs.

Vulnerable personalities
These form a less clear-cut group. They are potentially unstable people and bad psychiatric risks. They are all liable to breakdown, but to break down in various ways, and in different ways at different times. Handicapped by constitutional loading, they have a small margin of reserve, and when pinched by circumstances are liable to develop various neurotic reactions as well as 'short-circuit' uncontrolled or explosive outbursts. They may show one sort of reaction at one time, and another at a later one: or, if lucky, they may pass through life without overt symptoms. In general, they are inadequate.

Scrutiny of such a case is liable to show a poor heredity, neurotic behaviour in childhood, poor work and health record, and more or less in the way of previous breakdown.

Salient personality characteristics are a low physical and mental voltage with a lack of resilience and plasticity, with tendencies to disapprove of more, to be afraid of more, and to enjoy less than is normal. They often have difficulty in mixing, inferiority feelings, and an egocentric tendency to protect themselves from potentially stressful situations.

When breakdown occurs the commonest forms are states of anxiety or depression, or both combined, irritability and fatigue, poorly controlled emotionalism of non-specific sort, and explosive outbursts.

This is the first type of abnormal personality so far considered that may call for *treatment* in itself. The first thing to consider is the prevention of breakdown, and this must depend on the degree of vulnerability, and therefore the degree of shelter from the buffets of life that such a personality may require. The assessment is best made on consideration of the facts as shown by the life-history, and the main indications on which an opinion can be formed are discussed on pages 79–81. The practical value of preventing breakdown by trying to fit pegs into more or less appropriate holes was shown very clearly in the last war. Where breakdown has actually occurred, the treatment must be symptomatic in the first instance, with removal from the precipitating situation if the state is sufficiently severe to call for it. This may be followed by trying to make readjustments in the personality by better use of the assets, re-education of unsound attitudes, and an environmental re-arrangement designed to minimise the risk of further breakdown.

Finally, it may be well to point out that vulnerable personalities, though in varying degrees inadequate, may yet possess certain worthwhile qualities. They are by no means necessarily to be sneezed at, for they may have much value within their limitations. A medical education tends to encourage a certain distrust of the graces coupled with an inordinate appreciation of the homespun virtues, so that doctors are prone to deplore inadequacy. Yet a good ballet dancer and an intelligent but hypochondriacal leader-writer may be more unstable, but are likely to be more interesting and amusing than a good average-adjuster: nor contribute less to the gaiety or pleasure of nations.

Psychopathic (sociopathic) personalities

The cardinal feature of this group, as the term is used here, is seen in their asocial or antisocial behaviour. The psychopath acts without regard for the consequences, and in accord with his more or less immediate desires. He has a *very poor tolerance of frustration*, and whatever he wants—he wants it now! These desires frequently change, so that there is lack of perseverance and repeated change of goals. In following his own desires he is unwilling to subordinate himself to those of other people, and so is unscrupulous, egocentric and a misfit in society. As he acts without regard for the consequences, he frequently gets into difficulty and embroils others in difficulty also. The most remarkable feature is the failure to learn from experience, so that psychopaths make the *same mistakes* again and again, undeterred either by repeated failure or punishment. They are incapable of long-term plans, and are as débris on the sea of life, floating from job to job, but frequently submerged.

Emotional reactions of any sort may occur, such as sudden attacks of depression in response to some reverse, often ill-controlled and with much self-pity, sudden developments of anxiety when embroiled in some difficulty, uncontrolled rage which may result in throwing the china in a domstic tiff or in crimes of violence. Resort to alcohol (and less commonly to other drugs) often occurs. Impulsive suicidal gestures, especially in association with alcohol, are frequent, though actual suicide is uncommon.

It is easy to see how psychopaths, following their characteristic pattern of irresponsible behaviour, may drift into criminality. Not all criminals, of course, are psychopaths, but an appreciable proportion are, and number among their ranks seducers, bigamists, confidence men, prostitutes, common adventurers and *pathological liars* who talk without the least regard for truth however certain their detection, for the sake of the immediate impression that they like to be able to make.

There are, of course, degrees in these things. The foregoing account presents a reasonably characteristic picture. But there are also modified forms of psychopathy. For example, a man may be irresponsible, changeable and unreliable in his domestic relationships but yet may stick at a job which satisfies him; or he may repeatedly and irresponsibly change jobs, show no social conscience, and yet sometimes stick to the woman of his choice in defiance of the usual rule that psychopaths show no constant or satisfactory personal relationships.

The foregoing are the general features which are more or less common to all psychopaths, but the latter can be further subdivided and classified to some extent. It is common to divide them into those that are predominantly inadequate, and those that are predominantly aggressive.

The *predominantly inadequate* have something in common with the feebler types of vulnerable personality, but show additional features of irresponsibility, lack of social conscience, and inability to learn from experience. These features, together with their lack of will-power and determination, are shown in their careers. Weak-willed and easily tired, they provide many of life's failures.

The *predominantly aggressive* type is actively antisocial rather than merely a burden on others. The aggressiveness may take the form of the so-called 'short-circuit' (i.e. uncontrolled and explosive) reactions already mentioned. But that is not necessarily so. It may take more the form of a cold ruthlessness, with an unemotional absence of guilt or shame, which enables its possessor to prosecute unscrupulous schemes, and to pursue with complete sangfroid courses of action which he knows to spell ruin to others.

This brings us to a second conception of psychopaths, and one which is rather in fashion at the present time; that which takes special account of their emotional peculiarities. That they have emotional peculiarities is implicit in the above description, and these are usually seen in one of two forms; the emotions shown are either excessive or inadequate. These two peculiarities may be found in the same person, as when a psychopath may be quite untouched by some cruel and conscienceless act that he has committed, but may show an excessively emotional tantrum on being himself criticised. In general, however, it is possible to consider psychopaths under two headings in this connection: (1) those in whom emotional excesses predominate, (2) those who show poverty of emotion as a predominant feature. The former group comprises those who show most in the way of neurotic traits and neurotic reactions. The latter are less subject to breakdown, but may become the subjects of psychiatric care owing to collision with society or the law. The distinction along these lines may have implications of aetiological importance.

The *aetiology* of psychopathic personality is a difficult and un-solved problem. The family background of many is turbulent and chaotic, often marked by violence and poverty, and with no steady loving parent. It seems that to have a promiscuous and psychopa-thic mother is even more likely to have severe ill effects on a child than to have an equally disturbed father. Genetic factors are also important, as has been confirmed recently by studies of twins brought up together and apart. Everyone with psychiatric exper-ience has come across instances where a grossly psychopathic personality has emerged from circumstances which in themselves could in no way be incriminated for such a development. Other factors which seem to be relevant in some psychopaths include perinatal brain injury and encephalitis or other brain infections in childhood. In some large and muscular criminal psychopaths an abnormal chromosome pattern (XYY) seems more common than in the normal population.

The chances of psychopathic personalities developing is en-hanced by the frequency with which psychopathic persons marry each other. The subjects of this personality often feel inferior to, and therefore repelled by, more stable people, but are attracted by those ready to show an irresponsibility similar to their own; thus, a person who contracts an impulsive and ill-conceived marriage is likely to have chosen an impulsive and unstable partner. At once, the psychological factors may be set in train as far as the development of the children is concerned, as well as the hereditary ones.

As regards physical factors, there is similar variation. Physical anomalies are frequent in psychopathic personalities; such are an asthenic build, disproportion in physique, underdevelopment of secondary sex characteristics, vasomotor instability, and an allergic disposition. Many psychopaths, on the other hand, have excellent physiques. A special peculiarity worthy of note is the occurrence of cerebral dysrhythmia, i.e. of abnormal electrical discharges from the brain as recorded by the electroencephalograph. This is mainly found in the aggressive type of psychopath, and according to some authorities may occur in 65 per cent of them, as compared with 10 per cent in the ordinary population. The nature of the dysrhythmia has much in common with that shown by the chronologically immature, and so suggests some failure in the normal process of central nervous maturation.

In summary, it will be seen that the answers are not known. There are various clues, but there are no satisfactory formulae. Aetiologically, each case must be judged on its merits. Many will be found to have no satisfactory explanation.

As regards *course and prognosis* it is worth noting that a considerable number of cases who have shown erratic and difficult behaviour of a tiresome kind contrive to settle down despite every expectation to the contrary. This is especially so where persistent behaviour of a psychopathic kind has been shown by adolescents, and it is so to such an extent that those who are specially experienced in this field consider it imprudent to make a diagnosis of established psychopathic personality before the patient has reached twenty-five years of age. Remarkable transformations can occur in adolescence and early adulthood, and many authorities consider them to depend far more on the normal process of maturation than upon the effects of treatment. Of the cases who continue to show persistent psychopathic behaviour after the age of twenty-five, it is also true that an appreciable percentage show signs of increasing stability in the early thirties. Unfortunately, in the present state of knowledge it is not possible to predict which will do well and which will not, with few exceptions. In this connection, however, the point previously mentioned in relation to the affective peculiarities is of some consequence. There is more hope of improvement in those cases characterised by emotional excesses than in those characterised by emotional poverty. It is as though the latter have an essential deficiency which nothing can remedy: whereas the difficulties of the former arise not so much from an essential deficiency as from a relative failure of control which may be remedied by the normal process of maturation on which nervous integration depends, even though this may be delayed. Unfortunately, in many cases it seems to be delayed indefinitely.

The *differential diagnosis* is important between those cases who show *episodic* and those cases who show *persistent* psychopathic behaviour. It is only the latter who can properly be diagnosed as suffering from psychopathic personality. This is to say, some patients may legitimately be considered to show transient *psychopathic reactions*, between which episodes they may be relatively normal. Such come within the category of the vulnerable rather than the psychopathic personality. An essential feature of the latter is its persistence, and the point is of prognostic and therapeutic signficance in that the transient and episodic reactions are far more likely to respond to suitable environmental rearrangement.

As regards *treatment* of the psychopathic personality, much justifiable pessimism is felt. The inadequate psychopath may show greater steadiness under firm guidance, especially if under the thumb of a suitable wife. Some may be helped by periodic and regular attendance in an out-patients department, where they can ventilate their difficulties, discharge their emotions, and be subject to a steadying influence much as though they were reporting to a sympathetic probation officer. Aggressive psychopaths will be more difficult to manage as their explosions are liable to have taken place, and their consequences to have been set in train, so rapidly and unpredictably as to have anticipated any steadying influence that might otherwise have been offered. In essence the psychopathic person can be helped to feel better if he is anxious or depressed, and it can have a steadying influence if he becomes attached to a doctor or social worker who is prepared to give him some time. There is, however, no evidence that treatment affects the underlying personality disorder. In-patient treatment of psychopathic people should be kept as brief as possible, in for example the treatment of depression, as such patients often have a very disruptive effect on the ward. Certain special units have concentrated on providing help for psychopathic people, using intensive group therapy methods and trying to involve all the patients in the life and activities of the hospital community. Unfortunately no evidence has been produced which allows an assessment of the value of the method, although it has been very influential. In general, transformations through treatment do not occur in psychopathic personalities. Yet, the ultimate results are not always as bad as common sense would expect.

We have now considered these main abnormalities of personality that fall within recognised psychiatric categories, the schizoid, cycloid, hysterical, and obsessional personalities, who are all more or less clearly distinguishable: the vulnerable personalities, who are less homogeneous: and finally, the psychopathic personalities, which term has here been taken to indicate the persistence of essentially antisocial qualities.

It will be realised that, as part of Nature's untidiness, there will still remain a number of curious, unusual, and interesting people encountered from time to time who, refreshingly enough, cannot be properly fitted into the foregoing categories which represent no more than the run of the mill as it turns in medical practice.

MENTAL SUBNORMALITY

This term has replaced, since the introduction of the Mental Health Act, 1959, the old term 'mental deficiency'. Mental subnormality is defined as 'a state of arrested or incomplete development of mind (not amounting to severe subnormality) which includes subnormality of intelligence and is of a nature or degree which requires or is susceptible to medical treatment or other special care or training of the patient'. Severe subnormality is defined as 'a state of arrested or incomplete development of mind which includes subnormality of intelligence and is of such a nature or degree that the patient is incapable of living an independent life or of guarding himself against exploitation, or will be so incapable when of an age to do so'. Mental subnormality may also be referred to as *amentia*, as opposed to *dementia*, which last means intellectual defect occurring for the first time in later life.

As will be seen later, in the large majority of cases of amentia the subnormal development can be regarded as a variation of the normal, comparable with very short people; these cases have been distinguished as 'sub-cultural aments' (E. O. Lewis) from the much smaller group of aments whose abnormalities are so gross that they cannot be considered variations of the normal, and for which there tend to be more or less specific and clear-cut causes. To continue the analogy of height, these last cases are not comparable to very short people, so much as to pathological dwarfs.

The Mental Health Act, 1959, does away with the old subdivisions of mental deficiency into various groups. Yet, though criticisms could be levelled at the old classification, the new system does little to answer them, and the old classification was changed mainly because people felt that the old terms: idiot, imbecile, and feeble-minded (moron), were almost terms of abuse, and that a change of name might lead to changed attitudes.

Intelligence level and social incapacity

The legal definitions of the old classification were not based on intellectual deficiency as such, and nor are the new ones given on the previous page. The essential issue is the problem of social incapacity.

It is important to be quite clear on this point; while intellectual ability as measured by intelligence tests is an important factor that must be given consideration, the social incapacity that constitutes mental subnormality does not depend on that alone. Recent work has drawn attention to the wide range of factors which should be taken into account such as those proffered by one author: 'genetic and developmental history, *present* intellectual ability, emotionality, economic status, family composition, status in family group, moral standards, vocational skill, community tolerance and potential or latent capacity for the development of social competence under favourable conditions.'

It may be emphasised that in order to classify in such a way as to lead to appropriate action being taken in both the individual's and the community's interests, far more is involved than a simple judgment based on the result of intelligence tests.

The intelligence level can be estimated with reasonable accuracy by tests and is then referred to as the Intelligence Quotient, or IQ (see page 238). The IQ expresses the intelligence as a percentage of the normal, which is taken as 100 per cent. Persons of average intelligence are grouped around the mean of 100, and an IQ of 75 is usually taken as the borderline of subnormality. This is arbitrary, and it has been pointed out that many patients in hospitals for the mentally subnormal have IQs above 70. The mental subnormality hospitals contain most of the very severely handicapped, and many who are much less handicapped, who could probably manage in residential homes and hostels with relatively little supervision, if the accommodation were available.

As the IQ rises above 60, a diminishing proportion show such a degree of social incapacity as to warrant detention under the Mental Health Act, and the indications for compulsory detention then increasingly depend on the existence of factors other than mere intellectual backwardness, such as anti-social behaviour or marked instability. Very special reasons of this kind must be present before persons with IQs of above 75 are recommended for compulsory detention on the ground of subnormality. If such reservations are not made a wide variety of people could be compulsorily detained under the Mental Health Act on the grounds of social incompetence irrespective of their actual intelligence quotient. Apart from the legal dangers of such procedures, the establishment of rehabilitation schemes for such a heterogeneous group as might thus be lumped together would be a hopeless and impossible task.

Incidence

Careful investigations into mental subnormality have suggested an incidence of a minimum of 8 per 1000 of the population, but since a high proportion of subnormal patients, especially of the severer kinds, die early in life it is considered likely that as many as 5 per cent of all children born are aments of one sort or another. Severe subnormality is much less common, and only about 3 in every 1000 school children has an IQ of below 50.

As has already been said, the great majority of the intellectually handicapped belong to the group of subnormal aments, whose intellectual deficits are not gross and whose low intelligence is a relatively mild variation from the normal. In practice, therefore, the most frequent problem is that of the dullard. A certain percentage of these are in fact compulsorily detained in institutions although the justification for this may be dubious from both medical and legal standpoints. They are usually socially incapacitated rather than psychiatrically ill, and while they may benefit from some psychiatric aid also require a considerable amount of general social assistance. Those who are not compulsorily detained, yet show some social incapacity in varying degrees, live at large and comprise quite a large section of the community.

Of cases suffering from mental subnormality, about 75 per cent have an IQ between 60 and 75, the remainder being below 60.

Aetiology

The causes, both known and unknown, of mental subnormality are numerous. They may be considered under two headings, *intrinsic* causes which lie in the individual's innate endowment, and *extrinsic* causes which are not innate but arise from the environment, e.g. injury or acquired disease. Where the mental subnormality arises from intrinsic causes, it is spoken of as *primary amentia*; where it arises from accidents of the environment it is called *secondary amentia*. The latter is said to account for only about 20 per cent of cases, but includes the majority of the more severe forms, i.e. idiots and imbeciles.

Intrinsic causes. Heredity is of the greatest importance, but can be over-emphasised. It is self-evident that if environmental factors are fairly constant, intelligence differences are largely accounted for by heredity. But where the environment provides severe adversity as is frequently found in the backgrounds of the feeble-minded group, both IQ and social differences can be attributed in part to these adverse influences. It has been shown that in the feeble-minded group, adverse social conditions and severe neglect have been known to retard intellectual development by an average of 16 IQ points. One stresses this, nevertheless, bearing in mind that within the feeble-minded group, mental subnormality does result from the cumulative effects of many genes. In the lower grades the subnormality often results from specific genes of major effect. For example, phenyl-pyruvic amentia, microcephaly and amaurotic family idiocy (*vide infra*) all arise from single recessive genes; and tuberose sclerosis (see p. 235) and the rare naevoid amentia arise from single dominant genes. Mongolism is associated with chromosomal abnormalities that are mentioned on page 236. In yet other conditions that appear innate, such as some cases of Little's disease, the causes may remain obscure, and are probably different in different cases.

Extrinsic causes. These are numerous and may be considered under three headings (1) *damage before birth*, (2) *damage at birth*, and (3) *damage after birth*.

Among the causes of *damage before birth* are (*a*) incompatibility of blood groups (Rhesus factor), and (*b*) the occurrence of Rubella in the mother during the first three months of pregnancy. The last is so potent a cause of secondary amentia, usually associated with deafness and cataracts, that the chances of the foetus being born defective are high. Intra-uterine infection with syphilis is a much less common cause of secondary amentia than formerly. (*c*) Heavy drinking and smoking by the pregnant woman can have quite serious effects on the intellectual development of the child.

Damage during birth may result not only from trauma due to obstetrical manoeuvres and from intracranial haemorrhage occurring as the result of a difficult labour, but also from the prolonged anoxaemia that a difficult birth may involve.

Secondary amentia arising from causes operating *after birth* is most often due to infections that damage the brain, such as encephalitis or meningitis. It also occurs as an accompaniment of cretinism.

Pathology

In primary amentia the degree of pathological changes that are found varies with the severity of the mental defect. In the severe forms there are obvious abnormalities in the cerebral structure, such as in weight, size, under-development of the convolutions, etc. Microscopically, there is underdevelopment, imperfect arrangement and a relative absence of cortical cells. Such special forms of primary amentia as tuberose sclerosis and amaurotic familial idiocy show special pathological features that are mentioned later (p. 235). The pathological changes found in the lesser degrees of primary amentia are less striking, and as a rule surprisingly slight; indeed, in many cases there may be no obvious abnormality at all. This is presumably an indication of the imperfections in our histological knowledge and techniques.

The pathological changes found in cases of secondary amentia will vary widely according to the nature of the underlying cause, whether direct injury, haemorrhage, infection, etc.

Clinical pictures

Severe subnormality. The essential criterion is the degree of independence of which the child (or adult) is capable. The IQ will be mainly below 45, and the most severely affected will be almost inaccessible, capable of little more than grunts and moans, incapable of walking unsupported, incontinent of urine and faeces, and needing total care to preserve life. In the upper reaches of this grade the individual will be able to converse simply and will be quite active physically, but will still need guarding from dangers, especially fire and traffic. Some will be capable of concentrating on assembly tasks in occupational therapy, and enjoy social interchange, games, and so on—depending of course on the presence or absence of the physical handicaps which often exist. Epilepsy is also common.

In those of a calm and sunny disposition the burden of care is very different from those who are aggressive, prone to tantrums, or otherwise turbulent.

Subnormality. Most in this group will have an IQ between 50 and 70, and of course in the upper reaches are likely to be living in society without any special problems. They do need special schooling to help them learn to read and write, and many fail to cope with these skills. At work they are capable of enjoyable and productive jobs, and may live quite normally, including bringing up children. Their work is best simple and repetitive. There are many such jobs which are too boring for people of higher intelligence, although progressively fewer with technological change.

The medical profession has little need to be involved with the higher grade subnormals, unless they become ill or emotionally disturbed, and their care and supervision is largely the task of the educational and social services. In the lower grades there are often associated physical and mental anomalies which require nursing and medical care.

Psychiatric illness is common in the mentally subnormal, who are prone to psychotic episodes, often difficult to diagnose in the conventional categories; they are also rather more likely to develop schizophrenic illnesses than the intellectually better endowed. When schizophrenia does develop the prognosis is poor. Illnesses resembling bipolar manic-depressive psychoses are also quite common, and, depending on the level of verbal communication present, these may mainly present as episodes of over-activity or of retardation. In those of a higher grade of intelligence, depression often presents with bizarre hypochondriacal complaints. A careful comparative account by someone who knows the patient well is often most useful here.

The mentally subnormal do tend to find life difficult. Even the more intelligent are slow to learn and easily bewildered, and in many there is a lack of foresight, poor tolerance of frustration, and a tendency to be easily led astray. As a result they are often repeatedly involved in petty crime, sometimes by more intelligent people who exploit them for this purpose.

Low intelligence plays a large part in the self-perpetuating cycle of unplanned children who cannot be coped with, who thus themselves grow up dull and deprived, and who, for both genetic and environmental reasons, continue the cycle. Repeated production of illegitimate children and repeated petty crimes are often indications of mental handicap.

SPECIAL FORMS OF MENTAL SUBNORMALITY

These are numerous. It is proposed here to mention only a few of special interest.

Cerebral diplegia (Little's disease)

Various causes (birth injury, asphyxia, failure of myelination related to premature birth) for this condition have been advanced, but it is currently considered due to arrested development or degeneration of the nervous system in utero. The degree of handicap varies both as regards spasticity and intelligence, between which there is no real correlation. In many children the physical difficulties impede their mental development so that they seem duller than they really are, and of these quite a number will later display a high degree of intelligence. *Microcephaly* (the result rather than the cause of cerebral hypoplasia) occurs in about 35 per cent of cases and is characterised by a small skull (circumference usually about 17 inches or less) with flattened occiput and receding forehead. These, coupled with a receding chin, provide an unfortunate profile often called 'birdlike'. Most of those with microcephaly are severely sub-normal.

Amaurotic family idiocy

This is rare, but is mentioned because of its genetic interest (single recessive gene). It was originally thought to occur only in Jewish children. It is now realised, however, that it occurs in other races, and also in adults in a form that is pathologically indistinguishable. Special signs are muscular weakness and wasting, particularly involving the head and neck, blindness due to macular degeneration (seen as a grey patch with a cherry red spot at its centre) and progressive apathy with subnormality. Microscopically, cortical changes are the most marked and are characterised by ballooning of the cells by lipoid substances which replace the Nissl substances, while there is also an increase of neuroglia.

Tuberose sclerosis (Syn. Epiloia)

This is a heredito-familial disease transmitted by a single dominant gene. It is characterised by three groups of symptoms: nervous symptoms (mental subnormality and epilepsy); cutaneous symptoms (adenoma sebaceum, plaques of 'peau de chagrin', café-au-lait spots); and fibromata (tumours of the retina, the heart and the kidneys).

Mental subnormality is not present in all cases; where it exists its onset is always in the first two years of life, the first manifestation being development delay in speech, gait and habits. In a large proportion mental subnormality is very profound; in some cases superimposed psychotic (catatonic) features make it appear even worse than it may be. All types of epileptic manifestations, general convulsions, Jacksonian fits, and petit mal, may be observed. Adenoma sebaceum consists of a nodular rash of yellow-red or brownish colour which covers, if fully developed, a butterfly-shaped area over the nose, the naso-labial folds (where it often begins) and part of the cheeks.

Cretinism

Endemic as well as sporadic, is often combined with mental subnormality, the degree of which varies from mere dullness to the severest idiocy. The first definite symptoms, mainly physical, appear as a rule, within the first two years of life. The mental development is retarded. The main features of the cretin's psychological state are lack of initiative, slowness, and clumsiness. Cretins are claimed to be good natured and easily manageable. The physical appearance is very characteristic. The results of thyroid treatment on the mental state may be considerable if treatment is started early in life. Cretins are now rarely seen in hospitals for the mentally subnormal.

Mongolism (Down's syndrome)

This is much the most common of the special forms, comprising about one third of the severely subnormal. There are at least three forms. The so-called 'Regular Mongols' have 47 chromosomes instead of 46; the extra one is at chromosome 21 of which there are three instead of a pair (trisomy). This apparently happens through faulty division of the germ cell so that two 21-chromosomes appear in one daughter cell and none in the other; if a further 21-chromosome is added when fertilisation by the sperm cell occurs, trisomy and a Mongol child are the result. This is the type of Mongolism that is associated with increasing maternal age.

It sometimes happens that a 21-chromosome breaks, and that the broken segment fuses with another chromosome (translocation), usually of the 13–15 or 21–22 group. This results in a 'Translocation Mongol' with the normal 46 chromosomes but with an abnormally large one at one or other side. This type occurs independently of maternal age. Where there is a translocation in either parent the risk of a further child being a mongol is much above the random risk, about one in three.

'Mosaic Mongols' are those in whom not all the cells are abnormal; there is one normal stem-line, but the other is trisomic at chromosome 21. 'Familial Mongols' are not special entities but those with mongol sibs or other family history of mongolism.

For parents with one Mongol but no other affected relative the further risk is around 2 per cent regardless of maternal age.

Mongols have a characteristic appearance. They are all dwarfed. The face is flat with oblique palpebral fissures which suggest the name of the condition. The nose is short, the tongue large, fissured and often protruded. The skin is flabby, the muscles hypotonic, the joints abnormally flexible. There is often an umbilical hernia Congenital heart disease and severe myopia are common. The resistance to common infections is low but an increasing number survive to adult life with antibiotics, though they age early and seldom live over fifty.

As a group, Mongols show considerable variations. A few are quite intelligent and a few are very severely subnormal. The majority, though severely handicapped mentally, are docile, cheerful and trainable, so that they can look after their daily needs and live in a family. A minority are dull, introverted and untrainable. They are often said to show a special fondness for music. In fact, most of them like to join in music and dancing as part of play, but they have no special musical or rhythmical sense. It is very possible that the more pleasant qualities of Mongols have been exaggerated in the text books.

Phenylketonuria

Most sufferers from this condition are severely subnormal. Aetiologically, it appears to be due to the effect of a single recessive gene which results in biochemical abnormality, the essence of which is an enzyme failure to break down phenylalanine which accumulates in the blood with excretion of phenylpyruvic and other acids in the urine. Nearly all sufferers have fair hair and blue eyes and show muscular hypertonus with exaggerated reflexes. The diagnosis should be made immediately after birth by examination of the urine and estimation of phenylalanine in the blood. This is of some consequence as it may be possible to prevent mental subnormality from developing by a phenylalanine-free diet.

DIAGNOSIS OF MENTAL SUBNORMALITY

The ease or difficulty of diagnosis will depend on the age of the patient and the type of subnormality shown. Where the latter is one of the special types described above, with characteristic signs, the diagnosis can be made within the first year of life. Apart from these types, mental subnormality may be suspected (but cannot be diagnosed with certainty) if the child remains abnormally inert, uninterested and unresponsive, despite apparently sound physical health.

If, subsequently, there is a failure of the normal development in the second and third years, particularly as regards talking, walking and toilet training, the diagnosis of mental subnormality becomes very probable. During the ensuing years, the educational standard attained, the adjustment to school, and the results of intelligence tests (see p. 238) may clinch the diagnosis.

During adolescent and adult years the question of educability becomes of secondary importance compared with that of general social adaptation, as has been emphasised. This is especially so where compulsory detention under the Mental Health Act is involved. Intelligence tests may give a reasonably accurate indication of the degree of intellectual handicap, and therefore of the diagnostic category, but there would be no point in considering compulsory detention if the social adjustment of the patient were satisfactory.

In general, diagnostic difficulties will be encountered only among the higher grades.

To those who specialise in the psychiatry of the mentally subnormal, the problems of diagnosis and assessment are presented early, by family doctors, social workers, and from the schools. The more severe forms of mental handicap do not present to the general psychiatrist, but some degree of mental subnormality is quite a common feature, and is clinically important. The intellectually subnormal, as mentioned earlier, find life more difficult than do most people; and it is necessary to modify appropriately explanations, discussion, type of occupational therapy, and job expectations.

A careful psychiatric history and examination, which goes into schooling and job record, and follows up any clues by checking on literacy, general knowledge, and degree of understanding, is usually sufficient. Psychometric testing is advisable to check on clinical impressions.

The diagnosis of underlying mental handicap should also be suggested by certain types of breakdown, characterised by a mood which is shallow and inconsistent as well as by the fact that the history frequently discloses that the breakdown has been precipitated by very simple stress. In brief, these breakdowns are often very childish and naive and readily affected by changes in the environment. Frank hysterical conversion symptoms are frequently seen, the psychogenesis of which is often patently clear. These patients, as mentioned before, are also liable to short-lived psychotic episodes of an anomalous type which occurring in a more intelligent individual would be strongly suggestive of schizophrenia. Thus confusion and hallucinosis may be shown and paranoid ideas are very common.

Formal intelligence tests

Many of these have been devised. The first one of all was that devised by the Frenchmen, Binet and Simon. The most widely used in Britain are probably the Wechsler Adult Intelligence Scale (W.A.I.S.), and the Wechsler Intelligence Scale for Children (W.I.S.C.), but there are several other reputable ones. They consist of two main sections. A verbal scale measures vocabulary, which gives us the 'verbal IQ', and a scale based on various sub-tests, including mathematical, visuospatial, memory, logical problems and others, gives us the 'performance IQ'.

The tests consist of a series of questions. The questions are based on what intensive trial and experiment have shown that average children of each age level are capable of answering. Most tests take 16 as the age at which adult intelligence is achieved, which is an approximation only. If the eight-year-old child is unable to pass the tests geared to the eight-year level, then his mental age is considered to be less than his chronological age; on the other hand, if he can pass the tests at the nine-year level, his mental age is considered to be greater than his chronological age. The performances of different patients are rendered comparable by introducing a common denominator. This is done by dividing the mental age (MA) by the chronological age (CA) and multiplying by 100. This expresses the intelligence as a percentage of the normal, and is called the IQ or Intelligence Quotient. Thus, if a ten-year-old child achieves a mental age of thirteen years, the IQ = MA 13/CA 10 × 100 = 130. Similarly, if a child of twelve years and four months achieves a mental age of nine years and six months, the IQ = MA 114 months/CA 148 months × 100 = 77.

IQs between 90 and 110 can be considered within normal limits. IQs above or below these limits indicate superior or inferior intelligence. Medical students may be gratified to learn that they probably rank in the top 10 per cent of the population. IQs of 70 or below indicate that the patient is unlikely to be able to benefit from education in ordinary schools.

Many objections to the foregoing procedures have been raised. For example, the concept of MAs is obviously an artificial one if applied to adults. A grown-up person with a mental age of, say, ten years will be quite different from a normal child of ten. To say that he has the mentality of a child of ten is incorrect. All that a mental age of ten years means is that the patient is able to score on certain tests only what an average child of ten would score—which is quite a different thing. The W.A.I.S. and the W.I.S.C. use appropriate questions for adults and children respectively.

The number of available tests of all these kinds is very large indeed. The students must bear in mind, however, that such tests do not provide absolute answers to clinical problems, and there is no test that is free from involvement with a cultural background.

Finally, the student should be aware that the dissatisfaction of academic psychologists with the method of recording results in terms of MAs and IQs has led to the revival of the method of percentiles, which was invented by Galton in the last century. But percentiles are inconvenient to handle statistically, and they are not for many people a natural or easy way of thinking about the relationship of measurements. A percentile rank of say 30 means that 30 per cent of a representative population are below and 70 per cent above in regard to their performance in the particular test employed. The ranks between 25 and 75 may be accepted as normal, if it supposed that half of the population can be so regarded. But it is important to know against what objective criterion a test has been checked ('validated') in order to know what it means in terms of what is wanted—for example, the probabilities or possibilities of efficiency in some particular job.

Intelligence testing is also useful in the investigation of organic deterioration (p. 90); and in tracking down reasons for repeated job failure, as when we find someone who has a markedly higher verbal than performance I.Q., and thus at interview tends to appear more intelligent than he is in practical matters.

TREATMENT IN MENTAL SUBNORMALITY

(a) Severe subnormality

There have been advances in the last few decades in both understanding and treatment of some of the more specific forms of severe subnormality, especially phenylketonuria. Improved physical care, including orthopaedic, cardiac and neurological surgery, has improved the well-being of some physically extremely disabled children and adults. Improved anticonvulsant treatment of the epilepsy which is so common, and developments in phenothiazines, thioxanthenes, antidepressants and lithium therapy have helped those who are also psychotic or otherwise disturbed.

The fact that a 'purely' genetic condition like phenylketonuria has been shown to be preventable by a change of environment (in the broad sense) has stimulated research and the hope that other apparently inevitable disorders will also be preventable or treatable. (More could be done in the fields of antenatal and perinatal care, as a sizeable amount of irreversible damage occurs at these times, and mortality and morbidity rates in the United Kingdom are (in 1979) poor by comparison with most European countries).

There is, however, no way in which major improvements in intelligence can occur, unless some treatable condition such as cretinism or phenylketonuria is present, and then only if treatment is begun early.

(b) Subnormality (of less serious degree)

The main change in this field has been parallel to developments in psychiatry as a whole, in emphasising the benefit of community care, and trying to lessen the number and size of hospitals for the mentally handicapped. The present trend is to offer social support to the families keeping the child, or backward adult, at home; to provide more day centres and hostels; and to build small residential units where inpatient treatment can be offered.

Treatment for most of the affected individuals is not medical or psychiatric, but more educational and social. The traditional role of the medical profession in supervising and controlling the environment in which so many patients lived, that is in the large hospitals, has been strongly challenged by educationalists and social workers, who have highlighted the disadvantages of big hospitals for these patients.

For the very severely handicapped, especially those with associated physical disabilities or who need much nursing care, and for the mentally more disturbed who need psychiatric treatment, only the medical and nursing professions are really able to cope. For the less severely handicapped social training, appropriate special education, occupational therapy and training for work where possible, are the main aims.

As with the big mental hospitals, the dangers and difficulties of big, understaffed subnormality hospitals are easy to see. Institutionalisation, neglect of physical and psychological needs by overworked staff, and the inevitable morale and other problems of the staff themselves. However, it is naive to imagine that these problems cannot develop in small units run by social workers as the years pass and enthusiasm wanes. The burden on the family can also be considerable, as with chronic schizophrenics discharged from hospital under similar policies.

Governments tend to favour cheap alternatives in health care, and unless money is found to provide good facilities in the local communities, the big old hospitals will be run down and nothing suitable will take their place.

Many mentally handicapped individuals, especially if they have no associated psychiatric disturbance, can be trained to useful and stimulating work, although they are usually better placed in some form of sheltered workshop.

Information about the social and educational services available can be had from the National Association for Mental Health, 39 Queen Anne Street, London, W.1.

11

Personality reactions and neurotic states

In the previous chapter we have considered personality disorders, and have seen that personality is an enduring—or relatively enduring—feature of the constitution or make up of the individual. It is the result of the interaction of genetic and environmental factors, and is our starting point.

In this chapter we consider a broad range of abnormal personality reactions and neurotic states. We do not see neurotic disturbances as 'illnesses' in any sense, but as the reactions of people with more or less abnormal personalities to stresses with which they cannot adequately cope. Some of these reactions are due to overwhelming stress in normally robust and stable people, in others the personality is too fragile to cope with even the most minor disturbance, and, of course, the majority are somewhere in between these extremes.

Obsessional-compulsive disorders, usually grouped with the other neurotic conditions, seem to us to have important features in common with the major mental illnesses of schizophrenia and the affective psychoses, in that they cannot be conceived of so simply as reactions to stress, but have a more autonomous quality, and we therefore give them Chapter 12 to themselves. There is much overlap, however, and these classifications must be seen as matters of convenience, rather than as established entities.

As described in Chapter 9, we do not divide depressive states into two qualitatively distinct conditions—endogenous and reactive, or psychotic and neurotic. We think it more realistic to see all the major depressive states as a continuum, but we exclude from that continuum the minor transient depressive reactions which therefore find a place in this chapter, along with anxiety, phobic and hysterical reactions.

Anxiety, transient depressive reactions, and hysterical reactions are described separately, but in practice are quite rarely found in pure culture. Usually it is a question of anxiety with hysterical features, or mixed anxiety and depression, and so on.

SOME DEFINITIONS OF THE TERMS USED

One of the main stumbling blocks to an understanding of the neurotic states and neurotic personality problems lies in the use of the words 'neurosis' and 'neurotic', which have unfortunately several overlapping meanings. It might be better not to use them at all if they were not so firmly established.

Originally the word 'neurosis', which was first used in 1776, indicated the belief that various symptoms arose from disorders of the nervous system; but a hundred years later it had shifted its meaning to indicate some functional disorder without any organic pathology.

There are four main ways in which the word or its derivatives are used now:

Firstly, the adjective 'neurotic' is widely used, in and out of the medical profession, to indicate that someone overreacts to relatively trivial life events, either with anxiety, tension, depression, or some other complaint, and usually also means that the person is difficult to get on with. This use of the term is non-technical, but broadly includes its other meanings, which are, however, worth dissecting out.

The second main use is medical and psychiatric, referring to the principal neurotic states or syndromes as outlined in an earlier paragraph, and we can say, depending on our classification, that there are three or four neuroses or neurotic states. (We prefer not to use the term neurotic *illness*, as in our view the word illness is better kept for the more serious psychiatric disorders, or for conditions in which there is some known structural or biochemical pathology.)

A third use, slightly modified, is in the word 'neuroticism', introduced by psychologists in their attempts to measure how neurotic people are. A high neuroticism score means that someone has obtained a high score on a neuroticism questionnaire, and is analogous to a high score on an IQ test as a measure of intelligence. Most neuroticism questionnaires are heavily loaded with questions about palpitations, dry mouth, sweating hands, butterflies in the stomach, swimming sensations in the head, frequency of micturition, and others which are essentially related to autonomic overactivity. To this extent 'neuroticism' is a very limited concept, and is more or less the same as a constitutional tendency to become anxious with little provocation--what can also be called 'anxiety proneness'. It is important to realise that neuroticism as measured by questionnaires is not truly identical with any of the other concepts which the word neurotic covers, although closely related.

The fourth and last main use of the word is in 'neurotic character disorder'. So far the other three meanings outlined have all included the idea of some symptomatic disturbance, if only in the sense of autonomic overactivity leading to minor discomfort. In a neurotic character disorder, however, the disturbance lies in the way in which a person forms relationships with others, and there may never be any symptoms in the ordinary sense of the word. Perhaps the commonest example of such a neurotic problem is when a young man or young woman falls in love and marries, but does not see the spouse for what he or she really is—a fairly ordinary person. Instead, the young woman, for example, has reacted with feelings which more properly belong to her father, and she reads into her husband qualities of stability, protectiveness, reliability and so on which reflect her feelings for her father, and reflect also her emotional needs. This can be a complex and ambivalent situation and she may be reacting from a background of a very happy and loving relationship with her father, and unconsciously perpetuating it in marriage; or she may be seeking, and finding in an idealised way, qualities which were lacking in her own childhood. Similarly a young man may unconsciously seek a wife who provides him with a maternal kind of warmth and care. Marriages based on emotional needs like these can be stable, satisfying and happy, particularly if they choose people who are appropriate, and who do indeed provide the kind of parental love and support which is demanded. We can say that those involved in these relationships have transferred into adult life feelings which originally, and more properly, belonged to parents or to other important childhood figures such as siblings. As an example of this last we can take people who still behave in adult life as though they were competing with an older brother and react to people of approximately the same age with what is often called 'sibling rivalry'.

In everyone early childhood experiences mould personality, one aspect of which is the way in which we react to others and form relationships. In everyone some element remains of this 'transference' of emotion, and we should not be too quick to label it as neurotic but should reserve that term for people in whom there is such marked and inappropriate transfer of feelings that it causes difficulties in life. Obviously there is an important element of immaturity in those who have this kind of neurotic character problem, but they may be in other ways very stable and mature seeming, well able to handle the stresses and strains of life, and only having difficulties in certain specific relationships, usually in the home.

Serious trouble often develops in neurotic relationships of this kind at a stage when real life and the neurotic needs and demands are incompatible. A fairly common example is when a young man has enjoyed being mothered by his wife, but who feels relegated to a second place when a real baby comes along. Quite often such men become jealous and petulant, attention seeking in rather childish ways at times, become depressed, or even start to drink to excess. A neurotic conflict exists when strong but basically infantile needs of an individual are in conflict either with reality, with other important needs of his own, or with the needs (neurotic or otherwise) of another person. Depending on the situation the individual copes in various ways, including of course the possibility of maturation of character, the development of insight, and resolution of the conflict. (This happy outcome does not necessarily need skilled professional help.) In many cases no satisfactory resolution is arrived at, and some uneasy truce or intermittent warfare continues, in any one of the many ways in which a marriage or family can be unhappy.

When such neurotic character disorders and conflict filled relationships exist in people who are constitutionally anxiety prone, or vulnerable to depression, or who have hysterical personality traits, then we find the kind of neurotic state with symptoms which we have already mentioned and which are described in detail elsewhere in this chapter and in others. In other words these neurotic character problems, and the conflicts which they generate, are among the most important causes and precipitants of the neuroses (i.e. the neurotic states or syndromes)—the form of which depend mainly on constitutional factors. In addition to these internal psychological stresses, the neuroses may be precipitated by purely external factors, although of course many external problems in life, even including such matters as housing difficulties, are themselves partly or wholly caused by the personality of the sufferer.

In summary, the word neurotic has several meanings. First, it is used, often critically, about the generally over-reactive, difficult person who is unreasonably upset by day to day trivia, awkward and demanding in personal relationships. Second, it means connected with one of the main neurotic syndromes, as a proper medical diagnostic term. Third, it is closely related to the idea of being abnormally prone to anxiety, but not necessarily with other personality difficulties. Fourth, and last, it refers to a type of character disorder in which feelings about childhood figures are transferred to people in adult life, so distorting relationships and making life difficult for both parties.

We obviously need a better terminology, but none has so far been developed. Confusion persists.

ANXIETY STATES

Although the term 'anxiety state' (or anxiety neurosis) has a fairly precise meaning, it is very often abused. Anxiety itself may occur in almost any psychiatric syndrome. It may be a primary and integral part of the syndrome, as when an endogenous depression or a schizophrenic illness is ushered in by anxiety symptoms; or it may be secondary, as when a patient reacts with anxiety to the basic illness itself. Again, it may be an accompaniment of organic illness, as is often the case with Parkinsonism, or when an anxious tendency is released as a result of that diminished control that follows cerebral arteriosclerosis. Apart from these, many patients react to stressful situations by developing either anxiety or depression or both combined.

Anxiety is a normal part of life as a reaction to threat, and all medical students are aware that our feelings of anxiety are inseparable from the somatic changes produced by the surge of adrenalin in the 'fight or flight' reaction, which leads to heightened awareness and a readiness to cope with physical danger. In our society, in which escaping from a tiger is rarely necessary, the feelings have to be tolerated until they die down or are relieved by some treatment, and, as people differ in their tolerance of pain, so they differ in their tolerance of anxiety. (Some people actually enjoy feeling frightened, as the memoirs of mountain climbers make clear.) Many effective people carry a heavy load of anxiety without complaint, but the less robust are likely to regard it as intolerable, and as an 'illness'. The hysterical are more likely to make use of it. In neurotic states the anxiety does not have a clear-cut relationship to a dangerous situation, such as the climbers stimulating fear of falling, but is either diffuse and 'free floating', or attached to a situation which the patient regards as ridiculous, as in a phobic fear of going out into the street. The diffuse and apparently meaningless anxiety is particularly hard to bear, and one of the functions of psychotherapy is to try and find the underlying sources of it, which can help to make it much more tolerable.

We should only use the term 'Anxiety state' when we are sure that there is no underlying depression, schizophrenia, organic cerebral impairment, or alcohol problem, and the symptoms are purely those of anxiety, as described in detail later.

It is worth making a distinction here between the kind of minor and often recurrent anxiety states seen mainly in general practice, and the more severe and less tractable ones treated by psychiatrists. The former are common in people who have a life long proneness to anxiety, mainly women, but who may have no other personality problem. They may cope well with life in every way, but easily become anxious. If something out of the ordinary happens, such as a daughter's impending marriage to an undesirable combined with serious illness in the husband, then the anxiety threshold is exceeded and she goes to her doctor. With time, perhaps with some support and a tranquilliser, all this settles down, until the next time.

The more prolonged and difficult anxiety states arise when the precipitant is not some understandable and limited external stress, but where there is a complex problem of relationships due to an inner neurotic conflict, perhaps based on transference problems as outlined earlier in this section. It is unwise to give such patients tranquillisers freely, because with an enduring personality problem drug dependence is very likely. Psychotherapy is more likely to be the treatment of choice.

Aetiology
The general principle of multiple aetiology must be borne in mind; constitutional, physical and psychological factors will contribute to the condition.

Constitutional factors
There is a genetic predisposition to anxiety, and the genes involved are those of minor effect. It is presumably due to their influence that many people have brisk autonomic responses which readily raise their tension. Upbringing presumably also plays a part, although this is more difficult to demonstrate by research than the genetic aspect.

There is a much greater tendency to anxiety in women than in men, as there is for depressive reactions also. Traditionally in our culture, men have been more prone to 'act out' when under pressure, by fighting, getting drunk, kicking the cat, and so on. Women have been more likely to suffer inwardly with anxiety and depression. Differential rates of admission to prison and mental hospital support this distinction. It will be interesting to see if the changing rôle and attitudes of women alters this balance.

Physical factors
Cerebral arteriosclerosis and Parkinsonism have already been mentioned, but where anxiety arises in connection with these, the condition is best diagnosed under the heading of the physical disorder, since that will form the basis of the clinical picture. Apart from these, the main physical conditions that may give rise to

anxiety symptoms are (1) exhaustion, (2) head injury, (3) alcoholic excess, and (4) certain endocrine disturbances.

Exhaustion, whether from long continued stress, from genuine overwork, or from the debilitating effects of illness, encourages the development of anxiety because, as has already been said, 'worries get a hold' more easily on those who are run down from whatever cause; because an exhausted man is less master of himself, more suggestible, and therefore an easier prey to such worries as he may already have or which may suggest themselves, than is the same man in good health; and because the inactivity imposed by the exhaustion may prevent him from beguiling himself in the way that he was accustomed to from such worries as he may have. For these reasons anxiety is common after severe physical illnesses.

Head injury, especially when this is of a closed sort accompanied by concussion, is liable to give rise to an increased tendency to anxiety. This is commonly accompanied by irritability, and probably arises from a relative failure of autonomic control secondary to cerebral damage.

Anxiety is also often experienced by *alcoholics after drinking bouts*, and then appears to arise not so much from remorse as from actual toxic effect.

In spite of the fact that the production of anxiety depends on adrenalin, the relation of anxiety states to *endocrine disturbance* is nowhere clear cut, though some discern such a relationship in thyrotoxicosis and believe it to be reciprocal in that thyrotoxicosis causes anxiety as part of the clinical picture, and, in their view, anxiety states may lead to thyrotoxicosis which, if not too far advanced, may then yield to psychotherapy.

Psychological factors

The stresses that help to produce anxiety may be many and various, and, as has been said, what is psychologically stressful for one patient need not be so for another. The stresses may be external or internal, but usually both are combined. Thus, a man thrown out of work because his employer's business has failed may be anxious about his own and his family's future; that is external stress. But if he is inwardly prone to misgiving and to expect the worst rather than the best, these internal factors will increase his anxiety.

The commonest stresses arise in the family, very often from the kind of inner neurotic character problem described earlier. Others are found in such different connections as homosexuality, and frustrations in love and at work. The intensity of their effect will vary according to the patient's personality. The person who is by nature tense and over-conscientious is likely to develop more in the way of symptoms than the person who is happy-go-lucky. Indeed, the symptoms may arise much more from the personality than from the actual situation, since often it will be factors in the patient's personality that have brought the situation about. An obvious example is the type of patient occasionally seen who, tense, ambitious and perfectionistic by nature, makes his work his life; in pursuit of the satisfaction he gets from it, he takes more and more upon himself especially since his perfectionism deters him from delegating work to others, and so he keeps himself continually geared to effort; then, having been 'wound up' for so long, he cannot 'unwind', and therefore cannot relax although impending exhaustion bids him try to do so. In this way the patient may develop anxiety through the cumulative effect of stress. The process may be slow so that there is a latent interval between the original impact of the stress and the subsequent development of symptoms.

But anxiety can be engendered in another way that, though related to the foregoing, is rather different, namely by the sudden removal of stress. If a person is geared to effort, and the pressure upon him is suddenly relieved, he is deprived of those outlets for his accumulated tension to which he has become accustomed. He thus remains pent up. In acute form, this is well shown in the normal experience of feeling worse after danger than during it, and much the same thing may be observed, though less dramatically and in slower motion, in those who break down on retirement from a previously active life.

Thus, the main psychological factors in the production of anxiety are conflicts, frustrations and other situations that maintain tension with cumulative effect, and the sudden removal of stimulations, whether pleasant or unpleasant, to which the patient has become accustomed. The existence of such conflicts, frustrations and special situations may depend more on the patient's personality than on the outside circumstances themselves. Although the state of affairs may be clear to the outside observer, it is not necessarily plain to the patient, who may not realise the source of his difficulties to any appreciable extent, but may concentrate his attention on the symptoms themselves instead of on their causes.

Symptoms and signs
Since anxiety is a psychobiological response to stress, anxiety states show the physical signs of fear as well as its subjective experience. The mental symptoms vary according to the severity of the state, from a mild uneasiness coupled with a feeling that something is

going to happen, together with restlessness, to actual panic in which the patient is acutely afraid. In the typical case the fear is not clearly focused on any special object, but is general and permeates the whole mental state so that the patient experiences tension and disturbed concentration with inability to settle. Irritability is a common feature; the appetite is frequently impaired, so that loss of weight can be observed; and the patients find difficulty in getting off to sleep and wake unrefreshed after troubled dreams.

The more physical symptoms and the signs are an integral part of the emotional experience, and can easily be remembered by the fact that they are those produced by the increased output of adrenalin. The most constant are tachycardia with palpitation, increased muscular tension that leads to tremors, and sweating which is experienced in the palms of the hands and on the soles of the feet. These are usually accompanied by pallor, dilatation of the pupils and a rise in the systolic blood pressure, with increase in the tendon jerks, especially in the arms. Less constant but common features are other sensations associated with the 'adrenalin syndrome', such as dryness of the mouth, constriction of the chest leading to feelings of choking and suffocation, the gastric sensations of nervous dyspepsia ('butterflies in the stomach', 'the stomach turning over') with irritability of the gut, frequency of micturition, and a sense of weakness in the limbs ('india-rubber knees').

Complaints referred to the head are very common but may be of different kinds. (1) There may be a sense of tightness, often due to mere tension of the scalp muscles; (2) there may be a genuine headache of migrainous type set going by the emotional state; (3) the complaint of 'headache' may prove on analysis to be a mere verbal expression of psychic discomfort. There may also be dizziness and faintness which are often caused by over-breathing in an attempt to overcome the sense of impending suffocation. The symptoms and signs in general are mediated by the sympathetic and parasympathetic systems.

Anxiety may occur in acute attacks, the first of which can often be traced back to some special experience. Subsequent attacks may then be provoked by any event that comes to be associated with the original trauma. More and more events come to be so associated, so that finally, by a process analogous to facilitation, the 'conditioned reflex' may be set going by some stimulus with no obvious connection at all. This is specially liable to happen where the patient has interpreted the state as one of physical disease, and has become afraid of the symptoms themselves; his fear is then liable to lead to their recurrence with the development of a vicious circle.

Owing to these mechanisms, the patient with acute anxiety attacks of recurrent or episodic kind tends to develop a gradually more chronic condition in which the same symptoms, though generally milder, continue for long periods. The student is often puzzled because he seldom sees the full-blown picture of anxiety as described in the text-books. This is because the acute phase tends to be short-lived and to subside quickly. But the fact of its having occurred provides a nucleus for other developments, whose nature may vary considerably according to the personality of the individual patient.

In this development of anxiety states, three stages may be arbitrarily distinguished. In the first, the normal and physiologically appropriate adrenal-sympathetic response to stress is abnormally intense. The first stage is thus one of *over-reaction*. Over-sensitive and self-protective people may be rendered quite ineffective for the time being, and they commonly react to the anxiety symptoms in a hysterical way. Now, anxiety symptoms are biologically purposive, but they are not personally purposive in the same way that hysterical reactions are personally purposive. But in certain circumstances they can be used hysterically, and in practice it is common to find that anxiety symptoms that have arisen originally from stress are used hysterically as a means of escape from continuation of the stress. Thus, a clerk may develop anxiety symptoms manifesting themselves mainly in the form of supposed eye-strain, as the result of working for a difficult employer: and then use his supposed eye-strain as a means of changing his job, being genuinely unaware of the origin of his condition or the nature of the subsequent motivation. In the same fashion, over-sensitive and self-protective people may, through fear of the symptoms recurring, restrict their lives and activities and so fail to carry out their responsibilities and commitments on the score of invalidism. Such restriction may be continued in the absence of anxiety symptoms, and persist merely as a bad habit. Thus, the first stage of the anxiety state is liable to lead to *hysterical* developments.

If this does not happen, but the patient tries to carry on as before despite continuance of the stress, the second stage of the anxiety state is reached. This is the stage of *established tension*, and may be presumed to exist when normal relaxation does not follow relief from stress. The physical signs and symptoms remain generalised and prominent. The picture is one of tension with irritability and increased fatiguability, some dissatisfaction and unhappiness, with occasional exacerbations of more acute anxiety. The extent to which the symptoms interfere with the patient's life and activity depends upon their severity, and the patient's willingness or ability to cope with them.

The more stable and conscientious patients will continue to struggle on after the stage of established tension has been reached. As a rule, the objective evidence of anxiety and tension then becomes gradually less prominent, and the presenting symptoms become more those of fatigue, depression, with diminished emotional control and loss of weight. Irritability is marked, there may be difficulty in getting off to sleep with frequent waking, and the patient shows emotion more easily, often confessing rather shamefacedly that he feels moved to tears by sad stories, sentimental films and songs, and martial music. This third stage has been termed *anxiety with exhaustion*. It cannot be differentiated sharply from states of reactive depression with anxiety features.

The sequence through these three stages, as has been explained, is not invariable, but depends upon how ready is the individual patient to spare himself. Those who lose their lives by seeking to save them may not even enter the second phase, but may protect themselves from continued symptoms through a retreat into invalidism. More determined patients who are more ready to put up with symptoms will enter the second stage, that of established tension. But on the whole it will be only those patients with good personalities who do not spare themselves who arrive at the third stage of anxiety with exhaustion.

The remaining direction in which anxiety states may develop is in the formation of an '*organ neurosis*', and is usually determined by the way in which the patient interprets the anxiety symptoms. The patient may have attended primarily to specific physical symptoms, such as palpitation, breathlessness or headache, any one of which may have become his special concern. He may not complain of tension or fear at all; on questioning he will admit their existence but will probably attribute them to concern over his health and regard them as secondary to the physical symptoms. The physician is then apt to make the same mistake, and to believe that the complaint is evidence of organic disease. This is a common diagnostic error that often leads to prolonged, unnecessary and expensive investigations, which could have been avoided by more careful history-taking. The symptoms on which the patient chooses to focus attention are determined by the same sort of factors that determine the organ neuroses in hysteria (see p. 266). The chief of such factors are: (1) The patient's previous experience of illness, whether personal or second-hand. Thus, it is often found that headaches or nervous dyspepsia run in families. This may be both from constitutional causes or from the suggestive effect of example, and is likely to affect the direction in which the patient turns his attention when developing symptoms of his own. The same effect may follow seeing some friend or relative suffering from organic disease. (2) The patient's beliefs, arising from experience of illness, as to his physical strengths or weaknesses. Thus, the functional blindness from which Hitler suffered in time of stress during the 1914–18 war was doubtless conditioned by his conjunctivitis following exposure to gas. Symptoms connected with the head and heart are specially important to the patient on account of the importance of those structures. (3) The special importance of certain functions to certain people, often according to the occupational demands. A singer suffering from anxiety may be disturbed chiefly by respiratory symptoms, a watch-maker may be more concerned by tremor of the fingers. (4) The effect of emotion on function is such as to bring autonomic activities into special prominence. Hence the occurrence of such common phrases as: 'It gives me a headache', 'It makes me sick', 'I can't stomach it', 'It gives me cold feet', and so on. The existence of such sayings is no matter of chance; they express common psychosomatic relationships, and the effect of emotion on function is such as to make the patient abnormally aware of autonomic activity and of the organs influenced by the autonomic system.

Of recent years it has been fashionable to suppose that anxiety symptoms have in themselves a symbolic significance. For example, if a patient in some conflict develops diarrhoea, the latter may be interpreted by some people as a symbolic expression in physical terms of the patient's desire to get rid of something from his mind. We ourselves are unimpressed by interpretative exercises of this kind, and we do not believe that symptoms which are biologically purposive need be supposed also to be symbolically and personally purposive.

In summary, the symptoms and signs of anxiety states range subjectively from uneasiness to panic, from mild tension to severe restlessness, with the physical accompaniments that are associated with increased output of adrenalin. Such states may occur as acute episodes, but owing to association of ideas and the process of conditioning, the tendency is towards an increased chronicity, which may later be accompanied by exhaustion and diminished emotional control. Anxiety symptoms may also be increased by hysterical trends, and, if not recognised for what they are, may lead to unfounded fears of physical ill-health with the development of organ neuroses.

Differential diagnosis

The term anxiety state should not be applied indiscriminately to any case that shows the symptoms that have been described. To do this would be to include wrongly under such a diagnosis a large number of conditions that should be differentiated. Schizophrenic conditions may show much anxiety; anxiety may be prominent in depressive illnesses, and may accompany organic mental illnesses. In every case it is therefore necessary to consider: *What is there besides anxiety?* Where anxiety is an incident in some other and major condition, to call the case an anxiety state merely because anxiety features are present is to divert attention from what is important, with the probable effect of encouraging the wrong treatment. In fact, the diagnosis must be made on (1) the presence of symptoms and signs of anxiety, but (2) by exclusion of other syndromes. In this connection, it may be re-emphasised here that anxiety states in pure culture and full form are not common, and are seen with any frequency only under the acute stresses of war time.

The commonest thing is to find mixtures of anxiety and hysterical elaboration, and of anxiety and depression. The former will exist only where the intensification and prolongation of the anxiety symptoms serves some personal purpose. In such cases it may be better to diagnose 'Anxiety State with hysterical features'. Such a decision will rest upon the severity of the anxiety symptoms themselves, and the extent to which they are being purposively exploited.

Mixtures of anxiety and depression can come about in three ways. First, the patient may find the anxiety sufficiently distressing to react to it with depression. Second, and more commonly, the same stress may produce both anxiety and depression at the same time. Here again, it may be a matter of taste whether the case is considered one of 'Anxiety state with depressive features', or of 'Reactive depression with anxiety features'. In either event, the decision will not affect the treatment. But it may be otherwise in considering the third way in which anxiety and depression may be combined. This is when both are integral parts of a depressive illness of endogenous pattern. Differential diagnosis is very important here because effective antidepressant treatment will also clear up the anxiety symptoms, especially if a more sedative tricyclic drug is used; but treatment as a pure anxiety state might well make the depression worse. This is seen both with benzodiazepine tranquillisers and psychotherapy at times, as neither are suitable treatment for depression of endogenous pattern. The student should therefore be familiar with the clinical features of depressive illnesses, and the features which indicate appropriate treatment (p. 186).

Nor should an anxiety state be diagnosed simply because the patient shows an organ neurosis. The latter by no means necessarily arise on an anxiety basis. Some are frankly hysterical from the start, in that they serve some personal purpose; an example would be the persisting headaches of the 'delicate' woman who thus avoids her household duties. Others can be regarded as bad habits, as when a patient persistently complains of flatulence and a disordered stomach as the result of aerophagy. Again, some represent an exaggerated physiological response to an intense emotional experience which may be of a kind that affects everybody or, on the other hand, may have a special significance for the particular person concerned. Some people, for example, almost always faint at the sight of blood. It is unnecessary to suppose that a keen medical student who faints on his first experience of the operating theatre does so to escape from the unpleasant stimulus; nor need he show any other alleged anxiety symptoms at all.

Finally, where a patient shows persistent anxiety for the first time when over forty years of age, it is wise to bear in mind certain special diagnostic points. The highest probability is that the anxiety is an integral part of, and masking, an underlying depression (see p. 180). Other likely alternatives are that the anxiety arises in association with alcoholic excess or with the onset of an early dementia.

In sum, the diagnosis of anxiety state should be reserved for those conditions that show persistent symptoms and signs of anxiety in the absence of continuing adequate outside cause, and in the absence of other symptoms indicative of some other psychiatric syndrome.

Course and prognosis

It has been indicated that there is a tendency for even the recurrent and episodic forms of anxiety attack to show an increased chronicity with the passing of time. This is true, but need not give rise to too much prognostic pessimism since such a state of affairs can be considerably modified by treatment. In considering the prognosis it is convenient to consider each case under three headings: (1) predisposition, (2) stress, and (3) the type of reaction and resultant disability shown by the patient.

(1) *Predisposition*. This will best be shown by the family and past personal history. The past personal history in particular may give valuable indications of an objective kind as to the type and amount of stress that the patient can tolerate without developing symptoms, as to their severity when they have developed, and as to the extent that the patient has given way to or has overcome them. Over-sensitive and self-protective people are likely to develop hysterical additions. Only those with the better personalities will go through the phase of established tension to that of exhaustion.

(2) *The stress or load experienced*. Here the general principles previously outlined will apply. The slings and arrows of fortune that are outrageous for one man will not be so for another. Given a certain type of predisposition, the prognosis will largely depend upon the chances of avoiding similar stress in the future. Relevant questions are therefore; Is the stress that is responsible likely to continue or recur? Can or should attempts be made to avoid it? What can be done to make the patient realise more clearly its nature? And, since the stresses often

arise, as has been said, more from the patient's own personality than from the actual outside circumstances: What can be done to make the patient realise more clearly his own nature, including his capabilities, potentialities and limitations?

(3) *The type of reaction and resultant disability*. The disabilities imposed by anxiety symptoms and the extent to which they will be interpreted as evidence of illness will depend on (*a*) the ease of their provocation and their intensity and persistence, and (*b*) the patient's intelligence and personality and the many factors that affect his power of self-control. It is obvious that there is every possibility of variation in these respects, and, as in the rest of medicine, it is useful to separate as far as possible the patient's illness and his reaction to it. As has previously been emphasised, the latter rather than the former is an extremely common cause of the resultant disability. A fair indication of the severity of an anxiety state is afforded by the actual somatic manifestations. Where these are marked the actual disability is likely to be considerable and the patient must be considered to be under stress; where they are minimal despite much complaint it is likely that the patient's reaction to the condition is more marked than the severity of the state itself.

In general, the greater the predisposition the less good is the prognosis likely to be; the greater the patient's tolerance of stress the better is the prognosis likely to be. Favourable factors are therefore a personality with good capacity for relaxation and high tolerance of stress. Where the stress has arisen more from the personality and from inner conflicts than from external circumstances, the prognosis will depend on how far the patient may be brought to recognise those facts, and how far he can modify the attitudes that have led to symptom formation. Where the stress of outside circumstances has been severe, the prognosis will depend on how far environmental rearrangements can be made, and how far the personality can be brought do make the best use of such rearrangement.

Treatment
There are two essential preliminaries. The first is a good history, yielding a sound working knowledge of the patient's personality, habits of reaction, past performance and present difficulties, with an accurate chronological record of the onset of stress and the development of symptoms (see p. 73 ff.). The second is an equally careful physical examination, which may have great reassurance value.

The treatment of any given case must depend to some extent upon its causes. We may divide the patients into two broad groups: (1) those in whom the condition has arisen from external stress, whether from physical illness or from pressure of outside circumstances, and (2) those in whom the condition arises more from a personality disorder. It is a mistake to suppose that because a patient is anxious, such anxiety is essentially or even mainly psychogenic. Where the personality is a good one and the stress has been severe, it is likely that physical rather than psychological measures will be called for. On the other hand, where physical factors are of small importance and the external stress has not been marked, the approach must be psychological rather than physical. Hence the importance of an accurate history.

Admission to hospital

Very severe cases, arising from whatever cause, may need admission to hospital, though uncommonly. Where admission seems desirable, the patient may be inaccessible to psychological approach in the acute stage, owing to disturbance of concentration and pre-occupation with the symptoms. Heavy sedation may then be required, even to the point of continuous narcosis (see p. 403). In recent years barbiturates have fallen out of favour because of increasing dependence and addiction, as well as the prolonged hangover. A combination of chlorpromazine and dichloralphenazone is suitable (up to 300 mg and 4 G respectively every 4 or 6 hours).

Admission to a day hospital may well be useful, and helps to remove the patient from the pressures and conflicts of home, without encouraging the dependence and regression of admission as an inpatient.

Treatment as out-patient

In the much more commonly encountered case that is not so severe as to need admission to hospital, the first question that is likely to arise is: should the patient continue at work? The best guide to this is the extent to which the patient has actual physical manifestations (either of anxiety or of exhaustion, as observed by the physician and confirmed by the relatives), as opposed to the complaints that he may make. Where there are marked physical signs of anxiety, and especially where there is evidence of exhaustion time off work may well be indicated. But, as will later be explained, the patient should not be told merely to have a rest. Much benefit may be derived from a holiday, if it can be afforded, but it should be a holiday with opportunities for exercise and recreation.

In cases where there is much complaint, but no satisfactory evidence of either anxiety or exhaustion, continuance at work is likely to be the best policy. The doctor who allows the patient to persuade him of unfitness for work against his better judgment is doing the patient a disservice in encouraging habituation of symptoms. The decision should be made in the light of (1) the physical signs, (2) knowledge of the patient's personality. If the patient continues to insist that he feels unfit for work despite negative findings, the best course is to leave the decision to him, while insisting that there are no medical grounds for exempting him from his usual routine. In general, it is wise to err on the side of discouraging unnecessary restrictions on the patient's life and activity, where these arise because he is unwilling to put up with minor stresses.

Psychological approach

After these practical considerations, we must consider the psychological approach. The first necessity is to explain the nature of the symptoms and their relation to emotion. This in itself will often enable the patient to see them in better proportion and so to manage them more satisfactorily and with less in the way of secondary anxiety. It will also prepare the patient who needs it for the next stage in treatment, namely an examination of the underlying causes. In this connection many people believe that if they experience anxiety the cause must lie in their remote past, exerting its influence through some chain of events from childhood onwards. This is sometimes true, but on the whole applies to complex personalities only, and is not a belief to be encouraged unless there are good grounds for it. The amount and type of psychotherapy that is needed depends upon the patient's personality. Where this is sound, no more may be required than simple explanation of the symptoms and of their development in relation to the precipitating circumstances. Where the patient is an effective person, he will make the necessary environmental re-arrangements for himself. Less effective persons will need more in the way of psychotherapy and help in the management of their circumstances.

Psychotherapy

As to the psycho-therapeutic approach, it may be noted that sufferers from those anxiety states that arise mainly from personality difficulties are usually unaware of, or seldom face openly, the true nature of their problems, but turn their attention to what is less vital, the symptoms themselves, instead of the causes that give rise to them. The patient must be encouraged to look for these causes, especially by examining the setting in which the symptoms have occurred, and the emotions that such a setting has aroused in him. The explanation may not at first be apparent to the therapist. But even if it is, it should never be imposed upon the patient; the patient should be encouraged to produce it for himself, for it is only then that he will come to full realisation. The patient must search for the causes, though the therapist may help by indicating where best to look. The patient has thus to be led to realise—but to realise for himself—the true basis of his difficulties, and to try to re-adjust his standards to the requirements of his social environment, in so far as the latter cannot reasonably be modified by him or for him. When the conflicts which have contributed to the anxiety state involve the spouse it is often most useful to include both partners in the therapy, examining the relationship between them in this way.

Drug therapy

The most generally used drugs in anxiety states are minor tranquillisers, principally the benzodiazepines. They have the property of lessening anxiety and tension without much sedation, are non-addictive, although habituation and dependence can occur, and are very safe in the event of overdose. Details of their use is given in the chapter on treatment (Ch. 15).

Benzodiazepines also have serious disadvantages, especially if, as so often happens, they are relied on as the sole treatment. In a brief self limiting anxiety state, which arises as a result of transient stress, it is reasonable to use them to lessen anxiety. When someone has an enduring personality problem, or the anxiety is in response to long standing marital conflicts for example, then to use drugs alone is insufficient. The tranquillisers will do nothing to solve the problems, tolerance will develop so that the dose will be increased, and side effects such as ataxia and mental slowing then develop. Benzodiazepines also have an alcohol-like effect and often lessen self-control, and lead to instability of mood, especially in higher doses. After a time the patient may well be psychologically dependent on them, although true addiction does not develop. Many serious problems in people's lives cannot be helped by medical intervention, although much can be done by psychotherapy, advice, emotional support, help with environmental changes such as housing problems, and other social or personal measures. It is often better to do nothing than simply to put someone onto tranquillisers if there is no likelihood of a change in the life situation. Unfortunately there are great demands made on doctors for instant help, and many people expect to be given drugs when in any difficulty. There is also a temptation for the doctor to prescribe tranquillisers in order to satisfy the patient and cut short what seems to be an unproductive interview about an unchangeable life problem. Barbiturates should never be given to relieve anxiety in someone with long-term problems, as the dangers of addiction are considerable and the suicide potential high. They are best not used at all in psychiatric problems.

Another serious disadvantage of the routine use of tranquillisers for everyone with anxiety symptoms is that a sizeable proportion of the patients are likely to be suffering from unrecognised depression, and to be made worse by tranquillisers, or to have organic brain disease or some other physical illness presenting in the early stages with anxiety.

General management

At times the most useful changes are to be made in the patient's pattern of daily life, particularly in the kind of professional or managerial person to whom work has become the predominant preoccupation, who does not get adequate relaxation or exercise and who is continually wound up. Sometimes straightforward advice on these matters, after careful elucidation of the pattern of life, can be helpful. The exercise of going through the details with the patient may put his life in a new perspective, and make him see the need for change.

PHOBIC STATES

These conditions have much in common with obsessional states and are often classified with them for reasons which will be made clear. However, anxiety is one of their principal symptoms, and in many ways they more closely resemble the anxiety states, and are therefore considered here in this book.

A phobia is an irrational fear, in which the irrationality is recognised, realised (often) to be essentially ridiculous, and is struggled against with a sense of tension. These features are exactly parallel to those of obsessional thoughts with which these phobias overlap at times, and explain the alternative classification. Phobias do not lead to compulsive acts, although the patient may well modify his life in order to cope with them. They are of two main types: the simple and the complex, and this distinction is of great importance clinically in several ways. It is the simple monosymptomatic phobias which most closely resemble obsessional thoughts; the complex phobias arise mainly in people with neurotic character disorders in interaction with their spouses, or other family members. There is a borderland between the two where they merge. Much the commonest complex phobia is agoraphobia. Social phobias deserve separate consideration.

Simple phobias (monosymptomatic phobias)

Under this heading we can put all the very common fears of spiders, mice, insects of various sorts, heights, water, lifts or other confined spaces, wide open spaces, crowded streets, feathers and almost any other object one can think of. Less often there are such activities as vomiting, as described in the section on behaviour therapy (p. 385), or of certain diseases or types of dirt. They are described as 'simple' because the principal effect is only on the person who has the phobia, whose life may be made quite uncomfortable or unpleasant by them. In that they differ from the complex phobias, in which other people's lives are markedly affected, as described later, and into which they occasionally develop, depending on personalities and circumstances.

The simple phobias usually occur in people of rather tense and anxiety prone personality, who perhaps form conditioned reflexes rather easily. They have often been brought up by someone who has had a similar phobia and naturally inculcated it. In others there is a clear cut and convincing history of some earlier and fearful experience associated directly or indirectly with the phobic object. When there is a phobia of entering even shallow water for example, there is often a history of being thrown into the deep end of a pool or of feeling about to drown; and someone who has fainted in a tube train and woken up on the floor may be unable to travel by tube without anxiety after that. In other people no such clear account is given, but one can imagine some similar understandable chain of circumstances in many sufferers. In others the phobic object may seem to have some symbolic, particularly sexual, meaning, as with fear of snakes which may be reacted to as phallic symbols. In yet others, the underlying meaning may be related to some unacceptable and largely unconscious thought, as described in the next chapter on obsessions, when a phobic fear of knives arises from the repression of antagonistic feelings towards the children.

Another example of the importance of the unrecognised thought was of a man who suddenly developed a phobia of driving away from home in his car, unless accompanied by his wife. The fear began shortly after his wife had made a suicidal gesture by swallowing pills, complaining about the very long hours he was away from home as an insurance salesman. He did not spontaneously link the overdose and the phobia.

There are therefore various ways in which these simple phobias can arise, although the presenting symptoms are very alike. They can all be understood as over-learnt conditioned responses. Some of these phobias are very widespread, particularly that of spiders, and many otherwise stoical people are less happy about picking up a spider than a beetle, although why this should be so is not clear.

When confronted by the phobic object—for example a spider—the severely phobic individual feels rapidly mounting anxiety or fear, often to an unbearable degree, so that he has to leave the site. With pounding heart, sweating palms, tremor, dry mouth, vision blurred by pupillary dilatation, gooseflesh, unsteadiness, butterflies in the stomach, perhaps an urge to micturate or defaecate, and an overwhelming desire to run away, the patient can experience a full blown panic attack, and very often feels he is about to lose consciousness, lose control and 'go beserk', or even die. This extremity of fear is of course not so common as are milder attacks, but even the less severe panics are very unpleasant, and the patient naturally goes out of his way to avoid whatever situation seemed responsible. A process of generalisation can occur, using the terminology of learning theory to describe the development of further conditioned fear responses. For example someone with a phobia of snakes might at first be unable to go into the Reptile House at the Zoo, later be unable to visit the Zoo at all, and later feel a twinge of anxiety even at the sight of the word 'Zoo'.

Patients with these monosymptomatic phobias only present to doctors when they are severe, and a host of minor phobias are tolerated. Sometimes there is a severe exacerbation of a long-standing minor phobia, either in a setting of depression, or associated with some new emotionally stressful situation. A typical example was of a girl with a lifelong minor insect phobia who went on holiday with her boyfriend. He told her that he was attracted to another girl and left her on the beach; she developed a panic attack apparently focused on the flying insects nearby, which until then she had almost ignored. Over the next few months the phobia increased in intensity until her life was severely curtailed, and she was unable to go to college each day in case a flying insect brushed her face.

These phobias, of all psychiatric conditions, respond most rapidly and completely to behaviour therapy using desensitisation (p. 386). Benzodiazepine tranquillisers can help symptomatically, and the MAOI drug phenelzine (p. 401) can also be extremely helpful. It can be taken as a general rule that any phobia which does not affect the life of another person, and from which there is no secondary gain of hysterical type, such as can come from avoiding some responsibility, will respond well to treatment.

Complex phobias

This term is used here to describe phobias in which there are pronounced effects on other people's lives. The nature of the feelings of fear or panic is the same, although they are often more severe than are the simple phobias. They are very much more common in women. The actual phobic object need not be different, but in practice agoraphobia– –which literally means fear of the market place, but is mainly used for a fear of being out in the open away from home—is much the commonest. If an agoraphobic woman has no notice taken of her complaints by husband and family, and is left to 'get on with it', then it remains a simple phobia, and has a relatively better prognosis with treatment.

Much more commonly the situation develops as follows: for some reason a woman develops a fear of being out of the house on her own. It may begin with a severe panic attack while out shopping. There then develops, rapidly or slowly, a fear of going into that shop, then of approaching it, then of going to that part of town, and so on until she is unable even to go out of the house. Usually, but not always, those affected can manage to go out with the husband, or some other person. In some cases a child or a dog will do, or even an empty pram may be pushed along, and brings some security. The term 'housebound housewife' is used for this condition, which is extremely common, and may never come to medical attention in any way. Some people are housebound for decades at a time, and it is not uncommon to be told when taking a psychiatric history that some relative has not been able to go out alone since the birth of a child who is now grown up.

As the woman's symptoms develop, and she is progressively less able to go out, the husband, or less often another relative, has to start doing the shopping. At first this is only at the distant shop where the trouble began, but gradually he has to do more and more, until he is doing it all. He also is the one who attends parent-teacher meetings at the school, visits aged relatives, and fulfills all other demands of this type.

Quite commonly as the symptoms worsen in severity she either has to have the husband with her, or has to know exactly where he is, or if his whereabouts cannot be known because of his job, some other person has to be with her. A kindly neighbour may do this, but usually a sister, mother or child has to, and if necessary the child is kept off school for that period. Gradually the woman's symptoms come to dominate the lives of her husband and other members of the family, and their every action may need to be accounted for or controlled. If these demands are not met then the housebound woman may have a very severe panic attack, the idea of which is so disturbing to her and the family that it is never allowed to happen. In fact, in some of these cases the last true panic was years before, and the whole extraordinary life style they follow has been dictated by the fear of a panic attack developing.

The husbands in these situations have certain important things in common. They tend to be rather passive, gentle, kindly and indulgent men. One does not see these complex phobic developments in the wives of aggressive and harsh men, who would refuse to do the shopping unless the wife is ill enough to be in hospital. In those cases one sees agoraphobic women who manage to struggle to the nearby shops to get the rations, because they fear the consequences, but are unable to go out on their own for social purposes or to enjoy themselves.

The rôle of the husband in these cases is crucial. It is our experience that sexual factors play a major part in about two thirds of the fully developed complex phobias we see, in a curious manner. The husbands are usually not very active sexually, in keeping with the personalities described earlier. The wives have chosen men who are non-threatening sexually, but who are kind and 'understanding'. They appreciate these qualities, but at another level crave for a different type of sexual partner, romantic and passionate. It will often be found that the women concerned had been involved in important sexual affairs either just before the onset or actually at the time; or that fantasies about lovers from the past played an important part in their lives. Unlike the simple phobias, which can be mainly seen in terms of over development of conditioned responses, these complex agoraphobias have the quality of 'approach–avoidance' conflicts, to use the terms of experimental psychology. In other words the woman stays at home to remain secure from her own sexual temptations—an idea put forward by Freud many years ago. (These factors do not appear in those agoraphobias which remain simple.)

Two examples make the thesis plain. The first is of a woman whose husband was exactly as described above, and who had been severely housebound for many years. At the relevant time she was attending a day hospital, to which she was taken each morning by her husband and collected afterwards. Even the idea of going out of the house on her own provoked fear and nausea. She met, at the day hospital, a rather psychopathic man, and travelled alone to one of the main London railway stations where she met her intended lover by arrangement, and where both were fortuitously met also by the present author! She remained non-agoraphobic until her lover left her, when her symptoms returned. Shortly afterwards her long suffering husband finally turned, took a girl friend, and stopped cherishing and tolerating his wife, whereupon she again lost her agoraphobic symptoms, and became quite seriously depressed.

The second example is of a woman whose husband was again as described above, whom she had married about fifteen years before, for security, after the breakup of a passionate love affair with an Italian. She was completely housebound except for a long weekly rail trip into London to see a behaviour therapist, whom it turned out she had come to regard as a kind of fantasy substitute for her old lover. When this was realised and pointed out, she immediately left her husband, travelled to Italy, and sought out and found the other man—all without any serious anxiety. However, more years had passed than she had clearly thought about, and she found a middle aged married man, happily domesticated. She returned to England and her husband, reverted to severe agoraphobia, and gave up treatment.

The complexity and the presence of manipulative and controlling elements, with secondary emotional gains of hysterical type, make these agoraphobic syndromes very difficult to treat. Behaviour therapy using desensitisation methods and 'implosion' (q.v.) can be helpful, as can group and other psychotherapy. Drug treatment, using phenelzine, 45 to 60 mg daily, can be more helpful than any other, although it has to be continued for a long time and many relapse when it is stopped. It is our practise, in severe cases, to use phenelzine, and then to admit, if necessary and practicable, to a day hospital where both behaviour therapy and group psychotherapy can be offered. As with drug treatment alone there is a high relapse rate. This failure rate is understandable if the mechanisms and motives set out above are in fact operating, because there is no satisfactory resolution to the conflict. Quite a number of the women who do lose their symptoms go on to leave their husbands, although some return and again become phobic. In others the marriage breaks up permanently, and the new relationship rarely proves satisfactory. The patients then sometimes return later to the psychiatrist, no longer agoraphobic, but depressed and lonely, and sometimes dependent or even addicted to alcohol or other drugs.

It should again be emphasised that although a large proportion of severe complex agoraphobics have underlying conflicts of this type, it is not true of all. In some the syndrome dates from a puerperal depression, incompletely treated, and this group seems to do best with phenelzine or with other antidepressants. In yet other cases the original trigger to the phobia can be found in some physical illness. We have seen a patient in whom a virus infection of the inner ear (vestibular neuronitis) caused severe vertigo and some unpleasant falls in the street. The patient had always been of anxious and obsessional temperament, and a severe complex agoraphobia developed, aided by the oversolicitude of her husband, who was soon doing all the shopping. This disorder responded rapidly to simple explanation and advice about going out for a progressively longer distance each day, and it really belongs with the simple phobias as an overlearnt conditioned response, despite the effect on the husband's daily life.

Social phobia is a term used to describe a fear of confronting people in a public place such as a restaurant, and merges into ordinary shyness. It tends to improve with age and the normal social practice of life—although, unfortunately, not in everyone. It is commonest in young men of reserved and inhibited temperament, who suffer from marked feelings of inferiority and of diffidence with the opposite sex, and they usually have mild ideas of reference—that is, the feeling that people are taking some special and critical note of them. Occasionally such a phobia is prodromal to schizophrenia, in which case the ideas of reference develop into truly delusional beliefs. If such phobic people become depressed the ideas of reference can also become much more severe, and they can pose diagnostic difficulties, perhaps being considered as schizophrenic. However, they have none of the other characteristic symptoms of schizophrenia, the picture is otherwise depressive, and responds to antidepressants, although a phenothiazine can usefully be added. This is one of the borderlands of psychiatric diagnosis, where syndromes overlap, and the correct diagnosis may not be clear for a long time.

Common sense advice about mixing more with other people, making suggestions to join tennis clubs, or whatever is appropriate to the patient's interests, is usually worth while. The more severely affected are just incapable of following such advice, and may need more positive help, by a behaviour therapy approach such as social skills training, or by group psychotherapy where appropriate. With severe social phobias phenelzine can be useful, as described in Chapter 15.

HYSTERICAL STATES

The terms 'hysteria' and 'hysterical' are among the most ambiguous in psychiatry, owing to the looseness with which they are applied. In the first place, they are often used to describe behaviour that is merely uncontrolled; but the latter word is itself preferable for this purpose. Second, the word 'hysterical' is commonly but wrongly used as though it was synonymous with 'psychogenic', i.e. to denote any kind of state that is mainly of psychological origin. In our view, such use is too wide. We believe that it should be restricted to those psychogenic conditions that are initiated or maintained for the sake of some gain that the symptoms bring: such gain may be an escape from difficulty, or the fulfilment of some wish, or the satisfaction of some desire, whether in reality or fantasy. In brief we believe that the term 'hysteria' is too wide, and is usually better replaced by 'hysterical conversion state' and 'hysterical elaboration', as defined later. These are both conditions in which the symptoms lead to some personal benefit or gain.

That this concept is narrower and more specific than those implied by the words 'psychogenic' and 'functional' may be shown by the following examples. Suppose that we have a patient whose arm has been immobilised for some time in a plaster cast and who finds that he cannot use that arm when the plaster is removed, although there is no organic cause for such disability. His condition is functional, but it may or may not be hysterical. If his inability arises merely from a fear of permanent paralysis that he has gradually come to accept as a fact, the condition is functional but not hysterical. If such a state must be given a diagnostic label, we would prefer to call it a state of simple dissociation, or a functional paralysis. But such a state may become hysterical if its existence serves a particular purpose for the person, such as enabling him to avoid something that he does not wish to do, or gains him something that he desires whether material in the form of financial compensation, or more spiritual in the form of sympathy and consideration. Again, if a person reacts by fainting to some psychological shock, such as witnessing an unpleasant accident, we should regard that as psychogenic, but not as hysterical unless there were also some clear evidence of its serving some gainful purpose. Similarly, vomiting may be psychogenic, but becomes hysterical only if it is purposive, as, for example, if used to lead to termination of an unwanted pregnancy.

'Hysterical' is thus used here to describe psychogenic conditions that are initiated for some personal gain that they bring to the patient. It is, however, an essential characteristic of hysterical states that the patient is never clearly aware of his motive; otherwise hysteria would be synonymous with malingering. Often the motive may be very close to the patient's conscious knowledge, so that hysterical behaviour and malingering may shade into each other; indeed they may co-exist. But it is a mistake to suppose that frank malingering is at all common, except sometimes in the later stages of a hysterical conversion state, after the patient has gained insight into his condition, but before there has been any progress in the problems which precipitated the symptoms.

The hysterical patient's unawareness, or relative unawareness, of his motives depends essentially on *dissociation*, that is on a failure of the normally integrated function of the nervous system. We do not understand the nature of this dissociation, but there is good evidence of neurophysiological changes in some of these patients. In studies of the e.e.g. response to peripheral sensory stimulation (the cortical evoked potential) it has been found that in acute hysterical anaesthesia there is failure of the cortical evoked potential, indicating a block somewhere between the posterior nerve root and the cortex, as the peripheral nerves conduct normally. In chronic hysterical anaesthesia the cortical evoked potentials are present again, fitting in with the clinical impression, mentioned in the last paragraph, that the symptoms may be prolonged consciously.

It is as though the patient with dissociation manages to put his motives in some special compartment of his mind where they remain isolated in so far as he does not look at them. On the basis of 'out of sight, out of mind', he fails then to see either the motives or the connection between them and the symptoms, although they are accessible if he cares to look. But this is more than a mere act. Such dissociation can be very real, can be carried further than mere unawareness of motive, and can affect lower levels of function. For example, a patient with hysterical anaesthesia can so far dissociate his capacity for sensation as to be anaesthetic even to painful stimuli. The capacity for dissociation varies much from one person to another, but it tends to be especially marked in those who show hysterical trends to any considerable degree. In frank malingering there is no dissociation; the patient is fully integrated and it is his full knowledge of his motives that inspires his behaviour.

It can be extremely difficult, in fact impossible, to tell the difference between 'hysterical'—that is unconsciously motivated —dissociation, and deliberate malingering. The diagnosis in the end rests on whether or not you believe the patient is telling the truth.

Aetiology

Hysterical symptoms may occur in anyone. They are usually shown *par excellence* by those with the hysterical type of personality (see p. 221), but they may occur even in normal people under sufficient provocation of stress. In general, however, they are seen in the constitutionally pre-disposed.

Constitutional factors

Such constitutional predisposition may be genetically determined to some extent in that, although specific genes do not appear to be involved, it is common to find a history of marked personality disorders and minor forms of nervous instability in the sibs and antecedents of hysterical patients. Apart from the heredity, an over-protective upbringing calculated to encourage emotionalism, histrionic display, sentimentality, an avoidance of realism and dependence on others, is conducive to the development of the hysterical personality, and, even if this last has not occurred, predisposes the patient through acquired patterns of behaviour to reactions of a hysterical type.

Hysterical personalities tend to be characterised by a labile emotionalism of a shallow kind leading to rapid enthusiasms that are rapidly dropped, instability of mood reflected in a vocabulary that makes special use of exaggeration, an egocentricity that makes for possessiveness and selfish attitudes with self-display and exaggeration of such personal attainments as there may be, the whole being coloured by emotional dependence on others and a fondness for the dramatic. Hysterical personalities are not solid people but mirror others and so, while themselves trying to appear more than they are, are really easily influenced and abnormally suggestible. This suggestibility is itself an aid to self-deception. Such people are inclined to act emotionally rather than reasonably, and so to take flight into feeling rather than into effective action when confronted by difficulty. In this they resemble children, whose emotional immaturity they share.

In addition, hysterical personalities commonly show two physical findings also suggestive of immaturity: (1) underdevelopment of the secondary sexual characteristics, (2) lability of autonomic responses. The first, coupled with the emotional immaturity, suggests a general immaturity of the constitution, and is possibly related also to the sexual frigidity that such persons commonly show. The second, the autonomic lability, is also characteristic of the young or immature, as a reflection of their incomplete integration of emotional control. That it is common in hysterical personalities is presumably another indication of their constitutional immaturity. Such autonomic lability, especially when coupled with suggestibility, is largely responsible for the readiness with which psychological symptoms are converted into physical ones, e.g. by the ready production of palpitation on arousal of emotion, and by the elaboration into indigestion or vomiting of such gastric sensations as emotion may arouse. Hysterical women in particular have great difficulty in dealing with sexuality and sexual relationships at any level other than the mild flirtation, and it is very common for them to be intensely attached to their fathers, well into adult life, with transference problems of the type considered at the beginning of this chapter. Sexual frigidity is also common, but not invariable or essential to the diagnosis. Adolescence is a common time for the first development of hysterical reactions.

Physical factors
The development of hysterical behaviour is likely to be facilitated by physical damage to the brain, and especially to the frontal lobes which appear to play some part in emotional control. Thus, severe concussion or injuries resulting in more gross damage may often be followed by hysterical symptoms, even in those who have shown little or no such trends before. It is an excellent rule to suspect organic cerebral disease in patients who first develop hysterical conversion states in middle life, even if there is a clear emotional background and 'secondary gain' is apparent.

Again, hysterical symptoms are especially common in dullards and in the mentally subnormal; this partly because duller people can accept grossness of self-deception more easily than can educated and cultivated people, but also because the integration of their emotional control is less highly organised than in the normal, just as is their intellectual function.

Finally, the development of organic disease may precipitate hysterical symptoms though less directly than the foregoing mechanisms. A person debilitated by a long physical illness will, like anyone else suffering from exhaustion, become less master of himself than normally; he will then be less able to control himself or his worries, will become more suggestible and may in that way develop added symptoms as a result. The same may happen, though less commonly, with the development of any other organic disease or injury (not necessarily to the brain), if the patient is frightened or otherwise disorganised by its occurrence and the threat to his well-being. If, in this setting, the patient uses these added psychogenic symptoms to his own ends, they come within our definition of the hysterical: as, for example, if he regresses to a childish level of behaviour that leads him to exact increasing attention by making excessive demands. With predisposed people, organic lesions will often provide foci for further hysterical developments along these lines.

Psychological factors
We have already mentioned, in considering constitutional factors, the sort of upbringing and psychological attitudes that are conducive to hysterical developments. That crude hysterical reactions are commoner in women than in men may perhaps be accounted for by the less rigorous discipline to which women were subjected and the traditionally more sheltered life that a number were allowed to lead; for hysterical personalities crave for and thrive on protection so long as they get their own way. The daughter who is too delicate to leave home, and the clinging, femininely dependent, yet essentially selfish flutter-pate of the 'little woman' variety, are common hysterical types.

The more that a person is pre-disposed in such ways, the less is the stress required to provoke hysterical reactions. It would be impossible to provide a list of stresses which might provoke hysterical symptoms through their emotional effects, but common among them are engagements, matrimonial difficulties, unwanted pregnancies, bereavements and conflicts between duty and desire. As regards engagements, it is often found that the hysteric enjoys the romance and attention that usually accompany them, but shrinks from the responsibility and finality of marriage; hysterical symptoms may well provide opportunity for prolonging the engagement on the plausible ground that it would not be right to contract a marriage that might be jeopardised by ill-health. As regards matrimonial difficulties, hysterical patients often use their symptoms to get their own way, to keep the partner in subjection and their children in ministering attendance. Unwanted pregnancies, with their threat of the pains and dangers of childbirth and increased responsibilities, may induce hysterical behaviour directed towards securing termination of the pregnancy. Bereavements, by removing some source of protection or object of emotional dependence, may provoke hysterical manifestations designed to secure some substitute for what has been lost. Conflicts between duty and desire may often be solved by the development of hysterical symptoms whose continued presence provides grounds for excusing the patient from his obligations.

Apart from such specific and personal situations, there are others of a more general kind that facilitate hysterical developments. Any environment that increases emotional tension is liable to do this, so that the hysterical subject is more likely to break down in circumstances that subject him to many stimuli at once, as when working under undue pressure, or having to spend much time among crowds or traffic. Crowds are liable to exert a particular emotional and suggestive effect; hence the mass hysteria prone to occur at meetings of Faith Healers and Revivalists. Suggestibility, and therefore the liability to hysteria is also increased by being kept in a state of expectation; hence the suggestive effects, for better or for worse that may follow medical consultations.

In addition to all these more or less normal situations which may precipitate hysterical reactions, especially in the predisposed, we may remind ourselves that ill-health may do the same. We have already considered how the physical factors of organic illness may encourage hysteria both through the effects of physical debility and otherwise; psychiatric illnesses, without evidence of organic disease, may do the same, since the patient through being frightened or otherwise disorganised by the symptoms may develop secondary and hysterical ones as a reaction to the basic illness.

In summary, we may say that hysterical reactions may occur in anyone under sufficient stress, but tend especially to occur in the predisposed. To such predisposition both heredity and upbringing may contribute. Hysterical personalities, who show hysterical reactions *par excellence*, are emotionally immature and often physically immature also. Puberty and adolescence are favourite times for hysterical developments. These are also facilitated by such physical factors as head-injuries and organic illnesses, especially of a debilitating kind; and by such psychological factors as psychiatric illness, by difficulties, conflicts, and any situations that heighten emotional tension. Crude hysterical reactions are commoner in the immature, in women, and in people of dull intelligence.

Dangers in diagnosing hysterical states

Hysterical elaboration
This term refers simply to those rather common situations in which some physical or psychological illness or disability is exaggerated or prolonged in a manner which brings some benefit or 'secondary gain' to the patient. The motivation may be entirely unconscious, as was discussed earlier, but as with other hysterical reactions it shades imperceptibly into deliberate simulation or malingering.

The situation in which hysterical elaboration occurs may be of any clinical type. One often seen is when some elderly widow with a grown up family has a stroke which leads to hospital admission; when discharged she is left with a greater or lesser disability. Often enough before the stroke the family will have largely drifted apart, and visits to mother may have become increasingly rare. When she is taken ill every one begins to visit, daughters rally round to do the shopping, grandchildren arrive to do the garden, and the old parental home is fuller, busier and for the patient happier than for many years. It is natural then, that there are powerful forces preventing complete recovery, as that might only mean a return to isolation.

Similar elaboration can occur with industrial accidents when compensation is in the offing, or in many other situations, in which complete recovery from the original illness has disadvantages. An example of this was a 60-year-old man who had had a minor stroke, from which he had made a good recovery so far as could be judged neurologically. However, he remained unable to walk without falling down. He was a caretaker of a block of council flats, in which he had kept order among the near delinquent adolescents by his rough tongue and fists; and he believed he was correspondingly unpopular. He expected to be beaten up if he returned as a semi-invalid to his own home in the block, but recovered well when he was promised a transfer to a similar place elsewhere. Hysterical elaboration differs from hysterical conversion only in that the basis of the symptoms and signs is determined by some already existing pathology.

Hysterical conversion states

This term includes all those hysterical reactions in which emotional problems, tensions or conflicts are 'converted' into some physical or psychological disability; from which disability the patient obtains some benefit or 'secondary gain'.

There are three main dangers in making the diagnosis of hysteria, and they may be conveniently stated here.

(1) The mere absence of physical signs is never enough to justify the diagnosis. The hysterical reaction should be psychologically comprehensible in the light of (i) the form that it takes, (ii) the value of the symptoms to the patient, (iii) the setting in which it occurs. The diagnosis of hysteria is not therefore a diagnosis by exclusion; it is essential to find positive evidence in its favour as well. The student or physician should not suppose, because he cannot find any physical cause for a condition (and this perhaps especially applies to localised manifestations such as pains that are felt in particular sites) that the diagnosis is necessarily one of hysteria. In many somatic complaints of supposedly psychological origin, the psychiatrist is as unable to find anything positive from his point of view as is the internist from his point of view, and can contribute little to treatment except such benefit as may be derived from sensible psychological management.

(2) The 'escape into illness' notion has the attraction of a formula, and of a somewhat cynical formula, that is easy to remember and to apply, in the sense that it is easy to make what for many is this accusation. Further, since life is difficult and we all wish our world to

be somewhat different from what it is, some apparent justification
for applying the formula can often be conjured up. It is, therefore,
necessary to beware the danger of jumping to the conclusion that,
even if the formula does seem to apply, it necessarily gives a full or
complete explanation of a given case.

(3) A common fallacy is that an over-emphatic or histrionic
method of verbal expression or motor demonstration is necessarily
evidence of hysteria. This need not be so. It may be merely a cultural
manifestation as in many southern Europeans and Jews. In the past
it seems to have been the common enough form in Great Britain; our
eighteenth-century ancestors were unashamedly lacrimose. When
such over-emphasis is not a cultural manifestation, it is often the
sales talk of the simple arising from a genuine anxiety. The desire to
impress or to obtain the interest of the doctor can scarcely be
regarded as abnormal at all. This type of behaviour can frequently
be observed in socially admirable and hard-working, if perhaps
rather simple, men and women, with little evidence of either
hysterical personalities or of obtaining any gain in the sense of escape
from their difficulties. It is, therefore, necessary to look behind the
form of expression and try to determine its object, if any, whilst
realising that the patient need not be clearly aware of its object; few
patients are.

Symptoms and signs
These may be literally of any sort. In general it may be said that the
hysterical patient will complain of whatever pays him to complain
of. There are fashions in hysteria as in other forms of human
behaviour, and at the present time the trend is for hysterical
symptoms to be more subtle and vague and less obvious than they
were thirty years ago. That is why the symptoms and signs described
in the older textbooks seem surprising to the present-day reader.
The hysterical manifestations described by Charcot in the nineteenth century are now seldom, if ever, seen; the gross hysterical
phenomena seen in the 1914–18 war were seldom repeated in the war
of 1939–45. At the present time the commonest hysterical reaction is
the exploitation of some relatively minor physical symptom such as
headache or indigestion, coupled with a minor disturbance of mood,
and often with some anxiety. As other forms do still occur, however,
though much less often than in the past, it is necessary to describe
them, but the student should note that the more gross hysterical
manifestations are comparatively uncommon. Bearing this in mind,
hysterical symptoms may be conveniently considered under three
headings: (1) psychological, (2) motor, (3) sensory.

(1) *Psychologically*

Of the more gross hysterical symptoms, the commonest psychological one is perhaps loss of memory. Such loss of memory is usually of a convenient kind, which enables the patient to avoid some difficulty or to escape from some unpleasant situation; or it may occur after some imprudent behaviour which the patient prefers to forget. Such amnesias may lead to the development of fugues. In these the patient takes flight in a literal sense. He wanders off, and may be found later many miles from home, often alleging uncertainty as to his identity, and professing no knowledge of how he arrived where he did. These also are usually naïve escapes from difficulty. In the war, such fugues were common in the Army and tended to happen at the end of periods of leave; in the Navy they were rare, presumably because it was known that they were treated by disciplinary rather than medical methods. The genuineness of the amnesia varies from case to case. Often the memory is fully accessible and is regained completely. But where the patient has been under real psychological stress, wrestling with some insoluble conflict or grossly pre-occupied with some real difficulty to which he is reacting emotionally but with poor control, such pre-occupations may have so much absorbed his attention as to have rendered him unaware of his surroundings, at any rate for much of the time, and to that extent he may be only vaguely aware of what he has been doing. These amnesias and fugues are distinctly more common in those who have had head injuries with disturbances of memory in the past, perhaps years ago. It is as if that remembered experience provides a model for the hysterical reaction.

Allied to fugues are the so-called *trances* and *twilight-states*. Trances are dream-like states into which the patient withdraws so that he is temporarily insulated from the world about him. They resemble the hypnotic state not only clinically but also in that they are producible by suggestion and their development is facilitated by practice. Many mediums have developed very markedly the capacity to enter a trance. Hysterical twilight states, often called Ganser states after the Berlin prison doctor who first described them, are extremely rare even in prison practice. They consist of a mild disturbance of consciousness akin to the trance state, but with the addition of such symptoms as a lay person imagines a lunatic to show. The patient gives incorrect answers to questions, but his replies are of a kind to suggest that the correct answer exists somewhere in his mind. Thus, if asked to multiply 3 by 3 the patient will say 10 or 8, but never 9. The traditional example of how his answers are approximate but just wrong is the response to the question, 'How many legs has a cow?' Again, the patient answers three or five, but never four. Somewhat similar to the Ganser state, but differing from it in that there is no disturbance of consciousness, is hysterical pseudo-dementia. This is particularly prone to occur in those of subnormal mentality when under stress which has led them to suggest themselves into being more stupid than they really are. The condition may closely resemble an organic dementia, so that the differential diagnosis may not be easy, but depends on that accurate observation which will show that the performance of the hysteric is more patchy and less well sustained than that of the organic dement, and improves when his co-operation is gained.

A rare phenomenon that has much in common with amnesias, fugues, trances and twilight states, in that they all depend essentially on dissociation, is the occasional occurrence of so-called *dual* or *multiple personality*. The patient is usually a woman with a number of contrasting traits of character which she has not managed to combine harmoniously within herself, and so has a poorly integrated personality. Thus, there may be inferiority feelings leading to outward diffidence, but contrasting with an inner conceit and aggressiveness; likewise an external primness and conformity to convention may conceal passionate thoughts and longings of an unorthodox and unconventional sort. This is a not uncommon state of affairs which often causes patients to feel dissatisfaction. Given the tendency to dissociate, such a patient may express her inner self by allowing the appearance of the concealed personality traits while suppressing those that she is more accustomed to show. In this way, a mincing and prudish maiden, given to good works, may transform herself into a seductive Circe, out for a good time and affecting to be ready for any lark. Extreme cases have been recorded in which such patients would reserve different names and styles of dress for their different roles, and when playing them would deny their real identities or that they had undergone any change. On return to the normal personality there would commonly be an amnesia for the interlude. It will be seen that the self-deception required is great, and such rare cases seem to have resulted from suggestions made, whether wittingly or not, in course of treating persons with a marked capacity for dissociation and a strongly hysterical predisposition.

We have had a case in which a hysterically predisposed man, about to be ordained, was the subject of religious conflicts. He was a diffident, hesitant, insecure, inadequate man, given to histrionic but shallow emotionalism. After a trivial head injury he developed an amnesia for the previous four years of his life, which included his marriage and the period of his theological studies. He refused to regain his memory. After some weeks in hospital he was having a conversation about the hesitations with which he had approached marriage, when suddenly (within thirty seconds) he changed into a gay, swashbuckling, hearty type of undergraduate who slapped his doctor on the back, and was without a care in the world. This was presumably the role of jolly muscular Christian that he had always wanted to fulfi. The change was accompanied by a complete and instantaneous reversal of his amnesia. Before the change the only part of his *recent* life that he could remember, or would remember, was the month that he had spent with us in hospital. After the change he remembered the whole of his previous life (but denied that he had ever felt the least hesitation over marriage) but could recall nothing of the month that he had just been spending in hospital. He carried this so far as to insist that the doctor, who had seen him almost daily and with whom he had been talking for half an hour before the transformation took place, was a total stranger who had entered his life for the first time at that moment. All this was something more than an act, although it was certainly melodramatic and stagey; it indicated a capacity for dissociation that is fortunately denied to more normal people. The subject of dual or multiple personality, on account of its interest and fascination, bulks more largely in psychiatric literature than is warranted by its importance or the frequency with which it is encountered. Some of the more famous cases have probably been elaborated by the patient in response to the credulous enthusiasm of the doctors and journalists involved. It is mentioned at some length here because it is difficult to explain briefly, but it is emphasised that the condition is a very rare one.

All the foregoing have been psychological hysterical manifestations of a fairly gross kind. Minor and more common hysterical features are a fondness for making scenes, a liking for little quarrels and emotional reconciliations, stirring up emotional currents by encouraging other people to take offence where none is intended, and so forth. The emotional shallowness of the hysteric allows him to enjoy these without feeling the same degree of upset and exhaustion that they are liable to induce in people with more normal depth of affect who happen to get embroiled. The hysterical personality uses these devices either to express his own aggression, more or less subtly, or to exact attention and apologies from others. Such behaviour cannot be sharply differentiated from psychopathic reactions (see p. 228) except in so far as they are coloured by and are an expression of the hysterical personality. Where such hysterical psychopathic reactions are extreme and melodramatically coloured, involving hate to a degree suggestive of paranoia, or self-pity embellished with the addition of fanciful symptoms, they may sometimes simulate a psychosis and raise the suspicion of schizophrenia. But they are usually transient, experienced and related with some relish and the embellishments designed to add interest and colour, such as the appearance of gentle angels that whisper comforting advice, or the voice of the fiancé calling to the patient at night with a loving but urgent intensity. In some cases psychological symptoms of this kind are shown only in particular environment, and this may be a useful diagnostic and prognostic point.

(2) Motor symptoms

These may take the form either of paralysis or of abnormal movements. The paralysis may involve the limbs, trunk, or speech mechanism. The abnormal movements may take the form of jerks, spasms, tremors or fits.

Where paralyses are involved these are usually of a convenient kind, as in the dissatisfied machine-operator whose hysterical paralysis of the right leg prevented him from operating his treadle, or the girl who was 'struck dumb' with emotion when her fiancé found her less reliable than he had supposed. Disordered gaits, often of a fantastic kind, may be seen usually associated with hysterical ataxia.

Where jerks, spasms and tremors occur, the differential diagnosis from organic conditions may be difficult, e.g. choreiform movements. But observation will show that such manifestations change considerably according to the circumstances and setting in which the patient is placed and according to the suggestive effect of these upon the patient. The diaphragmatic spasm on which pseudo-cyesis (hysterical imitation of pregnancy) depends may, for instance, be abolished if the patient can be successfully induced to relax. Hysterical fits can usually be distinguished from epileptic ones without too great difficulty. The clouding of consciousness is usually much less; the patients generally do not hurt themselves, bite their tongues or pass water; they do not pass through the typical tonic and clonic phases, but tend instead to show purposive movements; and they seldom, if ever, have attacks when they are alone. The pupils are often widely dilated and respond poorly to light; the tendon reflexes are normal and equal, and a Babinski response is never seen. Finally, such fits are precipitated by emotional causes and tend to vary in intensity according to the presence and absence of spectators.

(3) Sensory symptoms

The more gross sensory symptoms in hysteria take the form of blindness, deafness or the production of areas of anaesthesia. Again, they are usually convenient and often their onset is dramatic. For example, a hysterical medical student who found dissection of the cadaver aesthetically offensive and failed in his anatomy examination, dramatically developed hysterical blindness on hearing the news, and was thus absolved from continuing with his studies. Deafness may similarly occur in an emotional setting, but has been known to develop gradually as a protection against a nagging partner, and to disappear when freedom has been gained. Areas of anaesthesia may occur in suggestible people after injuries, as the result of neurological consultations, and often after medical, and especially neurological, examinations. These occur more commonly in neurological practice than elsewhere, for obvious reasons. They are becoming increasingly rare with the increasing recognition of how they are produced.

All these hysterical imitations of illness are generally very rough, since they represent only the patient's guess as to what the illness is like. Thus, the hysterical anaesthesiae are usually of a glove and stocking type, i.e. limited to what the patient regards as a functional unit and without regard for the anatomical distribution of nerves. Hysterical paralysis is usually a rough and ready affair also, and some finer points in its differential diagnosis will be mentioned later. The more informed the patient, the better the imitation; greater difficulties may therefore arise when dealing with hysterical doctors and nurses, and especially with hysterical neurologists, who are luckily rare.

More subtle symptoms
With the increasing spread of medical knowledge, these cruder hysterical manifestations have tended to be confined to the more stupid and less educated patients. Those with higher intellectual and cultural endowments find, for the most part, that the self-deception is too gross to be easily tolerated. It is re-emphasised that they go in more for vaguer and more subtle complaints, such as headaches, giddiness and faintness. In these use is often made of physiological mechanisms, such as vomiting, while over-breathing, leading to dizziness and clouding of consciousness, may be used in the production of hysterical faintness.

Hysterical choice of symptoms
We have already seen that some patients with anxiety states may focus their anxiety on some particular organ with worry over its function. Hysterical patients may similarly focus their attention, and

then develop and exploit symptoms which they relate to the particular organ concerned. The direction of this is determined by the same sort of factors that determine the organ neuroses in anxiety states. The main ones are: (a) the patient's previous experience of illness, whether personal or second-hand, (b) some belief, derived from that experience, that certain parts of himself are specially vulnerable, (c) the special importance of certain functions to certain people (vision to precision-workers, hearing to telephonists, etc.), (d) the effect of emotion on function (excitement leading to palpitation, gastric disturbance or frequency of micturition) with consequent direction of attention to the affected parts.

The head, heart and alimentary tract are perhaps the favourite physical sites to which hysterical symptoms are referred. This is partly because of their special importance in the patient's conception of himself: the head as containing that core on which his personality and conscious existence depends, the heart as being that on which life itself depends, the bowels as the medium through which body and soul are kept together. It is partly also because the head, heart and bowels are so often affected by emotional upsets, with resultant headache, palpitation and vague aliminetary disturbance, so that the patient is more easily conscious of them.

The symptoms themselves may be of any kind, but are likely to be vague, variable and unaffected by treatment except where this has some special suggestive value.

Attitudes in hysteria

The whole clinical picture may be additionally coloured by the patient's attitudes. Thus, the patient often adopts a noticeably placid attitude towards the symptoms. This so-called 'belle indifference' is understandable in the light of the purposive nature of the condition. On the other hand, where the motive is to exact sympathy and attention and to make demands on others, this indifference may be replaced by ostentatious display. Some patients are able to combine both methods, employing melodramatic language or exhibiting fantastic physical contortions when asked to show their disability, with a brave, smug smile on a placid face. Hysterical patients also adopt a characteristic attitude towards the doctor, which after a little experience is often easy to recognise. The basis of it seems to be that they want to make a special impression and to strike up a specially personal and emotional rapport. They often start by politely belittling the help that they have previously received with an implication that they realise they are now in better hands; they seek to establish themselves as special favourites by the occasional introduction of coy flattery or by striking some more markedly personal note that is usual in the consulting room. In this way they are likely to show a mixture of something near obsequiousness that is coupled with over-familiarity. The student should be on his guard on observing this and should on no account be taken in by any tendencies to flattery. Meantime, the history is unfolded usually with a wealth of detail and the introduction of small dramatic touches. 'She said I had turned ashen, positively ashen, not a drop of blood left in me, and she thought it a miracle that I survived . . .' The observations attributed to doctors in such situations are often of an extraordinary sort. The patient will usually emphasise that he is 'particularly sensitive' (and may imply that this is meritorious, though a martyr-dom) and will often seek to reinforce this impression by jumping at noises and flinching when the cuff of the sphygmomanometer is inflated on his arm. The long-windedness of the history, unlike that of obsessional patients who are merely anxious to be careful and to avoid misleading the doctor, is determined by egocentricity and enjoyment of being the centre of affairs. A typical hysterical statement from a girl who had given up a long succession of jobs because of supposed physical ill-health, and who had found her last position in a nursery school too much for her, was: 'I was never one to spare myself. As my last doctor (such a nice man but a little old-fashioned in his treatment, and I do think it's better to come to a hospital like this where people are really up to date, don't you?) said to me some months ago. "For you to go on working in your present condition would be like trying to ride a bicycle up a steep hill with the brakes on". I should like nothing better than to go back to work. I love my work, I love children and I love doing good. But as my mother said to me only last night, it would be silly to do so until I am really fit again. I am afraid to say I think she was right. These headaches are just like a drill being driven in my head. It starts . . . and . . . and . . . And when I'm fit? Oh, I've always been artistic and interested in interior decoration—I'm thinking of taking up art.'

It will be realised that the extent to which these attitudes are shown will vary much from case to case. The normal personality who has suffered a hysterical breakdown under severe stress will probably show none of them. The moderately habitual hysteric will show some of them. They will be shown *par excellence* only by those in whom the hysterical personality is fully developed.

Chronic hysteria
Hysterical patients are not infrequently seen who complain of being chronic invalids. The main symptoms are usually weakness and

tiredness, of which there is little objective evidence, with the addition from time to time of transient but more specific physical symptoms. They lead restricted and self-centred lives and complain that their symptoms prevent them from carrying out duties which they would otherwise eagerly fulfil. The attitude is one not merely of acquiescence in the symptoms, but of steady insistence upon them as a matter of course. A characteristic remark is, 'Of course, I've suffered from my nerves all my life'. Paranoid and bitchy attitudes may be prominent.

Underlying depression

In some patients with hysterical conversion or elaboration, even those in whom 'belle indifference' is marked, there may be quite severe underlying depression. The motive or secondary gain of the hysterical reaction is basically an escape from intolerable feelings of guilt or depression, which seem to become 'unconscious' in the processes we call dissociation and 'conversion'. One young woman with hysterical paraparesis developed this after her closest friend had broken her neck while driving our patient's poorly maintained and almost brakeless car. Her own paralysis symbolised her friend's total quadriplegia. Only after months of unsuccessful treatment did we discover that the mother of the injured girl had been sending frequent 'poison pen' letters, constantly harping on the fact that our patient was to blame for the tragedy. When this came to light the bland affect and denial of problems was replaced by severe depression—essentially a more natural and adult reaction—and she rapidly improved.

The possibility of severe depression underlying the hysterical state should be borne in mind before trying dramatic 'cures' using hypnosis or drug induced suggestions, unless there is adequate supervision and control. Occasionally the removal of an hysterical disability in such a way, without doing anything for the underlying problem to which the disability is a response, leads to suicidal attempts. As was pointed out earlier, there is a wide range of susceptibility to hysterical reactions, and some develop them with little apparent provocation, others only when the stress is severe. It is obviously in the latter that serious underlying problems or depression may be present.

Differential diagnosis

It has already been emphasised (p. 273) that neither the absence of physical signs nor the presence of histrionic complaints is enough to justify the diagnosis of hysteria. The hysterical reaction should be psychologically comprehensible in terms of (1) the form that the symptoms take, (2) the value of the symptoms to the patient, (3) the setting in which they occur.

The form taken by the symptoms is unlikely to resemble that of any recognised organic condition unless the patient has had personal experience of that condition before. The more that the symptoms do resemble those of organic disease the less likely does the diagnosis of hysteria become. An account of the symptoms that is clear cut as regards their nature, localisation, onset, duration and relief, and that is given in substantially the same terms at different times, is on the whole unlikely to be an account of hysterical symptoms. The less that the symptoms resemble those of organic disease, and the more vague, widespread and variable that they are, the more likely does the diagnosis of hysteria become. The patient's choice of symptoms should be comprehensible in terms of his past experience and their suitability for whatever purpose they may be serving.

The value of the symptoms to the patient and the setting in which they occur can only be understood by taking a careful chronological history, supplemented by information from the relatives. This should show whether the symptoms can be reasonably construed as a reaction to circumstances, and whether such reaction can be reasonably construed as being purposive. A point of diagnostic value is that some cases show hysterical behaviour only in a particular environment. The occurrence of similar reactions in the past is of importance, although sometimes the history may reveal only a very sheltered and self-indulgent previous life, so that no gross hysterical manifestations appeared because there was no occasion for their display. A useful guide in the differential diagnosis is to ask oneself: does this breakdown come as a surprise? Most hysterical reactions do not come as a surprise, either to the patient's relatives or to the doctor who knows the case. In general, the reaction shown should be compatible with the personality that the history has revealed, and this judgment must be made on common-sense grounds.

The following case may illustrate the points involved. We were asked to see a man aged forty-three, who had been diagnosed as suffering from hysteria. His two children were ill, and one of them had cried incessantly for forty-eight hours, worrying both the patient and his wife, and causing them to feel worn out. In this setting the patient had suddenly, at ten minutes past eight in the morning and while trying to calm the child, felt faint and dazed, and had been obliged to sit down. He appeared confused and out of touch. He was brought to hospital where he was found to be lucid at some moments, but inaccessible at others, and at others again accessible but confused. In fact, there was fluctuation in his level of consciousness. Even if the sudden onset of the symptoms did not suggest a vascular accident, and even if it were not realised that such fluctuations of consciousness indicated some intracranial pathology (see pp. 50, 106), the history would have made the diagnosis of hysteria excessively improbable. From the wife's account the patient was a conscientious, hardworking man of responsible kind with an excellent work record, who had never shown hysterical trends before. To suppose that he was escaping by the sudden development of symptoms of this kind from the worry and fatigue caused by his child's illness was a naïve oversimplification of the clinical picture. In fact, he had a haemorrhage from an intracranial angioma.

Differential diagnosis of specific hysterical symptoms

Complaints of anxiety and depression are common symptoms in hysterical states, and may be the principal ones. A careful comparison of the subjective complaints and of the degree of objective disturbance, including pulse rate, sweating, fine tremor, pupil dilatation and weight loss may be helpful. If the depressive symptoms are of the endogenous pattern they should not be regarded as hysterical.

With regard to more specific hysterical symptoms, those of a psychological kind can usually be diagnosed without great difficulty if a satisfactory history has been obtained. This should enable hysterical amnesia to be distinguished from those caused by head-injury, alcohol or epilepsy. Fugues may have to be distinguished from post-epileptic automatism, and trances and twilight states from disturbances of consciousness due to other causes. The significant difference is that in post-epileptic automatism the behaviour is simple and purposeless compared with the complicated and purposive actions in the fugue, which show that the patient is still capable of using the higher levels of function in a coordinated way. Similarly, in trances and twilight states such disturbance of consciousness as there may be is of a partial kind that enables the patient to use the higher levels of function in a selective way that suits his needs. The hysteric is thus able to adapt himself rapidly to altering circumstances, which the patient in epileptic confusion is not. Ganser's syndrome (see p. 275) may simulate schizophrenia; prolonged observation may be necessary to establish the diagnosis, which may be clinched in the end by the variability of the condition, particularly in relation to different circumstances and the effects of suggestion. The diagnosis may be very difficult indeed when, as can happen, the Ganser state occurs in a patient who is actually schizophrenic as well. Hysterical pseudodementia may be hard to distinguish from true organic dementia, and observation may be required before the diagnosis becomes assured. In all these cases, should doubt persist, the position *may* be clarified by (1) investigation of the mental state under hypnosis or drugs (e.g. methohexitone given intravenously), and (2) the electro-encephalograph. The former method tends to lower the patient's resistance and enables relevant facts to be more easily ascertained; the latter may give indications of epileptic disturbance or brain disease. It is emphasised, however, that although these procedures may be helpful in some cases, they may also obscure the issue in others, since patients by no means always tell the truth even if their resistance is lowered, and since the electro-encephalograph sometimes produces findings that are confusing rather than helpful in our present state of knowledge.

With regard to the motor symptoms, hysterical paralyses can usually be distinguished from organic ones by the normality of the reflexes (the rare condition 'familial periodic paralysis' is sometimes mistaken for hysteria but is distinguishable, apart from on other grounds, by the disappearance of the reflexes in the paralytic phase), and by the fact that if asked to make a particular movement the patient will often actively prevent it by visible contraction of the antagonistic muscles that are also supposed to be paralysed. Hysterical paralysis of the forearm can usually be detected by flexing the supported elbow in supination and allowing the forearm to fall; in organic paralysis the forearm automatically undergoes pronation to fall with the palmar surface of the hand downwards, but the hysterical patient, unless forewarned, will allow the arm to fall in the same supine position in which it started. In paralysis of the leg, the diagnosis can be established by 'Babinski's second sign'. The recumbent patient is asked to sit up by using his trunk muscles and without using his hands. In the normal person both legs will rise off the ground equally. In the patient with organic paralysis the affected leg will rise higher than the normal one. The hysterical patient, unless forewarned, will keep his paralysed leg on the floor. Hysterical muscular weakness can usually be detected by encouraging the patient to move the affected part against resistance provided by the examiner. The force exerted by the patient usually increases or decreases according to the strength of the resistance that is applied. so that with suitable encouragement the patient may unthinkingly display considerable strength. Jerks, spasms and tremors may be very difficult to distinguish from choreic or extrapyramidal symptoms of organic type, but observation over a period will probably show that the hysterical forms vary very greatly in pattern and intensity, according to circumstances and the effects of suggestion. Disordered gait due to hysterical ataxia can usually be recognised through the patient's tendency to overdo it; such cases commonly show fantastic gaits, repeatedly nearly falling over (though seldom if ever hurting themselves) but saving themselves at the last moment by what the observer can recognise as skilled coordination and balance. The differential diagnosis of hysterical from epileptic fits has already been considered.

With regard to the sensory symptoms, hysterical blindness and deafness must be diagnosed on general grounds coupled with the absence of appropriate physical signs. Areas of hysterical anaesthesia can be detected, unless the patient is unusually well-informed, by the fact that they do not correspond with the anatomical distribution of the nerves that supply the area. It is possible to confuse a glove and stocking anaesthesia with peripheral neuritis but in the latter loss of tendon reflexes is almost invariable, and it is usually also possible to diminish or extend quite markedly the area of hysterical anaesthesia by suggestion so that the findings become quite inconstant.

The most subtle hysterical symptoms and the organ neuroses must be judged on their merits and differentiated from other conditions by their onset, development and course in the light of the patient's personality and circumstances, coupled with the physical findings.

In patients in whom there is hysterical elaboration of some already present condition, it can be most difficult to assess the patient's capacity accurately.

Finally, it must also be remembered that hysterical reactions can be facilitated by organic disease, and this factor should always be suspected when the past history is free from hysterical episodes and the personality is good. In particular, organic mental changes provide a fertile soil for physical conversion symptoms of all kinds. A comprehensive physical examination is therefore necessary in all patients, and should be repeated at intervals if necessary. Similarly memory and concentration should be carefully assessed, and the results recorded for later comparisons. Likewise, the differential diagnosis of severe hysterical reactions from schizophrenia can also be difficult, and all the more so since hysterical personalities may develop such illnesses. A fair rule is that if there is reasonable doubt between the diagnosis of hysteria and schizophrenia, the case is probably the latter.

Course and prognosis
The immediate prognosis of the individual hysterical reaction is good

and becomes all the better if the special difficulties that gave rise to it have passed or are capable of resolution. The immediate prognosis is bad only when the underlying motive has great force. The ultimate prognosis is more difficult to assess, but in general the better the personality and the greater the stress under which the breakdown has occurred, the less is the likelihood of relapse, provided that the same degree of stress can be avoided in the future. Those who have reacted hysterically to slight or negligible stress are more likely to relapse than those whose stress has been severe; the likelihood is increased if there has been a history of similar breakdowns before. In fact, the more the person is hysterically predisposed the less good is the ultimate prognosis. Hysterical reactions in childhood and adolescence need not give rise to undue pessimism—at any rate until the character can be regarded as set in established immaturity despite increasing age. It may not be possible to decide how ingrained hysterical trends may be without opportunity of trying the patient's reaction to the change of environment. There is no doubt that a hysterical predisposition can be influenced by the environment, and often diminishes or disappears after puberty or in later adolescence. Some cases show hysterical behaviour only in a particular environment; provided that the environment can be altered, this is a favourable prognostic sign.

In general, where the symptoms still show variability there is hope, and the chief prognostic point is the patient's level of performance between hysterical episodes. It is only where such level of performance is low that great pessimism need be felt. Where there is a history of successful performance between hysterical episodes the prognosis may be good. This is of much greater prognostic importance than the severity of the actual episode or the nuisance caused by the patient at the time of its occurrence. On the whole hysterical patients are liable to do better than might be expected and have a surprising capacity for pulling themselves together, except where the hysterical personality is established in full flower.

Treatment
One of the main difficulties in the treatment of hysteria derives from the fact that hysterical *personalities* are apt to arouse a strong emotion of irritation and dislike in the hearts of many doctors; they seem such selfish hypocrites and take up so much time. Medical men perhaps tend as a group to be practical and pragmatic in their views of life and to rate the capacity for efficient performance a good deal higher than the capacity for sensitive appreciation, feeling that the latter is only justified if it is translated into works. Both their temperament and training makes them distrust the mystical and subjective, and, like

good puritans, they hold that the proof of the pudding is not in its contemplation but in its eating, and that, when eaten, the value of the pudding lies in its power of sustenance rather than in its taste. With many hysterical personalities, however, the values of life reside in subjective experience and subjective development, without necessarily much urge for practical performance that does not directly nourish these needs. This scale of values, seen at its best in certain artists and mystics, is apt to be ill-mated with the demands of the work-a-day world, and to be highly antipathetic to different temperaments to whom it may appear as merely egotistic self-indulgence.

The tragedy of the persistent hysteric is that the immediate and short-term gains that are unconsciously sought are usually quite outweighed by the long-term losses. Hysterical behaviour in the end tends to alienate sympathy and affection; in that way the actual need for these may, through excessive demands, itself lead not to gratification but to ultimate indifference from other people.

As has previously been suggested, the affect engendered by the more difficult hysterical personalities is apt to be transferred to all cases who exhibit physical conversion symptoms, on the false assumption that all patients who exhibit these symptoms are of the same type; but as has been seen this is not true. Those, therefore, who are unable to conquer their revulsion towards hysterical personalities may be helped by bearing in mind that physical conversion symptoms can and often do develop in patients of quite a different type, who do not exhibit hysterical characteristics any more than they may do themselves. We are all capable of and have all practised some hysteria.

General management

In treatment the first question is: how seriously must the symptoms be regarded? This involves considerations of whether the patient should remain at work, should have a change of environment, should be further investigated, or should be admitted to hospital. The answer depends not only on the severity of the symptoms themselves but on how far they are likely to be benefited by such changes. It is not possible to supply a formula that will apply to all cases. In general, we think that in the treatment of hysteria it is necessary to take some risks. Of course, all patients must be properly examined, but it is wrong to suppose that because a patient has a complaint couched in physical terms it must necessarily be further investigated. If the physical examination elicits no evidence of organic illness and the psychiatric indications are in favour of hysteria, it is in general better to avoid investigations unless some special further indication arises later. Unnecessary investigations are not only wasteful, but encourage the hysterical patient to persist with the symptoms and to develop others. To admit a wavering hysteric into hospital for full but unnecessary investigations is to provide a focal point for the development of further symptoms both immediately and in the future, and to provide a landmark in his medical history that will be exploited and will obscure the issue in his future medical consultations. The error, if there must be one, should be on the side of encouraging the patient to keep at work. 'People are seldom better employed,' said Benjamin Jowett, 'than in earning their own living'. And this (though Jowett refused to recognise science or to believe in the existence of the knee-jerk) may be taken as the golden rule in the treatment of hysteria.

It may well be otherwise, however, as regards the advisability of changing the home environment. This is because some patients show hysterical behaviour only in one particular environment, as has already been said, and because the environment of some hysterics is specially calculated to encourage the continuance of hysterical behaviour, as will later be explained.

Having considered these general principles, we will now consider the removal of the actual symptoms themselves.

Treatment of specific symptoms

In this the first essential is that the patient should be accessible. Those in trances or twilight states can often be brought to full awareness by the application of some powerful stimulus that causes them fully to mobilise themselves; a suitable one is the application to the nostrils of cotton wool treated with strong ammonia. When full awareness is regained its continuance must be insisted on by obliging the patient to undertake some activity, such as conversing, washing, drinking a cup of tea or eating, after which it is much harder for him to sink into his former state with any plausibility.

The hysterically deaf can often be persuaded to hear by persuading them to listen to questions through a stethoscope; with any initial success the loudness of the stimuli is then gradually decreased until it is plain to the patient that he can hear better than he supposed. Again, he must not be given opportunity to lose his newly rediscovered auditory acuity.

Hysterical aphonia can often be overcome by squeezing the patient's chest very suddenly, which usually produces the distinct sound 'Oh' and 'Ah'. It is then pointed out that he can produce this sound and he is made to do it again. The syllables are then elaborated until words are formed. He must then be made to continue in conversation and also to talk to other people, which similarly makes relapse more difficult to achieve with plausibility.

Patients with amnesia, who are also inaccessible in so far as they are unable to furnish that account of themselves which is essential for understanding the case, may often be led to recover their memory by firm persuasion and encouragement. If the amnesia is for the whole past life it can soon be demonstrated that they have not forgotten everything and from small beginnings (such as what season of the year does it appear to be, roughly what year is it, is it A.D., or B.C., and what do those terms mean?) it may be possible to extend their memories indefinitely.

Where these methods do not succeed, simple and unsophisticated patients may often be successfully treated by crude methods of suggestion such as the application of galvanism or faradism. Alternatively, their suggestibility may be increased by hypnosis or narco-hypnosis (giving some hypnotic substance orally or intravenously) and the return of function then suggested to them. The resistance of amnesic patient to regaining their memory may often be broken down in this way.

The success of these methods largely depends, of course, on the cooperation of the patient, and in order to gain this, it is desirable to explain what is about to be done and with what object, at the same time offering some explanation, which may or may not be strictly scientific but should be geared to the patient's intelligence, of how the symptoms have come about. All of these rapid methods should be used without forgetting the possibility of serious underlying depression, as described earlier; and it should be made plain that help will be available for any such problem when appropriate.

In cooperative patients success should readily be achieved, especially if they are not faced with any specially difficult situation should the symptoms disappear. It is with uncooperative patients, with powerful motives for their symptoms, who are nearer the malingering end of the scale that the difficulties will occur.

Individual symptoms are best approached by firm and repeated persuasion, and 'jollying along', with praise and admiration for improvement, and a bored, uninterested response to failure.

When a patient has had some symptom or disability for some time he cannot be expected just to lose it, for no reason other than persuasion. It is necessary to have some face saving explanation and treatment, perhaps with some new (and harmless) drug treatment to which he can respond over the course of a week or two. No one relishes humiliation, and this is what a sudden loss of long-held symptoms can mean.

Rehabilitation

Removal of particular symptoms in this way, however, is only scratching at the surface of the problem. They will recur in one form or another unless an attack is made on the underlying psychological difficulty or unless the environmental stress is diminished. It is therefore necessary to study the difficulties that have been experienced in the patient's adaptation to life, and to plan treatment in accordance with the findings. In cases where the patient has a genuine problem, is aware of a need for help and is anxious for its solution even at some cost to himself—as opposed to requiring merely sympathy and attention from the doctor on whom he wishes to throw the whole onus of 'cure'—mutual discussion, with explanation of the pattern of reaction, and plans for the future mutually arrived at, may effect considerable improvement in attitudes and capacity for self-management, with consequently diminished likelihood of relapse. The chances of success depend largely upon the personality of the patient and on his possession of what may perhaps be called mental honesty. Markedly hysterical personalities are usually incapable of more than verbal insight, and this incapacity is a bar to successful psychotherapy. The most fruitful approach is usually then indirect and environmental.

A change of environment in young hysterics is often most desirable, not only in order to test their capacity for improvement, but also to remove them from an atmosphere which is often calculated to maintain such hysterical patterns of behaviour as they may show. Unfortunately, the relatives often show similar dispositions themselves, are unduly doting, or selfishly crave for the love of their children, and hence are sentimentally unwilling to permit the exhibition of that firmness and discipline that may be necessary. Even in older hysterics the relatives may have become so persuaded of the genuineness of the patient's 'invalidism', and may be so reluctant or unable to revise their concepts, that anything much in the way of that environmental change that may be essential to improvement may be unattainable through family opposition.

In considering environmental changes, however, it should be borne in mind that hysterical qualities may be of value in the patient's readaptation. Many hysterics do very well in positions where they may play-act (witness the stage) or duly indulge in self-demonstration or sacrifice (so long as this is not self-sacrifice so much as sacrifice to self), or where their work allows them to find such attachments as they may have been previously unable to form. A not uncommon sequence is that of a hysterical adolescence, an admirable if somewhat demanding motherhood, and once more a hysterical matronhood when the children have grown up and left home. This in itself suggests therapeutic environmental possibilities.

Relatives, and sometimes employers, will often ask for advice in handling the patient. There can be no set formula. But in general, over-solicitude is to be strongly discouraged; the symptoms should be disregarded as far as is compatible with reasonable humaneness and courtesy; and judicious firmness should be shown. Even so, it is a mistake to suppose that there is always a solution to every problem, for the really determined hysteric is likely to win in the long run and one must be resigned to it. The husband of a vain, silly woman of chronically and intractably hysterical disposition said to us, 'All through our married life friends have told me to be firm. But in the end I've found that it just doesn't pay.' In fact, resort must be had to bargaining.

SEXUAL DIFFICULTIES

The actual perversions are separately considered on page 216. We are concerned here with problems that are more incidental, but which may occur as part of a personality problem that is not necessarily specifically sexual in itself.

SEX PROBLEMS

Personal sexual problems leading to distress frequently occur in adolescents and young men and women. A number are disturbed by the continual awareness of sexual arousal and frustration, but the commonest complaint to doctors currently seems to be of feelings of sexual inadequacy, coupled with general feelings of inferiority, shyness of the opposite sex, and doubts about homosexual leanings. All aspects of sex are much more freely discussed nowadays, and sexual intercourse is commoner in younger people than only 10 or 15 years ago. There is great pressure on young people from all sides to be sexually active, and modern advertising and films seem to intensify feelings of inadequacy in the shy and slow to develop. At least in London we less commonly see young people in whom the problems arise from suppression or a refusal to recognise sexual drives and feelings, who have received no instruction, and have been brought up in an atmosphere of rigid sexual moralism. However, these sexual repressive problems are still not infrequent especially in older people, and the patients are prone to keep the whole topic of sex in some special separate compartment of their minds, and a compartment that they feel is better left unopened. They thus tend to split off from the rest of their conscious considerations such sexual stirrings as they may feel, and may do so to the extent of refusing to recognise them for what they are.

In general, the more frankly that sex is regarded, the more readily and unembarrassedly that the questions of children are answered as they are asked, and the more matter-of-factly that the subject is dealt with as a whole, the better adjusted will the child be to stirrings of puberty and the onset of menstruation, and the less difficulty will there be in regulation of the sex life in adolescence.

Where other attitudes have been adopted, leading to furtiveness of thought and approach, and even to refusal of recognition, problems may arise according to the conscientiousness and moral scruples of the individual. It can be helpful to discuss the problems with a sympathetic listener, and to have them put in a different perspective. For those people greatly troubled by sexual tension, who are against any pre-marital sexual experience or masturbation, the only sensible advice is to avoid sexual stimulation as much as possible, and to try and fill life with interesting and rewarding activities. It is not the place of psychiatry to undermine people's religious or moral beliefs on grounds of 'mental hygiene', although many people believe that it is.

An extremely common complaint in older people is that one sexual partner is much more interested in sex than the other. The increased freedom of discussion and journalistic publicity has led people to be less satisfied with an imperfect situation than they previously were, but unfortunately less can be done to alter libido and sexual activity than many have been led to expect, as these are so much a matter of basic constitution, and many are therefore disappointed. A similar problem of sexual dissatisfaction and frustration arises quite frequently in marriages in which the sexual drives of one partner decline with age more rapidly than those of the other. This decline seems to be more frequent in men, and can lead to great unhappiness if it intensifies feelings of inferiority, or becomes one of the battlegrounds in the marriage in which one is repeatedly criticising the other. The desire to test an apparently failing virility with another woman, having wondered how much his declining libido is the result of boredom or lack of attractiveness in the wife, is a very common cause of the breakup of apparently stable marriages. It is remarkable how often couples have not discussed the problem at all, and sometimes it helps them to do so jointly with a doctor or other suitable person. No change in sexual drive takes place, but the situation is often eased.

In recent years there has been much greater emphasis on the need for the education of sexually incompatible couples, for instance using the intensive techniques of Masters and Johnson, details of which should be sought in their books. Those authors made very detailed studies of male and female sexual physiology, and applied their findings to sexual technique; using counselling, detailed explanation and practical advice; and for some people even providing experienced sexual

partners for instruction. This last, although perhaps only a formalisa-
tion of what many people have done secretly throughout history, has
naturally led to much criticism, and has been largely dropped. Many
clinics have been set up in North America, and a few in Britain, to offer
treatment and help based on these lines. It is as yet too early for serious
assessment of their results. When the clinics are run by psychiatrists
and psychologists many other problems between the couple other than
the purely sexual ones come to light, and the work becomes closely
integrated with marital psychotherapy.

Masturbation

For many this is a source of distress, guilt and self-reproach. Such
feelings are not necessarily an anomaly but in some they may be quite
excessive. Since masturbation has been practised by practically
everyone at one time or another, the patient may be reassured that the
practice is normal rather than otherwise. If he has been taught that it
will drive him mad, send him blind, cause his eyes to drop out or totally
undermine his health (and we have known patients to have been taught
and to believe all of these), he may be reassured to the contrary. Over
emphasis on the benefits of masturbation should be avoided, as it can
become too permanent a substitute, and lessen the chances of
establishing a happy and more mature sexual life.

Shyness and anxiety in feminine company

These are often a source of worry to adolescents, and may sometimes be
coupled with a fear of homosexuality. They are by no means necessarily
an indication of the latter. Their occurrence depends much upon the
personality, upbringing and attitudes of the patient. In general,
discussion, explanation and reassurance will be indicated, together
with encouragement to mix and, where possible, the provision of
means of doing so. Specific help can be provided at times in
psychotherapeutic groups, and by behaviour therapy methods (q.v.)
aimed at easing social anxieties.

Homosexual arousals

These are a cause of concern to many adolescents who fear them to
indicate established homosexuality. In fact, they are common in
normal adolescents, are influenced largely by the environment (e.g. by
some pleasurable seduction, restriction to the company of the same sex,
adolescent hero-worship), and are not necessarily indications of a
homosexual constitution at all. If heterosexual arousals are also
experienced there need be no undue pessimism. What is really
ominous, on the other hand, is where the patient has never experienced

any heterosexual feelings, but is able to feel completely friendly and at ease in feminine company while sexually quite uninterested. Again, discussion and explanation will be indicated, with as much reassurance as may be justified. At the same time the patient may be encouraged to avoid situations or phantasies in which passionate homosexual emotions may be aroused, since the more intense and habitual these are the more satisfaction he is likely to derive from them: the more that he does so the more are they likely to be prolonged, and the less is he likely to be able to detach himself from such habits of thought and feeling. The advice will be much the same as in the management of sex tension (*vide supra*), but where the adolescent has heterosexual potentialities but is choosing to waver towards homosexuality, the disadvantages of the homosexual mode of life may be suitably emphasised in discussion, in the hope of counteracting his immediate homosexual temptations.

Sexual immaturity

Though patients seldom come for treatment on account of sexual immaturity alone, this often forms the foundation of a maladjustment that leads to other difficulties for which advice is sought.

It may show itself in various ways. Masturbation, though a normal transitional stage of sexual development, is usually a sign of immaturity if it persists. Other signs are undue prudishness: reluctance to participate in the sexual act through ignorance, apprehensiveness, or refusal to recognise it as a normal biological expression: frigidity: inability to find a sexual partner, and reluctance to bear children.

The ease with which such attitudes may lead to conflicts, dissatisfactions, inferiority feelings and matrimonial quarrels, will be readily appreciated. All these will have their effect in impairing the general social adjustment.

The causes of sexual immaturity, as of other sexual anomalies, are obscure. As always, all three groups of factors, constitutional, physical and psychological, must be considered. The importance of constitutional and physical factors is indicated by the commonness with which underdevelopment of the secondary sex characteristics is encountered in the sexually immature. In some cases, of course, the psychological effects of the upbringing in encouraging general as well as sexual immaturity will be obvious. In a few, immature sexual attitudes will have been encouraged by disagreeable and traumatic experiences, such as severe punishments for childish sex play, the inculcation of guilt-feelings for the same, emotional disturbances over seduction and rape with subsequent mistrust of men and misgivings over intercourse. But most often it will probably be found that these psychological factors have only reinforced constitutional trends already present.

Any treatment must depend, of course, not only on the cause but on the nature of the problem for which advice is sought. Where the predominant aetiological factors appear to be physical, little can be done since endocrine treatment, though it might be expected to achieve much, is largely ineffective. It is worth trying the effect of testosterone analogues such as Mesterolone 50 mg b.d. for four to six weeks, as in some men this does seem helpful.

On the other hand, where the predominant aetiological factors are psychological something may be achieved. Friendly discussion of the patient's attitudes and of the factors that have led to them may lead to some readjustment with beneficial effect. Where there have been previous traumatic experiences which have helped to 'condition' the patient unfavourably towards sexual expression, elicitation of the facts and ventilation of the associated emotions (if necessary implemented by abreaction, see p. 405) may provide relief and an easier frame of mind. Where the sexual difficulty is related to justified fear of pregnancy, or further pregnancy, contraceptive advice may be helpful. Where it seems due more to faulty technique, suitable advice to the patient or partner, as to considerateness, gentleness, the adequacy of preliminary wooing, forbearance in not making each attempt at intercourse a test situation, and so forth, may promote a more satisfactory state of affairs. In some cases of frigidity, where such advice is not likely to lead to undesirable complications, sedatives or even alcohol may be prescribed as a temporary measure in order to help in overcoming an initial resistance. Other cases will require help in readjustment in a more general and less specifically sexual way; this, again, can only be achieved—if at all—by mutual discussion of the difficulties, such re-education of the attitudes as may be practicable, and the planning of life along lines such as may yield more satisfaction than had previously been gained.

Impotence and premature ejaculation

These are very common problems. Impotence means an inability to achieve penetration during sexual intercourse. Premature ejaculation means, as it says, that an erection cannot be maintained as long as desired before ejaculation, and includes cases where ejaculation occurs both before and soon after penetration. In other words only some people with premature ejaculation are truly impotent; successful impregnation can easily occur with premature ejaculation if it takes place after penetration. Most importantly, the degree of prematurity is very variable, and the reaction of both man and woman to it depends on their expectations and needs. An easily aroused and satisfied woman may have no complaints about her sexual experiences with a man who may be unable to satisfy someone else. From the man's point of view both impotence and seriously premature ejaculation are very serious problems, in which there is a profound blow to self esteem. Very many men in this situation regard themselves as 'less than men', and their wives often take the same attitude.

The most important feature of all cases of persistent psychogenic impotence is the fear of failure, which in turn leads almost inevitably to the failure they dread. Few men can manage well sexually if they are haunted by the thought 'will I be able to do it this time?'. If the partner is abrupt, obviously disappointed, critical, or worst of all mocking, then matters are made much worse. A tolerant, loving, and encouraging sexual partner is much more likely to get the best out of the situation. The men affected are nearly always somewhat anxious sexually anyway, with doubts about their potency. One or two bad experiences of failure, felt as humiliating by the man, and perhaps triggered off by over-fatigue or unsuitable circumstances, can have disastrous effects in the long run. Over-anxiety and inexperience on the wedding night or the first sexual adventure; over excitement and anxiety after a long separation; some worrying thoughts about, for instance, homosexuality; attempts at intercourse in order to please a wife for whom at the time he has little feeling or with whom he has been quarrelling; or the inability to shed from the mind the cares of daily life, may all lead to failure. In most people, such a setback has little long-term effect; but in those sexually and otherwise unsure of themselves, with anxious and ruminative temperaments, a vicious circle is easily established in which the fear of failure is ever present, and the thought of love making is like an approaching serious examination which he expects to fail. If the man has rather low sexual drives in any case, the condition may well become intractable. Sometimes the man is suffering from an unrecognised depressive illness, from which the problem stems, and effective antidepressant treatment is all that is required.

From the foregoing it is clear that the key to successful treatment is the abolition of anxiety and restoration of confidence. Simple counselling of both husband and wife, with explanation and advice to her about the importance of her responses, is often helpful in cases which are not too serious; and alcohol or a tranquilliser before attempting intercourse may help, as may the use of a condom to lessen sensitivity.

A fair number of patients can be helped by the use of MAOI drugs, particularly phenelzine 15 mg q.d.s. and isocarboxazide 10 mg t.d.s. or q.d.s. These drugs have as a side effect the prolongation of erection and prevention of ejaculation, from a direct peripheral autonomic effect. In addition, these drugs, particularly phenelzine, lessen anxiety of phobic type, and in a way there is an element of phobic avoidance in the fear of sex and of failure which develops. In those who seem generally low in sexual drives mesterolone 25 mg q.d.s. can be added. If this drug treatment is going to work it does so within six weeks, and should not be prolonged beyond that time if unsuccessful. If it does help it should be continued for many months in long-standing cases, and then the dose gradually reduced.

In at least two thirds of cases this drug treatment will have little or no effect, and the patient should be offered behaviour therapy (q.v.), which is usually done by clinical psychologists. There are various behavioural approaches to these sexual problems, but all are based on desensitisation to the anxiety-provoking situation, by attempting to teach the patient to relax and enjoy the sensuous aspects of erotic contact without arousing the fear of failure in a 'test situation', so that the vicious circle of anxiety is interrupted. The full understanding and cooperation of the wife is almost essential to the success of these behavioural approaches, which are in their essence very like the techniques of Masters and Johnson mentioned before, although less physiological in emphasis. Formal psychotherapy, with detailed exploration of early life experiences usually does more harm than good in these patients.

It is essential to remember that organic factors may play an important role in these conditions. More rapid decline of libido with age in the man than in the woman has already been mentioned; and diabetic neuropathy is an occasional cause. A useful indicator is the total absence of dreaming or waking erections for months at a time. This strongly suggests that the problem is partly, if not mainly, organic. Any morning or other erection indicates that the mechanism is functioning and excludes diabetic neuropathy. Patients who have suffered head injuries or strokes often become partially or totally impotent, usually but not always with diminished libido, and no treatment seems helpful.

PERSONALITY PROBLEMS WITH PERSONALITY DISORDERS

We have considered personality problems arising in connection with anxiety, reactive depression, hysteria and minor sexual difficulties. Discussion would be incomplete without reminding the student of the added difficulties that may arise from the patient being also the possessor of one of those disorders of personality described in Chapter 10 which have not yet been the subject of special mention here. Thus, the aloofness of the *schizoid* personality may lead to special difficulty in social adaptation and awareness of it, which, despite the emotional coolness, may yet cause anxiety on that score. This may be hard to combat. The *cyclothymic* personality, with its tendency to alternating and sustained 'up' and 'down' swings of mood, may be handicapped by the periods of depressive inertia, lasting perhaps a week or two and interrupting the expansive activity of the contrasting phase; the treatment of his handicap may be very difficult, though perhaps aided by the use of a rapidly acting antidepressant (see p. 400). The rigid striving to perfection of the *obsessional* personality, if in some respects laudable, may call for psychotherapeutic influences aimed at lowering the standards, with discussion, even though it may turn out unfruitfully, of the lack of necessity for such standards to be maintained. The *paranoid* personality, once rapport is gained, may benefit from the repeated injection of doubt as to whether the environment is as hostile as was thought. The *vulnerable* personality may benefit from counselling and moral support. Possession of the *psychopathic* personality is liable to add to all the difficulties encountered by those subject to anxiety, neurotic depressive and hysterical states, as well as to the doctor's burden.

PERSONALITY PROBLEMS AND DULL INTELLIGENCE

Many of the difficulties of dullards have been mentioned in Chapter 10, and their special liability to the more gross hysterical manifestations has been mentioned on page 270. Dullards may, however, have some special liability to the development of other neurotic symptoms as part of that extra difficulty in coping with life that is commonly their lot. Although there are many who are cheerful and equable in spite of their handicap, there are more who are not. This is not surprising when one considers that they mostly have to put up with inferior jobs with inferior financial reward and poor future prospects, with, as a consequence, chronic marginal living in economic and other senses. This may make for feelings of grievance. To be aggrieved is to make for difficulty in social relationships, which the dullard's lack of general resources may have made difficult enough already. Their general lack of judgment, as regards expenditure and plans of action (including family planning) encourages financial hardship and impedes the introduction of other than transient pleasure, while it renders them liable to be exploited or cheated or fobbed off with second best.

Like other types of vulnerable personality, they have a special tendency to develop symptoms when pinched by circumstance, on which occasions, as has been said, they are prone to become 'intellectually out of breath'. This may be a frequent occurrence with people who have difficulty in finding the way, understanding time-tables, the numbering of streets, the operation of telephone-boxes, and who hesitate through diffidence to ask for help.

12

Obsessional states

These are described apart from 'personality reactions' and the other neurotic states in the previous chapter, because they cannot usually be seen as straightforward reactions of the personality.

Obsessions may be defined as thoughts and feelings that cannot be got rid of by voluntary effort, but which recur to the mind persistently and against the will, and into the abnormality of which the patient has insight. Since their repeated intrusion occurs not only involuntarily but against the will, the patient feels himself to be under compulsion. The involuntary and compulsive nature of the process is shown by the facts that the patient (a) recognises such intrusions to be illogical, and (b) finds that efforts to resist them lead to their more forcible return, as well as to uneasiness and anxiety.

The element of compulsion is the essence of the obsessional state, and distinguishes an obsession from a mere pre-occupation. The layman may consider that Romeo was 'obsessed' by Juliet, or that a person is 'obsessed' with a grievance if he airs it persistently, but such pre-occupations are not obsessional in the technical sense unless they cannot be resisted and unless their recurrence has a compulsive quality unreasonable to him who experiences it.

Obsessionalism may be confined to the realm of thought, but usually gives rise to obsessional impulses and acts, since thought so often prompts activity. Thus, an obsessional thought that the gas has not been turned off, with its accompanying feeling of uneasiness, may give rise to an impulse to go and see, and even to the act of inspection, although the person may know perfectly well that the gas has been turned off in fact. Such acts are known as *compulsions*, and when obsessions and compulsions co-exist (as is usual) the condition is often referred to as an *obsessive-compulsive neurosis*.

It thus happens that obsessional patients not only 'have to' think certain thoughts, but usually 'have to' perform certain acts prompted by those thoughts. At any rate, they experience uneasiness and anxiety until they have done so. There thus tends to be some correlation between obsessionalism on the one hand, and repetitive behaviour with the taking of precautions, on the other. These last are characteristic of the *obsessional personality* (see p. 222) with its tendency to weigh each *pro* and *con*, and to be meticulous and overconscientious. The correlation is, however, by no means exact. Obsessional symptoms often develop in people who do not have obsessional personalities. And, while the obsessional personality is more liable to become disabled by obsessional symptoms than is any other one personality type, the majority of its possessors escape the need for psychiatric care, while among those that do break down, it is usually the development of anxiety, depression and exhaustion (see p. 252) that calls for treatment rather than frank obsessionalism itself.

There is no sharp line of demarcation between obsessional symptoms and normal experiences. Everyone knows of the difficulty there may be in banishing a tune that runs persistently in the mind. All children experience certain compulsions; they 'have to' walk on or avoid the cracks in the pavement, and they 'have to' put their toys in certain places. Most adults order certain of their activities so that disturbance of the routine is disturbing to the mind. This varies in intensity, and when such disturbance occurs all transitions may be observed from momentary irritation, through the more obsessional state of being a slave to habit and forced to obey certain rules, up to full-blown obsessionalism.

It may be difficult, but usually is not, to decide when obsessionalism is within normal limits and when it becomes pathological. Most patients who seek advice for obsessional symptoms will be found to be dominated by them to an extent that constitutes a real handicap, although they have insight into its unreasonable nature.

Aetiology

This is complex and calls for the usual consideration of constitutional, physical and psychological factors. Among the *constitutional* factors, heredity is important; in any large group of obsessional patients, obsessional traits will be prominent in about one third of the parents and one fifth of the siblings. The personality has already been referred to, and it often appears that the upbringing has contributed to its obsessional elements. Thus, the inculcation of excessively regular habits, exposure to undue strictness and fussiness, emphasis on high moral standards and lofty ideals, and the expectation of especially good conduct, may often be found as part of the early history of obsessional patients; and where the person has been taught to feel anxious or insecure should he deviate from such standards, the likelihood of obsessional developments is increased.

That *physical* factors play their part is suggested by the fact that obsessional and compulsive symptoms may appear for the first time following organic disease, such as injury to the brain or encephalitis lethargica. The latter may lead not only to obsessive-compulsive phenomena in the ordinary sense, but to parallel developments in the motor field, such as coordinated tics and oculo-gyric crisis. It is uncertain, however, whether such symptoms arise *de novo* after the disease or injury, or arise on a hitherto unsuspected constitutional basis that the disease or injury has brought to light. For instance, it is occasionally found that organic cerebral changes in old age are accompanied by florid obsessional developments not previously in evidence; but careful investigation will then usually show that such trends were previously discernible in milder form, but appear more nakedly owing to diminished self-control.

Psychological factors have an obvious importance, but again it is difficult to know how far they are causal or how far they merely activate a constitutional predisposition. Whatever the basis, obsessional symptoms can often be traced to conflict, usually between the moral standards of the personality and more primitive urges, often of a sexual or aggressive sort. As one patient actually said, 'It's due to my wishes colliding with my conscience'. Such conflicts commonly produce anxiety; that they should lead to obsessional developments as well suggests that the constitutional background is an essential factor.

Psychoanalysts put the origin of obsessional symptoms at about the time of bowel control. It is not possible for those who have not descended so deeply into the evolution and workings at the unconscious mind to affirm or deny such a statement, but follow-up studies of children brought up in different ways of potty training do not show any clear association between any method and the development of obsessionalism.

Symptoms and signs
In the mental sphere obsessions are generally divided into ideas, impulses and phobias. *Obsessional ideas* are commonly connected with religious or philosophical problems. The patient may be unable to escape from brooding over the meaning of the Universe of the existence of God, or meaningless questions may recur repeatedly to his mind on negligible provocation, such as 'Why is that so?' 'Why is God?' 'Why is not nothing?' Inconclusive and repetitive brooding of this kind is often referred to as *obsessional rumination*. Other patients are unable to escape from ruminating on whether they should or should not have pursued some course of action, the idea repeatedly recurring to their minds without a decision being reached. This has something in common with the repetitive 'revolving in neutral

without getting into gear' of the depressive, and it is noteworthy that obsessional symptoms are particularly apt to flourish in depressive states. An extreme form of this indecisiveness is seen in *obsessional doubt*, in which a patient may feel so far compelled to examine every aspect of a course of action and to scrutinise its every disadvantage or advantage that he is not only unable to arrive at any decision, but is beset by increasing doubt as to whether the premises from which he started can be correct. In this way he may follow endless trains of thought, each raising further doubts until he even becomes uncertain of the existence of anything, and may become lost in a maze of thought involving questions as to the nature of reality. He may then seek re-assurance as to whether he has done things which he knows quite well that he has done, and corroboration of which he can quite well see for himself, e.g. whether he has or has not dropped food on the tablecloth or is or is not wearing his watch. Obsessional ideas, leading in this way to rumination and doubt, may in rare instances become completely paralysing.

Obsessional impulses are often sexual or aggressive. The patient may feel impulses, quite at variance with his ordinary feelings, to harm people, to assault them sexually or otherwise, to behave irreverently on solemn occasions, or to say or shout lewd or obscene things. Such patients rarely, if ever, give way to such impulses, but the experiences cause them anxiety and self-criticism, and lead often to fears of impending insanity. Perhaps the commonest and most distressing of this type of impulse is the urge to damage an infant, often a newborn baby in a setting of puerperal depression. Very rarely do such obsessional impulses lead to baby battering, which mainly occurs in psychopathic and poorly controlled women, but it is natural that such thoughts lead to great distress.

Obsessional phobias are irrational fears, which repeatedly recur and are commonly of open or closed spaces, heights, knives or sharp instruments, disease or contamination. Where they are severe they may interfere considerably with life, restricting travel and even causing confinement to the home, or limiting the amount of social intercourse owing to the difficulty of taking the necessary precautions or avoiding-action when in public places or in other people's houses. They are considered in more detail in the previous chapter, because anxiety is the principal symptom. The categories we use for convenience are not always mutually exclusive, and these phobias have elements of both anxiety states and obsessional disorders.

Apart from the mental sphere, obsessionalism may lead, as has been said, to *compulsive acts*. The obsessional patient is usually anxious, and compulsive acts are usually designed to reduce the anxiety. Where the patient develops the obsessional idea that the gas has not been turned off, even though he knows that it has, he may derive some re-assurance from going to see. Such patients will often feel restless and uneasy on retiring at night unless they have checked all the taps and switches, have ensured that the doors are locked and the windows bolted. Similarly, those with fears of contamination or disease may feel the need to wash repeatedly, and this may spread until it involves anything with which they have come in contact. They may thus feel obliged to wash and re-wash clothes, towels, bed-linen, shoes, money, cushion-covers, and even to scrub the upholstery of chairs and sofas. When this stage is reached, they usually persist in such activity despite recognition of its illogicality and its destructiveness. They may become dissatisfied with the way in which they have performed these acts, may take to using large quantities of disinfectants and antiseptics as an additional precaution, may have to go through the washing procedure in a set order, and then repeat it a set number of times. Behaviour of this sort is called *ritualistic*, and the patient may feel compelled to persist in it, against his better judgment and even to the exclusion of any useful activity.

Compulsive acts of this sort, however exaggerated, are aimed at allaying some more or less specific anxiety. Often, however, the obsessional patient's anxiety may not be specific but vague and generalised. The feeling, so common in states of anxiety, that some nebulous catastrophe is about to happen may then impel the patient to take steps to avoid it. But as his anxiety is not specific, there is no specific antidote. The usual course of action is then to put things straight, apparently on the basis that the more that things are in order, the less likely are things to go wrong. The fact that the things that may go wrong have no sort of relation to the things that he puts straight is recognised by the patient, but the sense of compulsion overrides the illogicality. Thus, the patient may take to straightening the curtains, eiderdown or tablecloth, ensuring that ornaments are in place, folding and re-folding clothes, towels and anything else that may be to hand. Such acts are superstitious, and superstition may be directly involved, so that the patient has to perform such acts three times, or in multiples of three, or in other ways, according to what his knowledge, experience and preference in superstitions may dictate. In severe cases these activities may also be completely disabling.

Deeper significance of obsessive-compulsive symptoms

These obsessional ideas, doubts, impulses and phobias, together with compulsive acts which may be ritualistic, are the main symptoms and signs found in obsessional states. In the occasional case they seem to occur as a phenomenon in themselves, without ulterior meaning. But as a rule they are only the outward manifestation of deeper disturbances, and have meaning in relation to the basic attitudes and emotional difficulties, even though the patient may be unaware, or only partially aware, of the relationship. In fact, obsessional behaviour is usually symbolic and a substitute in consciousness for something else, rather as such swear-words as 'dashed' and 'blooming' are substitutes for others whose real significance is readily forgotten.

The substitution may be partial and incomplete. In cases where respectable women of irreproachable behaviour experience impulses, which they cannot understand, to perform irreverent acts, to say lewd things, or to look suggestively at men in the street, it is likely to be found that underlying their scrupulous propriety there are contrary and rebellious trends which admit at most of only partial recognition. Likewise, where there are obsessional impulses to violence, to the surprise of a gentle personality, it is probable that there is underlying aggression whose recognition has been forbidden by a sense of duty. Again, where a patient ruminates obsessionally on religious or philosophical themes, it is likely that there is some underlying conflict of a religious or ethical kind, which there is such difficulty in solving that it is shelved, and its more remote and less personal implications become the subject of rumination instead. Shelving the problem has not altered its accompanying emotional currents, and the persistence of these, though their origin may be unrecognised, serves as a reminder of its existence, and stimulates the return into consciousness of the substituted activity.

In other cases the substitution may be more thorough. Fears of dirt and contamination are commonly related to the sex life, especially where there has been marked insistence on 'purity' and 'clean-living' with emotional effect on a conscientious personality. The emotional concern that may be engendered by conflict between moral standards and desire may be expressed more palatably in terms of fear of dirt and bacterial contamination. (Indeed, members of the so-called 'Oxford Group' have been known to speak of 'antiseptic relationships'.) Some patients with such conflicts have an obsessional preference for the right; they must use the right hand, enter by the right-hand door, walk on the right, turn to the right and so forth; the real antithesis in such states is not 'left' but 'wrong'. Other patients whose conflicts, however unrecognised, spur them to action find it preferable to touch palings, chair legs, pillars, and so forth, rather than yield to some baser desire.

Often there is a whole series of substitutions. The woman who, harassed by the children, dutifully repressed feelings of antagonism towards them, developed a fear of knives by which she might do them harm; she developed a ritual of putting away the cutlery and locking it so that the knives were out of sight, and then transferred her phobia to the key, and thence to keys in general. The substitutions are often, however, much more complicated than that, and may be simultaneously symbolic of many associated things. Thus, one patient felt obliged repeatedly to think 'The moon is turned to gold', a phrase which had no meaning to her, but whose significance was gradually, in part at least unravelled. It was a substitution for a phrase she had learned in a Bible class, 'The moon shall be turned to blood'. Blood was for her symbolic of menstruation, confinement, the sexual life, violence, her hatred of a relative and everything 'bloody' (a word which she would have liked to use, but did not permit herself), and her sex life and the relative concerned had been sources of perturbation. When she had violent and 'wicked' thoughts she was wont to distract herself from them by quotations from the Bible. One day, after an argument with her hated relative, the phrase that unfortunately occurred to her was 'The moon shall be turned to blood'. The emotional associations that it had for her increased her perturbation. She substituted for it 'The moon is turned to gold'. This was because 'gold' was to her symbolic of goodness, security and general worth, as opposed to violence and evil, and because the accomplished fact of the present tense was more re-assuring than the threat implied by the future one. She came to use this phrase as a talisman against evil. Over the years its origin and meaning had become quite lost to her, but in times of emotional stress it would recur automatically and involuntarily to her mind. In so far as its recurrence was meaningless it became a nuisance, and the more so since it was beyond her control and against her will. When, after patient search, its meaning and origin were regained it ceased to trouble her, though it would still recur from time to time.

Course and prognosis

In our view the obsessional states have been regarded with undue prognostic pessimism in psychiatric textbooks. These states are undeniably resistive to treatment, and it may be that the discouragement thus engendered has helped to promote an atmosphere of hopelessness. But in fact, and regardless of treatment, many cases seem to recover spontaneously.

It is generally agreed that where obsessional symptoms develop in association with recurrent depressive illnesses, as they often do, they may be expected to clear as the depression occurs. But apart from that, obsessional symptoms of pure kind and without such association will, in our opinion, clear spontaneously more often than seems generally to be supposed. Obsessional episodes occurring in childhood, at puberty, in adolescence and in the early twenties, quite often do so within a year and obsessional phobias of disease are often likewise episodic.

There seems to be some relationship between obsessionalism and age, in that the majority of patients referred to psychiatrists for obsessional disorders are young people, and the frequency of such referral diminishes with the decades. Similarly, studies of life histories show that although obsessional episodes are common in childhood, in the 'teens, twenties and thirties, they occur less commonly thereafter, and even obsessional illnesses of considerable severity in the earlier years tend to fade with the passing of time. To meet a severe obsessional episode in a patient in the early twenties need not, therefore, lead to undue pessimism since the majority get better, while even established conditions may wane in severity over the years.

A certain number of cases, however, do tend to be chronic. The difference between the episodic and chronic cases seems to depend largely on the extent to which the patient shows the obsessional personality. About 50 per cent of obsessional cases show this type of personality in more or less marked form, but about 50 per cent of cases do not. The more that the symptoms seem to arise from and to be bound up with the personality, the greater is the likelihood of chronicity. Conversely, the less that the symptoms seem related to the personality structure and the more that they seem related to some particular stress, the better is the prognosis. In brief, the possibility of a good prognosis is particularly true of those cases whose obsessional symptoms cannot reasonably be regarded as the cumulative result of the previous personality characteristics.

An ominous prognostic feature is the possession of a personality always lacking in drive, indecisive, and without serious interests in anything. Such people tend to be ineffective even without the burden of obsessional doubts, ruminations, or compulsive rituals, and with that burden they may be rendered incapable.

It is a bad sign when the patient does not really regard the obsession or compulsion as inappropriate or ridiculous, even though he knows that others do. For example, a woman who was continually washing and scrubbing her hands for fear of germs felt that others should really be doing the same; that her standards were the more desirable even if inconvenient. In this case there was no development of schizophrenia, which can occur in those who lack insight in this way.

Recurrences and fluctuations in the severity of obsessional symptoms may occur in relation to recurrent stresses such as lead to conflict or otherwise engender anxiety. Even so, such tendency seems to be reduced, as has been said, with increasing age.

Exceptions to the foregoing principles occur when (1) the symptoms appear for the first time after organic disease or cerebral injury or as part of a senile or pre-senile state. Though they may fluctuate, they then tend to be more chronic. (2) When the patient uses the symptoms in a hysterical way for the sake of some secondary gain that they may bring, and so encourages his invalidism. (3) When the pre-occupations, usually in a young patient, are specially bizarre or remote from reality and are held with less insight than would be expected. They may then be the heralds of a developing schizophrenia, in which the obsessional state gradually becomes a delusional one.

Differential diagnosis

Obsessional states have a characteristic quality that renders the diagnosis easy as a general rule. But, as with other conditions, mistakes are possible and these can be considered under the headings of (1) failing to recognise obsessionalism even though it may really be the foundation of the patient's complaints, (2) failing to recognise that the obsessionalism, though present, is incidental rather than fundamental.

The only cases in which the first of these mistakes is likely to be made with any frequency are those that present with hypochondriacal complaints. These last quite often arise on an obsessional basis, so that it is as well to be alive to this possibility. Persistent hypochondriasis, in the absence of depression and without marked previous concern over health, quite often occurs either in the form of a phobic state usually related to some more or less specific disease, or as an intensification and prolongation of symptoms that have had a genuine organic basis. Such cases will usually be found to have an underlying obsessional personality. Recognition of the basically obsessional nature of the complaints may not be of direct help as regards actual removal of the symptoms, but will help in the understanding and general management of the case.

The second mistake referred to, that of failing to recognise when the obsessionalism is incidental to some other condition rather than fundamental in itself, is liable to be made in two types of case quite different from the foregoing and from each other. The first and commoner type is where a depressive illness is accompanied by an efflorescence or exacerbation of obsessional symptoms to an extent that the latter dominate the clinical picture so that the depression goes unrecognised. It must be borne in mind that this association of depression with obsessionalism is a common one. Indeed, certain cases that show circumscribed recurrences of obsessional behaviour associated with mild mood disturbance are really recurrent depressions. The other type of case in which the obsessionalism is not basic but is incidental has been referred to in considering the course and prognosis. It is characterised by (1) the patient showing little affective response to the symptoms but tending to accept their presence apathetically, (2) the pre-occupations being of a kind that is either bizarre or remote from reality, (3) there being doubt as to the extent of the patient's insight into the abnormality of his symptoms. All these features may be suggestive of a developing schizophrenia.

Apart from these sources of possible difficulty, the diagnosis of obsessional states will depend on the presence of rumination from which the patient cannot escape, usually associated with compulsive acts which may be elaborated into rituals with a sense of struggle against the thoughts, associated with tension, and the whole accompanied by some anxiety but with insight into the irrational nature of the condition so that there is social preservation and usually every outward appearance of normality.

Treatment

This must depend on the setting in which the obsessional developments have occurred. For example, when a mildly obsessional person has shown an efflorescence of symptoms in relation to an attack of depression, the treatment should be directed towards the latter. Again, when there has been an increase of symptoms in relation to some special event or circumstance (e.g. the clerk who has had to spend specially long hours, and has genuinely been required to check and re-check his work in preparation for an annual audit over which there is cause of anxiety, so that he develops generally heightened tension with insomnia, and a spread of symptoms from work into other departments of life), nothing more may be required than some relaxation and distraction, coupled with re-assurance, encouragement and possibly some sedation. If the symptoms are markedly severe, and there has been excessive responsibility and undue overwork, a rest and change may be required as well.

It may be possible to do a good deal in this way by environmental management. Obsessional personalities may be admirable in positions where their conscientiousness and reliability are a valuable asset, yet useless in other positions where flexibility and rapid decisions are needed, and may indeed break down in a situation which others would find quite easy to cope with.

Psychotherapy gives disappointing results on the whole, and those of psychoanalysis are no better. Where the symptoms are of recent onset and plainly related to emotional conflict, something may be gained by discussion with a view to more precise formulation, which may help the patient to be more master of the situation. Obsessional symptoms, whether phobic or of other kinds, are notoriously resistant to treatment, however, and their complete removal is rarely achieved. Behaviour therapy can be very helpful, as described in a later chapter (p. 385), and is often the treatment of choice.

Tranquillisers may be useful in fortifying the patient to meet specific situations (e.g. train journeys) in which the symptoms are liable to be specially troublesome through temporary exacerbation.

Where the precipitating causes are more obscure, and the condition has developed insidiously with gradual elaboration of the symptoms, the treatment is liable to be very difficult indeed. A complete change of environment, such as admission to hospital, may sometimes be of help in breaking down the habits and pattern of life with which the symptoms have become associated; under such stimulus, the patient may find that he can do without the symptoms to a greater extent than he had believed.

Physical treatment
Antidepressant drugs are very helpful in those obsessional states which develop during depressive illnesses, and evidence of depression should be carefully sought in all obsessional states. Even in those in whom depressive mood is not obvious, and in whom symptoms are very long standing, the tricyclic drug clomipramine (Anafranil) can be strikingly successful. The usual full dose is 150 mg daily by any route, but side effects are common, and smaller doses are advisable to begin with. Very prolonged courses may be necessary, and in some the symptoms recur when the drug is stopped.

In view of the rather disappointing results of psychotherapy, it is the more unfortunate that electrical treatment has no place in dealing with obsessional states. Very striking symptomatic relief can be afforded, however, by psychosurgery. The symptoms do not disappear, but are less obtrusive and dominate the patient to a much less extent. The operation can be embarked upon more hopefully than in some other conditions, since the very qualities that make for an obsessional type of illness tend to hold the patient together after operation, and to prevent the untoward personality changes that may sometimes follow pre-frontal leucotomy. This procedure should be reserved, however, for those severe and long-standing cases who are seriously incapacitated and whose life is made miserable by their symptoms. As increasing experience has shown us that the prognosis in obsessional states tends to be better than is generally supposed, we have come increasingly to favour an expectant policy, although we should still be ready to consider operative intervention in any case where the symptoms had remained persistent and unvarying for a period of about two years, provided that these were of such severity as to call for drastic treatment.

In summary, drug treatment with clomipramine should be tried first, even in those in whom there is no significant depression, although much more successful when depression is present. If there is no benefit after four weeks of an adequate dose, behaviour therapy should be tried. Cerebral surgery is only indicated in those severely disabled, suffering great tension, and in whom at least two years have passed without improvement.

13

Alcoholism and drug addiction

ALCOHOLISM

Moderate drinking is a normal habit in these Isles. This habit becomes a medical problem only (1) if it leads to symptoms calling for medical aid, (2) if the individual develops symptoms when the supply of alcohol is interrupted, (3) when signs of organic deterioration appear, or (4) when the family is adversely affected.

Alcoholism is steadily increasing in almost all Western countries, and is a very serious health problem. It leads to cirrhosis of the liver and other physical diseases, as well as to the syndromes described in this chapter. Alcohol is a factor in road accidents, crime, baby battering, poverty, industrial inefficiency and, overwhelmingly, in unhappy family life. There is much unrecognised heavy drinking in all social classes, and heavy drinking occurs among much younger people than was the case a few years ago. Many people attending hospital, especially those with abdominal symptoms, are in fact alcoholics.

There are many social and psychological factors associated with heavy drinking as described later, but availability and cost are probably more important than any of them overall. Alcohol is much cheaper, in real terms, in the United Kingdom than it was before the Second World War, and is growing progressively cheaper. The best way to combat alcoholism would be to increase the tax on it, rather than rely on treatment methods of unproven efficacy.

Acute alcoholic intoxication

People vary much both in their tolerance to alcohol and in the sequence in which signs of intoxication appear. In some, physical signs such as slurred speech and other evidence of motor incoordination appear very early; in others mental changes alone may be observed until intoxication is severe. Usually, the first signs are those of disinhibition, i.e. increased talkativeness and mild euphoria. These are succeeded by impaired concentration with forgetfulness owing to defective registration of what is happening. Later, there is superficial thinking, lack of judgment and insight, with frank impairment of memory and often irritability. Patients with cerebral disease or injury, especially epilepsy, are liable to show severe intoxication (drowsiness, irritability, excitement) after quite small doses of alcohol, and this is a point to remember where there is some legal involvement.

Intoxication may lead to various legal and other difficulties. Psychotropic drugs, which are very commonly taken now, often increase the effects of alcohol. Both the benzodiazipines and tricyclic drugs can lead to unexpected drunkenness and even to confusional states with paranoid ideas, if taken with alcohol. No one on these, or other psychotropic drugs, should ever drink before driving.

The formerly frequent medico-legal problem of fitness or unfitness to drive a car after alcohol has become infrequent since the introduction of the Road Safety Act, 1967. This requires a suspected person to submit to breath tests and, if these are positive, to blood *or* urine testing, and it is an offence to refuse. Under this procedure the role of the medical man is confined to taking a blood sample. No examination is called for. Whatever his clinical state the driver will have committed an offence if the concentration of alcohol is more than 80 mg per 100 ml of blood or urine. If, however, the police choose to proceed under the Road Traffic Act, 1960, (e.g. if they think the 'breathalyser' has failed in its purpose) the subject *may* refuse medical examination. If he does not, special attention should be paid to the smell of the breath, the presence of flushed face, full and rapid pulse, dilated and sluggish pupils, and evidence of motor incoordination e.g. the ability to walk straight, to write adequately, and to pronounce test phrases such as 'Baby hippopotamus', 'West Register Street', 'British Constitution', 'The Leith police dismisseth us', 'Red leather, yellow leather'. As regards the mental state, note should be taken of the mood, type of language used, memory for recent events and the ability to do simple arithmetic.

Treatment
This is seldom called for in simple intoxication, except for the occasional case who shows violence and excitement. Such have sometimes been referred to as *mania a potu*, an unfortunate term since it has nothing to do with mania. These are usually explosive reactions occurring in people liable to be explosive whether drunk or sober, and who are specially susceptible to alcohol. The prime necessity is to get enough help to restrain the patient and to remove anything potentially dangerous to himself or others. The excitement

can then be reduced by intramuscular injection of chlorpromazine, 250–500 mg depending on the size of the patient.

Alcoholic coma

All comatose cases require careful examination. It is most unwise to attribute a comatose state to alcohol unless it seems certain from the history that the condition can be explained on that ground alone. The development of symptoms after an overdose of insulin may be very similar to that of alcoholic intoxication. Nor is the smell of the patient's breath a reliable guide; a drunk person may be diabetic, or may have sustained a head injury through falling; and people are often given brandy or whisky on feeling faint, though they may have had no other drinks.

Treatment

The only immediate practical measure is to aspirate the stomach and examine the contents. So long as there is doubt as to the cause of coma, the patient should be kept under observation, with repeated attention to temperature, pulse, respiration, blood pressure and the development of eye signs.

Acute alcoholic hallucinosis

This is a rare condition which generally starts after a heavy drinking bout. The patient hears hallucinatory voices, usually reproachful or threatening, without much clouding of consciousness. The mood is usually one of fear (as in delirium tremens which, indeed, may subsequently develop) though there may be traces of alcoholic jocularity. Some cases turn out to be schizophrenics who have taken alcohol to drug themselves in the first stage of an acute schizophrenic episode.

CHRONIC ALCOHOLISM

This condition develops in recognisable stages. It is possible to be a heavy drinker without being an addict to alcohol; indeed, it is estimated that only about one heavy drinker in twenty becomes addicted. The difference is that the heavy drinker can do without alcohol if he chooses; the addict can not, because he has become habituated to and physiologically dependent on it. It is difficult to know why this happens, although genetic factors are probably responsible in part.

The definition of alcoholism is uncertain, and there are two main approaches: First, we can define it narrowly by the existence of physiological addiction with tremor or withdrawal ('morning shakes'); or by the development of some clear cut alcoholic syndrome such as delirium tremens, cirrhosis of the liver, Korsakoff's psychosis, dementia, hallucinosis, and so on. This leads to fairly low incidence figures, but has the benefit of being more easy to identify accurately. It is also reasonable to consider alcoholism as a 'disease' using this limited definition.

Second, we can use a looser definition and say that a person is an alcoholic if the drinking damages his or her health, or adversely affects the lives of others. This is the view taken by the World Health Organization. It has obvious advantages in recognising the effects of alcoholism on others, but means that reliable statistics are almost impossible to collect, particularly for any international or historical comparisons; and makes the 'disease' concept of alcoholism less appropriate. It is wise to keep these two different attitudes to diagnosis clear in one's mind, as many people confuse them.

Aetiology
Alcohol is an inherent part of our culture, and almost everyone has taken alcohol by late adolescence or early adulthood. Only a few go on to become heavy drinkers, and even fewer to develop physiological addiction or one of the recognised complicating syndromes. Price and availability, as mentioned earlier, are extremely important in determining the general level of alcohol consumption in any community, and other environmental factors affect the individual.

Recently in Britain the Royal College of Psychiatrists have suggested that the following should be regarded as the daily upper level of safe drinking: four pints of beer, four doubles of spirits; or one bottle of wine. Although there is very great individual variation, above these levels alcoholism becomes increasingly frequent.

There are some simple environmental factors. Thus, publicans, bar-keepers and commercial travellers often drink as a normal part of their occupations. Businessmen and women with frequent expense account lunches are very much at risk. Drinking is also a normal function of certain social sets, especially among those who live in outposts which are often in difficult climates with few distractions, and among colleagues whom they would not ordinarily have chosen as associates. Such may have quite normal personalities. Social factors of a more general kind, such as poverty and slum life, that used to encourage periodic trips to Nirvana, are less important than they used to be.

More commonly, the reasons for excessive drinking must be

sought in the personality of the patient rather than in his environment. Thus, many alcoholics are *psychopathic personalities*, especially inadequate psychopaths, whose impulsiveness, poor control, inability to take a long-term view, tendency to feel a few drinks below par and awareness of their inadequacy, may combine to encourage the habit. In other people, not necessarily psychopathic, excessive drinking may arise from *personal problems*. Some may be constitutionally anxious, yet determined to overcome fear. Others experience dissatisfaction and frustration through, for example, marital difficulties, homosexuality, failure to achieve ambition and to adjust to that failure. These may use alcohol because it is a powerful solvent of reality—for the time being. As a once talented actor, less successful than his wife, expressed it: 'Once I'd had that failure it was difficult to meet my equals as I had before, and frankly I preferred to be cock of my own dunghill in the local.' Such drinking comes under the heading of *neurotic reaction*.

Some excessive drinking is *symptomatic* of more specific psychiatric illness. The lack of restraint in early GPI or other organic deterioration may facilitate alcoholism, as may hypomania. Certain cases with recurrent depression turn to alcohol for relief of symptoms. Some manic-depressive patients thus show that recurrent and periodic form of drinking known as *dipsomania*; others, having started the habit, may drink between attacks. In all symptomatic cases a history of symptoms *preceding* the alcoholism may be of diagnostic importance, particularly for forensic purposes.

There are also very important cultural factors in alcoholism. The Irish for example are much more prone to heavy drinking and alcoholism than are the other inhabitants of the British Isles, a fact which is related to cultural attitudes to alcohol and its place in life. Traditionally Irish men associate heavy drinking with manliness, despise the non-drinker, and centre all their social life around alcohol. These attitudes of mind persist for several generations after emigration, so that in the United States second and third generation Irish Americans still have higher alcoholism rates than, for instance, Italian Americans. The Italians can also be compared interestingly to the French. Both Italy and France produce large quantities of wine, and there are no significant racial differences, yet alcoholism is very much commoner in France than Italy.

Women traditionally have had a lower alcohol intake than men, and have had much lower alcoholism rates. The woman alcoholic usually has a more disordered personality, which has led to the abnormal drinking, and they do correspondingly worse with treatment. With women increasingly competitive with men in life outside the home, more and more alcoholism in women is seen, but in people of relatively more normal personality.

The development of heavy drinking is thus dependent on many factors, both personal and social. The development of alcoholic addiction, but not that of heavy drinking alone, is known to be largely influenced by genetic factors; an old idea recently confirmed by Scandinavian studies of twins and of adopted children similar to those used to unravel the genetic component in schizophrenia. There are probably inherited differences in the way in which alcohol is handled by the body, as there are known to be for several other drugs. It has also recently been claimed that peoples of Mongolian extraction, including Red Indians and Eskimos, metabolise alcohol differently, and are more prone to ill effects from alcohol; which if true partly explains the ease of conquest of the West, and the high alcoholism rates of the North American Indian now, although there are also many unfavourable social factors acting in their case.

Symptoms and signs

The first or *premonitory* phase is usually marked by alcohol forming a keynote in the patient's life. An agreeable event calls for celebration by, and a difficulty calls for consolation from, a drink. A bar is regarded as the only conceivable place for a rendezvous. A drink is essential in the transaction of business. Drinks are a necessary preliminary to meals even if the latter have to be delayed. Social occasions are preceded by a drink or two before setting out, 'to gain flying speed'. Anxiety is felt as to whether the supply of alcohol will be adequate, and further 'flying speed' is sought rapidly on arrival. When travelling, thought is given to reserve supplies and flasks. More time tends to be spent away from home. There is a reduction, at first hardly noticeable, in initiative, efficiency and amount of trouble taken, with a tendency to be behindhand and uncommunicative in the mornings. At this stage the patient may worry about his alcoholic intake, and may express this in the form of jocose references to the subject.

The *established* stage is marked by the patient finding himself unable to feel comfortable in the absence of alcohol. Patients have difficulty in describing this, but they seem to suffer from a restless, irritable malaise, with a sense of discontentment and difficulty in settling to things. This is temporarily dissolved by alcohol so that a need for it is felt. One drink now leads to the need for another, and the patient does not control the quantity even when he has reached a 'comfortable concentration'. He therefore subsequently experiences a different malaise of the hang-over type. If this is severe, it may cause him to stop drinking for a day or so, but he will almost immediately start again. He needs to drink more, and more quickly than his former associates; while with them, he may excuse himself and sneak extra drinks elsewhere. His application and initiative are now more definitely affected; he does less work and does it less effectively and attentively. Any originality in thinking or conversational adroitness disappears; he relies on his former stock-in-trade and speaks in clichés. He drops his outside interests and forms no new ones. Financial difficulties now often arise; he becomes less scrupulous and may indulge in gambling with poor judgment. In the home he is self-centred, inconsiderate, and evasive of his responsibilities, often with more or less plausible excuses. If taken to task he may show an aggressive irritability, often expressing a morbid jealousy that may be related to increasing impotence; this may alternate with a maudlin self-pity and remorse if he is feeling physically prostrated.

The *advanced* stage of chronic alcoholism is marked by anorexia, with failure to take enough food, morning nausea often with vomiting, tremor, a constant preoccupation over supplies, and the necessity for drinks in the morning before activity is undertaken and the tremor can be controlled. A morning tremor ('shakes') controlled by alcohol, is a definite sign of addiction. Alcohol is also necessary to achieve sleep, although alcohol is itself a cause of early morning wakefulness. Abstinence leads at once to anxiety, which may be severe.

The stage of *alcoholic breakdown* is then reached, with almost chronic intoxication, weakness arising from lack of food, vomiting and toxic effect, sometimes with signs of peripheral neuritis. Lack of initiative is total, except for getting more drink about which there may be every unscrupulousness. The mood is one of anxiety, depression and remorse. The patient thinks only of himself, how he feels, and the next drink, shows a reduced tolerance so that he is drunk on little, with impaired time-sense and only a vague appreciation of recent events. There is now commonly a considerable aversion to alcohol and a full recognition that he wishes to dispense with it but cannot.

Accompanying these developments there will have been various degrees of upset both at work and at home. Complaints will have been made, and relations will have become strained. Paranoid developments may have occurred, with suspiciousness and actual delusions (p. 322), with possible attempts at testing the fidelity of the spouse by traps and detective work almost always based on the patient's alcohol-induced impotence. These may have encouraged increased consumption of alcohol as a solace, with the creation of a vicious circle.

Specially ominous indications in the foregoing sequence are: (1) a falling off in the patient's capacity to hold his liquor, (2) the occurrence of patches of amnesia after only small amounts of alcohol; these are evidence of cerebral damage, (3) enlargement and tenderness of the liver (which may later give place to shrinkage and induration), (4) tenderness of the muscles and nerve trunks with defects of sensation, referable to peripheral neuritis.

Alcoholics tend to be singularly deficient in insight, cannot be convinced that their troubles arise from their habits, refuse to admit defeat ('Give it up? Why, that would be giving in'), and insist that they can manage the situation in the teeth of overwhelming evidence to the contrary. They are plausible and almost always untruthful as to the extent of their consumption. Women have a greater tendency to drink secretly than do men, and many have more opportunity of doing so.

Many alcoholics are men and women of the world with remnants of a personality that was once engaging. This may lead them to show an apparent frankness, with a spurious charm that is really allied to shamelessness, and connected with a vain refusal to face the 'humiliation of confessing the facts'. Phrases like 'To be perfectly frank . . .', 'To be quite candid . . .', 'If I'm really honest . . .', may help to put the doctor on his guard and to recognise, even if his fellow club-members do not, that when an alcoholic claims to have put all his cards on the table, a number are probably face down.

Course and prognosis

A few resolute souls are able to wean themselves from spirits before the established stage is reached. But the course of many alcoholics from the premonitory stage onwards is ever downwards.

In some cases this downward progress is punctuated by attacks of *delirium tremens* (p. 322); a few end with *Korsakoff's psychosis* (p. 112). The extent to which these occur varies much from one country to another; for example, the incidence of delirium tremens and Korsakoff's psychosis is high in Switzerland; in these Isles it is very low.

With determination, however, the course and prognosis are far from hopeless. The most important prognostic points are (1) the personality of the patient, and (2) his willingness for treatment. The sounder the personality, and the more comprehensible the addiction in the light of the situation in which it developed, the better is the outlook likely to be. Willingness for treatment, however, may be apparent rather than real. The patient who comes for help on his own initiative and will face a future of total abstinence, will do better than the patient whose real object in coming is to gain temporary respite from the moral pressure of relatives by making an appeasing gesture. The patient's plans for the future may be some index of his genuineness. Where these are realistic the prognosis is not unfavourable; where they have a fatuous optimism coloured by wishful thinking the prognosis is bad.

With the better personalities, whose addiction has been situationally determined to an appreciable extent, and where there are realistic plans for future alterations, good results can be achieved, though there are often disappointments. Where the patient, coming under pressure, adopts the attitude: 'They say I need a cure, well, you give it me and we'll see if it's any good', satisfactory results are not to be expected. Intermediate mixtures of sincerity and goodwill are likely to meet with intermediate results. By the time that a patient has lost his home, wife, and possessions as well as his work, the outlook is very bad.

Many alcoholics become severely depressed, as their life disintegrates around them, and their usual reaction is to drink even more. Suicide is many times more common among them than among normal drinkers, and in many the drinking itself may seem to be a form of slow suicide.

Many cases relapse once. That is not necessarily ground for pessimism. When a second relapse has occurred, however, the natural discouragement of the therapist has some basis in reality. But even in cases with frequent relapses something may be gained by reducing both the intensity and frequency of alcohol intake, and so prolonging life and usefulness, even though such efforts may not amount to much more than making the patient fit enough to start drinking again.

OTHER ALCOHOLIC SYNDROMES

Chronic alcoholic hallucinosis

This is also rare. It may develop from an acute hallucinosis or it may be insidious in onset. In either event the patient hears hallucinatory voices in clear consciousness and without much disturbance of behaviour. Characteristically, these are repetitive and rhythmical —'idiot, idiot, idiot', or 'beggar, beggar, beggar'. The condition tends to be very persistent. Some patients get used to the voices and carry on in spite of them, but most develop paranoid misinterpretations as a result of the voices and come to need institutional care. Such patients may, however, be appreciably helped by phenothiazines (p. 391).

Alcoholic paranoid states

Alcohol can play a part in the production of states that may closely resemble paranoid schizophrenia, or, when a grandiose colouring is added, general paralysis of the insane, but with a much better prognosis. Jealousy is usually a prominent feature, and the delusions are usually related to it; the paranoid alcoholic accuses his spouse of infidelity, especially when impotence has occurred as part of the alcoholism. Important points to look for are (a) the alcoholism, and development of symptoms in relation to it, (b) a greater variability in the clinical picture than occurs in paranoid schizophrenia or general paralysis, (c) organic mental features (p. 50). The differential diagnosis from general paralysis may only be possible after serological investigations; for example, slurred speech and sluggish pupils may be present in both.

Delirium tremens

This is most often precipitated by sudden alcohol withdrawal, and is more common in spirit drinkers. It occurs especially in those whose diet has led to deficiency of vitamins. The onset is often acute, precipitated by a drinking bout with insufficient food intake, by a physical illness or injury, or admission to hospital with consequent alcohol withdrawal. On the other hand, the onset may be subacute and preceded by nocturnal anxiety, nightmares, hypnagogic hallucinations, sometimes with confusion at night, though in the waking state. This may happen for a few nights before the delirium begins; such an occurrence should at once bring to mind the possibility of an incipient delirium, however normal the patient may seem during the daylight hours. A few cases start with an epileptic fit.

The clinical picture does not differ materially from that of other delirious states (p. 106). Special features characteristic, though not diagnostic, of the alcoholic delirium are: *physically*, tremor of the tongue, lips, fingers and hands, often coupled with signs of polyneuritis, and *mentally*, a mixture of anxiety with jocularity, the occurrence of rapidly moving hallucinations of small animals (mice, rats, insects), and the imaginary pursuit of his own occupation by the delirious patient. References to alcohol, intentional or inadvertent, in the patient's remarks, and requests for gin, whisky or brandy, are diagnostic pointers.

It is not always realised that this is a serious condition. The mortality used to be about 10 per cent, though this has been reduced by modern methods of treatment. The commonest cause of death is circulatory failure. The length of the attack can now be reduced to about three days or less; formerly, it was three to seven days, and usually five. Of the survivors, about one-third may be left with Korsakoff's psychosis (p. 112).

More details of the clinical features and treatment of the delirium are given on page 111. When that has recovered the problem of alcoholism has to be dealt with if possible, as described below.

Alcoholic dementia

In addition to Korsakoff's psychosis, which is secondary to thiamin deficincy, alcohol can cause direct brain damage, a fact that has been increasingly recognised recently. Very many alcoholics show slight permanent intellectual impairment, even after prolonged abstinence; and a few show quite severe decline, with demonstrable cerebral atrophy. The lack of insight and will to cooperate which many advanced alcoholics show may well be due in part to some degree of dementia.

Epileptiform fits

Grand mal convulsions can occur in alcoholics in more than one setting. Principally they occur on sudden withdrawal in chronic alcoholics, during a period of delirium tremens for example. In this way they are like the withdrawal fits of barbiturate abusers. They can also occur in acute severe alcohol intoxication—'rum fits'.

Treatment

It is a sad fact that we cannot yet be confident that any particular type of treatment regime is of any overall value, although special units for alcoholics are frequently established. Their main function should really be in research into treatment methods. That is not to say that no alcoholic can be helped, but the results depend mostly on the personality of the patient, and particularly on genuine motivation and determination, on the personalities of those offering help, and on the family and work setting in which he lives.

The alcoholics who do best with treatment are those whose drinking is secondary to some treatable psychiatric syndrome, especially depression; and those in whom some relevant clear cut environmental problem can be overcome. The more abnormal the underlying personality, the worse the outlook.

It is important to give clear and accurate information about the risks of his drinking to every alcoholic, with details of liver and other damage, as this can be the necessary motivational spur.

Before the established stage is reached, attempts should be made at encouraging moderation. Difficulties, anxieties and situations that encourage drinking should be discussed, and clarification of the whole problem and possible means of dealing with it should be attempted, in the hope of altering the habit-pattern and devising alternative satisfactions.

It is also necessary to be quite clear that, once the patient has entered the established stage of chronic alcoholism, total abstinence is going to be essential for the rest of his life. Every alcoholic patient who comes for treatment hopes to be turned into a controlled drinker, but this is only possible for a few, and people entering treatment should not be aiming at it. Though treatment does not often succeed unless the patient comes actually asking for help, usually as the result of some crisis, there are some patients who after admission to hospital has enabled them to 'dry out' and regain perspective, will see the light although they may have come reluctantly in the first place. Such cases may be deterred from accepting treatment if the need for total abstinence is stressed too soon. But a patient seen in the premonitory phase, before his addiction is actually established, may be sobered into changing his habits if the ultimate need for total abstinence is put to him with sufficient cogency.

It is so difficult to control alcoholism outside hospital that admission is almost always essential if addiction or some other complicating syndrome is present. Even then, many patients show a facile optimism about their future and discharge themselves too soon. In hospital, care should be taken to ensure that the patient does not have a secret supply of alcohol. Sudden withdrawal may precipitate delirium tremens and/or epileptic fits. Full doses of vitamin B complex by intravenous or intramuscular injection, and diazepam for its anticonvulsant action and calming effect are very useful. Chlormethiazole (Heminevrin) is perhaps the most useful drug for control of withdrawal symptoms, producing a kind of light narcosis in adequate doses, of about 4 to 6 g daily, gradually diminishing over the course of a week. The drug can rapidly induce dependence itself, and should not be continued for long, or used for outpatients.

The withdrawal symptoms are relatively mild as long as delirium does not supervene. Restlessness, irritability, emotional lability and anxiety may be shown, with anorexia, tremulousness, sweating and diarrhoea. These should be reduced by sedation with phenothiazines (see p. 381) or chlormethiazole and large doses of vitamins such as are given in delirium tremens (see p. 112), which may also help to prevent delirium from developing.

When the patient's general condition has been improved, specific *physical* treatments may be considered as an adjunct to the general psychological management.

Detoxication units. For some years many North American hospitals have had special wards for drying out alcoholics, many of whom are severely deteriorated and have been taken there by the police who might otherwise have arrested them as 'drunk and disorderly', or under some equivalent charge. Suitable patients are then offered more prolonged treatment. There are some similar units in the United Kingdom. They will lessen the burden on the prison service, but most of those admitted are likely to be untreatable by current methods, so it is to be hoped that they will be developed for research purposes at first.

Aversion treatments. These are also discussed in the section on behaviour therapy (p. 385). Details of the methods are given in *An Introduction to Physical Methods of Treatment* by Sargant and Slater (see bibliography). They are included here principally for historical reasons, as they are very rarely used now. The most widely used method of aversion in alcoholism was for many years apormorphine. It was claimed by many of those with most experience that the therapeutic effect depends more on the correction through the central action of apormorphine, of metabolic abnormalities caused by the alcohol, than on simple conditioning, although the psychological effects are also important. Nevertheless, the treatment as given followed the general pattern of other aversion treatments, building up an atmosphere of disgust and degradation as the alcoholic lay surrounded by his vomit perhaps for several days, given injections of from 5–30 mg apormorphine every two hours, day and night, while alcoholic drinks were offered to him. This treatment is physically as well as emotionally rigorous; the subjects must be reasonably fit to start it, and their condition must be carefully watched.

Another widely used method of setting up a conditioned response against alcohol was by emetine hydrochloride or a mixture of emetine hydrochloride, pilocarpine and ephedrine sulphate, using the same technique as for apormorphine. Both of these methods were very successful at times in the hands of enthusiastic and experienced doctors, but how much of the success was due to the treatment and how much to less tangible emotional factors of support and rapport and encouragement, is impossible to say. They have fallen out of use, partly because of their physical dangers and partly because of disappointing results. Nor have units specialising in alcoholism replaced them by electrical aversion techniques, but mainly concentrate on group psychotherapy, work rehabilitation, antabuse and referral to Alcoholics Anonymous. The results of these latter methods are still not at all convincing, although each of them seems to benefit some people, especially Alcoholics Anonymous.

Disulfiram treatment. Antabuse, disulfiram, interferes with the metabolic breakdown of alcohol with the effect of causing acetaldehyde to accumulate in the blood-stream. This can be fatal. Disulfiram should, therefore, never be given to an intoxicated person. The treatment is best begun in hospital. The patient, detoxicated, is given 800–1200 mg daily for one or two days, and the dose then reduced day by day to about 200 mg (one tablet). On the fifth day alcohol is given as a test, in the form which the patient prefers. A suitable quantity is 50 ml of gin or whisky. Some degree of acetaldehyde poisoning develops. Its extent depends on the amount of antabuse given, on the amount of alcohol given and the rate at which it is absorbed. It may be unwise to let the patient pour drinks for himself and drink at his normal rate. We prefer to give repeated 50 ml doses of spirits every ten or twenty minutes according to the effect or lack of it. We prefer to give the treatment in bed, and to have the pulse rate taken every ten minutes and the blood pressure every twenty minutes, though some people would consider this fussy. Most patients experience some effect after about fifteen minutes; those who do not should be given more alcohol.

The initial effect is that the patient feels hot in the face with flushing that extends to the conjunctivae, giving rise the 'bull-eyed' appearance which makes him look more uncomfortable than he really is. This is followed by palpitation, a sense of constriction in the chest and neck, with pounding of the vessels in the neck and head leading to headache. The patient now feels ill, uncomfortable and apprehensive, even in fear of death. There is a rise in pulse rate and a fall in blood pressure that is usually gradual, but occasionally rapid. In course of this the flushing gives place to pallor with general malaise, nausea and sometimes vomiting, while the patient may say he is experiencing the worst 'hang-over' he has ever known.

If the patient shows a satisfactory reaction and drinks are given every ten minutes, the stage of pallor will usually be reached in 45–60 minutes. We do not give alcohol beyond this point and most patients will already have refused to continue.

The patient should be kept under supervision in bed for the rest of the day as delayed reactions of fainting or vomiting may occur.

Many patients will go to sleep an hour or so after the start of treatment, and they tend to wake up feeling particularly well.

If the effects have not been sufficiently unpleasant to make an impression on the patient, the procedure may be repeated with increased dosage or antabuse and/or alcohol, or with more rapid alcoholic intake.

The patient then has to be persuaded to take maintenance doses of antabuse (200–400 mg daily), if necessary under supervision, in the hope that knowledge of what will happen if he drinks will deter him from doing so. Disulfiram is of most help when the patient takes it himself daily as a kind of commitment 'to be sober today'.

The commonest complications are (a) cardio-vascular collapse, and (b) coronary thrombosis. The former may be alarming and blood pressure elevating drugs (e.g. mephentermine sulphate 15 mg) should be at hand during treatment. It should be avoidable by controlling the rate of intake of alcohol. That coronary thrombosis can occur owing to the antabuse-alcohol reaction dictates caution where there is a suspicion of coronary arterial disease. Other indications for caution are other cardiac disorders, cirrhosis of the liver, nephritis, diabetes and thyrotoxicosis. Patients on mainten-ance doses may sometimes complain that they feel rather less alert. A rare but startling complication is the occasional development of psychotic states in patients who have had antabuse in large doses or over a long period of time; these take the form of organic confusional states but they may also have markedly schizophrenic features. They may last for some days after withdrawal of the drug, but show spontaneous recovery. Citrated calcium carbimide (Abstem), is a less severe and more rapidly acting drug of similar type. The dose is 50–100 mg daily by mouth.

Rehabilitation. This is essential. Without it nothing will be achieved save improving the patient's physical condition sufficiently to encourage further drinking.

The uselessness of attempting to dissolve difficulties with alcohol may profitably be discussed with intelligent and cooperative patients, and plans made for the adoption of more satisfactory attitudes. In fact, the treatment will call for some psycho-therapy, the underlying principles of which are discussed in Chapter 15.

It is usual in alcoholic units to see the treatment in two stages: first is 'drying out', with correction of any vitamin lack, tranquillising drugs, antidepressants if needed, and physical improvement. This stage usually lasts from one to three weeks. Second, a longer inpatient period, perhaps of several months, in which underlying personal problems can be discussed, especially in group psychotherapy with other alcoholics, and work and other aspects of personal rehabilitation can start, with regular hours, exercise, and an attempt to rebuild damaged family relationships if possible.

In many alcoholics the family not only suffers from the drinking, but contributes to it, and a good many alcoholics find it easier to remain abstinent if they separate from their spouses. This is particularly so when the male drinker feels humiliated by his wife, either sexually because of low potency which precedes or follows the alcoholism, or for some other personal feeling of inadequacy.

The return to the outside world often has to be gradual, as by going to work but returning to hospital at night for a few weeks. The hospital unit can also usefully offer a social focus for the discharged alcoholic, to which he can return for regular group meetings and social events; and many of them also provide a base for the local Alcoholics Anonymous group.

Families can also be involved by discussing joint problems and airing conflicts in a professional situation, instead of attempting only to blot them out with alcohol; and many wives of alcoholics find support and help from Alanon, a kind of parallel organisation to Alcoholics Anonymous itself. Alcoholics Anonymous (A.A.) can be of great help to some drinkers, and every alcoholic should be informed about them, and told how to contact the local branch. The members have for the most part considerable knowledge of alcoholism through previous personal experience and have acquired a certain *expertise* in helping to prevent recurrences of the habit. They hold meetings, discussions and social occasions, and individual members can be called on by the drinker who feels he is relapsing. Patients who are introduced will find themselves welcome as new members and may also find a niche in which they may be useful to others, which is always helpful in restoring self-esteem. There are various branches, and particulars may be obtained from the London Office, at present at 11 Redcliffe Gardens, S.W.10.

Follow up after discharge, offering personal support, encouragement and advice, is also very important. If possible, the outpatient should see the same individual doctors, nurses, psychologists, or social workers (all of whom have active treatment roles in most alcoholic units) as during his inpatient stay.

During this after-treatment, care may be required to tide the patient over special events, and the better one knows the patient the more will one be prepared. Festive occasions such as Christmas may call for special precautions, as may such other events as anniversaries, births, marriages and wakes.

DRUG ADDICTION

Drug addictions can be divided into two main groups. The first comprises addiction to those drugs which involve only an *emotional* dependence, such as marihuana, cocaine, analeptics such as the amphetamines and phenmetrazine (Preludin), and bromides. True physiological addiction does not develop, so that they can give them up without physical symptoms.

The other group comprises addiction to those drugs which involve a *physical* dependence, and this is a very real thing in that the patients develop abstinence symptoms of a physical kind if supply of the drug is discontinued. The nature of the withdrawal symptoms varies according to the drugs to which the patient is addicted, but these fall easily into two sub-groups, namely (1) the opiate group, and (2) the alcohol-barbiturate group. The withdrawal symptoms of the opiate group are characterised by 'nervous instability'—and this is no fancy on the part of the patient or the observers—with autonomic dysfunction but *without* the development of convulsions or delirium. The withdrawal symptoms of the alcohol-barbiturate group are characterised, if the addiction is sufficiently severe, by the development of convulsions and delirium.

The growth of opiate addiction in Great Britain has been parallel to that in the rest of the western world, although not so great as in some countries. Between 1936 and 1960 the average number of opiate addicts annually was 336; with a high of 620 in 1937 and a low of 199 in 1947. The figures were reliable because there were no illegal sources of morphine and heroin. Most of those on these drugs were patients who had been given the drugs for some severe pain and became addicted; and many were doctors, nurses, pharmacists and so on who had easy access to the drugs. There was no 'drug culture' and young people were rarely involved.

The new wave of drug takers developed here from 1960 onwards, much increased by North American heroin addicts who came to this country because here the drugs could be legally prescribed for addicts, whereas in their own countries it was a crime to take and to prescribe them. By 1965 there were 259 new cases of heroin addiction known, of whom 145 were under 20 years. There was no significant change in morphine and pethidine addiction, all the increase was with heroin, though later Methadone became important.

The rate continued to climb, and in 1968 there were 2624 new notifications in Great Britain of narcotic addicts. Of this total 2096 were on heroin, 214 on Methadone, and 314 were on other drugs. As

330 PSYCHOLOGICAL MEDICINE

a response to the extremely rapid growth of heroin addiction new legislation was brought in. Heroin prescribing became restricted to a very few doctors, centred almost exclusively in special drug clinics in hospital outpatients departments, and with special inpatient units to back them up, which stopped over-prescribing by 'rogue' doctors, many of whom were just too credulous and unable to say 'No'. The effect of the new (1968) legislation and organisation of drug clinics was striking: by 1970 there were 762 new notifications, of whom only 353 were on heroin; but there has been a subsequent rise and in 1977 there were 1149 new notifications, of whom 615 were on heroin.

An unknown number of addicts remain outside the system, variously estimated as between 20 and 100 per cent of the known totals, and it is possible that some addicts manage to register themselves at more than one clinic. Narcotic addiction is largely centred still in London. Of the 1977 total of 1149 new notifications, only 39 were from Scotland, even fewer from Wales, and more than two thirds of the England total were in London. Most provincial addicts migrate to London, where an anonymous shiftless life is easier, and where they can find more of their own type. In 1979, at the time of writing, there is disturbing evidence that the situation is again getting out of control.

Many other drugs are turned to by opiate addicts, especially if heroin is in short supply, and by drug abusers who have never been on heroin. A growing practice has been to crush up barbiturates and inject the incomplete solution intravenously—with frequent local abscesses, septicaemia, and a fairly high mortality as consequences. Intravenous methedrine has been withdrawn from the market by the manufacturers, and oral amphetamines are at present being voluntarily outlawed in many areas and hospitals. Mandrax, a mixture of methaqualone and diphenhydramine, has many devotees and should in our opinion not be prescribed either. We have no exact knowledge of the numbers of addicts, even of heroin, because we do not know how many others each known addict may be supplying. There is no machinery to ascertain the frequency of barbiturate addiction, but surveys of various populations have indicated it to be very common, especially in middle aged housewives who have little, other than their addiction, in common with the younger addicts. Barbiturates are still overprescribed, although amphetamines are less often prescribed by doctors now. Barbiturates are in bathroom lockers, handbags, available in clubs and cafés, and even brought by parents to their children in remand homes. In recent years large and small scale thefts of drugs from chemists' shops and hospital pharmacies have increased the amounts in circulation, but careless over-prescribing remains the chief source.

Aetiology

Here, many factors are involved, and it is not a simple matter at all. There are social, personal, physical and pharmacological factors.

Under *social* factors, the first is availability; addiction starts where the drugs are to be found, and the best way to become an addict is to know one. Addiction is almost a contagious disease.

So the basic *social* factors are availability and the sort of person who takes to addiction. In the United States the great majority of addicts belong to minority groups from the same areas of the same cities, slum areas with a high incidence of other social problems, delinquency, crime, venereal disease, and unstable family structures. It looks as though addiction, like delinquency when that occurs on any large scale, is a social function of a problem population, stemming from contact with each other and so handed on by local tradition. However, the drug culture also attracts large numbers of young people from quite privileged backgrounds, but of unstable and inadequate personality. Addiction in Great Britain, by comparison on a small scale, has not yet assumed the fixity of the American social pattern. Many of our young currently view drug-taking with complacency, even approval, and there is evidence of a Rakes' Progress from marijuana and amphetamines to 'hard' (opiate) drugs.

So much for the basic social factors of availability, and the social problem group which spreads the contagion. But since enormous numbers of people subjected to the same social circumstances do not become addicts there must be *personal* factors also. As regards these, it would appear that anyone *can* become addicted. But just as alcohol is a 'detector of psychic weakness' the same is true of drugs, and the more the 'psychic weaknesses', the more is the person at risk. Fundamentally, it seems to us that addicts are people who just like taking things in accordance with a narcissistic, childlike preoccupation with their own needs. Safeguards against addiction are to be obsessionally careful and emotionally cold. Dangers are to be incautious, impulsive, unduly emotional and of a dependent type. Some *young* addicts are impulsive hedonists out for a thrill who get into bad company, part of the 'teenage explosion'. Others may be serious students with adolescent needs, hoping to achieve creativeness and greater self-knowledge, questing for new sensations and experience in an attempt at greater self-fulfilment. Among those of more complex psychopathology, some may take drugs as an aggressive protest against reactionary society. The more tormented may take them to reduce the moodiness arising from their awareness of the difference between their ideal and actual selves, or from their sexual and interpersonal problems, finding themselves more bearable and life less threatening, however transiently, under the effect of drugs.

Most *adult* addicts seem to be immature and dependent people who look for and expect props, who take flight into feeling rather than effective action in face of difficulty, and the self-centred dependence of many encourages a selfish possessiveness of others that renders relationships complicated and unsatisfactory. There may then be a tendency to flight into pseudo-illness with demand for drugs and increasing use of those as solvents of the reality they do not wish to face. These are the anxious-hysterical group. Addiction becomes even commoner where there is an admixture of psychopathy. Then, having got into the company of addicts the patient finds, in Isbell's words, he has entered a 'distinct social group with its own language, customs and code'; he feels himself to belong, he is at less disadvantage than in ordinary company, and if he tries to extract himself, he is lonely, bored, has lost his friends and 'feels nothing in common with the squares who are not hep to drugs'. Even so, many addicts resent their dependence on the drug, are liable to feel inferior and in the gutter on that account, like to equalise by dragging others down to their level and so persuade them to share and in that act may feel some possession of that power which they like but otherwise will lack.

Narcotic drug users have a high crime rate, even before they start on drugs, and nearly all of them are convicted of an offence at some time. The female addicts have relatively higher delinquency rates, before the addiction starts, than do the males; an expression of disordered personality in another field.

Next, we come to *physical* factors. Some patients have genuinely developed an addiction through attempts to relieve genuine pain, but this is also often put forward as an excuse, with the alleged condition having been elusive and obscure, defying diagnosis in a way that creates scepticism as to how founded in reality it was.

Last, we come to *pharmacological* factors. It is usually thought that the choice of the drug has been more rather than less accidental, depending on chance and availability, but this may not be altogether so, in that opiate addicts like the reduction of general (including erotic) appetite, while experiencing from intravenous injection a transient thrill akin to orgasm though centred in the abdomen, after which they feel a tranquil freedom to get on with what they want to do; whereas barbiturate addicts are more often aggressive people (even though also immature and inadequate) who like a high degree of sexual stimulation and to live in an emotional vortex, for which the disinhibiting effect of barbiturates may be useful.

Symptoms and signs

Emotional dependence group

Marijuana (Cannabis indica), also known as pot, hash, grass and by other names, is mainly smoked but can be eaten. Various types are produced from different countries, but the main active ingredient of each is delta tetra hydrocannabinol. It leads to a wide variety of effects, partly depending on what the drug taker is expecting, his stage of mind, and the social setting. Often there is a sense of calm elation, with distortions of space and time, and perceptual distortions with illusions or even hallucinations can occur. Outwardly the subject looks distant and dreamy, 'stoned', and may be giggling over little things. As with many drugs there may be a sense of deep creative thinking or of cosmic awareness, but the ideas are usually flat and obvious to the unintoxicated, and even to the subject afterwards.

Occasionally, cannabis is followed by an intense feeling of anxiety, amounting to terror, which usually settles down with time, aided by chlorpromazine. This seems to happen if the subject takes a much stronger preparation than usual, or one prepared in a different way, as for example when an American smokes Algerian hash for the first time.

Cannabis is now taken very frequently in the western world, and probably has no more serious ill effects than alcohol, which has plenty. There is a strong movement to make it legal. One serious disadvantage, not widely recognised, is that there is a cannabis 'hangover', a not unpleasant apathy, unlike the subjective distress caused by alcohol. Students in particular can be affected badly, because a weekend heavy session may be followed by two or three days in which no work gets done. When the apathy wears off the student starts to worry about not having done enough work, and too often smokes more pot to assuage his anxiety. The drug is implicated in many student failures.

Cocaine can confer a sense of extreme well-being with increase of psychomotor activity and abolition of fatigue and hunger. This is very short-lived. When the dose is repeated toxic symptoms may appear with central nervous stimulation and autonomic sensitisation: elevation of blood pressure, pulse and respiration, with sweating, exophthalmos and mydriasis, increased reflexes with tremors, twitches and even spasms of muscle groups. Finally, a toxic psychosis may appear with disorientation and failure of grasp, visual, auditory and tactile hallucinations, a persecuted suspiciousness—a sub-delirium that may become a full delirium.

The picture with *amphetamine* is similar but the symptoms develop much more slowly, the effects are far less intense and last longer. With *bromide* there is an increasing calm with intervals of somnolence and, as the dose climbs, a gradually increasing sub-delirious state, starting at night, which may progress to full delirium; there may or may not be acneiform eruptions. With none of these drugs is there any abstinence syndrome.

With the *alcohol barbiturate* group, (main members other than alcohol: barbiturates, paraldehyde, chloral, meprobamate (Equanil) glutethimide (doriden)) true addiction can occur. The clinical picture is one of more or less chronic intoxication. At high levels of intoxication there will be a muddled, fuddled confusion, with impaired intellectual function and diminished emotional control, and neurological manifestations such as dysarthria, nystagmus, ataxia and other evidence of incoordination, perhaps with the physical accompaniment of unexplained bruises, grazes or burns sustained through falls. At lower levels of intoxication, diagnostic pointers include the following:

Reluctance to tolerate reduction of the dose with or without devices aimed at preventing it, e.g. statements that the prescription or the pills have been lost, or short measure given. A general falling off of efficiency and effort; the housework does not get done, letters are unanswered, bills are unpaid or paid twice through memory impairment, meals are delayed. Oscillation of mood from an anxious, irritable, depressed disgruntlement and then back to equable cheerfulness, without obvious external cause. Oscillations of behaviour from a disinhibited over-talkativeness with restlessness to a slow, forgetful fuddledness with somnolence at the wrong times, but sometimes with night being turned into day by the added introduction of analeptics, for many barbiturate addicts like to offset the sedative barbiturate effect. There may be also the development of an aggrieved antagonism with grumbling accusations, sometimes with a germ of twisted truth achieved by altering the emphasis of something that has been said or the motive of something that has been done. In general, such changed behaviour may reveal something of the underlying discontent that may have led to taking drugs in the first place, its expression being released by their disinhibiting effect. Particularly, in the more purely intellectual sphere, there may be rambling conversation that does not reach a point, telling the same story twice, asking the same thing again and again, repeatedly seeking confirmation, muddles over dates, missing appointments, forgetting to relay messages or making telephone calls at extraordinary hours through impairment of time sense or judgement, finding entries in diaries with inability to remember when they were made and to what they refer, or a story of seeing a client on a Thursday without recollection of having seen him on Tuesday, even though notes had been made.

With the *opiate* group, (main members: morphine, diacetylmorphine (heroin), methadone (physeptone), hydromorphone (dilaudid), levorphanol (dromoran), pethidine and phenadoxone (heptalgin)), morphine may be taken as the paradigm. The intoxication that occurs with alcohol and barbiturates is not seen. The initial effects of depression of blood pressure, pulse rate, temperature and respiration are not maintained as tolerance is acquired, but the pupils remain constricted, constipation is always present, sexual function remains depressed, and there is continued irritability of the longer reflex arcs. In the early stages the candidate for addiction may show increased activity followed by drifting into a light sleep, from which he may wake suddenly and then drift back again. It is in this stage of drift from sleep to wakefulness that the opium dreams occur. But as tolerance increases, this tendency to light sleep decreases. To outward observation the opiate addict is not abnormal as long as he can continue to take a satisfactory dose, and he will be quite able to carry on a skilled technical job. The only outward evidence may be constricted pupils, injection marks, and loss of weight secondary to reduced food intake—though in general the productivity, is likely to be less and more time may be spent in daydreaming. The moral decay emphasised by the older text-books need not occur except in so far as the addict may be unscrupulous over trying to maintain supplies.

Withdrawal symptoms
As regards the first group—those drugs involving emotional dependence only—the only withdrawal symptoms of note are moodiness and malaise and withdrawal may be abrupt without danger. With the alcohol-barbiturate group, the withdrawal symptoms may be serious. Their severity varies with the dose taken, the degree of intoxication and its length. Withdrawal symptoms are to be expected if the patient has been taking more than 800 mg of barbiturate per day for any significant length of time, but as regards alcohol there is more individual variations so that it is less easy to be precise. With

barbiturates, the usual course of events is that after a latent interval of about eight hours, anxiety, restlessness, headache, tremor, twitching of various muscle groups, weakness, vomiting and postural dizziness make their appearance. These increase, accompanied by electro-encephalographic changes in the form of slow waves with spike and wave formation. Between about the thirtieth and forty-eighth hour of withdrawal epileptiform fits may be expected in about three cases out of four. Thereafter, the patient may begin to recover, but, on the other hand, about two out of every three are liable to increasing insomnia with the development of delirium, usually starting at night. Barbiturate delirium does not differ significantly from delirium tremens, and the attitude of the patient towards it may vary between, occasionally, amusement at the queer things that he is observing and, more often, fear that may become desperate with frantic efforts to escape from imaginary enemies. Agitation may lead to exhaustion and exhaustion to death. While the onset of delirium may be prevented by judicious use of barbiturate or alcohol, its course cannot be so influenced after it has begun.

On withdrawal of morphine and other opiates the symptoms are less dangerous but are distressing both to experience and to observe. Their intensity depends to some extent on the dose that the patient has been accustomed to take, but a critical level seems to be reached at about 500 mg a day. Higher doses do not lead to significant increase in development of withdrawal symptoms, which last may be quite mild in patients taking less than about 300 mg. For the first fourteen hours the patient feels reasonably well, but there then develop yawning, lacrimation, rhinorrhoea and perspiration with a restless, uneasy sleepiness. After about twenty-four hours the patient awakens to a persistent insomnia, with intensification of the foregoing symptoms now coupled with severe cramp-like pains in the back and legs and 'cold flashes' which lead to curling up with demand for more blankets whatever the atmospheric temperature. Objectively, there are recurring waves of gooseflesh with twitching of various muscle groups. After about thirty-six hours there is an intense increase of restlessness, with retching, vomiting, diarrhoea, total anorexia and increase of temperature, respiration and blood pressure, with loss of body weight. This state reaches its height at about forty-eight hours after withdrawal, continues much the same until about the seventy second hour of abstinence, and then starts to abate. After a week or so objective signs have disappeared, but the patients may yet complain of weakness, aches and difficulty in sleeping.

Treatment
In this, whatever the addiction, there are several stages. The first is
to get the patient to see the need for treatment. This may be
difficult. The second is to wean the patient from the drug. This can
only be done satisfactorily in a controlled environment, i.e. an
institution, away from sources of supply. Even so many patients
will cheat, or try to, by bringing in supplies more or less cunningly
concealed or by claiming to need more than was stated at the
preliminary consultation.

With the cocaine, marijuana, amphetamine and bromide group
this will not much matter since immediate withdrawal carries no
ill-effects. With the alcohol-barbiturate group to withdraw abruptly
may be to endanger life. A few diminishing doses of alcohol should
suffice to avoid delirium tremens, and, since the drugs within each
group are more or less interchangeable some added barbiturate may
help. The patient should be out of hazard if he survives without
discomfort an alcohol-free period of about twenty-four hours. With
barbiturates, the best practice seems to be to substitute pentobarbi-
tone (nembutal) since its length of action is such that four oral
doses daily should suffice to prevent withdrawal symptoms without
producing more than mild intoxication. The 'stabilising dose' can
be established by observing the patient over a period of about
forty-eight hours. Tremulousness and postural hypotension are the
main indicators of underdosage. When the patient appears comfortable on the stabilising dose, this should be gradually reduced by
100–200 mg each day. If tremulousness, twitching, hypotension
and weakness occur, the reduction should be suspended for
twenty-four hours, and it may be advisable to nurse the patient on
a mattress on the floor. Severely addicted patients may require
gradual withdrawal over a month or more, specially if there are
cardiovascular or other organic complications. Since the barbiturate
delirium cannot be reversed once it occurs, it is best to err on the
side of caution and even to increase the dose if the warning signs
are marked. Phenothiazines are best avoided owing to risk of their
potentiating the liability to epileptic developments. Benzodiazepines can relieve some of the symptoms, and have an anticonvulsant effect.

With the opiate group, immediate withdrawal (the so-called 'cold
turkey' treatment, having reference to the cold flashes and the
goose-flesh) rarely involves risk to life but may be considered cruel.
Since it has no deterrent effect against relapse the insistence by
some hospitals on immediate withdrawal may be considered puni-
tive. The substitution method is again to be preferred. Methadone

is the drug of choice because it is a sufficient substitute for the others of the opiate group, its effects are of quite long duration, and its own abstinence symptoms are milder. It is best given orally to wean the patient away from his liking for syringes and whatever symbolic significance they may have. The patient should be observed on what seems to be the suitable minimum dose. If the guess is a good one, two doses a day should keep the patient comfortable and enable 'stabilisation' to be achieved within forty-eight hours. It is usual to substitute 1 mg of methadone for every 3 mg of morphine, and 1 mg of methadone for every 2 mg of heroin that the patient claims to have been taking. The stabilising dose may then be halved and gradual reduction carried out, arriving at complete withdrawal within seven to ten days. This can be achieved with only slight discomfort. Some practitioners add barbiturates or phenothiazines which, though without effect on the withdrawal symptoms themselves, may help the patient to tolerate them better.

The withdrawal is easy enough, but the next stage is to get the patient to see the necessity for forswearing once and for all time the use of his drug, and this may be very difficult. At the same time the patient must be rehabilitated, first into suitable physical activity and occupation, and second, into suitable attitudes of mind. In this last, the therapist and patient have mutually to consider what were the factors that led to addiction in the first place, how they may be corrected and what alternative satisfactions can be found. In this, of course, the patient's life situation and personality structure (those parts of it, in Meyer's homely words, that work, those that don't work so well, and those that don't work at all) must be considered, and attempts made to adjust both situational and personality factors. This is usually in fact a matter that is very difficult to bring to a satisfactory conclusion. On leaving hospital the patient must have somewhere to go, a job and some friendly and continuing supervision. For the occasional patient whose motivation and cooperation are good but who fears temptation while precariously adjusted, the administration of the opiate-antagonist cyclazozine may be helpful in that it counteracts the thrills engendered by opiates and renders unexciting the effects of taking them, so that their neutralisation in that setting makes them not worth while.

Finally in treatment, the best method is prevention, and the best prophylaxis is to have a law-abiding society and a firm legal control.

Prognosis
This is apparently better than is generally thought, though accurate figures are hard to obtain since addicts are notoriously shiftless,

changeable and unreliable so it is difficult to follow them up. Many die prematurely, occasionally of an acute, massive pulmonary oedema, the cause of which is hard to explain, more often through failure of antiseptic precautions in self-injection leading to liver failure, bacterial endocarditis, septicaemia, etc. Many seem abnormally susceptible to intercurrent infections. Of the survivors, the prognosis seems to depend on two main factors. One is the length of the treatment. Early relapse is associated with its brevity. The second main factor is concerned with the social circumstances to which the patient has to return. Those with satisfactory personal relationships and some qualification to undertake interesting work have a better chance than the thrill-seeking, restless, personality-disordered addicts who neither work nor have social attachments except to other addicts. It is probably because of this that of those who started addiction for *medical* reasons 60–70 per cent were able to make some more or less satisfactory drug-free adjustment. The results with doctors and nurses in the United States who had satisfactory and interesting work to which to return and who by law had to be followed up for five years, were even better and reached the surprisingly high figure of about 90 per cent. So, prognostically, there is great variation from case to case. It has been estimated that over a longer period of ten to twelve years, about half the 'teen-age addicts will be off all drugs for no obvious reason except perhaps that the process of maturation enables them to dispense with thrills, props and artificial aids to a better adjustment.

LSD (lysergic acid diethylamide)

This, though not properly a drug of addictive type, may be mentioned here because its indiscriminate use—mainly by personality-disordered adolescents—has created much anxiety. Although chemically unrelated to mescal (see p. 137) its effects are similar. Visual illusions and hallucinations occur, but visual experience of the actual scene is also enriched and enhanced, while movement and changing relationship of the surroundings may appear to be happening. Time sense is disturbed. Memories may be recaptured with a special vividness and intensity of feeling. These, and the visual experiences and the emotions felt, may become invested with a special significance and importance, so that a new world may be felt to have been revealed.

LSD has been used therapeutically in attempts to 'explore the personality in depth' and as treatment for alcoholism and various neurotic disturbances. Its value is not established, and acute psychotic episodes and chronic schizophrenia-like psychoses have followed

340 PSYCHOLOGICAL MEDICINE

its use. Both LSD and marijuana are sometimes followed by anxiety states with depersonalisation and fears of permanent mental damage which can be very distressing. They usually respond to chlorpromazine. 'Flashbacks', with the sudden onset of severe anxiety and perceptual disturbances even months after taking the drug, are a distressing complication, the mechanisms of which are not understood.

The 'opening of a new world' idea has led the intellectually curious as well as the personality-disordered into experimentation with LSD. Certainly this may be fascinating; certainly it is also dangerous. The altered judgements under its influence may lead to difficult situations, e.g., accidents involving innocent people, unwanted pregnancies, things said and acts done that are later regretted. There have also been reports of serious self-damage through lack of judgement, as by walking out of a window in the belief that he can fly. 'Trip-takers' and devotees of 'psychedelic experience' should be discouraged from taking LSD.

Amphetamine psychosis

In a certain number of people who take large doses of amphetamines, the tense, restless, excited state which the drug taker aims at develops into a full blown psychosis, closely resembling paranoid schizophrenia. Unlike the toxic confusional states consciousness remains clear. The patients are fearful, sweating, often with dilated pupils; they feel they are spied upon and persecuted, and have auditory hallucinations; and they often try to run and hide from their persecutors. They are usually brought to medical attention by their friends or by the police. If the diagnosis is suspected the urine can be tested for amphetamine-like substances.

Treatment is based on phenothiazines and time, but some fail to clear up completely, suffering apparently from chronic paranoid schizophrenia. Whether or not these people might have been developing schizophrenia anyway is not known.

14

Peripheral psychiatry

We stated at the beginning of the book that the question of whether or not a case come under psychiatric care should depend on the practical consideration of who is best qualified to treat it. This may often be a matter of doubt, and even of dispute. It is proposed in this chapter to discuss such 'borderland' cases. Since opinions differ, the relegation of some of the conditions about to be discussed to the periphery of psychiatry may seem unorthodox and surprising to some critics; others may be surprised that such conditions are included at all. The first matter for consideration is so-called 'Psychosomatic illness'. (See also Chapter 1, p. 12 *et seq*.)

Psychosomatic medicine

This term, like others in psychiatry, has several almost distinct meanings, so that discussion of the subject often generates more heat than light. We do not intend to go into much detail in this book, but would like to consider the various uses of the term, and mention some of the basic principles. The bibliography contains some references to the subject.

(1) The commonest use of the term psychosomatic illness refers to illnesses of proven structural or biochemical pathology, regarded as caused—to some important degree—by psychological factors. Many physicians, and more psychiatrists, believe that emotional factors play an important role in the development of duodenal ulcer, coronary thrombosis and coronary artery disease, hypertension, asthma, ulcerative colitis, and eczema and some other skin diseases. Others believe that there is no sound reason for believing that emotional factors play a more than secondary role, although everyone recognises that emotional disturbances will worsen the symptoms, and often the prognosis, of all of the above named illnesses, and many more.

It is difficult to prove a causal relationship between emotional disturbances and these illnesses, and much of the research work done in the past has been of poor quality, based too often on a clinical hunch after seeing only a few patients. It is nearly always possible to find the sort of emotional factor in which you are interested if you look hard enough and have no controls. For instance many psychiatrists and psychoanalysts were struck by the frequency of obsessional characteristics and of 'over control' of emotions in those with various physical illnesses, largely because they studied no control subjects and were not aware how common such characteristics are in the normal population. Yet others saw causal associations between emotional immaturity and dependency in, for example, ulcerative colitis, without allowing properly for the effect on personality and behaviour of a debilitating illness.

In recent years, however, some more careful research has been done and the writers believe that the following associations are among those well established: subarachnoid haemorrhage, especially that not due to aneurysm or angioma, is often precipitated by emotional turmoil; the death rate from heart disease and other causes is markedly raised in those whose spouse has recently died; and an episode of agitated depression leads to some permanent rise in blood pressure.

There are a good many illnesses in which emotional factors play an important part in many cases, even if they are not what is often called 'the necessary cause'. These include coronary artery disease and coronary thrombosis, asthma, hypertension, and a good deal of skin disease. The writer is not convinced that emotional factors are of much importance in the genesis of ulcerative colitis, rheumatoid arthritis, and duodenal ulcer, although they certainly affect the patient once he has developed the illness.

It is well established, though not widely known, that physical and mental illnesses tend to affect the same individuals. Patients who present in early life with anxiety and depression have higher physical morbidity and mortality rates, with a shorter life expectation than their happier peers. Intelligent and happy children are more likely to have healthy adult lives than are less well-adjusted children. University students who are calm, cheerful and sociable, have less serious illness in their later lives than their more anxious and reserved contemporaries.

The use of life events schedules to study the causes of depression and schizophrenia has been mentioned in the appropriate chapters (p. 166 and p. 134), and they have been used similarly for some physical diseases. There is growing evidence that some physical illnesses, in some people at least, can be a response to emotionally disturbing events, even though the life events may be acting only as triggers in those already predisposed and ripe for the illness.

It is rather naive to think of any illness as resulting from a single cause. Even in the infectious diseases, one must consider host resistance, in which genetics, early feeding experiences, and very many other factors play a part. Emotional disturbances were long thought to determine host resistance in tuberculosis, if the operas of the nineteenth century are anything to go by; and all experienced physicians and surgeons know that some patients seem to die because they have given up the struggle to live, and 'turn their faces to the wall'.

There have been a good many theories about the possible mechanisms which relate emotional and physical disturbances, mainly based naturally enough on autonomic nervous system function. Everyone knows that transient physical changes occur constantly, in response to emotional changes, or even to changes in alertness and concentration. Pulse rate, blood pressure and skeletal blood flow, e.e.g. patterns, gut motility and visceral blood flow, skin conductance, and many biochemical and hormonal changes have been extensively studied, and their relationship to various emotional states and personality types charted. As yet the studies are mainly of emotional and physical 'parallels', and even in cases where the causal association is clear, the nature of the mechanism is not understood.

Recently there have been claims that autonomic nervous system responses can be conditioned, so that, for example, an animal could be trained to raise or lower its blood pressure in order to gain food or avoid electric shock. The implications of this are very wide, in the treatment of hypertension, for example. Similarly, the new subject of 'Biofeedback' sprang up, concerned with the deliberate alteration of the subject's own autonomic functions. The best known application of this was in the modification of e.e.g. rhythms, by being given feedback in some form to indicate success or failure.

In fact the experimental work on which all this was based has been severely criticised, but it is included as an example of the trend of psychosomatic investigations, which are increasingly sophisticated.

(2) Another common use of the term 'psychosomatic' refers to the physical symptoms of anxiety or of some other powerful emotion, which are due to overactivity or dysfunction of the autonomic nervous system. Palpitations, dyspnoea, sweating, butterflies in the stomach or other unpleasant sensations, nausea and vomiting, colicky lower abdominal pain, frequency of micturition or of bowel function—the latter often amounting to diarrhoea—dry mouth and choking sensations are the commonest. These complaints make up a large number of those for which people consult their general practitioners.

(3) A related aspect is the study and intercorrelation of various somatic and psychological measures, not necessarily studying patients or illness, but in a psycho-physiological way. One example is the study of the effects of different mood states on endocrine function and,

conversely, the effect of hormone changes on mood states, such as those in women throughout the menstrual cycle. This type of study is increasingly frequent, and should help to provide a firmer basis for clinical psychosomatic medicine.

(4) An important field, not usually considered under the heading of psychosomatic medicine, but reasonably mentioned here, is the patient's emotional reaction to any illness. This is especially important in those with long illnesses which affect earning prospects, and lead to prolonged hospitalisation. Likewise, the reactions to mutilation, to the threat to life of a heart attack or stroke with the inevitable fear of recurrence, or to a diagnosis of cancer, must all be taken into account by those caring for such patients in any way. The reactions depend of course on the personality and life situation of the patient as well as on the nature of his illness, and include denial of the truth, depression, anxiety, despair, anger, frustration, hopeless 'giving up', hysterical manipulation, and of course include also constructive coping and realistic acceptance of the situation.

(5) The broadest application of the term psychosomatic is concerned with the relationship between emotional and personality factors and a wide range of accidents and physical illnesses. For example: the emotional aspects of heavy cigarette smoking mean that cancer of the lung has a psychosomatic background in many cases; motor cycle accidents and injuries are commoner in rather psychopathic and aggressive young men; alcoholics and heavy drinkers have many more road accidents than others; physical fitness, including control of body weight, is related to coronary heart disease, and obviously depends largely on personality and attitudes. Many more examples could be adduced to illustrate the point, which does not need labouring.

Having outlined various ways in which emotional factors can be involved in the development of physical illness, it must be made clear that even in cases where the importance of these factors seems obvious, psychiatric and psychological treatment has not been shown to be of much help. It can be taken as a good working rule that if someone has psychiatric symptoms which justify treatment in their own right, and also has some physical illness, successful treatment of the former often helps the latter. If the patient is not aware of any emotional disturbance, psychiatric treatment is likely to have no effect or may even be harmful. The former is seen clearly in those cases of eczema and hypertension who come to psychiatric attention for coexisting depression or anxiety, and improve a great deal physically after psychiatric treatment. Even malignant hypertension, with papilloedema, has been known to be reversed by pre-frontal leucotomy carried out for a coexisting psychiatric illness.

Anorexia nervosa

This illness is a serious one in many cases, and perhaps does not comfortably fit in a chapter like this one, followed by enuresis, stammering and sleep walking, but it is not a large enough subject for a chapter of its own. References to the extensive literature are given in the bibliography.

The illness is one of those in which emotional and physical factors are continuously, and obviously interacting. The patient, nearly always an adolescent girl or single young woman, becomes emaciated through persistent refusal of food, the condition often beginning with a normal seeming slimming diet which then gets out of control. The appetite may be in abeyance, even with revulsion at the thought or sight of food; but more often the patient feels ready to eat, but complains of feeling distended after only a mouthful, and resists all efforts to make her eat more. When pressed to eat, such patients usually resort to vomiting, and almost always show both determination and ingenuity in hiding or otherwise disposing of food that they pretend to have eaten. The degree of emaciation may be quite alarming, and is the more striking in view of the remarkable energy and activity that such patients usually contrive to sustain. Amenorrhoea is part of the syndrome. A certain number of patients vary between overeating with obesity, overeating with vomiting, and food avoidance.

Anorexia nervosa seems to be increasing in frequency in the Western World, a fact perhaps related to the increase in overeating and obesity in our societies, and the parallel fashionable interest in being thin; and perhaps related also to the increasing cultural pressure on young people to be sexually active even if they are not ready for it. In many families of anorexic girls food and eating seem to play a very large part; and in nearly all the patients affected there is a fear of sexuality, and a feeling of inability to cope with sex or even with sexually toned relationships. The sexually unappealing skinniness and the amenorrhoea can be seen as a way of removing oneself from the fray, and prolonging childhood; and many patients worry a great deal as they begin to gain weight with treatment, that they will attract sexual attention. In many of the sufferers there is a distorted image of their own body size and shape, and they seem to see themselves as larger than they really are.

In some cases the illness seems to have the function of keeping the parents together as a married couple, if the patient believes that they are likely to split up 'when the children have grown up'. This kind of manipulative hysterical element is common in anorexia nervosa, and makes treatment more difficult.

Another common background factor is depression, perhaps precipitated by an unhappy love affair, which at first seems much like any other depression with anorexia and weight loss, but in which a kind of 'gear change' occurs. The depressive feelings fade into the background as the anorexic syndrome develops, and attention is more and more centred on food and weight. This sub-type of the illness is commoner in those with a relatively normal personality and family background, with onset later rather than earlier, and is the most responsive to treatment, often being helped by antidepressants.

Another common feature is marked obsessionalism, affecting various aspects of life, and associated with a tendency to brooding rumination on all the details of calories, grams gained and lost, and on various unhappy experiences of the past. Patients in whom there is marked obsessionalism do rather badly.

Course and prognosis are very variable, but overall this is a serious illness, with a mortality of up to 10 per cent in the long run, in those who come to specialist attention. There are many milder cases who do not reach specialist units because they recover spontaneously or respond rapidly to treatment. Death occurs from malnutrition with electrolyte imbalances, intercurrent infections, the complications of alcoholism which often develops in long standing anorexia, and from suicide. In some cases the starvation has a suicidal quality in itself.

These girls and, rarely, boys avoid all food, especially carbohydrates, and are sometimes described as having a 'phobia' of weight or of fatness. It is important to realise that the starvation itself affects the mental state profoundly, so that one is not only having to deal with the underlying emotional problems, but with mental abnormalities which arise secondarily from the starvation and consequent metabolic changes. These secondary changes are often difficult to understand and to empathise with, and, combined with the dishonesty about refusal and hiding of food, make these patients difficult to like, so that nursing staff and doctors tend to get irritated by them.

Treatment must be aimed at restoring weight to normal levels, and then trying to prevent relapse. In any but a mild case it is best to admit to hospital, as these patients need skilled nursing, and the situation in the family may be extremely disturbed and disturbing;

the patient is often playing one parent off against another, as well as causing concern by her illness. In a mild case it may be worth agreeing a 'contract' with the patient, that if she manages to attain a certain weight by a certain date admission may not be necessary. The same type of treatment contract is useful in hospital, in that the patient is kept in bed until a certain agreed weight is reached; and a programme is drawn up in which various privileges and rewards are gained as weight is gained. Drug treatment is usually necessary especially at first and chlorpromazine or other sedative phenothiazine may be used and has the benefits of lessening tension and agitation, and also lessening the tendency to vomit which many of the patients have. Antidepressants are indicated if depression is marked; and psychotherapeutic discussions, involving the family where appropriate, are very important. Psychotherapy may be impossible in the early stages, but as the mental state improves with better feeding and restoration of normal metabolism, it becomes easier.

In a few patients, in whom all other treatments have failed, some psychosurgical procedure such as prefrontal leucotomy may be necessary as a last resort.

Prevention of relapse in those who have responded to treatment is another problem. Essentially, these girls must be helped to develop and mature emotionally, a process which takes time, but can be aided. Emotional support over a long period is helpful with discussions aimed at developing a different view about life problems, especially about sexual relationships and family tensions, and interviews with the family where appropriate. Even in those who do fairly well there are often prolonged difficulties in the ensuing years, including depression and phobic states, and many abuse alcohol.

Nocturnal enuresis
This term is generally taken to apply to bed-wetting that persists after the age of five years. Recent large scale surveys show that the condition is very common, most cases show no psychological disturbance, and the problem is largely one of maturation of bladder control. Doctors, and psychiatrists especially, see a selected series in which psychological factors are prominent.

Perhaps the simplest possible cause is lack of adequate training, owing to the symptom having been passively accepted as inevitable so that it has persisted as a habit. This must be a rare state of affairs except in young children, but it seems occasionally to happen. We treated successfully a man of twenty-seven, who had never had one dry night in his life. His parents and all their siblings, and all his own siblings suffered from the same complaint. For them, enuresis was not only a family weakness but a family tradition. Explanation, persuasion and re-education relieved the patient of the symptom. Overall enuresis is commoner in boys than girls and a positive family history is common.

From the physical point of view, enuresis is sometimes associated in children with other conditions causing local irritation. If only for this reason, a proper examination must always be made, including testing of the urine.

From the psychological point of view, there seems some tendency for enuresis to occur in two contrasting types of children, those who are babyish and unduly submissive, and those who are notably aggressive. It is often held that in the former group the symptom represents one part of a general reluctance to accept the responsibilities of growing up and of achieving independence; however this may be, there does often seem to be some relation between enuresis and anxiety in such children. As regards the latter group, it is often held, and sometimes plausibly, that the symptom is an expression of aggressive feelings, of which the patient is only partly aware, directed usually either against the person responsible for the laundering or against the brother with whom the bed is shared.

The symptom certainly improves with age, and seems more likely to do so the less the patient is troubled by it or by other things. It usually ceases by the time puberty is reached, but is commoner in adults than might be supposed. Where it does persist, we are struck by the apparent absence of adequate psychogenesis, and by the frequent, though not invariable, association with other symptoms. Thus, the patients very commonly have 'irritable' bladders, in the sense that they are liable both to frequency and urgency of micturition, while they usually sleep abnormally heavily. It is usual to find that they were accustomed to leave the schoolroom for the lavatory more often than their schoolmates, that they prefer aisle seats in cinemas, theatres and churches, and are unable to sit through lengthy performances of any sort. They are peculiarly difficult to arouse at night, and often have to be dragged from their beds when due to get up in the morning. This is suggestive of physiological abnormality. It is said that enuresis in children usually occurs within two hours of going to sleep and that the volume of urine passed is remarkable in view of the short lapse of time since the bladder was emptied. We agree that the volume of fluid passed is often remarkable, but, on the other hand, we are much struck by the extreme inconstancy of the time at which it occurs. We also agree that the volume of fluid passed, and the part played by the hypothalamus, both in the regulation of sleep and in the liberation of anti-diuretic hormone from the posterior part of the pituitary, which is ineffective in deep sleep, are relevant considerations in the aetiology of enuresis as a whole.

Regular arousal at night in order to ensure emptying of the bladder is usually ineffectual. If the patient has not passed water before being aroused, he seems just as likely to do so after it. The most generally useful treatment, effective in about 75 per cent of sufferers, is the electric alarm apparatus set off by the first few drops of urine allowing current to flow through a circuit. The apparatus is now widely available commercially and through child welfare clinics.

Drugs are useful in some cases, especially in those who sleep very deeply. Amphetamines (e.g. 15–30 mg Amphetamine sulphate at night) are well proven; but their use is being generally discouraged now. Imipramine 25 mg at night is sometimes helpful, also on the basis of lessening the depth of sleep.

We regard most cases of adult enuresis as having some physiological disturbance rather than a primarily psychological one.

Stammering

This, again, is commonly considered a psychogenic disability, but is far more probably a condition to which psychological factors make only a partial contribution. Those who have studied it most fully ascribe it to an instability of integrated cortico-vocal function, probably related to a failure of either of the cerebral hemispheres to become the clearly dominant one. This is, however, another unsolved problem. The instability of function becomes more obvious when the patient is under stress. Such stress is commonly afforded by the feelings of diffidence and inferiority that the stammering itself arouses in the sufferer. Recent intensive study by psychologists (as opposed to psychiatrists) has rendered this a highly specialised field with the development of new and widely differing techniques which have changed the prognosis much for the better.

The most effective treatment is speech therapy, but psychotherapy and psychological management may be of help where there is an associated personality disorder, whether arising from the difficulties engendered by the stammer or from other causes.

We have occasionally treated stammerers with more or less success by hypnosis, since they may speak well under conditions of relaxation and may be so far encouraged by their success as then to feel more confident, but the effects have not been lasting.

Sleepwalking

This, though fairly common in children, is rare in adults. In children it may be associated with so-called 'night terrors', in which the child starts up from sleep, apparently terrified, but in a stage of consciousness intermediate between sleeping and waking in which he remains inaccessible. If there is such association, the condition will usually yield to glucose drinks taken at bedtime, since it apparently arises in relation to glycopenia. In other instances, it may represent the acting out, in a semi-sleeping state, of some conflict with which the child is preoccupied. In that event, the behaviour is more or less purposive, though not executed in full consciousness, and is likely to indicate the nature of the conflict. Treatment should be directed towards resolving this. The sleepwalking is unlikely to lead to danger, but for reassurance purposes it may be wise to prescribe small doses of sedatives, gradually to be discontinued as the psychological adjustments are effected.

In adults, we have encountered sleepwalking of two kinds, quite different from each other. One form has occurred in hysterical and exhibitionistic patients, whose hysterical symptoms verged on malingering. In their nocturnal disturbances they did appear to be asleep, but their behaviour was purposive, and had a stagey quality that encouraged one to suppose that they could have arrived at full wakefulness with very little effort. It appeared to be a dissociated state, comparable with that of the fugue (p. 275), but coloured by some degree of sleepiness. No fears were felt that such behaviour would involve any danger.

The other form occured in stable men, who were known to have been quite sober, and whose sleepwalking seemed quite without motive or conscious direction. In these, danger was certainly involved. One patient fell forty feet out of a window; another was rescued when found by a nurse hanging over the edge of a balcony. Both had a complete amnesia up to the moment when they were found, and each gave a history of having walked in his sleep on more than one occasion before. There was no evidence of epilepsy in either. The nature of the disturbance was not understood, but was not believed to be psychogenic. Beyond giving advice to sleep on the ground floor whenever possible, and otherwise to play for safety by taking hypnotics when sleeping above that level, it is difficult to know what treatment to prescribe for cases of this sort.

Tics and spasmodic torticollis

Tics are commoner in children but may persist into adult life. They occur most commonly in states of fatigue and debility or in situations in which the patient feels self-conscious or is under other stress. They are thus influenced by both physical and emotional factors. Sometimes a case may be considered essentially psychogenic, in that the tic may represent symbolically some aspect of a conflict with which the patient is preoccupied; for instance, a patient not previously subject to tics, developed a sudden jerking of the right forearm in a setting of conflict over whether or not to get engaged. He had long been in the habit of urging himself to action by saying to himself 'Get a jerk on'. He saw the connection for himself, and the tic stopped as soon as he had done so, although he remained in conflict for some time. In some patients tics and facial grimaces seem to represent suppressed anger directed at some close family member, and in many there seems to be some instability of cortical motor activity enhanced by emotional stress. Many cases of tic, especially in children, respond to haloperiodol. The dose should be built up steadily from 0.5 mg b.d. until benefit is achieved or Parkinsonian side effects appear. As emotional tension and anxiety make tics worse other psychological help may be useful.

Spasmodic torticollis, which is also often considered essentially psychogenic, appears to us to arise from an instability of motor function manifesting itself in periodic disturbances of tone. It occurs only in adults and is commonest in middle age. It may or may not be associated with emotional stress; where it is, such stress appears contributory rather than causal. The condition is peculiarly resistant to treatment of any sort. Psychological treatment seems to exert no influence on the basic condition, though it may sometimes improve the patient's adjustment to it. Recently, promising surgical techniques have been devised in the form of a stereotactic attack on the ventromedial region of the thalamus in which small, distinctive lesions can be made by thermocoagulation, electrolysis, or chemical means.

Acute intermittent porphyria

This rare, dominantly inherited abnormality of pyrrole metabolism, commoner in women than in men, may come to psychiatric notice either because of mental symptoms or because 'attacks' otherwise hard to explain have encouraged an erroneous diagnosis of hysteria. The 'attacks' may involve abdominal, neurological or mental symptoms, but these may occur separately or together. Most noteworthy are bouts of unlocalised abdominal pain with severe vomiting and constipation (occasionally diarrhoea), which may previously have led to laparotomy; they usually subside after about forty-eight hours. Apart from or together with those, there may be focal lesions of the central nervous system, e.g. peripheral neuritis, facial palsy, optic atrophy, wasting. Possible mental symptoms, occurring in association with the foregoing or independently, range from those of organic neurasthenia (p. 90), through histrionic display and aggressive contrariness, to confusional states and delirium. The 'attacks' are often precipitated by the patient having taken barbiturates —sometimes sulphonamides. The best hope in diagnosis lies in finding porphyrins in the urine, though a history of having taken barbiturates and/or a family history may be suggestive. There is no specific treatment, though phenothiazines (e.g. chlorpromazine 25–100 mg q.d.s.) may allay excitement and confusion. Barbiturates are to be avoided. The condition is rare, but should come to mind when otherwise inexplicable periodic abdominal and/or mental symptoms are encountered.

15

Treatment

We have repeatedly emphasised that in every patient there are constitutional, physical and psychological factors in aetiology. Our treatment should bear this in mind. Although there are as yet no treatments which will change the constitution, constitutional factors will often determine response.

All treatments in psychiatry can be considered under three main headings: (a) environmental change, (b) psychological treatment, and (c) physical treatments, and these should not be considered as in any way mutually exclusive. In nearly every patient each of them is relevant to some extent, althogh in many one will be more important than the others, and we hope to make clear in this chapter what is included under each heading.

As an example we can take the case of a middle-aged woman with a serious depressive illness of mixed endogenous and reactive pattern—as so many are. She has been increasingly failing to cope with her husband, a chronic invalid since a fall while drinking. Their relationship has always been turbulent, and just before his accident she had told him to 'go away or die' and leave her in peace. Her guilt about her ill wishes to him, which were immediately almost fulfilled, have led her to refuse a home help from the local authority. In this case an important environmental change is brought about by admitting her to hospital, where she is given physical treatment by antidepressants and e.c.t. successfully. She is then helped psycho-therapeutically by discussions of the problems with her husband. Her guilt, already lessened by the improvement in depression, is further helped, and she is persuaded to have a home help on discharge. If her husband still has a drink problem, or needs further treatment for his disabilities, to do something about these is again part of the therapeutic environmental change. This kind of combined approach is the essence of psychiatric treatment, and the three main headings should always be in the back of the doctor's mind in planning treatment.

It is important not to view physical and psychological treatments as mutually exclusive, as too often happens when people have dogmatic theoretical views: our theories are not good enough to justify dogmatism.

We should not take the naive view that a disorder precipitated by psychological stresses must of necessity be treated by psychological means. We know, for example, that many depressions precipitated by grief respond to physical treatments. The view is naive because by ignoring constitutional and physical factors it regards 'precipitation' and 'cause' as interchangeable concepts. Nor should we fall into the opposite error, and think that physically determined illnesses can only be treated by physical means. If someone has a pre-senile dementia, environmental change by hospital admission and support for the family are among the most useful things we have to offer.

There are two more very important points to appreciate in considering psychiatric treatment, which are much less obvious in the field of general medicine. The first is the aspect of 'social trouble', the sheer nuisance value to relatives, neighbours, friends and society at large, caused by the behaviour of some patients—including those with organic dementia and confusional states, and also many psychotic and psychopathic people. This is not often a problem in, for example, the surgical wards. If it is, and someone's behaviour is too troublesome to be borne, the psychiatrist will often be asked to cope, and the diagnosis will indeed usually be of dementia, confusional state, schizophrenia, mania or personality disorder. All this means that the way we have to treat many of our more disturbed patients is determined by society's dislike of them or of their behaviour, as well as by what is actually best for them.

The second of these general difficulties is the problem of psychopathic disorders of personality (p. 224). These are rarely amenable to treatment, being so much a part of the constitution. When severe they can cause unhappiness for the individual and others, and can lead to behaviour which seems to the ordinary person so strange and 'crazy', so infuriating and disturbing, that people feel that they must be 'ill' and therefore a psychiatric case. The personality of the patient and of those treating him always interact, and the relationships which develop, and the nature of the people concerned, have a marked influence on the type of treatment offered, and on many aspects of it. If the patient has a severe personality disorder, accompanying a psychiatric illness, then the usual treatments may be impossible to carry out, because, for example, of unreliability with appointments or medication, or because the patient is just unable to sustain interest in anything long enough. The personality, whether seriously disordered or not, also sets limits to the results of treatment. The habitually gloomy and anxious remain so even after the successful treatment of a serious depression. This is a limitation which is not always recognised, and often it is only by talking with someone who knows the patient well that we realise that we have made as much progress as we are likely to. The same applies in the opposite sense. We may not realise how much potential for improvement the patient has until we speak to someone else, who may make it plain that the patient has not at all returned to normal, that further efforts must be made, and that it is our treatment which is at fault, rather than the patient's personality. This is an important message.

The therapeutic plan
When a diagnosis has been made, and the patient's personality and life situation assessed, a therapeutic plan must be made and environmental change, psychological treatment, physical treatment, or the desired combination of the three, decided upon.

In some cases rather different treatment is needed for the immediate relief of distressing symptoms, from that aimed at the underlying illness. For example, in a patient with a depressive illness there might be marked anxiety symptoms. *Symptomatic* treatment for the latter with a benzodiazepine could start before the more *specific* electrical treatment (e.c.t.) for the former. Similarly, we may have to treat intercurrent infections, or make up for a prolonged period of poor appetite by adding vitamins. All this should be part of the therapeutic plan.

ENVIRONMENTAL CHANGE

The ideal therapeutic plan is that which combines the best chance of benefiting the patient with the least dislocation of his normal life. The first consideration is likely to be whether or not the patient needs to be off work. Most psychiatric patients do not; the great majority are better at work, and they should be encouraged to continue. It may even be said that minor symptoms are indications to stay at work rather than otherwise. Many claims of unfitness for work are based on reluctance rather than inability, and many patients have different views from the doctor on the value and meaning of work. In such cases, the answer must be that there are no psychiatric grounds for exemption. In taking such a decision the essential thing is to look for evidence of some definite psychiatric syndrome, e.g. depression or anxiety with objective signs, in addition to the patient's mere statement that he feels unfit—and always supposing that there is no evidence of organic disease. In fact, the guides are (1) what the patient's previous personality has been, and (2) what positive symptoms and signs does he show.

The next consideration is likely to be whether or not the patient needs to be treated in hospital. With the foregoing principles in mind, we may briefly consider the sort of cases that do best in hospital and the indications for admitting them.

Indications for hospital treatment

The main indications for inpatient treatment are:

(1) *To remove the patient from a stressful or harmful environment*, such as a very tense home situation.

(2) *For the patient's own protection*, e.g. to prevent suicide, to prevent social embarrassments which the patient and family might have difficulty in living down, to prevent undue expenditure and extravagance arising from mental illness.

(3) *For the protection of others*, usually to avoid violence or the threat of it, or where the patient is socially a public nuisance, e.g. if delusional beliefs lead him repeatedly to make complaints or to threaten legal action, or if he repeatedly shows deteriorated behaviour in public, e.g. exposing himself or appearing unclad.

(4) *For providing treatment* which offers reasonable chance of benefit, without which the patient would get worse or would recover more slowly and with greater suffering.

In practice, the majority of cases that come under these headings are those with the major illnesses, i.e. the psychotic cases. Under this heading we include those with the so-called functional psychoses (schizophrenia and affective psychoses), and those with organic psychoses, e.g. toxic deliria, organic confusional states, and those cases of senile and pre-senile deterioration who are unable to manage their own affairs and have no one who can satisfactorily look after them.

With regard to *schizophrenic* cases, those who are young and have not undergone appropriate treatment should usually be sent to hospital, in view of the seriousness of the illness. Chronic schizophrenics who have been treated but with limited success, may do better outside hospital than in, according to the amount they can do, the amount of satisfaction they can get from life, the adequacy of their social adjustment, and their living conditions. But the more they live in isolation and have to fend for themselves without supervision, the more they are likely to deteriorate. For cases of schizophrenia with late onset, in early middle age, usually of the paranoid or paraphrenic variety, admission to hospital is less essential; if their circumstances are suitable, it may be best for them to live at large, especially if they are socially well-preserved and able to remain acceptable to their associates.

As to *manic-depressive* cases, it may be said that the manic patient should always be in hospital since he will be unmanageable in the outside world; the hypomanic should be placed in hospital, if possible, when he is wearing out himself, his relatives and his bank-balance, as well as when he is drinking to excess. The depressive should be admitted to hospital when there are (*a*) serious risks of *suicide*, (*b*) *delusions, ideas of reference*, or *guilt feelings*. These mean that the case is beyond ordinary conversational approach and requires special handling.

With regard to cases with *organic psychoses*, the necessity for admission to hospital may be very variable. Admission to hospital is often necessary for detailed diagnostic observation and investigation. After that, it depends on the state of the patient and the home situation. (More details are given in Chapter 7, on the problems of the demented old.) The disposal of those with toxic deliria or organic confusional states depends on the underlying cause and the physical condition of the patient.

While the foregoing psychotic cases constitute the bulk of those who will require admission, there are of course many others, perhaps with relatively minor conditions, who may benefit from hospital care. Such are cases of *reactive depression* who have become suicidal risks, or who require removal to a sheltered environment before improvement can be expected. *Severe hysterics* may require hospital care, and something of the control that goes with it, especially where their relatives are unable to manage them satisfactorily, or encourage them into invalidism through mistaken beliefs or undue solicitude. Cases of *anxiety with exhaustion* who have become debilitated and demoralised may benefit from rehabilitation carried on in the supportive atmosphere of hospital. *Severe obsessionals*, and other neurotic cases (including alcoholics) whose symptoms have become conditioned by, and habitually related to, their daily routine, may be helped by the de-conditioning effect of removal to hospital, and an inpatient programme of behaviour therapy (p. 385). Finally, a certain number of cases in whom the diagnosis remains doubtful may need to be admitted for investigation and further observation before any satisfactory treatment can be begun.

Environmental adjustment in hospital

Admission to hospital involves, apart from anything else, a sudden and complete change of environment; such a simple measure may bring about a striking change in the clinical picture. To effect this to best advantage care should be devoted to such questions as which ward would be the most suitable, whether the patient would be better in a single room, whether he is favourably or unfavourably influenced by certain other patients or nurses. His reactions should be observed carefully and suitable alterations made accordingly, as far as may be possible. The extent to which they are possible is often surprising.

The desirability of some occupation has already been stressed. In hospital this is met by *'Occupational Therapy'*. The name is perhaps unfortunate as tending to emphasise the aspect of filling in time, whereas stress should be laid on the far more important aspects of relieving unhappiness or discomfort by distraction, affording an opportunity for the recovery of real pleasure in activity, increasing self-confidence by tangible evidence of a capacity that had been doubted or unrealised, and often enough frank training in better habits of concentration and work. For patients in hospital, and for chronic patients of whatever sort whether in hospital or not, this form of treatment is invaluable. It is not achieved by suggesting a little knitting as an alternative to brooding or the depressing exchange of rival symptoms with other patients. It should be definitely organised and recognised as a form of treatment which the patient is expected to undergo, just as he is expected to take his medicines and whatever else may be prescribed. In this way a corporate spirit is developed, and handicraft classes come to develop a sociable atmosphere that has a value of its own. Apart from arts and crafts, occupational therapy includes *industrial units* (manufacturing and assembly work), games and recreations, which do much to reduce the patient's isolation, all an integral part of the occupational programme.

Resocialisation of the shy and isolated is another important aspect in occupational therapy; in work-like situations, domestic activities such as cooking and baby-care where appropriate, and in more purely recreational pursuits, the occupational therapists try to foster social contact, interest, and self-respect.

Apart from its value in treatment, occupational therapy can have even some diagnostic value in doubtful cases, and it can throw considerable light on the extent to which the individual patient has progressed. The patient's behaviour in the work or occupational situation can be very revealing.

The more chronic the condition of the patient the more should his occupation serve some useful function to the community in which he lives. Thus, in mental hospitals the employment of suitable patients on the farm, in the gardens, about the house, and in maintenance work, is of mutual benefit in that the patient's own self-esteem is maintained through service to the community. The more such work resembles that which the patient will resume on discharge from hospital, the more valuable it is in his rehabilitation. The setting-up of industrial units in the hospitals themselves has been a valuable innovation. The transition to a fully independent life can also be aided if facilities can be arranged for the patient to work outside the hospital for a time before discharge, whilst spending his leisure time under its medical supervision and within its sheltered atmosphere.

Day hospitals, hostels, and rehabilitation centres
Day hospitals are increasingly recognised as very useful treatment centres, not only for chronic patients, but for a wide range of acute disorders. A well run and well staffed day hospital can cope with all but the most severely disturbed, and the list of indications for admission as an in-patient also applies to day patients. In some cases the patient is too severely ill, the home environment too unsuitable, or daily travel impractical in which situations inpatient care is better. The benefits of a day hospital over inpatient treatment are several: most importantly there is less emotional regression and institutionalisation, and family and social life are much less disrupted when the patient is only in hospital during normal work or school hours; nursing and medical staff work shorter hours without the need to provide 24 hour care; and there are economies in all other areas too. The current policy of the Department of Health and Social Security is to provide 40 day hospital and 30 inpatient places for each 60 000 of catchment area population, excluding provision for psychogeriatric patients, which indicates well the recognition now given to day care.

Hostels and Halfway Houses. These are provided for those who are able to live outside hospital and work, but are liable to relapse if left to fend for themselves, or if they return to an emotionally intense home with which they cannot cope—and which cannot cope with them. They are therefore principally for chronic schizophrenic patients. Unfortunately, although many promises have been made by the government and by local authorities, far too few of these hostels have been provided, and charitable organisations such as the Cheshire Homes and Richmond Fellowship have done most of what has been achieved.

Group homes. These are mainly for patients who have spent many years in mental hospitals, usually with chronic schizophrenia, and who are markedly institutionalised. They are provided with a house in the community, shared between four or five ex-patients, and look after themselves, but are visited by social workers, community nurses or voluntary helpers, or by all three. A good deal of preparatory rehabilitation, especially in domestic training, shopping, and so on, is needed before they move into the group home.

Rehabilitation Centres likewise offer a haven to psychiatric patients who are not too disturbed for an active regime, in which treatment, whether psycho-therapeutic or physical, is combined with an elaborate occupational and recreational programme, the former involving the use of workshops where new skills or trades may be learned and the latter providing educational facilities in the form of films, lectures and discussion groups which, to a varying extent, may be organised and run by the patients themselves. Some areas have *Training Centres* for subnormals; and other types of *Day Centres* are provided by go-ahead Local Authorities.

Mention may also be made of *Industrial Rehabilitation Units*, which may or may not be residential, and which are designed to cater for those who, having been obliged to change their employment for physical or other reasons or having been industrial misfits for whatever cause (including subnormality), need help in their readjustment. Their aptitudes can be tested, decisions can be made as to the best use to which these can be put, and instruction given accordingly in the establishment's workshops.

Day hospitals, hostels, rehabilitation centres and industrial rehabilitation units are attempts to answer social problems that cannot be dealt with individually but need to be dealt with *en masse*. As such, they are or should be functions of the community, and it is to be hoped that such facilities will be extended as the need for them is increasingly recognised.

Care of the patient at home

The following professionals may be involved in the care of the patient in the community, either at home or in a hostel, group home, or other accommodation: the general practitioner, psychiatrist, community psychiatric nurse, social worker, district nurse, health visitor, and home help. It is the demented elderly person who is likely to have the greatest number of services offered, and the chronic schizophrenic also often needs a lot. If the patient is at home, dependent on relatives, the relatives themselves may need much help and support, as the burdens borne by them are often great. With so many different helpers, from several agencies, confusion and inefficiency are common, and a close watch should be kept on this.

The post of community psychiatric nurse is a recent development, and has turned out to be extremely useful, especially in the care of the chronic schizophrenic, but also with other types of patients. In some areas the nurses are attached to general practices and in others to the psychiatric teams which deal with the catchment area. These nurses have already had psychiatric training. They are able to assess the patient in the home and thus be aware early of relapse, give treatment injections of depot phenothiazines, for example, advise and support the relatives, discuss with the patient and family ways of becoming increasingly independent, help with behaviour therapy programmes devised for agoraphobic and other neurotic patients, and much else besides. They can certainly cut down the rate of relapse and readmission among schizophrenics, by close supervision of the patient and his medication.

Links with community services

For patients with chronic or relapsing illnesses, especially schizophrenia, and for those members of vulnerable and problem families who are so often psychiatric casualties, inpatient and outpatient treatment are only part of the network of services which must be used. Increasingly social workers may be called on to help. They can visit the home regularly, provide emotional support, try and reduce emotional tensions in the family, encourage the patient to take his medication and to attend outpatients, and keep in touch with both G.P. and hospital doctor. They are able to note the development of emotional disturbance in other members of the family and give appropriate advice or refer for treatment; and they are also able to guide patients through the intricacies of the state industrial and sickness benefit schemes etc. In providing a psychiatric service to an area it is essential to have effective links with the local authority and its social workers. A few years ago the recommendations of the Seebohm Committee for the reorganisation of the social services were implemented. The divisions between mental welfare, child care, and other specialised skills were largely abolished; and 'social work skills' of a generic type are supposed to be offered by one social worker only to a family or person. The effects, from the viewpoint of psychiatry, were almost entirely harmful; and the administrative disruption and growth of bureaucracy in social service departments generally led to less efficiency. Recently however, there has been a return in practice to the more specialised social worker, after a basic training in common with other members of the profession.

Agreement and refusal to enter hospital

If admission to hospital is advised, the majority of patients will accept the idea readily enough. A certain number, however, will refuse. Of these, a few will be quite sensible people with reasons of their own. These need not be pressed. A few will have hysterical personalities and take pleasure in making themselves the centre of other people's difficulties. These need not be pressed unless they are proving an intolerable burden to others. Other patients will be rigid and obstinate people who refuse 'on principle' because they feel such a step would be 'giving in'. More or less trouble should be taken to persuade them according to the benefits that are likely to be gained. Others again will be vacillatingly indecisive depressives whose illness prevents them from making up their minds to any course of action. With these much trouble should be taken and they will usually respond to firm pressure, especially if the support of the relatives is enlisted. Alcoholics will often agree to enter hospital, but will change their minds at the last moment with various plausible excuses; the relatives should be warned of this contingency so that they are prepared for it. The remainder of those patients who refuse will be psychotic cases, hypomanic, manic, schizophrenic or with organic brain damage, who lack insight into the seriousness or abnormality of their condition. They may sometimes be persuaded to enter hospital on the score of treatment or investigation of some physical symptoms from which they may incidentally complain; but where this is not feasible compulsory detention in hospital must be considered. (This is considered in Ch. 16.)

Thus, the main questions are: Is the patient willing? If not, can he be persuaded to go to hospital voluntarily, if reluctantly? If he agrees, though reluctantly, will he adhere to his decision? If he is not willing, and cannot be persuaded, or if he agrees but is certain to change his mind, does the situation justify the exercise of compulsory detection?

Disposal. It is always desirable that patients should be admitted to hospital informally whenever possible, and this is emphasised by the Mental Health Act, 1959, which came into operation in 1960. Under this Act patients can, however, be compulsorily detained, and this can be done in any hospital that is willing to accept them (see p. 419), but the extent to which there are suitable facilities for psychiatric patients varies from one area to another. Information about these can be obtained from the Local Authority or the Regional Board. The range includes psychiatric units of general hospitals and neurosis centres, as well as mental hospitals, while for those willing to pay fees there are a number of private institutions ascertainable from the Medical Directory. Arrangements for the reception of patients, whether to be compulsorily detained or not, must always be made in advance.

The psychiatric emergency

These sometimes arise, such as the sudden development of catatonic excitement or threats of and attempts at suicide. The assessment of suicidal risk is described on page 199. An immediate decision may be required as to the patient's fitness to remain at large. If unfit, admission to hospital should be arranged forthwith, if necessary, under compulsion.

In the meantime, until the necessary arrangements have been made, the patient should be put to bed, where he can best be controlled, and his clothes removed. In dealing with excited patients, drugs will be needed in most cases in which hospital admission is necessary, although very often excitement dies down in a calm atmosphere after the opportunity to talk. The most widely used drug is intramuscular chlorpromazine, of which up to 600 mg may be used for a very excited strong man. Intramuscular haloperidol, in large doses of up to 60 mg, has the benefit of causing less hypotension and somnolence, and is extremely effective against psychotic delusions and hallucinations. It should be remembered that violent excitement and agitation most often follows fear and paranoid misinterpretation, and all concerned should be as calm and non-threatening to the patient as possible. Other helpers should be recruited, if necessary from neighbours or police, but should keep out of sight unless finally needed. The patient must be carefully watched (e.g. accompanied to the lavatory), with help remaining at hand, especially as some time may elapse before arrival of suitable transport or the local authority employed Social Worker whose help may be called upon (see p. 420). Suicidally inclined patients need equally careful watching, but milder sedation should suffice.

General problems of adjustment

The patient's environmental adjustment may conveniently be considered under the three headings of his working life, his social life, and his sex life. Ideally, he should be satisfied in each, but the less he is satisfied in any one, the more important is it that he should derive satisfaction from the others. His working life may be unsatisfactory because the job is too far below or above the intellectual level of which he is capable, because it involves unsuitable conditions or excessive hours of travel, or because he does not get on with the people concerned, which may or may not be justified. His social life may be unsatisfactory on account of social isolation, lack of stimulation, or unsuitable use of leisure, or because of inadequate housing conditions or domestic friction—at present these last are in combination a frequent cause of symptoms, especially where several generations are obliged to live at close quarters in the same house or flat.

A patient's sexual life may be disturbed by personal conflicts or timidity, faulty technique, homosexuality, or other sexual deviations, which are considered elsewhere in the book. Environmental factors can be important, most commonly when a couple are separated only by a thin wall from their own parents or children, and are embarassed by the noise produced by their lovemaking. Women in particular may be frigid in such a setting, and yet never think clearly about the cause of the problem until they discuss it with someone else.

As regards *minor modifications*, it is often essential that both patient and relatives should obtain at least temporarily that peace which, as the hymnist informs us, only comes 'with loved ones far away'. Apart from such fairly common situations, the oft held belief that those who are run down just need a holiday has some justification in psychiatric experience with minor disorders. Domestic friction may call for discussion with the family, and sometimes suitable advice as to dealing with the patient's emotional difficulties has more curative and preventive value than any approach that is confined to the patient himself. The same may be true where marital disharmony has had its repercussions on the sex life.

Insufficient occupation, lack of stimulation and social isolation are frequently the cause of symptoms. Insufficient occupation may thus be an indication for voluntary, part-time or even whole-time work. Lack of stimulation (usually arising from unsuitable use of leisure) and social isolation may be indications for the same, as well as for the development of new interests and fresh social contacts. Certain opportunities for such developments exist in the form of welfare organisations, clubs, educational classes, lectures, discussions and public recreational opportunities. Mere advice that opportunities of this kind should be seized, however, is seldom good enough, for the sort of personality difficulties that have led to the situation in which the patient develops symptoms will probably also deter him from acting on the proffered advice, even if he knows where such social and recreational activities are available. More active steps must be taken. Consequently, there has been a movement to base occupational, recreational, educational and social facilities on the hospital, and hence the origin of social clubs and activities as an integral part of psychiatric out-patient departments. In them, the services of the patients themselves are enlisted in organising the activities, which form a part of what is sometimes known as group or social treatment. Where such facilities do not exist, information as to how some of the patient's needs may be supplied can be gleaned from social workers, Citizens' Advice Bureaux, the clergy, and through local knowledge which the good practitioner will make it his business to possess. The patient may require much specific help and encouragement in these directions.

Major and more sweeping environmental modifications, such as change of home or work, require very careful consideration. The indications for such important changes should be clear rather than speculative. As regards work, the suitability of the man for the job is the first consideration; this depends on his intelligence, aptitudes and handicaps, as well as his emotional stability; these must be reviewed in the light of the intellectual and technical requirements of the job, and the emotional stresses that it may involve. Patients with chronic disabilities, psychiatric or otherwise, may be helped by being placed on the disabled persons register and receiving the aid of the local Disablement Resettlement Officer. With regard to changes of home, patients should generally be discouraged from hare-brained or impulsive schemes, but where the living conditions are genuinely bad the social worker may be an invaluable guide through the maze of agencies which may be dealing with the administrative problems involved. Where the question is one of changing not only the home but the partner, decisions should never be reached in a hurry. The decision can be reached only by the parties concerned. It is not for the doctor to advise, though he may legitimately discuss the relation of the patient's symptoms to the situation, and the pros and cons of the various courses of action. It is often wise for the parties to have a temporary period apart, to allow tempers to cool, and to allow any final decision to be taken in a calmer frame of mind.

PSYCHOLOGICAL TREATMENT

This heading covers a wide range of activities and approaches, including various types of formal psychotherapy, several of which are described in more or less detail in this section, including psychoanalysis, group psychotherapy, behaviour therapy and so on. In its broadest sense, psychological treatment also includes all those interactions between people which go on day by day in the doctors' surgery, outpatient clinics and in hospital wards, and which are often difficult to identify and describe, but which play so important a part in creating the right atmosphere, and in helping people to feel better and to respond to treatment.

The beginning of the first interview with the patient is perhaps the most important time of all. It determines whether the patient will feel able to talk freely, will be able to trust the doctor, and will later follow the recommended treatment. Even the contact between patient and reception staff or nurses has an influence in this way, and to a lesser extent so do the physical characteristics of waiting rooms, consulting rooms, hospital wards, and the whole general setting. These continue to exert an influence throughout the patient's visit or hospital stay. The importance of them, and of many other factors, should not be underestimated.

Interview technique is briefly described in Chapter 5, the essentials being adequate time, good listening by the doctor, and the avoidance of leading questions and moralising. Privacy and quiet are also needed. It is almost impossible to make a detailed assessment of a patient's problems and mental state in a busy medical ward, separated from the next patient by only a curtain and a few feet of space.

Simple psychotherapy

Psychotherapy aims at relieving symptoms of psychic origin by adjusting the attitudes that have led to their development. It is an art rather than a science, and cannot be learned from books any more than can surgical technique. It is, however, possible to state some underlying principles of general applicability.

There are two essential preliminaries. The first is to gain the patient's confidence. Successful psychotherapy must depend basically on obtaining a good grasp of the case, and the facts cannot be gained without the patient's confidence being gained also. The sort of approach that is necessary for gaining a good history has been outlined on page 73. Some course must be steered between a booming heartiness under which the patient remains submerged but unsatisfied, and a nervous diffidence which he will come quickly to reflect. The second essential preliminary is the careful collection of the facts. The sort of facts that are required are listed on pages 74–79, and the sort of conclusion that should be reached is outlined in general terms on pages 79–81. A detailed study of this kind may render the symptoms immediately intelligible in the light of what has been going on in the patient's mind, whether the connection is recognised by him or not. But this is, of course, by no means always so, and in complex cases several interviews may be necessary before the case becomes reasonably intelligible in psychological terms. It is unwise to jump to conclusions; careful ascertainment of the facts must always precede any attempts at interpretation of the symptoms.

Even these essential preliminaries are not without therapeutic value in themselves. The opportunity of discussion may have come to the patient as a relief, and the formulation of the trouble into words will have helped towards a more objective view. The combined effect is to reduce the size of the difficulties in that the patient sees both them and the symptoms in better proportion, with the effect that he can face them more easily and constructively. In a sense, therefore, the treatment has already begun, with *ventilation* of feelings and *clarification* of problems.

When these essential preliminaries have been completed the

treatment proceeds by stages which are often referred to as *explanation, suggestion, persuasion* and *re-education*.

Explanation consists in interpreting the symptoms to the patient in the light of the psychological processes that have led to their development. Many patients, although they should not be told that there is 'nothing wrong with them' or that 'it is only nerves', are able and even pleased to accept the reassurance that their symptoms are due only to psychological causes and will not seriously affect their physical fitness or mental faculties. Many sufferers from states of anxiety have no difficulty in grasping the principle that the mind affects the body, that their symptoms are the *normal* accompaniments of emotional disturbance, and find that the symptoms cease or are tolerable once their origin has been understood. Where technical matters are involved, such as that muscular tension leads to tremor, the explanation will have to be direct. The art of this depends on the ability to adapt explanation not only to the patient's intellectual level but also to his emotional needs. Hence the importance of the manner that is adopted. But aside from such technical matters as the relation between anxiety and autonomic function, it is wise to proceed by a Socratic method so that the patient, stimulated and encouraged by the therapist, looks for and finds the explanations for himself. It is only thus that he will fully realise the connection between his symptoms and his situation. If such explanations are imposed upon the patient he may reject them. If he finds them for himself, they are the more convincing to him, and his understanding of them will be both more complete and lasting. In explanation, therefore, the patient should play an active role; the role of the therapist should be confined to helping the patient where to look to find the causes.

Explanation, as has been indicated, may provide relief in simple cases, but there will usually remain decisions as to future action. These are likely to be necessary for such reasons as mitigating the stress to which the patient has been subject, or preventing its recurrence. In general, it is best not to give direct advice, but to help the patient to form his own course of action by discussion of the advantages and disadvantages of the possible alternatives. It may be necessary also to encourage the patient towards the development of firmer, or more yielding, or different attitudes, as the case may be. In making these adjustments, both internal and external, *persuasion* will play its part. This is usually considered to mean influencing the patient by reasoning. But in persuasion, there is always also a large element of *suggestion*. This may be indirect, arising from the doctor's personality, and from the atmosphere of the hospital or consulting room; it may be more or less indirect, as when matters are put subtly to the patient so that he brings forward as his own idea something constructive that has been hinted at by the therapist; or it may be altogether direct, in the form of plain advice, where other methods have failed, or when implanted in the patient's mind under hypnosis (p. 404).

When adjustments have been made in these ways, continued supervision in the form of periodic interviews may be necessary in order to ensure that such gains as may have been made are maintained. It is this process of helping the patient to apply his newly acquired attitudes and understanding of himself to the life-situation, and so to maintain his improvement, that is referred to as *re-education*.

Supportive psychotherapy is the term used to describe the 'propping up' of patients who can be helped to cope with the difficulties of life by regular, if infrequent, interviews with their doctor, psychiatrist or any other suitable person. An example is found with those elderly ladies, recovered from depression after the death of husbands on whom they were emotionally dependent, but who gain a surprising confidence from the knowledge that in a few weeks' time they will be able to see their doctor, tell him some of their problems, and thus share some of their burdens.

Supportive psychotherapy should concentrate on the positive aspects of the patient's character whenever possible. It should encourage independence of thought and action by the rewards of discreet flattery and approval, and generally aim at supporting self-esteem. It should not, if at all possible, be purely an occasion for repetitive complaints which are answered by non-constructive sympathy. The importance of some of these relationships is shown by the very marked deterioration which can follow the death or unexpected departure of the doctor, and the danger of creating unnecessary dependence should be remembered when arranging supportive interviews.

Psychoanalysis
This is sometimes equated with psychiatry as a whole by those who are ill-informed, and it has been variously described as 'the greatest discovery of modern times' and as 'the biggest hoax in history'. Its origins have been mentioned page 10. It requires a special training for the understanding of its concepts and technique. On this account it has become somewhat divorced from medicine and from the rest of psychiatry, and the mystery surrounding it has been enhanced by the use of a special jargon which is difficult to understand. This last, together with the meagreness of published data, makes its results difficult to assess. Increasingly it has been supplanted, for treatment, by more brief psychotherapies often based on psychoanalytic theory.

Theory

Mental illness is regarded by most psychoanalysists as arising from abnormality of emotional development thought to be largely determined by early childhood experiences. The underlying theory was developed by Freud from the study of cases believed to have been hysterical, but now thought by some possibly to have been chronic schizophrenics. Although Freud included physical and constitutional factors in his original concepts, these have come to be increasingly ignored by his disciples and the emphasis is heavily on the psychological.

As psychoanalysis has been extremely influential, and is still a very prominent feature of psychiatry as practised in the United States, the student may welcome a brief presentation of the Freudian theory. Freud believed the mainspring of human behaviour to be an urge, which he called the *libido*, and which he considered to be an urge to gain satisfaction in accordance with the 'pleasure-pain principle'. And Freud believed this urge to have a fundamentally sexual basis. The underlying idea, derived from the fantasies and infantile experiences of his patients, is that the libido is the basic factor underlying the pleasure-pain principle of life. Freud believed that other methods of gaining satisfaction, of a not specifically sexual kind, were substitutes for the fundamental and universal one, but arising from the same driving force. In this sense, all satisfactions came to be sexual, and Freud included under this heading much that would ordinarily be called 'sensual', and that is *far* removed from sexual as the latter word would ordinarily be used.

Freud believed this libido to be present in all people from birth onwards, but that the form in which it found expression varied at different ages. He shocked public opinion by drawing attention to the fact that even infants experience enjoyment that may legitimately be considered to be of a sexual kind. He described the development of the sex life through a series of phases. The newly born child was called *auto-erotic*, receiving sexual (or sensual) pleasure through stimulation of the skin, as when caressed. Later in the auto-erotic phase came satisfactions derived from the stimulation of particular areas or 'erogenous zones', first the mouth and later the anus. Oral satisfaction was gained first through sucking, later through biting. Anal satisfaction was gained first through retention of the faeces, later through their expulsion. Subsequently, the genital area became the main erogenous zone. Having passed through these oral, anal and genital phases of the auto-erotic phase, the child became, after about the first eighteen months of life, able to distinguish between himself and his environment, so that his desires became attached to things outside himself.

This was the *allo-erotic* phase. His interest, however, was still mainly directed towards himself, with derivation of pleasure from exhibiting his own body, calling for approval from those around him, and sensual (or frankly sexual) self-stimulation. This, the narcissistic phase, was characterised by such overtly sexual pleasure as masturbation and love-play, but also by attraction towards the parent of the opposite sex. From about the age of five or six, there followed the so-called 'latency period', during which the more frankly sexual feelings remained for the most part in abeyance under the influence of repression until revived by pubescence. The child was believed then to pass, in the natural course of events, through a homosexual phase in adolescence, followed by the final establishment of heterosexuality.

As to the less specifically sexual development, Freud conceived of the personality as coming to consist of three parts, which he called the *id*, the *ego* and the *superego*. The *id* was basic, and consisted of the individual's general energy, instinctively and unconsciously directed towards gaining satisfaction in accord with the pleasure-pain principle. He regarded the *ego* as responsible for the individual's adaptation to life in so far as it provided, through knowledge and reasoning, a conscious regulation and control over the rest of the personality; and also responsible for coping with the reality of the outer world. He believed the *superego* also to be a controlling force, but in an unconscious way, as being derived from those standards and injunctions inculcated into the child by parents or other authorities and accepted so that they became an automatic regulating force exerting control without the intermediary of conscious reasoning.

Freud conceived that tension between these three aspects of the personality could result in mental symptoms in certain circumstances: for example, if conflicts of the ego, under the influence of id impulses and superego limitations, could not be satisfactorily resolved.

The smooth progress of the individual from one phase of development to the next depended on sublimation, i.e. the libido is redirected into channels permitted by the superego that are acceptable substitutes. When such normal development was unsuccessful, *fixation* occurred, and the individual remained fixated at a more primitive level of development than normal. Thus, according to the Freudian theory, the sexual perversions arise from fixations that have occurred in the oral or anal phases of development, so that the individual is left with a lingering inclination to oral or anal satisfactions, as opposed to genital ones. It will be realised further that such fixations are believed to take place at a very early age, so that according to psychoanalytic views the development of the person may be determined to a very considerable extent by the age of, say, eighteen months. By then the seeds of personality traits may have been sown, particularly with regard to attitudes towards authority and the subsequent development of *complexes*, i.e. systems of reaction to conflicting feelings, tending to lead to the development of symptoms and arising from repressed sentiments.

Two of these at least may be mentioned, since their names are so well known, even if their meaning is seldom understood; these are the *Oedipus* and *Electra complexes*. (There seems nowadays to be some trend towards using the former to cover both sexes.) Freud believed, as already stated, that in the allo-erotic phase the child experienced attraction towards the parent of the opposite sex, with the effect that he wishes the other parent out of the way and experiences jealousy and resentment. The sexual attraction is frustrated because adequate satisfaction is impossible, the jealousy and resentment may give rise to conflict and, if sublimation fails, the sentiments may then be repressed into the unconscious in an attempt to resolve that conflict. When, after the latency period, the sex life begins again at puberty, the old conflicts are revived although at an unconscious level, with renewal of attraction towards the same parent, and revival of mixed feelings that include resentment towards the other parent. The individual has difficulty in managing these feelings through unawareness of their origin, and their persistence causes him difficulty both in social adaptation and in arriving at emotional independence. It will be remembered that Oedipus, though unaware of the parental relationships, paved the way for marrying his mother by killing his father, while Electra gained revenge for the murder of her father by her mother, by assisting in the subsequent murder of the latter.*

Treatment
The above are some of the main points of psychoanalytic theory. The analysis consists of interviews, lasting about an hour at a time, repeated up to six times a week, and continuing—it may be—for years. Traditionally, but subject to modern modification, the patient lies on a couch and is asked to say whatever comes into his mind, however apparently irrelevant and objectionable. The analyst is meantime

* It has been a source of surprise to us that no place seems to have been found in the warp and woof of psycho-analytic theory for Dymphna, a Princess of Ireland, who escaped from her father in the seventh century, and eluded his pursuit as far as Gheel in Belgium, where he overtook and murdered her because she refused to yield to his incestuous desires. The apparent omission is the more striking since she was later canonised and became the tutelar saint of the mentally afflicted, so that her shrine became a psychiatric Lourdes and formed the nucleus of the now famous Gheel colony, where psychotic patients live at large under the care and in the private houses of the residents of that town.

behind the patient and out of sight. He encourages the patient to continue, taking special note when the stream of talk fails as this is thought to indicate resistance and therefore the proximity of repressed material. Apart from such stoppages, the patient's talk is supposed to depend on 'free association', one idea suggesting the next without conscious direction or control, so that dominant topics ordinarily kept under the patient's 'mental censor' are allowed to rise to the surface.

The data thus provided are interpreted by the analyst to the patient in the light of psychoanalytic theory, leading to further trains of thought and further exploration. In course of this, old situations are re-lived, the emotions associated with them are ventilated and the reasons for symptoms are exhibited. Meanwhile, the patient develops a special attitude towards the analyst who, as the person encouraging the revival of these experiences, comes to be associated in the patient's mind with the various persons, parents, siblings, bosses, etc., involved in them. This attitude of patient to analyst is known as *transference*, and the nature of the transference changes from time to time according to the emotions that are activated. In fact, it is the transference situation that reveals the patient's basic attitudes, and the belief has now come about that it is on the analysis of this transference between patient and analyst that the success of analytic treatment depends. At the present time there seems much more emphasis than formerly on dealing with current as well as past experiences in course of the analysis, while current stresses and situations as well as the analytical relationship itself are regarded as factors in the recovery of repressed material. It is supposed that through the treatment the patient is enabled to understand his own emotional development, and through understanding to make appropriate adjustments. Apart from this, and in the absence of a formal course of treatment, analytic techniques may be of use in providing explanations for unexpected behaviour or attitudes that have developed in particular situations.

It will be seen that the theory, even as judged by this presentation of its bare outline, is elaborate and at some points far-fetched. Unfortunately, many of its later adherents have come to regard it not as a theory but as a creed or dogma, with consequent failure to review its shortcomings. This adds to the danger that any given case may be moulded to fit the preconceptions of the therapist. Its application has also come to be extended far beyond Freud's original intentions. Such attitudes and excursions have done nothing to enhance its reputation. Its aims are laudable, and especially in this respect, that the intention is to equip the patient to deal with life in whatever form and without stooping to those manipulations and adjustments of the environment that must sometimes be advocated by those, including ourselves, who practice other methods. In this respect its aims are basic and radical, but whether or not they are achieved is quite another matter.

Offshoots. The psychoanalytic schools of Adler and Jung are offspring of the Freudian school, whose legitimacy is not accepted by the parent. They differ in being far less specifically directed towards the sexual aspects of life. That of Jung makes a wider use of symbolism, and involves the conception of the 'collective unconscious',—an 'unconscious' mind that is inherited and common to all mankind, that gives rise to common urges, not specifically sexual, that are not conscious nor related to rational thinking but are symbolically expressed in dreams, myths and legends; it is the collective unconscious, according to Jung, that is responsible for all the alleged essential similarity in the myths and legends of all races.

The Adlerian school is based mainly on the two concepts of 'organ-inferiority' and the 'will-to-power'. Here the prime motive force in human behaviour is believed to be the will to power, i.e. desire for mastery of the environment, failure to satisfy which leads to conflict. Conflict results in the formation of symptoms which, by a sort of 'escape into illness', are an attempt at its solution. Both the pattern of the symptoms, and the fears of failure that give rise to them, are believed to be determined by 'organ inferiority', arising in gross form from some actual physical disability, or less obviously from some more subtle defect that has led to over-sensitiveness.

Whether the theories of the various psychoanalytic schools find general acceptance or not, whether their claims are justified or not, and whatever their limitations in practice, they have made contributions to a further understanding of the mind and its more subtle mechanisms. It is important, however, that these claims should not be pressed too far either in the explanation or in the treatment of mental illness.

Formal psychotherapy (major psychotherapy)

By the term 'formal psychotherapy' we mean that the patient is taken on for a course of treatment, consisting of a series of interviews or meetings, which are devoted to helping him by purely psychological means. There is no clear cut distinction from simple psychotherapy (p. 366), but the latter usually takes place during the course of interviews devoted also to other matters, such as the result of drug treatment, and is essentially brief and limited. Formal psychotherapy is usually carried out by someone with special training, or by someone gaining that special training and being supervised in so doing. In practice, the general psychiatrist usually refers a patient for psychotherapy, or for an opinion on its desirability, rather in the way that a physician will refer a patient to a surgeon—seeking specialist knowledge and skills. If he is suitably trained he can do it himself.

There have been many changes in the field of psychotherapy in the last twenty years. A large number of therapies, mainly originating in the United States, have sprung up, and in some cases have spread to this country, but remain quite outside the range of psychiatry as it is usually practised. We will mainly describe the well established.

Formal psychotherapy really began with *psychoanalysis*, as developed by Freud (see p. 368), and as modified by many other psychoanalysts. Psychoanalysis includes several different schools of thought and dogma, which often differ sharply, and is a very long drawn out procedure nowadays, taking an hour at a time, three, four or five days weekly, for several years. In our opinion it should not be regarded as a therapeutic procedure, but more as part of the training of those interested in practising as psychoanalysts or psychotherapists of that school. It can be seen as a voyage of exploration of the human psyche which can lead to shipwreck, as well as to a sense of knowledge and satisfaction at journey's end.

Psychoanalytic (dynamic) psychotherapy implies that the therapy is based on psychoanalytic concepts and practice, usually by people who have been analysed, who may or may not be medically qualified. It is the original form of what can be called '*insight-directed*' psychotherapy, as opposed to supportive psychotherapy and behaviour therapy (q.v.). 'Insight-directed' means that the therapist tries to give the patient's symptoms and problems in adult life a deeper psychological meaning, very often relating them to problems in early life experiences with the parents or other important childhood figures. These are so-called 'transference' problems (see p. 244), and the therapist uses *interpretations* in dealing with them, and with other types of conflict or problem.

Interpretations are used to lead the patient to realise the unconscious forces which are at work, affecting and often distorting his emotional responses to other people. They are better illustrated than defined: for example, if a man loves and marries an older, rather motherly woman, is sexually impotent with her but is potent with other women, for whom he cannot feel strong affection, his therapist might comment that he has married someone like his mother —answering some deep need—and that this has inhibited his sexuality because of an unconscious feeling that this would be incestuous. The therapist's remarks, however phrased, are the interpretation, and the ability to profit from such interpretations is regarded as a precondition for successful insight directed therapy.

In psychoanalytic psychotherapy, as in psychoanalysis itself, the relationship which grows between patient and therapist is regarded as extremely important, because of the development of transference (p. 372). The patient is seen as responding to the therapist in a way which is more appropriate to his parents, or to someone else important in his childhood, and the interpretation of these transference feelings is another of the main features of this type of therapy.

Some schools of psychotherapy avoid interpretations of the psychoanalytic type, as in the American 'client-centred' psychotherapy of Carl Rogers and his school. This concentrates on helping the patient (or 'client' to these non-medical therapists) to express and recognise his feelings by putting them into words. The therapist tries to help in this process of clarification, to share the distressing feelings, and to aid the client in coming to terms with his past and present.

This group has done some of the most important research in psychotherapy of recent years by identifying three of the personal characteristics of the therapist which are related to improvement. These personal characteristics they identified as 'accurate empathy' 'non-possessive warmth' and 'genuineness'. It has long been evident to those outside the main schools of psychotherapy that the personality of the therapist is more important than any theory used, but the Rogerian school were the first to go into this seriously. They do not claim that these are the only factors which count, just that they are the only ones they have so far identified. (Studies elsewhere have shown that the enthusiasm of relatively untrained therapists can at times outweigh the experience of their seniors, who are, perhaps, more world weary).

'Accurate empathy' is the ability to express in words to the patient what he is feeling at that time—a clarification and a demonstration that the therapist understands. 'Non-possessive warmth' means that the patient does not have to earn the therapist's regard and personal interest by being pleasant or worthwhile, and that he feels a sense of warmth and interest without any sense of possessiveness or attempt at control. 'Genuineness' means that the therapist seems to mean what he says, is not putting on an act of, for example, simulated interest and compassion. These characteristics presumably apply to all forms of psychotherapy, and are stressed here for that reason, although the Rogerian school is not very active in Britain. These findings contrast fascinatingly with the classical manner of the psychoanalyst, which was supposed to be essentially blank and impersonal, so that the patient could more freely react as though to his parents, or with some expression of transferred emotions in keeping with the central role of transference and its interpretations in psychoanalysis.

Brief psychotherapy is a term used for a form of dynamic (psychoanalytic) therapy, increasingly popular recently in this country, in which only a limited number of sessions are used—perhaps twenty or thirty—and only certain specified personal problems tackled. Other forms of insight directed therapy have tended to have more diffuse and often unrealistic aims of causing major change in the personality, and have usually been unlimited in time. As such, they tend to stretch out for years, with the risk of harmful effects from excessive dependence and continual brooding introspection. Full scale psychoanalysis, lasting for years and years, is the most prone to produce these side effects.

Marital and family therapy. A family approach to the problems of children has been in use for very many years, as the effect of family problems and conflict on children has long been obvious, and to extend the idea to the treatment of adults is a natural step. One of the main emphases of family therapy is to see the patient who actually presents with symptoms as a kind of scapegoat, who carries the burdens and problems of the family, and who, in some way, helps to keep the rest of the family functioning smoothly by being 'sick'. Therapists of this persuasion use the phrase 'the sick rôle' a good deal, and put less emphasis on the personal characteristics which have led that particular family member to break down and develop symptoms, although he might have behaved differently if he had been different in his constitutional make-up. A family approach can be very illuminating and helpful, even though it is not suitable in every case, because it is certainly in the family that passions and problems tend to be most intensely felt.

In family therapy both husband and wife and any suitable children are usually present, but other relatives and even neighbours and friends are brought in by some enthusiastic therapists.

In marital therapy only husband and wife are involved, and it merges into the kind of counselling offered by the Marriage Guidance Council and similar organisations. A recent development is the use of behaviour therapy techniques, which sound comically simple but can be helpful, as when one spouse gives the other tokens (which may be pieces of wood or printed paper) to 'reward' the other for something which has been pleasant—such as not nagging for twelve hours or helping with the washing up. People often do not realise the harm they do by continuing in habitual ways, and an approach of this type, undertaken in a light-hearted manner though with serious intent, can help people to adjust to each other.

Parallel to these family and marital therapy developments, and closely associated in theory and practice, has been the growth of the sexual therapies, especially that based on the techniques of Masters and Johnson (see Bibliography). All of these methods and approaches are used flexibly, and have remained free from the kind of isolated dogmatism which developed in the various schools of psychoanalysis, especially between the two world wars. There is, however, the disadvantage that their protagonists tend to see all psychiatric disturbances in terms of family pathology, and inter-relationships, ignoring much else of personal meaning, and ignoring also the physical and constitutional aspects.

In the western world marriages and family life have been breaking up with increasing frequency, as divorce gets easier and easier, and the increasing interest in these marital and family therapies is perhaps a natural consequence. It seems to this writer however, paradoxically, that the therapies are themselves part of that same philosophy, or attitude to life, which is leading to the breakdown. The point is that too much emphasis is put on marriage as an institution designed to make people happy, with the assumption that if it does not do so then it should be mended or 'treated', and that if the treatment is of no avail, then the marriage might as well be scrapped.

Marriage as a social contract and institution has developed in some form in all societies, as a way of providing a stable environment for the vulnerable human young. When it also led to happiness that was good fortune. Now that its principle function has been diverted into the manufacture of happiness, and it can so easily be scrapped if not successful in that, the young are not getting the stable environment they need. Nor do the divorced and remarried necessarily find their second and third marriages any more successful. In marriages the commonest form of unhappiness lies in the unrealistic demands the partners so often make of each other. We see this for example when immature couples, marrying very young, seek qualities of security and stability in each other—like some ideal parent, always loving, tolerant and reliable—which they are quite incapable of providing. At the same time, each may be wanting an exciting companion and a perfect lover, such as they have been led to expect by our culture and its media of communication, and, of course, by serious minded marriage guidance counsellors, marital therapists and psychiatrists!

Group therapy. Group therapy became popular in the armed services in the Second World War, although sporadically used before that. It was at first mainly seen as a way of educating groups of neurotically disabled servicemen into the nature and cause of their symptoms, but soon lost this didactic quality. It became more a way of sharing experiences and emotions, of thus gaining relief from distress and more knowledge about others and oneself; and, as a group forms a kind of microcosm of life in which the relationship problems of the world outside are repeated relatively harmlessly, the therapy offered a way in which people could learn to react differently to others.

Group therapy has been extremely popular with the organisers of psychiatric treatment because of its economy and flexibility. Therapeutic groups can be held for outpatients and inpatients, can be supportive and relatively superficial, or can deal with the most intimate and distressing personal matters as in individual therapy. There are several theoretical schools, which differ sharply from each other. Some more or less conduct individual psychotherapy in public, as it were; others have an almost mystical view of the existence of a group spirit or matrix, which is seen as the most important therapeutic agent. Some have a closed membership once they start, others are 'open', and new members come in as others leave. Some have one therapist, others have two, preferably one of each sex; some are officially leaderless, with no therapist in charge, although one can be consulted if necessary. Many have sprung up quite independently of psychiatric services or psychological schools, and have developed into the encounter groups so common in the U.S.A., in which people come together, sometimes for a day or more at a time, in some of which physical and even sexual exploration is encouraged and expected. *Sensitivity groups* are also common, in which groups of interested people, perhaps would-be counsellors, personal advisers, psychotherapists and so on, discuss their own and the others feelings, trying to enhance their sensitivity and openness to others.

Most commonly in this country, free discussion and straightforward self-disclosure are encouraged among not more than eight patients at a time—the ideal number, as Lord Houghton declared, for 'a polite dinner party', though, especially as the interactions develop, the groups are not always 'polite'. They usually meet weekly, for about one and a half hours at a time, and after overcoming initial diffidence those attending may be eased by finding that they are not alone in their difficulties, and the belonging and participating helps those who feel isolated and unneeded. In a cohesive group in which people are working well together, the group influence may be remarkably powerful, but suitable selection of patients is essential for this.

Group therapy has the advantages over individual therapy that the patient is not in such a subservient rôle; he may accept insight and criticism better from his peers than from an authoritarian-seeming therapist; unhealthy dependence on the therapist is much less likely; and he can contribute to the welfare of the others by his own contributions, which enhances self-esteem. For many more sensitive individuals, groups provide too rough and tumble an experience, as people battle for dominance or express their anger, and many drop out for this reason.

Indications and contra-indications for formal insight directed psychotherapy

Unfortunately there is no general agreement about what type of patient is most suitable for psychotherapy, nor which particular type of psychotherapy is most suitable in various conditions. We do know, however, that the personality of the therapist is of great importance.

Many psychotherapists, especially in the U.S.A., have taken the view that almost all patients should be treated by psychotherapy, even those with florid psychoses such as schizophrenia or mania, believing that by so doing they were treating the fundamental problems, while drug therapy could only treat symptoms. This misconception arises from viewing all mental illness as a purely psychological reaction to stress and conflict, and ignoring the physical and constitutional aspects, including genetic and biochemical factors; and also from ignoring the accumulated published evidence. On the whole, those who have taken that view, which has been less popular in recent years, have not had many dealings with psychotic patients in fact.

In our opinion, the role of psychotherapy in the psychoses is a limited one, and only useful after the acute illness has settled down. It can then undoubtedly be helpful in the resolution of conflicts, both internal and in the family, which may be adding to the difficulties of life and raising the patient's level of anxiety or arousal. If such problems can be more clearly understood and thus ameliorated, not necessarily by prolonged or elaborate psychotherapy, the chance of relapse can be lessened. A common example of this is in the young schizophrenic, in conflict with one or both of his parents, and continually 'stirred up' emotionally. Sometimes family attitudes and reactions can be usefully modified; more often it is best for the young patient to leave home for some more neutral emotional atmosphere. Psychotherapeutic help can ease this move for both patient and parents.

The following case report provides another example of the useful, but limited, role of psychotherapy in the psychoses:

A thirty-year old woman had had recurrent schizophrenic illnesses, remained well on depôt injections of fluphenazine decanoate, but relapsed each time the drugs were stopped. She was in continual conflict with her mother with whom she and her husband continued to live. The latter was rather like her dead father, and was an unassertive man who suffered from premature ejaculation, and she was continually angry at him for this, and for his inability to stand up to her mother and to herself. After a series of individual and joint therapy sessions and successful sexual therapy, the couple were much better adjusted and found their own place to live. They were both happier and calmer, and her medication was reduced successfully, but when the drugs were stopped completely as a trial a year later, she again relapsed, exactly as before, and with no apparent precipitant. There is no doubt the psychotherapy was worthwhile in its own right, but it did not affect the basic course of the schizophrenia. In other rather similar cases longer drug-free remissions can be produced by psychotherapy and environmental change, but the patient remains vulnerable to any upheaval or 'life event', as described in Chapter 8, and not just to specific conflicts or problems.

The psychotherapy used in these schizophrenic patients should usually avoid the more challenging interpretations, for example, about infantile sexual drives and the Oedipus complex, which may be appropriate in neurotic patients who have stronger defences, and are better able to make use of such interpretations. To the schizophrenic, with his disturbance of abstract thought and fragmented psyche, 'deep' interpretations can be distressing and harmful. Support, explanation, and guidance of a somewhat prosaic kind, is usually more appropriate.

In bipolar manic-depressive psychoses, psychotherapy can again be helpful in dealing with conflicts and problems if any can be identified which deserve treatment in their own right, or which have a rôle in precipitating the major mood swings. If no relevant neurotic problems or conflicts can be identified, as is more often the case, there is no point in offering formal psychotherapy for manic depressive illnesses as such. The important stresses in this group of illnesses are, in practice, more commonly environmental, as described in Chapter 9, but the environment does include other family members, and psychotherapy can be useful here at times.

Formal insight directed psychotherapy is very rarely helpful in people with obsessional disorders, because of the ruminative style of thinking of these patients, as described later. For obsessional and compulsive symptoms behaviour therapy is usually more appropriate.

In individuals with marked psychopathic disorders outpatient psychotherapy is more or less useless, and only some kind of group in a special inpatient unit is likely to be helpful. Special units for psychopaths have been developed throughout the world, some firmly disciplined, as in prison psychotherapy units, some more or less run by the patients on group therapy lines. Unfortunately, because of the lack of well-controlled studies, it is impossible to know what, if anything, such attempts at treatment achieve. Similar scientific assessment problems afflict the whole of psychotherapy, as is outlined later, but most would agree that a good response to treatment in psychopathic personality disorder is hard to find.

Another important contraindication is found when the patient is too seriously depressed to begin the psychotherapeutic exploration of any underlying problems which may exist. If someone is having serious suicidal ideas or is unable to cope with the business of daily life, he or she is almost certainly too depressed to cope with psychotherapy, which may indeed lead to deterioration, and treatment is best aimed first at symptoms by antidepressant drugs, and psychotherapy can appropriately be started after discharge. Most psychiatric hospital admission wards are not well suited to formal insight directed psychotherapy, as they are more geared to coping with seriously disturbed people who need symptomatic treatment and support. A prolonged stay in such a ward while having psychotherapy can lead to rapid institutionalisation, sapping energy and initiative. Some special inpatient psychotherapy units do exist, but they are run on different lines. Inpatient behaviour therapy (p. 385) is, however, sometimes advisable because of the controlled environment which may be needed.

The principal uses of insight directed psychotherapy are in people with neurotic personality reactions and neurotic character disorders, as described in Chapter 11. Some of those described in Chapter 10 under the heading 'Developmental disorder of personality' can be helped to come to terms with their own nature, and gain other benefits, and the vulnerable can gain from support although they run the danger of excessive dependence.

The first essential is that the patient should regard himself as someone who has personal problems or conflicts, and not just symptoms, and he must be eager to change. If motivation to change is lacking, and the patient is more interested in talking about himself because he is such a fascinating subject, no useful result is likely. He must be reasonably capable of introspection. The first realisation that the problems exist quite commonly follows discussion with the psychiatrist, and one of the main functions of the diagnostic interview is indeed to seek for such problems.

In psychotherapy the personality of the therapist is one of the important factors, as described earlier, and the relationship which develops between therapist and patient, or between members of a group, is crucial. Another essential is an adequate grasp of the language. The patient need not be of superior intelligence as is often thought, but must be bright enough to cope with the situation verbally. It is interesting to know that most studies of those to whom psychotherapy is offered, at least in the United States, show that young, attractive, well-educated females of the upper social classes are the most favoured, even when fees are not involved. The poor, and poorly educated, the less personally attractive, less intelligent and the generally deprived, are less likely to get psychotherapy. It is presumably the same in this country.

It is also advisable that there should be a limited number of identifiable neurotic conflicts or problems, and that the patient should otherwise function fairly well in society. The more areas of life which are disturbed—work, social, sexual, family relationships—the worse the outlook. The impulsive and lacking in forethought—that is, the somewhat psychopathic—do badly, as already mentioned. He should be able to accept and benefit from interpretations, assuming they are appropriately made, being able to see something in a new light, with a new emotional response. It is not bad for the patient to put up some reasoned resistance to interpretations, and argue about them, so long as the discussion is constructive, and not purely obstructive. (Unconsciously determined resistance to psychotherapy is something the therapist must be alert to.)

The patient's style of thought should not be too ruminative and indecisive, as happens so often with obsessional personalities. Psychotherapy can become bogged down in endless, pointless theorising, or painful brooding on some sad episode or inadequacy; and unsuccessful psychotherapy, if prolonged, seems to intensify this type of problem.

Indications for group psychotherapy. These are similar to those for individual psychotherapy on the whole, but a group is a socialising influence, especially for the shy and those who are socially inept. Benefit can come simply from the regular social interactions, independent of more specific insights and so on, and this forms, therefore, a supporting indication. The realisation that many other people have similar problems can also be a great relief. As groups lead to less individual dependence on the therapist, they may be preferred in passive and dependent-seeming people for this reason.

Results of psychotherapy

In the past twenty years in all branches of medicine and surgery there has been an increasing sophistication in the assessment of results, and many well established treatments have been scrutinised and discarded. The use of random allocation trials helps to overcome problems of comparability of patients and of diagnosis, and double-blind methods in drug trials help with observer bias; but in assessing the results of psychotherapy double-blind methods are not appropriate, and random allocation trials have proved very difficult to organise on a big scale although some informative small ones have been done.

There have been several large scale studies of patients referred for psychotherapy who never received it, but who, when followed up, showed the same degree of improvement (roughly two thirds improved, one third not) that has appeared in many small scale studies as a result of treatment. From this many writers have concluded that psychotherapy has no sizeable effects and that this improvement rate represents the natural history of neurotic disorders. This has provoked supporters of the various therapies into passionate defence, but sadly not into the organisation of random allocation studies on a large scale.

Every doctor who has practised any form of psychotherapy has seen patients who have clearly been helped, sometimes with dramatic rapidity, and therefore most practising psychiatrists, as well as non-medical psychotherapists, have found the large scale 'no benefit' studies mentioned difficult to accept, as they seem to contradict daily clinical experiences. It is always difficult for anyone to be cold-bloodedly objective about something like this, and almost impossible to ask them to contemplate as useless something to which they have devoted themselves personally and professionally. A surgeon informed that radical mastectomy is a useless and unnecessarily traumatic procedure, as is now said by some, must experience the same difficulty; and similarly that surgeon must have seen patients in whom it was 'obvious' that the operation had been marvellously successful, even though a random allocation study might suggest otherwise.

There is much more evidence to support the usefulness of psychotherapy than clinical impression alone. Many studies show that identifiable, and measurable change, can come about through interpretations for example; and small scale studies have shown greater symptomatic relief from therapy in patients than occurs in controls, but in most of the studies there have unfortunately been flaws in the methods of assessment.

One very important factor in all psychotherapy which makes a medical type of assessment more difficult, is that many patients who enter psychotherapy do not in fact have symptoms as such, and even if they do the therapist might well consider these of little importance. A simple example is provided by someone referred after recovery from a depressive illness because the referring psychiatrist thinks that neurotic conflicts within the marriage have been among the factors leading to the depression. A symptom-free patient therefore begins therapy with the aim of discussing and sorting out various marital and personal conflicts, during the course of which therapy much distressing discussion may take place, leading to anxiety and even depression in the patient. Nevertheless, the therapy may be experienced as helpful, although a standard symptom rating scale might suggest the opposite.

Many people go into psychotherapy who have never been overtly disturbed at all psychiatrically, and have certainly not been 'ill'. They may feel unhappily inhibited in personal relationships or unable to form an enduring sexual relationship, be lonely and fearful, feel that they are achieving less in life than they should do, wish to experience things more deeply, or just want to find out more about themselves. In this country the National Health Service does not cater much for these people, but in private practice they form a large part of those in psychotherapy and psychoanalysis, and in the U.S.A. an enormous number of people have had psychotherapy of one kind or another for problems like these, and have invested much time and money in it. There is some evidence that the public's enthusiasm for orthodox psychotherapy for the mentally not-too-bad is waning now in the U.S.A., but other methods of 'life enhancing' therapy keep springing up, most of which appeal principally to the young.

Psychotherapy, which began as part of medicine, offering treatment to the ill, has slowly become seen as a way of helping people to happiness and fulfillment. In a society in which most people do not have to worry about satisfying the need for food, warmth and shelter, there is progressively less to be concerned with apart from problems which probably would have seemed incomprehensible to our early ancestors; and people seem increasingly dissatisfied with the quality of their lives as their standard of living improves. In this setting of personal and social dissatisfaction it can be imagined that an objective assessment of the effect of psychotherapy is extremely difficult. It is also of little importance to us here. What we do need is to clarify its contribution in the more limited field of psychiatric disturbance.

There remains another important aspect to consider when trying to make sense of the negative findings of some large scale studies, and the way these contradict smaller studies and personal experience. In the research work by the Rogerian school already referred to, in which accurate empathy, genuineness and non-possessive warmth were confirmed as valuable, it was found in the early studies that many patients offered psychotherapy actually became worse during treatment. Deterioration was associated with an absence of the three desirable characteristics mentioned; but we should consider this in a broader way. Most treatment studies in all branches of medicine use categories such as: No change; improved; much improved, and cured. The idea that some people might be made worse is too often not seriously contemplated, and that has certainly been true of many psychotherapy, and other, outcome studies, although with increasing sophistication has gone an increasing honesty about this. In some groups of patients as many may be harmed as helped. In any follow-up study there are many patients who cannot be contacted for various reasons, and also many drop outs; we can assume that these will include many of those who feel that the treatment is irrelevant or positively harmful, but their absence is easily ignored in the final statistics.

It is probable that the personal and clinical impressions of individual improvement are correct but that those who do badly are not recognised as so doing, or if they are, we naturally tend to forget them. This is at least a partial explanation of the contradictory results. Our response should be further research into the refinements of psychotherapy. Patients should not be referred for 'psychotherapy', any more than they are for 'surgery', but we should consider the details of which type of treatment, when, under what conditions, for how long, and by whom. The last is perhaps the most important consideration, and indicates the importance of the training of the psychotherapist, as well as of the need for further research.

Behaviour therapy
This term covers several disparate methods of treatment, all based on psychological theories of learning derived essentially from Pavlov's work on conditioning. They aim to abolish old, or to set up new, conditioned reflexes, and are aimed entirely at symptoms, deliberately avoiding attempts to treat 'the cause'. Behaviour therapists see neurotic symptoms simply as learned patterns of behaviour; a very different approach from that of psychoanalysts and psychotherapists, who tend to see symptoms as superficial manifestations of deep seated conflict and personality disturbances. There has been much unnecessary and unwise argument between behaviour therapists and psychotherapists, both claiming to be members of the only true church, and both making excessive claims for the efficacy of their treatments, but recently there have been some joint studies by behaviour therapists and psychotherapists trying to establish which method is most suitable for particular patients in particular situations.

Aversion therapies
These were the earliest behavioural treatments to become popular and were used extensively in alcoholism in the form of apomorphine and

emetine regimes. Their importance now is mainly historical. The aim of the treatment is to produce a conditioned avoidance response to alcohol so powerful that it outweighs the patient's craving to drink. This is done by giving intramuscular apomorphine 5–30 mg and offering the patient his favourite drink shortly afterwards, seconds before the apomorphine causes violent nausea and vomiting. This is continued day and night, in an atmosphere of increasing exhaustion and disgust, the patient sitting surrounded by unemptied vomit bowls, being exhorted and preached at (sometimes by tape recorded messages), until the very idea of alcohol is sufficient to provoke nausea and vomiting. The technique has physical dangers, is distressing both for patients and staff, is no more effective than less traumatic methods, and has been largely abandoned.

Faradic stimulation is now the most popular method of aversion therapy, and is used mainly in sexual disorders—transvestism, fetishism and homosexuality particularly. As an example of the technique, a homosexual would be shown photographs which he had previously selected as being erotically exciting, and would be given a painful shock to his forearm by the therapist at appropriate times. It is usually more effective not to give a shock every time a picture is shown, but to give it intermittently, so that the patient never quite knows what is going to happen. A refinement is to use the penis plethysmograph, which indicates even minimal penile enlargement on a mercury gauge like a sphygmomanometer, so that the therapist has some guide to the patient's feelings other than his statements. As the treatment proceeds, usually with daily one hour sessions, the patient's sexual interest in the photographs wanes, and in successful cases, his general homosexual interest wanes.

One of the greatest problems with this technique in treating any sexual deviation, is that it is purely negative, and heterosexual feelings do not necessarily fill the emotional void created by the loss of homosexual or other urges. The patient's life is to that extent emptier, and he may be more lonely and unhappy with no sexual life at all than as a homosexual, fetishist or transvestist. Positive conditioning techniques cannot yet help much, and so the most successful treatment is in those in whom normal sexual feelings and behaviour have also been clearly present.

During the course of treatment, depression and anger directed at the therapist quite often develop, and unstable and aggressive or psychopathic people do badly with these techniques, as with all others.

Desensitisation therapies
These are more generally used than aversion techniques, mainly in the

treatment of phobic or other anxiety. The aim is to lessen the anxiety which is associated with some particular situation by getting the patient to relax while in a situation which would usually provoke anxiety. As Wolpe, who largely developed these methods, said 'if a response inhibitory to anxiety can be made to occur in the presence of anxiety evoking stimuli, it will weaken the bond between these stimuli and the anxiety'. The provocation of anxiety can be either by putting the patient directly in contact with the real life object or situation, or by the patient using his imagination to conjure it up.

Real life desensitisation. If the patient has a single monosymptomatic phobia of, say, spiders, he can, in many cases, be rapidly desensitised to them. He is taught to relax on a couch or in a chair, and is presented with a graded series of small pictures of spiders, working up through small dead spiders in glass boxes, through a series of progressively larger and nearer spiders. At each stage he deliberately relaxes, and does not pass on to the next until he is quite comfortable and free from anxiety. It is with these simple phobias, which rarely come to psychiatric attention, that the most successful results from behaviour therapy are obtained.

Real life desensitisation is much less successful in agoraphobic syndromes, which are difficult to treat effectively by any means. They are usually complex neurotic syndromes, with major disturbances in the relationships between family members, and the syndromes are usually only the tip of an iceberg. The treatment consists of taking the patient, usually a 'housebound housewife' for progressively longer trips out of the house. This may be effective, but often does not last beyond the period of treatment. The patient frequently becomes over-dependent on and emotionally over-involved with the therapist, who may become a kind of substitute for the husband in the mind of the patient. There is often an hysterical element in the agoraphobias, and the patients tend to manipulate the treatment situation—including the therapist—for more attention or some other secondary gain. However, as part of a wider treatment regime, as for instance when a patient is being treated with phenelzine (p. 401) and chlordiazepoxide (p. 397), or with psychotherapy, the patient should always be encouraged to go out for gradually increasing distances, either on her own, with a nurse, or with a group of other patients.

Desensitisation in imagination. This technique can be used in patients who can, while lying on a couch, produce a fantasy vivid enough to make them anxious, of their own particular phobic object or situation. They first work out, with the aid of the therapist, a finely graded hierarchy of anxiety provoking situations. Having been taught to relax on the couch, which may take several sessions using, if necessary, a semihypnotic technique, they then imagine the fear inspiring situations. Starting at the bottom of the hierarchy with the mildest situation, and only moving up to the next when completely relaxed and comfortable with each lower stage, they work up to the top.

A simple example is that of a young girl student, with a fear of vomitus and of people vomiting. Her grandmother apparently had had the same fear to a milder extent, but in the patient it limited her life quite markedly. She was unable to travel on a bus, sit in a lecture hall or cinema, etc., or sit in someone else's house, except in the seat nearest the door. Thus, if by chance someone began to vomit she could escape without having to go past the vomitus. She felt unable to marry and have children in case she had to cope with husband or child vomiting. This last situation was at the very top of the hierarchy, and even talking about it during an interview made her feel faint and dizzy with anxiety. She was taught to relax, using a mental image of a pleasant hillside scene where she had been very happy as a child, and she could bring this into her mind at will, with an immediate sense of calm and happiness. In eight weekly one-hour sessions, she lost all her fears of travel and cinemas, etc., and could contemplate child care with only slight anxiety; she remained well six months later.

Desensitisation in imagination can be used both in simple mono-symptomatic phobias like that just described, and in the more complex agoraphobic states, but the latter respond less effectively. As a general rule, treatment in neurotic states is less successful the more other people's lives are affected by the patient's symptoms: as for example, when a husband has to stay at home a great deal in order to lessen his wife's feelings of anxiety, and there is therefore the possibility of hysterical secondary gain arising from the symptoms.

Desensitisation with drugs. Another way of inducing relaxation is to use intravenous shortacting barbiturates (methohexitone). The patient lies on a couch, with the syringe needle inserted in an arm vein, and imagines the anxiety provoking situations as described earlier. As his anxiety rises it is quelled by very small doses of the drug, insufficient to cause clouding of consciousness. This method is very rapidly effective in some patients, and has the benefit that those who find it difficult to relax to order can still be treated.

Flooding and implosion techniques. These are more recently intro-duced desensitisation techniques, in which the patient is subjected immediately to massive 'doses' of the anxiety producing objects or situations, either in real life or in imagination, instead of gradually moving up the hierarchy to more difficult situations when free from anxiety. They seem to work more successfully for some patients than the more gradual desensitisation techniques.

Positive conditioning therapies

These differ from aversion techniques in that the desired behaviour is rewarded rather than undesired behaviour—e.g. drinking, being punished (positive as opposed to negative reinforcement). The electric alarm bell and pad widely used for enuresis fits into this category in a way, in that the alarm produces the reward of a dry bed, and there is no 'punishment' for wetting. A *Token economy* is a method of running a psychiatric hospital ward in which the patients are rewarded for good behaviour by being given tokens with which they can buy sweets, cigarettes or certain privileges. The technique is used mainly for chronic and regressed schizophrenics who are withdrawn and possibly mute. Each time they speak or make any personal contact they are rewarded with a token, but undesired behaviour is ignored as far as possible. There is no evidence that the method produces better results than skilled nursing and occupational therapy of conventional type, but these are often in short supply in mental hospitals, and the token method is still experimental. Similar 'operant conditioning' techniques have been used in disturbed children, and have also been applied to other neurotic conditions. It is too early to assess their value.

Another recent development in behaviour therapy is the teaching of *social skills*. The shy and socially inept person who feels unable to chat to others, especially if attractive and of the opposite sex, can often be helped by quite simple instruction. How long to look someone in the eyes before turning away, how to shake hands, how to develop and practise a few introductory phrases, how to be a bit more assertive and stand up for one's rights in a shop (or with one's spouse) and many other applications. They can be done individually or in small groups. The need for this training is clearly related to deficiencies in early training in many cases, especially when the patient has socially withdrawn parents, who never learnt the skills and so could not pass them on. For the prosperous classes in Britain the public schools have long seen this type of training as one of their proper functions.

Modelling techniques are increasingly used in behaviour therapy. They essentially rely on imitation and practice, so that, for example, the patient who has an obsessional fear of dirt watches the therapist picking up objects from the floor and is encouraged to copy him, while being given approval and support. Modelling of this type can lead to marked changes in behaviour, and there are complex psychological mechanisms at work, including desensitisation and social rewards.

Side effects and contra-indications of behaviour therapy

If the psychoanalytic approach is correct, then purely behavioural treatment of neurotic symptoms, without attempting to treat the underlying conflicts, could lead to some other symptom developing as a substitute. In fact, this does not seem to happen in the simple monosymptomatic phobias at all, probably because they are rarely the expression of deep seated underlying conflicts, and are mainly examples of 'over learning' in anxiety prone individuals. In more complex neurotic states, particularly agoraphobia, behaviour therapy is not very successful on its own anyway, and is mainly used in conjunction with other methods of treatment. In our experience, the main side effects in agoraphobia follow improvement in the patient, and arise from changes within the family—as, for example, when a woman loses her symptoms and then leaves her husband. We have known such patients later return to the husband and settle down again with agoraphobic symptoms as housebound housewives. In others, quite severe depression has followed otherwise successful treatment, but agoraphobia often runs a fluctuating course and depressive episodes are common without treatment. Altogether, true symptom substitutes seem to be rare.

In the aversive treatments for alcoholism and sexual deviations, aggressive outbursts and depressive spells are common. The therapist must always be able to deal with these himself, or have suitable help if he is a psychologist trained only in behavioural techniques. Aggressive and psychopathic people do badly, as do those with severely obsessional or hysterical personalities.

PHYSICAL METHODS OF TREATMENT

These are the most important in the psychotic illnesses, but have applications throughout psychiatry. They can be considered under three main headings: treatment by drugs; electrical treatment: and cerebral surgery, in order of importance.

Treatment by drugs
Before 1953 the drugs most used in psychiatry were (1) sedatives, for allaying agitation, restlessness or excitement, (2) hypnotics, for promoting sleep, and less often (3) analeptics, for stimulating those who suffered from lassitude and variable depression.

Chlorpromazine, a phenothiazine, was introduced in 1953, and found to be of great value in schizophrenia especially; and later the monoamine oxidase inhibiting (MAOI) and tricyclic compounds were developed as antidepressants. By 1960 the treatment of both schizophrenic and affective illnesses had been revolutionised, and many advances have been made since then.

Phenothiazines and other antipsychotic drugs

These now form the mainstay of drug treatment in schizophrenic illnesses, in which they calm agitation and fear, allay restlessness and excitement, lead to detachment from and then often to actual loss of delusions, hallucinations and ideas of reference, and control thought disorder and passivity experiences. They are therefore much more than 'tranquillisers', a term now used mainly for the 'minor' tranquillisers named in a later section. On the negative symptoms—loss of drive and of affect—they have little or no effect. It is currently thought that their antipsychotic effects stem from their anti-dopaminergic actions on the meso-limbic system.

All schizophrenic patients should have an adequate trial of these drugs, and most of them will be helped. Some are suited more by one than the other, and as a general rule the more sedative members of the group (chlorpromazine and thioridazine) are indicated in markedly disturbed patients in whom the sedative controlling action calms them subjectively and objectively. In less florid illnesses, and particularly in patients during rehabilitation and after discharge from hospital, the less sedative trifluoperazine or fluphenazine, or one of the non-phenothiazine drugs such as flupenthixol, may be preferred.

The phenothiazines act quickly. The sedative and controlling effect of intramuscular chlorpromazine in adequate dosage occurs within a few minutes in even the most disturbed patients; and oral doses on an empty stomach take effect within 10 or 15 minutes. After weeks or months of normal dosage a patient may stop the drugs only to suffer a relapse, sometimes after a delay of several months. The failure to take continued phenothiazines after discharge from hospital is a common cause of relapse leading to readmission, a fact which all doctors should know, as it is not uncommon for the drugs to be stopped on advice from a doctor who does not realise the importance of continued medication. Most often however, the patient stops them because he feels so well, or because he very understandably resents the idea of being dependent on drugs. It is well worth while spending time with patients and relatives in explaining the need to take the drugs. If this is still unsuccessful long acting depôt injections may be useful (see p. 395).

We do not yet know how long it may be necessary to continue these drugs, but it is our practice to advise permanent phenothiazines to those who have twice needed readmission after stopping them. In patients admitted for a first illness, who remain well on discharge, it seems reasonable to withdraw the drugs under supervision after 12 months. If they relapse on drug withdrawal after a full year of good symptomatic recovery, a longer period—two or three years on medication—should be tried before stopping it again.

In some schizophrenic patients the 'activity' of the illness seems so great that continuous drug treatment is necessary, whatever the living conditions of the patient. In most, however, the drug treatment protects against relapse brought about by the patients' abnormally intense reaction to environmental stresses, often quite trivial seeming to the onlooker, but none the less sufficient to disturb the patients' equilibrium. Most often relapse in the non-medicated occurs about three weeks after the stressful event, which may be something like a move of house or change of job. The rôle of these 'life events' in the course of schizophrenia is considered in Chapter 8.

In practice drug therapy may be found continuously necessary in some patients until they change their environment in some important way: perhaps by leaving an unhappy home, making a happy marriage, being admitted to hospital or in some other way.

The phenothiazines are also valuable in other psychiatric patients. Chlorpromazine in particular is useful in calming and controlling the manic or hypomanic patient; it helps to relieve the agitation of the melancholic; and the restlessness and paranoid ideas of the demented, confused and delirious. Phenothiazines also potentiate the use of barbiturates and other hypnotics, help reduce the distress of intractable pain, partially control withdrawal symptoms in drug addiction, and are useful antiemetics.

On the whole the phenothiazines are of little value in the minor neurotic and depressive states mainly treated by general practitioners, despite some of the claims of their manufacturers. In the major mental illnesses they are invaluable, and they have replaced deep insulin treatment for schizophrenia, almost abolished the use of pre-frontal leucotomy for conduct disturbance in chronic schizophrenia, and greatly reduced the need for electrical treatment in mania and hypomania.

There are so many phenothiazines available that any clinician can develop experience of only a few of them. Those mentioned in more detail are therefore those which we have mainly used.

Undesirable side effects are common but rarely serious. They include postural hypotension with occasional syncope; and drowsiness, dullness, and apathy. These are most common with high dosage of chlorpromazine and thioridazine, as is excessive weight gain. All these foregoing side effects suggest that the dosage needs to be reduced.

Extrapyramidal disturbances ranging from a curious pottering restlessness to muscular rigidity and frank Parkinsonism are common with all phenothiazines, but especially with the less sedative members of the group, such as trifluoperazine (Stelazine) and fluphenazine (Moditen), and others which contain a piperazine ring and a fluorine atom. In some patients more severe and dramatic extrapyramidal disturbances occur, with continued restless movements of the legs (akathisia); or writhing, forced athetoid like movements particularly of the neck, and also of limbs, trunk, facial, tongue and pharyngeal muscles; and sometimes oculogyric crises occur. These disturbances are accompanied by feelings of great anxiety and tension. These extrapyramidal disturbances respond to antiparkinsonian agents such as orphenadrine (Disipal) 50–150 mg daily; benzhexol (Artane) 4–20 mg daily; or benztropine (Cogentin) 2–4 mg daily. Benztropine 2 mg and procyclidine (Kemadrin) 10 mg can be given intravenously for the more severe disturbances with immediate relief. Some patients, especially older or brain damaged, develop permanent abnormal muscular movements, affecting mainly the tongue, pharynx and face, known as *tardive dyskinesia*. This is an increasingly serious problem, much commoner with long term treatment, and very difficult to treat.

The extrapyramidal side effects are thought to be due to the dopamine-blocking effect of the drugs on the striato-nigral system. An uncommon side effect is galactorrhoea (milk secretion from the breast), secondary to a rise in circulating prolactin, which in turn results from dopamine blockade in the hypothalamus, where a prolactin-inhibiting factor is usually produced.

The anti-parkinsonian drugs sometimes produce a feeling of euphoria, and some patients became dependent on them, and may take excessive amounts leading to confusional states.

Phenothiazines may facilitate epileptic disturbances; and fluid retention with dependent oedema can occur. Patients on chlorpromazine may develop marked photosensitivity leading to unexpected and severe sunburn; and all phenothiazines may lead to pyrexia, and occasionally to urinary retention. On prolonged treatment opacities may appear in the lens and cornea, due to melanin also accumulated in the skin. Thioridazine can cause retinal degeneration. Cholestatic jaundice occurs particularly with chlorpromazine, and may lead on to hepatocellular damage; and rarely blood dyscrasias of various types develop due to marrow suppression.

Liver damage and blood dyscrasias have been responsible for most of the deaths reported. Phenothiazines should be avoided in those with liver and renal damage, leucopenia, persistent tachycardia, and marked hypotension. Their tendency to potentiate the action of other central nervous system depressants (barbiturates, alcohol, general anaesthetics), and their epileptogenic properties should be remembered.

The side effects and complications may sound formidable, but should be seen against the enormous extent to which these drugs are prescribed without incident throughout the world. In particular jaundice and blood dyscrasias now seem very rare.

Chlorpromazine. (Largactil. Thorazine.) This is the oldest and most thoroughly tried. It can be given by mouth or by intramuscular injection, but intravenous injection can be fatal. The useful dosage range varies from 25–50 mg at night for restless and disturbed senile cases to the relatively enormous doses sometimes necessary in young and very disturbed psychotic patients in whom up to 1000 mg daily may be given. Normally dosage should be increased gradually from 50 mg b.d. or t.d.s., and most schizophrenic patients will need not more than 150–500 mg daily in divided doses. In schizophrenia dosage must be prolonged, as mentioned before, but in other conditions the dose can be gradually withdrawn as symptoms abate.

Thioridazine (Melleril). This drug is similar to chlorpromazine in its sedative effect, and in dosage. Prolonged use may lead to retinal degeneration, but otherwise it is relatively free from side effects.

Promazine (Sparine) is less potent than chlorpromazine, and the dosage is approximately double, but it is claimed to have no toxic effect on the liver and has less hypotensive effect. It is therefore useful in the management of alcoholic patients as well as for the elderly. It can be injected painlessly.

Perphenazine (Fentazin) is about five times as potent as chlorpromazine, seems very free from toxic effects and causes little drowsiness, but extrapyramidal disturbances are common. Dosage ranges from 2 mg t.d.s. to 60 mg daily, and antiparkinsonian agents are often needed with the bigger doses.

Trifluoperazine (Stelazine) is of very high potency, leads to little drowsiness, and of all phenothiazines seems to us the most effective against the hallucinatory, delusional, thought disturbance and passivity experiences of schizophrenia. Liver damage and other toxic effects are rare but extrapyramidal disturbances common and sometimes severe. Doses ranging from 5–30 mg per day are usual, and antiparkinsonian agents are again often needed. A very useful proprietary preparation is the delayed release capsule of Stelazine 'spansule' 10 or 15 mg which need only be given once in 24 hours, preferably at night.

Thioxanthenes

This group of drugs has been developed in Scandinavia as a parallel range to the phenothiazines, with less sedative and more sedative members. They are, like the phenothiazines and all drugs useful against schizophrenic symptoms, dopamine blocking agents. Only two, flupenthixol and clopenthixol, are in use in Britain.

Flupenthixol (Fluanxol). By mouth, this drug is not much used in schizophrenia, although as flupenthixol decanoate it is a widely used depôt injection described later. It has useful antidepressant and tranquillising properties when given by mouth in a dose of 1–3 mg daily (in 0.5 mg tablets).

Depôt injections

Although phenothiazines are so valuable in the treatment and maintenance of schizophrenic patients, many stop their drugs, often because they feel well and are convinced that drugs are not necessary, or because of an objection to being dependent on medication. Others simply forget them. Depôt injections of fluphenazine and of two thioxanthenes, are available, which slowly release the active drug into the circulation for several weeks after deep intramuscular injection.

These depôt drugs are most useful in patients who are unreliable about their medication. Slowly developing over-dosage can be a problem, leading to apathy and dullness, as well as to extrapyramidal side effects. A careful watch must be kept, and dosage can usually be reduced as time passes. An upheaval in life might need a temporary increase in dose to protect the patient from the overreaction, leading to relapse a few weeks later, which is so characteristic of the schizophrenic.

When first used these depôt drugs were said to precipitate severe depression and suicide, but in fact this is not so, and the incidence of depression is no greater than in those on oral medication, and less than that in the untreated.

Fluphenazine enanthate (Moditen). Fluphenazine is a well established phenothiazine by mouth. As a depôt injection, the enanthate was the first to be introduced; it needs to be repeated every two to three weeks. After a test dose of 12.5 mg to exclude oversensitivity, the usual starting dose in a seriously disturbed young person might be 50–100 mg, and an average maintenance dose 25 mg fortnightly.

Fluphenazine decanoate (Modecate). This preparation lasts longer than the enanthate, and is preferable for maintenance, with monthly injections. Again, a 12.5 mg test dose is advisable and dosage usually settles down at 25–37.5 mg monthly.

Flupenthixol decanoate (Depixol). This is a thioxanthene. The injections need to be repeated every two to four weeks; a test dose of 10 mg is advisable, and the average maintenance dose is 20–40 mg every two, three, or four weeks.

Some patients are suited better by this preparation, which seems rather less sedative, but it is probably not quite so effective in controlling severe schizophrenia as is fluphenazine.

Clopenthixol decanoate (Clopixol). This is a more sedative and longer acting thioxanthene, recently introduced in Britain but well established in Scandinavia. A 50 mg test dose is needed, and the average maintenance dose is 200–400 mg every three or four weeks.

Haloperidol (Serenace; Haldol). This is not a phenothiazine but a substituted butyrophenone. It is potent and rapid acting, and most useful in the control of very excited and disturbed schizophrenics and in hypomania and mania. Intravenous injection of 5–30 mg will rapidly reduce major excitement, but most patients will respond to divided oral doses of 4.5–15 mg daily. Extrapyramidal disturbances are common and severe, but otherwise it seems a safe drug. It has a distinctly depressant effect and as hypomanic patients improve the dose should be gradually reduced. It is sometimes used as a minor tranquilliser for which it seems ill-suited to us.

Pimozide (Orap). This drug is related to haloperidol. It helps maintain some patients symptom free, without sedation, although of little use in treating disturbed patients. The dosage varies from 4 to 10 mgm daily by mouth. It is relatively free of side effects.

Very high dosage therapy. The usual range of doses of antipsychotic drugs has been outlined above, but very much greater doses of some phenothiazines and of haloperidol can be given, and at times prove extremely useful. Schizophrenic patients, resistant to more usual doses, can be given steadily increasing doses either until adequate improvement occurs, or until unacceptable side effects develop. Several hundred milligrams every two weeks of fluphenazine enanthate, or even up to 140 mg daily of haloperidol can be given. It is very remarkable that extrapyramidal side effects are not marked with these huge doses. It is thought that the anticholinergic effect of these drugs makes them act as their own antiparkinsonian agent when given in such large amounts.

Rauwolfia serpentina. Alkaloids of rauwolfia (e.g. reserpine) are also included under the major tranquillisers, but have largely been abandoned owing to their marked tendency to cause severe depression, and because of the superior effectiveness of the phenothiazines.

Minor tranquillisers (Ataractics)

This category includes drugs of widely different composition, but in recent years the benzodiazepines have almost supplanted the others, and are the only ones considered here.

Benzodiazpines. The most commonly prescribed are diazepam (Valium), chlordiazepoxide (Librium), oxazepam (Serenid-D), and lorazepam (Ativan). Most are metabolised through diazepam, which prolongs the duration of activity, but not lorazepam. There are few clinical differences except that lorazepam acts more briefly; and the cheapest is generally preferable. They lessen anxiety and tension without causing as much drowsiness as barbiturates or hypnotics generally, although the benzodiazepines are effective hypnotics when anxiety prevents sleep. Nitrazepam (Mogadon) is a safe and popular hypnotic of the same series.

These drugs do not cause physiological addiction, but they do lead to psychological dependence. They are grossly over-prescribed, and doctors should make a real effort to correct this. Some of them are slowly cumulative, such as flurazepam, prescribed widely as a hypnotic.

Because of the immediate relief of distress they provide, they lead to emotional dependence; and as tolerance develops the dose often creeps up, and the side effects become more serious as the dose increases. There is mental slowing, and physical unsteadiness, and dysarthria is common. As with alcohol, there is often release of normally inhibited aggression, as well as impairment of judgment; and many cases of baby battering are associated with benzodiazepines. Recent evidence incriminates them in road accidents too. They have a summative effect with alcohol, of a rather unpredictable type.

It should be more widely known that benzodiazepines interfere with learning, and their use for students with examination nerves quite often calms the fears, but prevents useful study. A sedative tricyclic drug such as trimipramine to help the student sleep in the days before the examination is safer than diazepam. It is possible that too free use of a benzodiazepine also prevents the individual learning from experience, or from psychotherapy, and thus can prolong the very conflict or neurotic problem which is causing the anxiety.

These drugs are often prescribed by doctors in the mistaken belief that they have an antidepressant effect. In fact, they often worsen depression, and if taken by a patient in whom anxiety symptoms are part of a depressive illness they can be positively harmful. Worst of all they are handed out much too freely to the chronically worrying and vulnerable members of our society, to lessen the impact of day to day stresses. As such, they induce drug dependence, lessen the ability to cope and encourage the belief—much too widely held—that any discomfort or distress is an affront and must be relieved by someone.

Benzodiazepines are powerful anticonvulsants, and intravenous diazepam 10–20 mg is useful in status epilepticus. Sudden withdrawal after prolonged use can precipitate convulsions.

The use of these drugs should be restricted to brief courses in moderate dosage, for example, diazepam 2–5 mg up to three times daily for some self limited condition. Thus, they can usefully be given in depressed patients who are already on an antidepressant if anxiety symptoms are prominent; or can be used to allay a phobia of flying so that someone can go abroad. They should not be given for a long standing problem, nor to lower the general level of anxiety in someone who is chronically tense and anxious.

Beta-blockers
Beta-blocking drugs have been in use for several years in the treatment of anxiety symptoms, and more recently have been tried, in very large doses, for schizophrenia. They block the activity of the ß-adrenergic fibres, thus lessening the intensity—in theory—of all those anxiety symptoms which are mediated through this system. These are particularly palpitations, tremor, and gastrointestinal symptoms such as 'butterflies in the stomach'. The most commonly used is propanolol, 80–160 mg daily. They seem to help some patients, but our experience of them is disappointing.

Indications for drug therapy in depressive states
It is not always clear which patients will benefit from antidepressants. There are many chronically unhappy and low spirited people, vulnerable to the pressures of life, in whom these drugs are useless; and there are people with neurotic personality problems who become depressed in a purely reactive manner in certain situations who similarly cannot be helped with drugs. Antidepressants are most clearly indicated in those in whom the depression has a clear cut onset, arising in a person whose spirits are usually good. The more the depression resembles the classical endogenous pattern the more likely it is to respond to physical treatments, and the relevant symptoms should be carefully enquired into (see Ch. 9.)

In patients with severe depressive illnesses, with delusions, marked psychomotor retardation or agitation, impaired fluid intake, marked weight loss, or who present an immediate suicide risk, it is better to use electrical treatment (described later) without delay.

When antidepressants are given a trial they should not be persevered with unchanged for more than four weeks if there is no response to full dosage. After successful treatment the drugs should not be stopped too soon, as relapses may occur, and they should be continued for at least four months before tapering them off. The longer the illness has lasted before successful treatment, the longer should be the period on the medication. Twelve months of an antidepressant is not uncommonly needed.

Amphetamines

The use of amphetamines (Benzedrine) and dextroamphetamine (Dexedrine) or mixtures of these drugs with barbiturates (e.g. Drinamyl) is not recommended. They often lead to addiction, and their action is brief and frequently followed by tension and worsening in the depression. Amphetamines are necessary in narcolepsy and at times in hyperkinetic children in whom they are paradoxically sedative, but should otherwise not be prescribed.

Antidepressants (thymoleptics)

The principal antidepressants used now belong to three main groups: Tricyclic drugs, Monoamine oxidase inhibitors (MAOI) and tetracyclic compounds.

The modes of action of these drugs are not really understood, but they have been linked with the so-called 'Catecholamine' hypothesis of depression. This postulates that depressive illnesses are caused by a fall in the level of available monoamines (noradrenalin, 5-hydroxytryptamine)—as illustrated for example by the depression which often follows the use of reserpine, a known cause of monoamine depletion of platelets. It is thought that tricyclic drugs work by inhibiting the re-uptake of nor-adrenaline and 5-hydroxytryptamine from the synaptic cleft; while MAOI drugs inhibit breakdown by monoamine oxidase centrally. The two main tetracyclic antidepressants, maprotiline and mianserin, differ from each other. Maprotiline is more like a tricyclic in structure and actions; mianserin seems to act by blockade of pre-synaptic α-adrenoceptors. All of these explanations of how antidepressants work should be regarded as hypothetical.

Tricyclic drugs

These are closely related chemically to chlorpromazine. Imipramine

(Tofranil) and amitriptyline (Tryptizol) are the best known, and in double blind trials have been effective in from 60–80 per cent of outpatient depressives, compared to 40–55 per cent of patients given placebo. The effective dose is about 150 mg daily, although less should be given to the elderly. The antidepressant effect is delayed for 10 to 21 days usually. Other well tried tricyclic drugs are doxepin (Sinequan), desipramine (Pertofran), nortriptyline (Aventyl) and trimipramine (Surmontil). The last is the most sedative, amitriptyline slightly less so. These more sedative drugs can be very useful as hypnotics. Protriptyline (Concordin) is given in the smaller dosage of up to 60 mg daily, and is non-sedative. Clomipramine (Anafranil) is worth special mention because of its striking effectiveness in obsessional disorders, and in phobic states to a lesser extent.

The side effects of the tricyclic drugs are largely due to their central anti-cholinergic actions: with dry mouth, constipation, retention of urine, impaired visual accommodation, sweating, and occasional impotence. Postural hypotension is common and may be serious, especially in the old, in whom they also cause ataxia at times, and in whom the atropine-like effect may precipitate glaucoma. Rarely a toxic confusional state develops, especially with amitriptyline; and alcohol may lead to unexpected and prolonged drunkenness. Epileptic fits are another rare complication. Major toxic effects on liver or other body systems are very uncommon, and these drugs are relatively safe, except in overdosage, when they can cause cardiac dysrhythmias and death. Doxepin is the only tricyclic which should be given to people with any history which suggests cardiac dysrhythmia; including therefore patients who have had a myocardial infarct within the previous four months or so. Although minor side effects are common they are usually transient and need not be feared, except in the elderly.

Tetracyclic drugs
Until recently there has been general agreement that the tricyclics were the antidepressants of first choice, but in our opinion mianserin, a tetracyclic drug, is probably preferable. It is as effective an antidepressant as amitriptyline and has almost no anticholinergic effects. Consequently, it does not lead to the unpleasant, and in the elderly, dangerous atropine-like side effects of the tricyclics. It is also non-toxic to the heart, and therefore much safer in accidental or suicidal overdose. As it has been in use only a few years some caution is reasonable before assuming that the tricyclics have been genuinely supplanted.

Mianserin causes drowsiness and some postural hypertension,

particularly in the first few days. It is advisable to build the dose up from 10 to 20 mg to 60 mg, though up to 120 mg can be used, increasing as the drowsiness allows. It is as effective taken all at night as in divided doses.

The tetracyclic drug maprotiline is more like a tricyclic drug in structure and actions, and is also an effective antidepressant. It has some atropine-like side effects, and occasionally causes convulsions, like the tricyclics. It seems safe in those with cardiac dysrhythmias. The usual dose is 150 mg daily for an adult.

Monoamine oxidase inhibitors (MAOI)

The first of this group to be used was iproniazid (Marsilid), but although effective it is also toxic, especially to the liver, and is now rarely prescribed. The most generally effective seems to us isocarboxazid (Marplan), of which the dose is 20–40 mg daily in divided doses. Phenelzine (Nardil) (30–60 mg daily) is also valuable, and is rather more sedative. It is widely recommended for phobic anxiety states and agoraphobia, and for the latter it is the drug of choice. In both of these drugs the benefits appear only after about 7 to 21 days.

The most serious side effect of the MAOI group is the *hypertensive crisis*, in which a rise in blood pressure occurs which is so rapid and severe that subarachnoid or intracerebral haemorrhage may occur. This happens when the MAOI drug has inactivated those enzymes which destroy pressor amines, and the usually innocuous amines thus accumulate in large amounts. These pressor amines include tyramine (found in cheese, and to a lesser extent in Marmite, Bovril, broad beans, Chianti, pickled herring and yoghurt); others are ephedrine, amphetamines, and various substances used as nasal decongestants or 'cold cures'. Other drugs are potentiated by MAOI compounds, in particular morphine, pethidine, and related drugs, and some hypotensives. These may all lead to sudden *vasomotor collapse* with *respiratory failure and coma*. Anaesthetists, surgeons, and dentists should be told when patients are having MAOI treatment. It is extremely important that patients should be warned of these foods and drugs, and deaths still occur, although less frequently. Tranylcypromine (Parnate) was most often incriminated in the hypertensive crises. Tricyclic drugs have been included on the list of drugs to avoid, but in our experience and that of many others, a combination of amitriptyline and isocarboxazid at least is safe and often effective, as is trimipramine and tranylcypromine.

Apart from these serious drawbacks the MAOI drugs are relatively free from side effects, although they have been suspected of causing jaundice; and fluid retention may occur.

Lithium carbonate

In the last few years lithium carbonate has been shown to lessen the frequency and severity of recurrent hypomanic and manic illnesses, and, although less markedly, the depressive episodes in people with bipolar manic depressive illnesses. In some patients it is also useful in the immediate control of hypomania. It is less useful in the prevention of recurrent depressive illnesses alone, although worth trying in many cases.

Lithium salts are toxic; and regular serum lithium estimations are necessary. The optimal levels are between 0.8 and 1.2 milli-equivalents per litre. Above 1.6 mEq toxic effects become more common, and 2.0 mEq is dangerously high as cardiac arrhythmias or renal damage may develop. Signs of toxicity include anorexia, coarse tremor, vomiting, diarrhoea, and marked thirst. Lithium salts may also cause direct gastric irritation. Longer term side effects include hypothyroidism and nephrogenic diabetes insipidus. Both are revers-ible when the drug is stopped, except that two cases of permanent renal damage have been described. A suitable preparation is Priadel, a delayed release form. Initial dosage is 800–1600 mg daily for up to a week, to reach a suitable blood level, followed by 400–800 mg daily as a maintenance dose, depending on the serum estimations.

Lithium probably acts by virtue of its close chemical resemblance to sodium and potassium, interfering with the cellular metabolism and transport of these ions.

Sedatives

The use of daytime sedatives in the old fashioned sense has been replaced by tranquillising drugs. These have relatively less effect on the level of consciousness than, say, barbiturates, which calm the acutely distressed at the cost of sedation. In our opinion barbiturates should not be prescribed except as anticonvulsants or anaesthetics, except in patients who have taken them in a stable dosage for a long time, and in whom it is not worth trying to wean them off. They are too often addictive to be used freely.

Paraldehyde should also not be used. By injection it is painful and can cause sterile abscesses; by mouth it smells and tastes disgusting.

Chlorpromazine, if necessary by intramuscular injection, up to 500 mg or more, will calm the most excited psychotic patient. A benzodiazepine, such as diazepam, by mouth or injection, of up to 20 mg will adequately tranquillise, and sedate to some extent as well.

Chlormethiazole (Heminevrin) is a very useful drug for controlling withdrawal symptoms in alcoholics, and is powerfully sedative. It is unfortunately also addictive, and can cause nocturnal confusion, especially in the elderly. It is best kept for use in alcoholics, in short courses only.

Hypnotics

Hypnotics are too freely prescribed, and doctors have been slow in recognising this. With all hypnotics there is a tendency for the dose to be slowly increased as they gradually lose their effect, with the disadvantages of increased 'hangover' effects and the risk of addiction. Recently studies have shown that hypnotics affect the e.e.g. for weeks or months after they have been stopped.

The most generally suitable hypnotics now in use are nitrazepam (Mogadon) 5–10 mg, and dichloralphenazone (Welldorm) 650–1300 mg. Both are safe in the event of overdosage, particularly nitrazepam, and have little hangover effect or addiction risk. Some benzodiazepines, such as flurazepam are cumulative, and can interfere with memory and judgment. It should be avoided. Mandrax, a combination of methaqualone 250 mg and diphenhydramine 25 mg, has recently been popular but in our opinion should not be prescribed. It is addictive, is unpredictable and overdoses are dangerous. Barbiturates are effective and well proven, but their disadvantages have been outlined above. In depressed patients a useful hypnotic effect can be produced by a sedative antidepressant, such as mianserin or trimipramine, in full dosage, at night. The risk of suicide in the depressed should always be considered when deciding on the type and quantity of drugs to be prescribed; and sometimes they are better doled out by a relative.

Continuous narcosis

This, sometimes called sleep treatment, is of use in some patients with severe chronic tension and anxiety, not responding to simpler régimes. The aim is to keep the patient asleep for from 16–20 hours a day, for 7–12 days, and a combination of chlorpromazine 200–400 mg and dichloralphenazone (Welldorm) 2 G can be given every six hours or so to produce this. Antidepressant drugs and e.c.t. may be given concurrently. The method is of least value in those who clamour for it most on the basis of 'if I could only get away from it all'.

Narco-analysis and hypnosis

Situations sometimes arise in which the persistence, despite treatment, of symptoms believed to be psychogenic leads to the suspicion that there are operative factors that the patient has not disclosed. The patient can often be helped to talk more freely under the influence of drugs, as is known to every reader of spy stories. In reality, however, there is no such thing as the 'truth drug', and the patient may not only continue to conceal facts, but may tell eye-opening lies when drugged. Some care is therefore called for in interpretation of what is said, and it is advised that reliance should not be placed on the statements of drugged patients where legal issues are involved. There are, however, a number of cases in which the increased communicativeness of patients, achieved by this means, may be useful in treatment, though it will be realised that sympathetic doctors who secure good rapport will need to use this method less often than other therapists.

Methohexitone or thiopentone are useful for narco-analysis, and are given intravenously. The amount required will vary from case to case, and the most satisfactory method is probably to encourage the patient to count while the injection is made slowly, and to stop at the point at which speech becomes markedly slurred. This can be of particular value for the recovery of episodes for which the patient is amnesic, and the elicitation of other factors that have been repressed, or which the patient has been unable to bring himself to disclose. While the patient is under the influence of the drug it is often possible to undertake treatment by suggestion.

The principle of narco-analysis is the same as that underlying hypnosis. There are various hypnotic techniques, most of which depend on getting the patient to fix his attention on some particular object while disregarding the rest of the environment. Suggestions are then made to him, in a confident but soothing fashion, that he is relaxed and comfortable. The idea is then gradually instilled, by repetition of suitable phrases, that this relaxation is giving place to sleep. The patient may then be told that his eyelids are becoming increasingly heavy, are gradually closing, and that when they do close he will be asleep. If the patient is cooperative and suggestion skilfully made, the desired result will be achieved. The depth of the hypnosis can then be further increased by suggestion that the sleep is 'deeper and deeper'. In this state the patient's suggestibility is much increased and, with suitable encouragement, information may be obtained from him in much the same way as under the influence of drugs. While this is done the 'depth of sleep' must be maintained by repeating the suggestion. The heightened sugges-tibility of this state may also be useful in removing symptoms, e.g. by implanting the idea that the patient will waken free from anxiety, buoyant, and confident. In cases of hysterical paralysis and aphonia the patient can often be brought rapidly to full use of the affected parts while in the hypnotic state, during which it can also be suggested that this recovered function will continue on wakening. Although the results can be dramatic, the value of hypnosis is very limited, except when used by someone particularly skilled or gifted, and with suitable patients.

Abreaction

The release of pent-up emotion is called abreaction, for which the above methods can be used. Patients carrying a heavy emotional load and unable to discharge it may be helped thus in much the same way as some people 'get it off their chest' by having a drinking bout. Some prefer ether inhalations for this, in that these seem specially to facilitate emotional release. The main indication for abreaction is the suspected repression of painful traumatic memories or experiences. It must be realised that hypnosis, narco-analysis, and abreaction constitute only a part of treatment which will require to be carried further. Abreaction was more valuable for the dramatic traumata of war time than it is for the milder stresses of peace.

Deep insulin treatment

This, also called Insulin Coma Treatment, was introduced by Sakel of Vienna in 1935. It had for some time been known that insulin was effective in improving both the physical and mental state in cases of severe anorexia, and it was with this in view that Sakel tried its effect in combating withdrawal symptoms in cases of morphine addiction. The results were encouraging, especially when the doses used were sufficient to produce clinical evidence of hypoglycaemia, which was found to be controllable without difficulty if adequate precautions were taken. Sakel was encouraged to try the method empirically on schizophrenics. Its *modus operandi* was considered to be through biochemical changes occurring as a result of the hypoglycaemia. For many years this method was the accepted way of treating schizophrenia, and generated much the therapeutic enthusiasm, which was of great value to psychiatry generally at the time. The method fell rapidly into disuse after a controlled trial in which patients treated with insulin coma therapy were found to fare no better than those given intravenous barbiturate coma.

Electrical treatment

This is often known as e.c.t., standing for 'Electrical Convulsant Treatment' or 'Electroconvulsive Therapy'. It is also commonly known as 'Electric Shock Treatment'. We feel this last term is unfortunate owing to the alarming emphasis. For the same reason, the alternative term 'electroplexy' has been coined. We prefer the still simpler 'electrical treatment', which stresses the therapeutic aspect without alarming the patient, since electricity is familar enough not to be frightening, while still mysterious enough to most people to convey an encouraging suggestion of science allied to magic. However, 'e.c.t.' is firmly entrenched in British use.

The treatment consists in passing an electric current through the skull between electrodes placed on the temples. It is generally held that the current should be of such strength as to produce a convulsion, since weaker currents tend to be inadequate in their effects. Despite the strength of the current, the convulsion itself can be prevented from occurring by special means which will later be described.

If reasonable precautions are taken, there need be nothing alarming about the treatment, either to those who give or receive it. It is very safe, and carries little more risk than that of being run over in the street. Nor need there be any complications of note.

Development

In 1933 von Meduna of Budapest, when studying a large number of case records, was struck by the low incidence of epilepsy in schizophrenics and by the rarity of schizophrenia in epileptics. He found this sufficiently striking to formulate the hypothesis that the two conditions were 'biologically antagonistic' to each other. The corollary was that to induce fits in a schizophrenic might lead to improvement of the schizophrenia. Such fits were induced chemically, usually by the intravenous administration of camphor compounds. Despite the unsoundness of the underlying theory, considerable improvement was often found to occur. With increasing experience it came to be realised that such improvement depended, in the main, on controlling disturbed behaviour and in clearing those disorders of the mood, whether of excitement or depression, with which schizophrenia is so often associated. That is, the improvement was for the most part symptomatic rather than affecting the essential underlying illness. This led to the use of the treatment, on a symptomatic basis, in the treatment of mood disorders, whether related to schizophrenia or not. In these, it proved considerably effective. Indeed, this treatment revolutionised the treatment of severe depressive illness, and it is in this field that its chief use lies. But it has also been found of unexpected benefit in certain rarer conditions which will be described.

In 1937, as the value of the treatment was becoming established, Cerletti and Bini devised a machine for giving fits electrically.

These are more easily induced, are less severe, and produce fewer complications, so that this has become the method of choice. Electrophysiological research is still being conducted with a view to finding improved forms of current and technique, but the existing machines, though capable of refinement, are therapeutically effective.

Even with electrically induced fits, there remained a certain group of patients with co-existing physical disabilities that were a contraindication to convulsive treatment. Efforts were therefore made to devise means of abolishing or attenuating the actual fit. This was achieved by the use of curare and its derivatives, and later by polarising agents, each of which prevents the peripheral spread to the muscles of the electrical impulses initiated by the current. In this way the treatment has come to be virtually without physical hazards.

Modus operandi

This is an empirical treatment. As its success became established, various theories to account for its action were sought in psychological terms, such as that it satisfied a desire for punishment, was an expiation of guilt-feelings, was a symbolic re-birth after death, and so forth. These have been discarded, and no doubt is felt that the treatment works through its physiological effects, presumably on hypothalamic and brain stem functions. There is some evidence that it affects brain mono-amines, and some that it enhances post-synaptic receptor responses to the amines, so that the effects are similar to those of the antidepressant drugs.

Indications

Although it has been used in a wide variety of conditions, often more in despair than in hope, the treatment is of established value only in (1) states of depression, (2) states of excitement, (3) confusional states. As to (1), electrical treatment is of remarkable value in those depressive illnesses of endogenous pattern, leading to recovery in about 70 per cent and marked improvement in about 90 per cent of cases. The sort of syndromes that benefit *par excellence* are described on pages 171 to 175, but the treatment can also be effective in some schizophrenics with depressive colouring, particularly if there is any suggestion of clouding of consciousness, or much anergia. As to (2), electrical treatment is of value in controlling acute schizophrenic excitement, hypomanic and manic excitement, and the periodically disturbed and violent behaviour of chronic schizophrenics but is rarely needed now because of the more effective use of anti-psychotic drugs. As to (3), confusional states, it is odd that electrical treatment, which itself may produce confusion, should confer benefit, but it can certainly do so. It is occasionally needed when a confusional state, of any severity, persists after the responsible physical illness has apparently settled down.

Contraindications
Wisdom must naturally dictate caution in the treatment of cases who are feeble, frail or suffering from organic disease, especially where the psychiatric state justifies expectant treatment. Age is no barrier, and good results have been obtained in patients over eighty. Patients advanced in pregnancy have also been successfully treated. Almost the only physical contraindications are recent coronary thrombosis, heart failure, and active chest infection. Apart from physical contraindications, the treatment is best withheld from patients in whom the pattern of symptoms is more reactive, especially if important neurotic conflicts are present. It is a mistake to use it in doubtfully depressed people of hysterical or markedly obsessional temperament.

Complications
Serious complications are rare, with about three deaths yearly in England and Wales, where about 80 000–90 000 treatments are probably given annually. This is no greater than the death rate associated with anaesthetics in minor medical or surgical procedures, but should not be accepted as inevitable. The commonest cause of death is vagal inhibition leading to cardiac arrest. (It must be remembered that there is a sizeable death rate from suicide in depression.)

In the last few years, beginning in the U.S.A. but spreading to Europe, there has been a strangely passionate movement against the use of e.c.t., mainly outside the medical profession. The treatment has been criticised for causing severe mental impairment, especially of memory; regarded as an assault on the patient by an authoritarian psychiatric profession which is interested more in controlling and subduing innocent victims than in helping distressed patients, and said to be useless as a treatment in any case.

The campaign against e.c.t. has had some harmful effects, in that psychiatrists in the U.S.A. have become afraid to use it even when it is obviously needed, for fear of litigation. Unfortunately, the campaigners have tended to be equally passionate in their belief that psychotherapy or some social change is always the treatment of choice, whatever the nature of the depression, and in the U.S.A. many deeply depressed patients who really need a physical treatment have had to continue with non-productive psychotherapy because of the power of this particular lobby.

There is, however, no doubt that e.c.t., like any treatment, can be abused. There is no justification for giving large numbers of treatments close together as memory disturbances do then become increasingly likely. Between six and ten e.c.t., given at a rate of one treatment twice or thrice weekly is enough for almost any patient, and 12 treatments should be regarded as the maximum unless there are very good reasons, such as a previous genuinely good response to a larger number than that. Memory disturbance is common after a course of e.c.t., but is nearly always transient, and it is often forgotten that depression is associated with impaired concentration and memory in many cases. In older patients, and with bilateral rather than unilateral treatment, more persistent complaints of forgetfulness are commoner. Psychometric testing often fails to demonstrate the deficit, but this may be a reflection on the tests used.

Complaints of memory disorder are overwhelmingly more common in patients who did not have the classical indications for e.c.t.—that is, the presence of an endogenous pattern of symptoms, as described on page 171. People prone to obsessional ruminations, continually examining themselves by minute introspection, are also likely to focus on quite minor and transient memory loss, and worry about this so much that it becomes another symptom.

Another major group of patients who may complain bitterly are people who, even in good health, find it difficult to live up to the intellectual demands made on them by their jobs, or who have intellectual ambitions and interests which outrun their capacities. A course of e.c.t. is then seen as the cause of their failure to achieve the success which eludes them, even if to the onlooker it seems more likely that the failure to achieve was a factor in causing the depression. There are many men and women of high intellectual calibre who return to productive and creative life after e.c.t., but they rarely talk or write about it.

The campaign against e.c.t. also casts doubt on its efficacy, and as a result a number of controlled experiments have been done, and more are under way. This is never a bad thing in medicine, and one must remember that insulin coma therapy (q.v.) was also considered very effective until it was found to be no more so than an intravenous barbiturate anaesthetic. (Perhaps it would have been logical to have used barbiturate coma as a treatment, but this was not done. The experiment was done in the early years of phenothiazine treatment, the efficiency of which has been proven in sophisticated trials.) Most controlled trials have shown clear evidence in favour of e.c.t., and the weight of evidence is still firmly on the side of the treatment.

It is not wise to give e.c.t. to a patient against his or her will, except in exceptional circumstances of danger to life where other treatments are not helpful or appropriate, such as suicide by refusing all fluids. In such a case, a second opinion would be advisable, and the patient should be placed under a compulsory section of the Mental Health Act. This is advisable from the doctors' point of view, and currently necessary for nurses in the United Kingdom, as most of them are not prepared to give treatment to a patient against his will unless he is subject to a compulsory order.

Despite all that has been devoted to this problem here, in daily clinical practice e.c.t. is given usefully, and without disagreement, to many patients every year, although it has been progressively less used as antidepressants have improved.

Use with out-patients

Patients not sufficiently ill to need admission to hospital may be satisfactorily treated as out-patients. All patients should be escorted home after electrical treatment, but, apart from questions of memory disturbance, many may feel unable to fend for themselves in an empty house, especially if at all inclined to the development of hysterical or anxiety reactions. Patients with any suggestion of schizophrenia should be given phenothiazines or other anti-psychotic drugs at the same time, as occasionally schizophrenic symptoms may be released by the electrical treatment.

Technique

The patient should wear loose clothing and should have had no food for four hours, and no fluids for two and a half hours. His bowels and bladder should be evacuated before treatment. Metal hair clips and dentures should be removed. The presence of loose teeth should be noted for fear of their being dislodged. The anaesthetic and relaxant are given intravenously. The electrodes, soaked in saline, are placed on the temples to which a little 'contact paste' may previously have been applied. A gag may be placed in the mouth before the current is applied, or at the moment when the patient opens his mouth as the tonic phase of the attenuated 'fit' begins.

The current must be sufficient to induce a generalised epileptic convulsion, although the convulsive movements themselves are almost totally abolished by the use of a muscle relaxant. Increasing the duration of the current increases memory disturbance, without improving the antidepressant effect. Many contemporary e.c.t. machines are not correctly designed with this in mind. A minimum of 10 Joules of electrical energy is advisable, as lower quantities may fail to produce a fit. A brief pulse is desirable.

The best anaesthetic is probably intravenous methohexitone, with suxamethonium chloride or bromide (30–60 mg) from a different syringe, through the same needle, as a muscle relaxant. Intravenous atropine can be given with the methohexitone, to lessen the bradycardia and the likelihood of vagal inhibition leading to cardiac arrest.

Artificial inflation of the lungs with oxygen is necessary on account of the respiratory paralysis; various types of machine are available for this. Very occasionally, *laryngeal spasm* may occur, so that it is advisable for those giving the relaxant to have experience of passing a laryngeal tube.

After the treatment the patient must be kept under supervision and lying down until consciousness is fully restored.

Unilateral application is advisable for routine use, although it seems to us to work rather more slowly and in some patients bilateral application is still necessary. In the unilateral method both electrodes are applied to the skull on the non-dominant side, in the frontal and temporal regions. The benefit is that there is much less immediate memory loss and confusion.

Frequency and duration of treatment

A series of such treatments is given, the number being determined by the clinical improvement. It is usual to give two or three in the first seven days, and two in each subsequent week as far as may be necessary. The number required may be reduced if thymoleptic drugs are also given, but without them it varies as a rule between three and ten; with an average of six, if bilateral and eight if unilateral. It is fairly often the case that the markedly depressed patient experiences no subjective improvement from the first two treatments, even though it may be apparent to those around that improvement has actually occurred. Where the diagnosis is certain, therefore, it is a mistake to abandon the treatment too soon. Improvement in sleep and in spontaneous activity are usually the first signs of response, and these are later followed by subjective awareness of improvement. Even where recovery is apparent, the patient should be kept under observation for a period as relapses may occur. If the improvement is held over a period of two weeks from the last treatment, it will be maintained for at least a year in over 90 per cent of cases.

The estimated recovery rate with electrical treatment in uncomplicated cases varies from about 70 per cent to about 90 per cent, according to the criteria adopted. About 90 per cent of cases can expect considerable improvement at least. A curious feature is that the treatment sometimes succeeds later in the attack when it has failed to confer benefit before. This is usually so only when the previous attacks have been lengthy, and is a contraindication to undue therapeutic pessimism.

The only substantial disadvantage is that the treatment does not prevent recurrence of subsequent attacks, and antidepressants should usually be continued for several months after the electrical treatment has been given. Attempts to prevent relapse by giving, say, monthly treatments over long periods regardless of whether the patient is ill or well (such a measure being reserved, of course, only for the rapidly recurrent cases) have sometimes been reported to be successful, but are often disappointing. A possibility to beware of is that a depressive phase may sometimes be converted to a hypomanic one in course of this treatment.

Psychosurgery (cerebral surgery)

Cerebral surgery was previously limited to pre-frontal leucotomy, but several different operations are now available. They are rarely performed, but still have a place in psychiatric treatment for those patients disabled by severe tension or depression, from whom no other treatment offers relief. In earlier years chronic schizophrenia was treated by leucotomy, but this is no longer advisable, unless the patient has severe tension as well as schizophrenic symptoms.

Although the surgical treatment of mental illness had been attempted in the 1880s, this operation was conceived by Moniz, the professor of neurology at Lisbon and father of angiography. He developed the idea that where a patient had fixed delusions, it might be possible to disorganise them by disorganising the neural substrate that he supposed to be responsible for their formation. The frontal lobes seemed the logical point of attack, both because they were then believed to be the seat of the intellectual life and because they had no other clearly assignable function. Moniz was further encouraged by experimental work reported at a neurological congress held in London in 1935, in which extensive ablation of the frontal areas in apes was shown to have improved their emotional stability at small cost to their intellectual function. He initiated the work in the same year. It was found that the delusions and hallucinations were virtually unaltered, but that, as in apes, the emotional stability was improved in that the patients were much less disturbed by their symptoms and acquired a greater ease of mind.

Techniques

Several different techniques were developed over the decades. For years the standard operation was a free hand and essentially blind procedure aimed at severing the white matter of the centrum ovale just in front of the anterior horns of the lateral ventricles; and various other less extensive freehand operations followed this. They have been replaced by stereotactic procedures in which small lesions are placed accurately, or by open operations such as removal of parts of the temporal lobe for temporal lobe epilepsy. (Stereotactic procedures in neurosurgery are those in which X-rays outline the skull and cerebral ventricles, so that a guided probe can be exactly placed in relation to certain 'landmarks'. They are very safe.) These small accurately placed lesions are much less likely to cause harmful personality change, such as apathy or excessive disinhibition, than the older blind operations.

The most favoured operations in this country are: (a) stereotactic tractotomy, in which fibres from the orbital cortex are interrupted by radioactive yttrium seeds; and (b) stereotactic limbic leucotomy, in which lesions are made in the fronto-limbic pathways, and in the cingulum. Both of these operations are aimed at the relief of symptoms, namely depression, anxiety, and tension—especially that associated with obsessional-compulsive states. Operations such as amygdalotomy and hypothalamotomy have been used, mainly in other countries, to lessen aggressive and violent behaviour. There are major ethical problems with these latter operations, particularly as they tend to be offered mainly to prisoners rather than to patients.

The tractotomy and limbic leucotomy interrupt fronto-limbic connections, which are involved in emotional and autonomic functions centred in the limbic system.

General effects

Clinically, the usual physical effects are improvement of appetite and sleep, restoration of lost weight and of regularity of previously irregular menstruation. The mental effects may be summarised under the headings of: (1) Reduction of the patient's emotional charge, so that he feels and reacts less intensely, with a reduced tendency to worry; in line with this there is liable to be some reduction in spontaneous activity and initiative. (2) Release of inhibition, so that the patient feels less restrained, imposes less check upon himself than before and may say and do things more impulsively and with less deliberation than he would have shown before operation. (3) Intellectual changes, which are often of a subtle kind. The patient tends to think more in concrete than in abstract terms, to attend to the immediate rather than the remote, to have some difficulty in the adroit distribution of his attention when attending to the various aspects of any complex matter, so that his judgments tend to be simpler and made with less deliberation and thoroughness. These are not absolute changes but are broad, general trends. The extent to which they occur depends on the amount of damage done by the operation, and on the pre-morbid personality, of which the post-operative one is a modification. The better the pre-morbid personality the better the post-operative results are likely to be. The difficulty is to devise an operation which gives adequate relief of symptoms without causing untoward personality and intellectual changes. The more extensive operations tended to do both, but the more accurate and limited modern operations cause less damage. Many patients who would otherwise have been hopeless chronic invalids have been enabled to lead useful lives after operation at a cost that is small by comparison, and may be apparent only to those who knew the patient well before. In brief, there are always changes, but it should not be supposed that the operation reduces the patients to robots or renders them necessarily difficult to live with. On the contrary, many are pleasanter to live with than they were before, and we have known clergymen, university professors, business executives, etc., resume their work satisfactorily even after the standard operation.

Indications

This is a symptomatic treatment and must be used on a symptomatic basis. The main indications are, therefore, afforded by cases incapacitated by tension, agitation and distress. It is rare to offer these operations to patients who have been intractably ill for less than five years, and have had every other appropriate form of treatment.

Among the *affective disorders*, states of severe anxiety with tension, and of depression with agitation, are those that do best. Manic-depressive illnesses of classical kind with regularly recurrent manic and depressive phases show disappointing results in that, though there is less post-operative tendency for recurrence of depression, the recurrence of manic phases is little influenced, though it is true that the severity of the recurrences is usually reduced. Nor is the operation as effective as might be hoped in cases of chronic or recurrent mania without depression. In cases of recurrent depression without manic attacks the results are much better.

In the *schizophrenic illnesses*, only those with severe depressive or tension symptoms are likely to be helped, and the operation is rarely performed.

Incapacitating *obsessional states*, notoriously resistant to other forms of treatment, are among the cases that do best of all, and the chances are better the more the symptoms are confined to rumination and the less they involve repetitive rituals.

In some patients with severe intractable pain cerebral surgery may be necessary to make life bearable; and in cases of severe anorexia nervosa it may be necessary to preserve life. The operations are regularly but uncommonly performed for both conditions.

Contraindications

Operation is an irreversible procedure, and should be regarded as a treatment of last resort. There are, therefore, two absolute contraindications: (1) If there still remains untried some form of treatment from which benefit may reasonably be expected. (2) If there remains any serious chance of spontaneous recovery occurring before permanent deterioration has set in.

The other contraindications are only of a relative sort. Physically, hypertension increases the risk of haemorrhage at or after operation. But many patients with severe hypertension have been operated on successfully; it is wise, however, to keep them at rest and in bed for a few weeks as a preliminary. Psychiatrically, cerebral surgery should be avoided in patients who have been aggressive or lacking in drive and in the capacity to struggle against adversity. Lessened restraint can lead to troublesome aggression; the apathetic will became more so.

The lessened restraint may also be of importance in cases with homosexual trends, since operation may lead to their frank release; whether it does so or not will depend on the patient's recognition of and pre-operative attitude towards them, as well as on the extent of his social conscience and powers of self-control. People who are well controlled before operation are likely to remain reasonably well controlled after it. People who are naturally self-indulgent are likely post-operatively to be more so.

The patients who are likely to be difficult after operation are those who have always shown poor social adjustment, who do not adapt themselves, are egocentric with lack of regard for others, have poor powers of effort, hold grudges, and show little depth of feeling. The possession of such a personality cannot in itself be considered a contraindication to operation, if the symptoms experienced are totally disabling and of a kind from which operation might confer relief. But where the symptoms are not totally disabling and the patient is able to lead some sort of a life, even though under handicap, it may be better for him to continue as he is rather than become an even less satisfactory personality though with fewer symptoms. Such decisions may be very difficult indeed.

Complications
The overall mortality using modern techniques is very small. Any intracranial operation carries some risk of post-operative epilepsy, and the more extensive the approach the greater is the risk. Thus, post-operative epilepsy occurs in about 16 per cent of cases after gyrectomy or topectomy, but in only about 10 per cent of cases after simpler operations. Even so, many of these have but one single attack, and we have never known post-operative epilepsy to constitute any serious problem. Urinary incontinence is an occasional complication but is nearly always transient. Urgency and frequency of micturition may persist but seldom to any degree that causes embarrassment. Such formidable complications as rectal incontinence, hemiparesis, etc., that were reported after some of the early cases, are so rare as to be negligible.

After-care
The post-operative rehabilitation is very important. The patients are usually in an accessible, tractable and accepting frame of mind after operation, and every advantage should be taken of this to encourage them into more satisfactory attitudes and habits, both as regards occupying themselves, attending to their duties, and learning to live with and to manage their residual symptoms. Behaviour therapy may be more effective, as may drug treatment, after operation. A considerable amount of re-education may be necessary, especially in those who have long been psychotic. Occupational therapy is indispensable.

We are of the opinion that, if the home situation is suitable and the relatives show reasonable understanding, the patients do best if they are discharged as soon as their condition allows, rather than kept in hospital for a lengthy period.

Most neuro-surgeons advise that the patient should take small doses of anti-convulsants; many patients, however, will not bother about this if it is left to themselves.

It is always advisable to follow up the patients after discharge until one is satisfied that the maximum improvement has been gained and the patients' stability established. In this connection, it must be borne in mind that the immediate post-operative result is no guide to what the future holds; many patients continue to improve slowly and to make further adjustments over periods of many months and even years after operation.

16

The legal aspects of mental illness

The Mental Health Act 1959, which came into force in 1960, brought about various changes both in official terminology and procedure. At the time this ninth edition is going to press some revisions of the 1959 Act are being considered, of a minor nature principally.

With regard to terminology, there used to be two states called respectively 'unsoundness of mind' and 'mental deficiency', either of which might call for 'certification'. These terms have been superseded. Both unsoundness of mind and mental deficiency now come together under the official heading of *Mental disorder*, and patients whose mental disorder is such as to call for detention in hospital against their will are no longer 'certified' but may be *'compulsorily detained'*.

This general term *mental disorder* is subdivided into four categories: (1) *mental illness*, (2) *severe subnormality*, (3) *subnormality*, (4) *psychopathic disorder*.

The first category, *mental illness*, is not defined in the Act, so that its interpretation may be elastic.

Severe subnormality is defined as 'a state of arrested or incomplete development of mind which includes subnormality of intelligence and is of such a nature or degree that the patient is incapable of living an independent life or of guarding himself against exploitation, or will be so incapable when of an age to do so'.

The third category, *subnormality*, is defined as 'a state of arrested or incomplete development of mind (not amounting to severe subnormality) which includes subnormality of intelligence and is of a nature or degree which requires or is susceptible to medical treatment or other special care or training of the patient'.

The remaining category, *psychopathic disorder* (the legal recognition of which is a notable innovation), is defined as 'a persistent disorder or disability of mind (whether or not including subnormality of intelligence) which results in abnormally aggressive or seriously irresponsible conduct on the part of the patient, and requires or is susceptible to medical treatment'.

A main emphasis of the 1959 Act is that psychiatric treatment should be given as far as possible on a voluntary, called *informal*, basis. Methods of compulsory admission and detention are described later.

Admission to hospital

Under the Mental Health Act of 1959 any psychiatric patient may in theory be treated in any hospital. It is unnecessary to say that the hospital should be a suitable one. Nothing is likely to be gained by sending a severely subnormal patient to a general hospital, and many hospitals with psychiatric facilities are unsuited for the reception of violent and difficult patients, and do not attempt it. Further, there is no provision in the Act that obliges a hospital to accept a patient, even though a recommendation for compulsory detention may have been signed. There is, however, a responsibility on Regional Hospital Boards to ensure as far as possible that beds are available for patients who need admission. Under the commonest arrangement made by such boards, psychiatric hospitals are expected to admit all suitable cases from a particular 'catchment' area. Hospitals are often unwilling to accept patients from outside that area. In any event, they are not obliged to accept patients, even from their own area, and even though compulsory detention has been recommended. It is, therefore, essential in all cases to make prior arrangements for every patient's admission with the hospital that is chosen.

Informal admission

This is always to be preferred. No forms are required. All that is necessary is that the patient should be not unwilling to enter the hospital and that the hospital should be willing to accept the patient.

Compulsory detention

The reasons for this have been summarised as (1) for the patient's own protection, (2) for protection of the public, (3) for the provision of necessary treatment. The indications have been discussed on pages 356 and 357. Under the Mental Health Act of 1959 compulsory detention can be arranged in three ways: (1) *In emergency*; this enables the patient to be detained for *three days*. (2) *For observation*; this enables the patient to be detained for *twenty-eight days*. (3) *For treatment*; this does not apply to all types of patient, but enables the patient to be detained for *twelve months*, though with a right of appeal within the first six months. The hospitals receiving patients subject to compulsory detention can discharge them before these periods of time have elapsed, or alternatively, can make arrangements for such periods to be extended if necessary.

The procedure to be followed differs somewhat according to the method used, and details are given later, but in *every* case there must be (1) an *application* to the hospital to receive the patient, and (2) a *medical recommendatiion* or recommendations. These are made by filling in printed forms, which can be obtained from H.M. Stationery Office, from the local authority social worker, or from the hospital concerned. The *application* may not be signed by the doctor, but must be signed by the patient's nearest available relative, or in an emergency any relative, or by the local Social Worker who, except in cases of emergency admission, must where practicable consult the nearest relative. Details of the different types of *medical recommendation* are given below. Both the application and the medical recommendation or recommendations should accompany the patient to the hospital, with which, it is re-emphasised, prior arrangements for admission must have been made in all cases.

There are certain general prohibitions, designed to safeguard the liberty of the patient, concerning relationship between the person signing the application and the doctor or doctors signing the medical recommendation or recommendations. Thus, the doctor signing the medical recommendation may not also be the applicant; nor may he be the partner or assistant of the applicant; nor may he be related either to the patient or to the applicant in any of the following ways: husband, wife, father, father-in-law, mother, mother-in-law, son, son-in-law, daughter, daughter-in-law, brother, brother-in-law, sister, sister-in-law. Nor may he have any pecuniary interests in payments for the patient's maintenance in hospital. The same prohibitions apply where two medical recommendations are required, in which event the doctors signing these may not be partners or assistants of each other, nor related to each other in any of the foregoing ways.

If the doctor is in difficulty or doubt as to procedure, he can get information and help from the local authority social worker, who may also assist in conducting the patient to hospital. The Department of Health and Social Services (Alexander Fleming House, Elephant and Castle, London, SE1) also expresses willingness to provide help and information, but is not able to pronounce whether a patient should be compulsorily detained. If the suitability of a patient for compulsory detention is questioned after he has been so detained, legal proceedings may ensue. For this reason, among others, full notes of the occasion should always be kept. 'Persons signing medical certificates will not be liable to any civil or criminal proceeding if they act in good faith and with reasonable care.'

Admission for observation (other than in emergency) (Section 25)
This calls for (1) an *application* for the patient's admission addressed to
the managers of the hospital on a form called Form 1, signed by the
patient's nearest relative, or by someone authorised to act for the
nearest relative (in which case a copy of the authority must be attached),
or by a local authority social worker who should, if feasible, have had
prior consultation with the patient's nearest relative, and (2) a joint
medical recommendation by two doctors. This may be done individually
on separate forms (Form 3A) or jointly on the same form (Form 3B).
They sign under a printed statement to the effect that the patient is
suffering from such mental disorder as to warrant detention in hospital,
that the patient ought to be so detained either in the interest of his own
health or safety or for the protection of others, and that informal
admission is not appropriate. No other reasons are called for, and apart
from filling in the particulars the doctors are merely expressing
agreement that what is printed on the form applies to their patient.
Where practicable, one of the recommendations should be made by a
doctor who has known the patient prior to the examination, and the
other must be given by a doctor approved by some local authority as
being a suitable person to act in this fashion by virtue of special
experience. Lists of doctors so approved can be obtained from the local
authorities or from the Regional Boards. The following provisions
must be complied with:

1. The medical recommendations must have been signed on or
before the date of the application.
2. The doctors may have examined the patient together, or, if
separately, must have done so within seven days of each other.
3. The applicant and the doctors must have seen the patient within
fourteen days of the application being made.
4. The patient must be admitted to hospital within fourteen days of
the application being made.
5. The relationship, or lack of it, between the applicant, the patient
and the doctor must come within the provisions stated on page 420, and
neither of the doctors may have any pecuniary interest in the payments
made for the patient's maintenance or treatment in hospital.

This procedure enables the patient to be compulsorily detained for a
period of *twenty-eight* days from his admission. The period can be
prolonged by an application for admission for *treatment* under the
procedure that is described later on.

Admission for observation in case of emergency (Section 29)
There are required: (1) an *application* calling for the patient's admission

and addressed to the managers of the hospital; this is made on Form 2 and can be done by any relative of the patient or by a social worker; the terms of the form require the applicant to sign that the patient's admission and detention is a matter of urgent necessity and that the alternative procedures would involve undue delay. (2) One *medical recommendation*, which is to be made on Form 3A. Wherever practicable, this should be done by a practitioner who has known the patient before. Form 3A requires the doctor to sign that the patient is suffering from mental disorder of such a degree as to warrant detention in hospital and that informal admission is unsuitable, while measures other than emergency ones would involve undue delay. The following provisions must be complied with:

1. The medical recommendation must be signed on or before the date of the application.
2. The applicant must have seen the patient within three days of making the application.
3. The patient must be admitted to hospital within three days of the examination on which the medical recommendation is based.
4. The relationship, or lack of it, between the applicant, the patient and the doctor must come within the provisions stated on page 420, and the doctor may not have an interest in any payment made for the patient's maintenance or treatment in hospital.

This procedure enables the patient to be detained for a period of *seventy-two hours* after admission but, if a second medical recommendation is furnished within that time, the patient can be detained for twenty-eight days as in admission for observation.

Compulsory detention in hospital
A patient already in hospital may be compulsorily detained wherever he is for three days under Section 30(2). The report is made by the 'responsible medical officer' (not clearly defined) to the managers of the hospital.

Admission for treatment (Section 26)
The procedure for this is more elaborate and is not applicable to all types of case, probably because it enables the patient to be compulsorily detained for *twelve months*. There are, however, provisions (*vide infra*) for the nearest relative to seek the patient's discharge, and for the patient to appeal against continued detention, before that period of time has elapsed. Under the sections of the Mental Health Act, 1959, which we have hitherto considered, namely Section 25 dealing with admission for observation and Section 29 dealing with admission for

observation in case of emergency (enabling compulsory detention for twenty-eight days and seventy two hours respectively), the doctors are not required to do more than state their opinion that the patient's mental disorder is such as to warrant detention in hospital and that informal admission is unsuitable. Under Section 26, which we are at present considering and which deals with the patient's admission for treatment such as might involve detention for twelve months (or more if the authority is renewed), the doctors are required to state not only the reasons for their opinions, but their opinions as to the type of mental disorder from which the patient is suffering, i.e. whether mental illness, severe subnormality, subnormality or psychopathic disorder (see p. 418). It may be noted at the outset that patients *over twenty-one years of age* are not eligible for the compulsory detention under this section of the Act if *subnormality* or *psychopathic disorder* is the ground on which it is sought. Patients suffering from subnormality or psychopathic disorder *under* the age of *twenty-one* may be eligible for compulsory detention for treatment, but patients *over* the age of twenty-one need to be suffering from *mental illness* or *severe subnormality*.

The following documents are required (1) an application, (2) two medical recommendations. The *application*, made on Form 4A, is addressed to the managers of the hospital and signed by the patient's nearest relative or, in the absence of such, by the social worker who should have consulted with the patient's nearest relative, and who may not proceed if the latter objects. The *medical recommendations* may be made individually (Form 5A) or jointly on the same form (Form 5B). These forms require the doctors to state the official category of mental disorder from which the patient suffers, namely whether this is mental illness, severe subnormality, subnormality or psychopathic disorder. More than one of the four official categories may be given if desired (e.g. mental illness with subnormality, severe subnormality with psychopathic disorder, etc.), but one of the four official categories must be common to each of the medical recommendations, though the latter may differ in other respects. The forms also require the doctors to give their reasons for believing detention in hospital to be necessary (this in the shape of a clinical description of the patient's state), and their reasons for believing out-patient treatment or informal admission to be unsuitable. The clinical description should, therefore, indicate that the condition is of a degree which warrants detention in hospital. Such observations may be supplemented by facts supplied by others, but the two should be clearly distinguished. Full notes should be made and kept, together with the names and addresses of other informants, for reference in the event of subsequent litigation. The whole should show clearly that the patient is in need of compulsory detention, and ideally should be such as would convince the most stupid and bigoted member of a jury to that effect.

The same provisions must be observed, as regards dates of seeing the patient, signing the application and medical recommendations, and relationships of the various parties, as are required in the foregoing Section 25 where the patient is admitted for observation. It is again emphasised that patients over the age of twenty-one years are not eligible for admission for treatment under Section 26 unless suffering from mental illness and/or severe subnormality, as opposed merely to subnormality or psychopathic disorder. Apart from medical recommendations, however, subnormal and psychopathic cases may be admitted and compulsorily detained whatever their age, if they are the subject of a Court order.

Admission by a police officer (Section 136)
Police constables have the power under Section 136 to take to 'a place of safety' any person whom they find in a public place and who appears to be suffering from mental disorder, and to be in immediate need of care or control, in his own interests or for the safety of others. The place of safety is usually a hospital. Admission under this section is for three days.

The role of social workers
Social workers have an important role to play in compulsory admissions under Section 25, 26, and 29 in particular. They act as representatives of the public in a way, if there is no suitable relative available, and also guide the concerned relatives.

Under the legislation initiated by the Seebohm report the old specialists in mental illness which every local authority employed (the Mental Welfare Officers or MWO), lost their particular speciality, and took on a more diverse case load. Many departments are reverting to the older style, without the older name, as the loss of the specialists was felt increasingly. Special training is usually now offered to those who are called on for this emergency psychiatric work, and certain social workers in each department hold a warrant to act in such cases.

Discharge from psychiatric hospitals
Old ideas die hard, and the unfounded notion is still occasionally expressed that 'once you get into one of those places you can never get out again'. Relatives will, therefore, sometimes consult the family doctor or specialist as to the means of discharge, either before or after

agreeing to the patient's admission. Some knowledge of procedure may, therefore, be useful.

It may be stressed that no one wishes to increase work or expense by keeping patients in hospital unnecessarily, while psychiatric hospitals, like others, take a natural pride in their recovery rate. Indeed, the present-day trend is towards returning to the community even chronic cases who have not fully recovered so long as there is a reasonable chance of their making some satisfactory social adjustment.

Apart from the foregoing, (1) patients admitted informally may discharge themselves at any time. (2) Patients compulsorily detained under an application for observation in case of emergency (Section 29) must be discharged within three days of their admission unless further arrangements are made; the patient may agree to stay in hospital, if this is thought advisable, on an informal basis; if he does not agree to stay informally, although this is thought advisable, the relatives will be consulted before further steps are taken. (3) Patients compulsorily detained under an application for observation (other than in case of emergency) (Section 25) must be discharged within twenty-eight days of their admission unless further arrangements are made, in which event the foregoing remarks apply. (4) Patients compulsorily detained under an application for treatment (Section 26) must be discharged within twelve months of their admission unless, if a further stay is thought advisable, they agree to stay informally, or other arrangements are made, in which event the relatives will be consulted. But in this connection there is more to be said. The nearest relative of any patient compulsorily detained under this Section 26, carrying liability to detention for twelve months, may at any time write an order for the patient's discharge. This is addressed to the managers of the hospital, but must be preceded by seventy-two hours' warning that it is to be presented. The patient must then be discharged unless the responsible medical officer furnishes a report, within the seventy-two hour period following the warning, that the patient would be dangerous to himself or others if discharged. If this is done, the nearest relative may then apply to a Mental Health Review Tribunal. If the Mental Health Review Tribunal upholds the medical officer's opinion and refuses to sanction the patient's discharge, the nearest relative must then wait for a further six months before raising the matter again. Apart, however, from intervention by the nearest relative, any patient compulsorily detained under this Section 26 may himself appeal to a Mental Health Review Tribunal for his discharge within six months of his admission.

Another special provision relating to the discharge of patients is that those who have been compulsorily detained, under whatever section of the Act, on ground of *psychopathic disorder* or *mental subnormality* (but *not* on grounds of mental illness or severe subnormality) cease to be liable to compulsory detention on attaining the age of twenty-five; they must then be discharged unless the responsible medical officer furnishes a report that they would be dangerous to themselves or others.

The Mental Health Review Tribunals referred to are appointed by the Lord Chancellor and consist of at least one medical, one lay and one legal representative.

It is perhaps unnecessary to re-emphasise that, apart from appeals by patients or relatives, the responsible medical officer or the managers of the hospital may authorise the discharge of patients at any time, regardless of the section of the Act under which they may have been compulsorily detained.

Patients may also be allowed leave of absence from hospital on trial, during which time they may receive a cash allowance if in need.

Facilities provided by local authorities

Another main emphasis of the new Act is on the provision by local authorities of residential and training centres for patients whose condition does not call for full hospital care, but who yet require some form of rehabilitation, shelter or supervision. Although few of these have been developed at the time of writing, further provision is envisaged according to the extent of local needs.

PROCEDURES IN SCOTLAND

The Mental Health (Scotland) Act, 1960, in force from June 1962, is broadly similar in conception to the English Act of 1959, but there are some terminological and procedural differences. The Board of Control for Scotland is replaced by the Mental Welfare Commission. As in the English Act, the general term *mental disorder* is used, but the subdivisions are different; these are (1) *mental deficiency* such that the patient is incapable of living an independent life or of guarding himself against serious exploitation, (2) *mental illness* which is a persistent disorder manifested only by abnormally aggressive or seriously irresponsible conduct, (3) *other mental illness*.

The Scottish Act thus retains the old term 'mental deficiency', which is equivalent to the new term 'severe subnormality' in the English Act; like the English Act it recognises 'psychopathic disorder' by implication, but avoids use of the actual term; as in the English Act 'mental illness' is undefined.

As in England, patients may be admitted to hospital without formality, but the term 'informal admission' does not appear in the

Scottish Act. There are also provisions for the patient to be compulsorily detained, but the words 'compulsory' and 'compulsorily' do not appear in the Scottish Act.

Patients in Scotland can be detained in hospital through legal provisions in the following two ways: (1) *Emergency Admission*, (2) *Application for Admission*.

Emergency admission (Section 31)

A recommendation, known as an *emergency recommendation*, is made on a printed form by one medical practitioner, who is required to sign that admission in pursuance of an application would involve undue delay, and that admission and detention are urgently necessary. The consent of a relative of the patient or a mental health officer should be obtained, and the recommendation should be accompanied by a signed statement that this has been done; alternatively, it must be accompanied by a statement of the reasons for failure to obtain such consent. An emergency recommendation authorises the patient's removal to hospital at any time within three days of its having been made, and his detention for a period of up to seven days. The medical practitioner must have examined the patient on the day on which he makes the emergency recommendation. It is the duty of the board of management of the receiving hospital to notify without delay the patient's nearest relative or other responsible person.

Application for admission (Section 24)

This calls for (1) *an application*, (2) two *medical recommendations*, and (3) *approval of the application by the sheriff*. The *application* is addressed on a printed form to the board of management of the appropriate hospital, and is signed either by the patient's nearest relative or by a mental health officer. The mental health officer must take such steps as are reasonably practicable to inform the patient's nearest relative of the proposed application and of his right to object to it. Whoever the applicant, he must have seen the patient within fourteen days of submitting the application to the sheriff for approval. The *medical recommendations* must have been signed on or before the date of the application. The doctors may have examined the patient separately, or together if the patient has made no objection to the latter procedure. If they have examined the patient separately, they must have done so within seven days of each other. One of the doctors must be approved by the Regional Hospital Board as having special experience in the diagnosis or treatment of mental disorder. The other should be the patient's general practitioner, if practicable, or should have had previous acquaintance with the patient. If the patient is destined for *private* accommodation, neither of the doctors may be on the staff of the hospital named in the application; if the patient is to be accommodated other than privately, one of the recommending doctors, but only one, may be on the staff of the hospital named in the application. Also, only one of the medical recommendations may be made by a medical officer in the service of a local authority. Neither of the doctors may be the applicant. Contrary to the procedure in England, either or both of the doctors may be related to the patient and may have a pecuniary interest in his admission to hospital, but such relationship and/or pecuniary interest must be stated. The recommendations, made on a printed form, must state the form of mental disorder (i.e. whether mental deficiency, mental illness which is a persistent disorder manifested only by abnormally aggressive or seriously irresponsible conduct or other mental illness), that the disorder requires or is susceptible to medical treatment and is of a nature or degree which warrants the patient's detention in a hospital for such treatment: and that the interests of the health or safety of the patient or the protection of other persons cannot be secured otherwise than by the detention recommended. One form of the mental disorder mentioned must be common to both of the recommendations, though the patient may be described as suffering from the other forms in either or both. There is, however, one important reservation. *No person over the age of twenty-one years* shall be admitted *under application* (Section 24) unless suffering from (1) *mental deficiency* such that he is incapable of living an independent life or of guarding himself against serious exploitation, or (2) *mental illness other than* a persistent disorder which is manifested only by abnormally aggressive or seriously irresponsible conduct. The implication is that patients suffering from what would amount to 'psychopathic disorder' in the English Act may *not*, if over the age of twenty-one years, be the subjects of application for admission on that ground alone under the Scottish Act, though they may be the subjects of emergency admission, or the subjects of application for admission if *under* the age of twenty-one. This reservation is essentially similar to that pertaining to the compulsory detention of patients suffering from subnormality or psychopathic disorder under the English Act.

For *approval by the sheriff* to be obtained, the following conditions must have been observed. The applicant must have seen the patient within fourteen days of submitting the application. Both medical recommendations must have been signed on or before the date of the application. The application must be submitted to the sheriff within seven days of the last date on which the patient was examined for the purposes of a medical recommendation. The sheriff may make such enquiries and see such persons (including the patient) as he thinks fit.

In the event of objection by the nearest relative of the patient, he shall hear that relative and any witness whom that relative wishes to call. Equally, before he withholds approval of an application he must give opportunity of being heard to the applicant and to any witness the applicant may wish to call. The proceedings may be conducted in private if the sheriff, applicant or patient so desires.

Discharge of patients detained in Scotland

Patients detained under an emergency application must be discharged within seven days of admission unless an application for admission is made (see p. 427).

A patient detained under an application for admission must be discharged within twelve months of admission unless the responsible medical officer obtains from another medical practitioner a report on the patient to the effect that continued detention is necessary in the interests of the latter's health or safety or for the protection of others. If such a report is obtained, the patient's nearest relative must be informed, and the patient may appeal to the sheriff.

A patient detained solely on the ground of (a) mental deficiency, or (b) mental illness which is a persistent disorder manifested only by abnormally aggressive or seriously irresponsible conduct, must be discharged on attaining the age of twenty-five years unless the responsible medical officer obtains from another medical practitioner a report on the patient to the effect that the latter is suffering from mental disorder such as would warrant his admission to hospital if he were not already in one, or that he would be likely to be dangerous to himself or others if discharged. If such a report is obtained, the patient's nearest relative must be informed and may appeal to the sheriff for the patient's discharge.

Unlike the English Act which allows the nearest relative to make an order for any patient's discharge (though, as explained above, this may not necessarily be acceded to), the Scottish Act allows this only in the case of patients who are not in a State hospital, i.e. private patients.

Apart from the above, patients may also be discharged at any time by order of the Mental Welfare Commission, the board of management of the hospital concerned, or, in the case of State hospitals, by the responsible medical officer with the consent of the board of management. Patients may also be discharged by order of the sheriff if he is appealed to in the situations mentioned above, or, in the case of private patients, if he consents to an order for discharge made by the nearest relative. In this last instance, if the sheriff does not consent the nearest relative may not make another order for the patient's discharge until a further six months have elapsed.

As in England, patients may be granted leave of absence from hospital even though liable to be legally detained there.

Facilities provided by local authorities

As in England, the new Scottish Act provides for the delegation from central to local authorities of the responsibility for establishing residential or training centres for patients whose condition may not call for full hospital care, but who yet may require some form of shelter, supervision or rehabilitation.

CRIMINAL RESPONSIBILITY

A person who is found to be obviously insane at the time of trial is found 'unfit to plead' and is not tried. Main issues here are whether the person is capable of giving instructions for his defence and of following the evidence. When during the trial of an accused person he is found to have been insane at the time of the commission of the act, the jury shall, if satisfied that he committed the offence, return a verdict of 'Guilty but insane'. In either case the person may be detained in custody during Her Majesty's pleasure.

In dealing with insanity, the Courts follow the rules laid down by the judges in connection with the case of McNaghten, a paranoid patient, who had been tried for the wilful murder of Sir Robert Peel's private secretary. The important points in these rules are:

1. 'In order to establish a defence on the ground of insanity it must be clearly proved that at the time of committing the act the party accused was labouring under such defect of reason from disease of the mind as not to know the nature and quality of the act he was doing, or if he did know it, that he did not know he was doing what was wrong.'

2. 'If the accused labours under "partial delusions" only, and is in all other respects sane, he should be considered in the same situation as to responsibility as if the facts with respect to which the delusion exists were real.'

These rules have been subjected to much criticism. The words 'nature and quality' refer essentially to the physical aspects of the act, i.e. if a man has a gun, does he know that it is a gun? Does he know that, if he discharges it, the effect may be damaging to other people? The word 'wrong' does not refer to any question of abstract values, but as used here is synonymous with 'punishable by law'. Thus, the question 'Does he know that it is wrong?' must be taken legalistically to mean 'Does he know that it is wrong in law and punishable accordingly?'

From these considerations it is clear that the first of the rules quoted has the possible advantage of rendering it almost impossible for any guilty person to escape the rigours of the law on the ground of insanity. The rule may be considered liable, however, to fall rather hardly on some people who, though guilty of the act, were fully insane in a medical sense without fulfilling the legal criteria of insanity as laid down in the rule. As a learned judge put it 'Hardly anyone is mad enough to come under the McNaghten Rules'.

The second of the rules quoted is unrealistic, since the idea of partial insanity takes no cognisance of the necessity for assessing people in terms of the total personality, nor of the fact that instinctual and emotional factors are far more important in controlling a person's actions than are intellectual processes or ratiocinations.

In themselves, therefore, the rules may be considered unsatisfactory. But no one has been able to devise a better alternative, or at any rate one that has met with acceptance. In practice, the difficulty is overcome by the Courts now interpreting the rules with an increasing elasticity, so that those with most experience believe that the system works quite well. The Homicide Act of 1957 (before capital punishment was suspended) made provision for the defence of 'substantially diminished' responsibility as the result of mental abnormality. The Mental Health Act, 1959, Section 60, provided that persons involved in criminal proceedings may be made the subjects of a 'hospital order' by the Courts, where the latter are satisfied by medical evidence that the offender is suffering from one of the offical forms of mental disorder such as would justify his detention in hospital, or that detention in hospital (as opposed to prison) is the most suitable form of disposal. These provisions have increased the flexibility of Court procedures.

Medico-legal reports

It is traditional that a doctor should help his patient. Indeed, most doctors feel some obligation to try to do so. The fact that a person has sought medical advice is thus liable to create a special personal relationship. But where the doctor, patient and the law are all concerned together, the relationship is not bilateral but triangular. Students and doctors who are inexperienced but show enthusiasm for the normal professional role are not always at ease in the triangular situation. In making reports or recommendations they are sometimes liable to assume something of the role of advocate instead of that of impartial observer, owing to a certain sense of obligation to the patient. But it should not be supposed that a man is better treated by medical than legal measures merely because he has sought medical advice. Conversely, even though punishment may sometimes be valuable, it should never be prescribed by a doctor.

CIVIL LAW

The question of mental disorder may arise in all provinces of Civil Law, but only three aspects will be mentioned here:

(1) Management of property and the court of protection

The function of the Court of Protection is to manage the property and affairs of persons who, by reason of mental disorder, are unable to do so themselves. The Court is only directly concerned with patient's property, not with their persons; but through control of their property, or so to speak of the money bags, it is able to exercise considerable control over such questions as to where the patient shall live or whether the patient shall enter or leave hospital or nursing home.

The need for protection of this kind is obvious in many old people who, owing to confusion or forgetfulness, may make a hash of their finances, e.g. by leaving bills unpaid or cheques or dividends uncashed; or who may neglect themselves or be imposed upon or sponged upon by others. But the need for protection is not confined to the senile. It is also, for example, evident in many subnormals and in that ever-enlarging group of the brain-damaged as the result of head injuries.

Except for temporary relief in emergencies, the Court must have medical evidence to establish its jurisdiction. The relevant section (Section 101) of the Mental Health Act 1959 is in effect so all-embracing that any form of mental illness, or any disorder or disability of mind, suffices to give the Court jurisdiction if by reason thereof a person is incapable of managing his property and affairs.

It should be clearly understood that, in providing a medical certificate or affidavit to this effect (1) the responsibility of taking action, or not taking action, falls entirely on the shoulders of the Court, the doctor merely being the reporting agent; and (2) the issue in question, namely whether the patient is capable of managing his property and affairs, is quite a separate issue from the desirability of compulsory detention in hospital under Sections 25 and 26 of the new Act of 1959. The majority of the patients under the jurisdiction of the Court of Protection are not in hospital, nor could they or should they be compulsorily detained in hospital. Conversely, the fact that a patient is in hospital, whether voluntarily or compulsorily, is not in itself sufficient to establish that he is incapable of managing his affairs.

It is most important that both doctors and relatives should realise that incapacity to manage affairs and the need for compulsory admission to hospital are quite unrelated.

The normal procedure of the Court—and except in most exceptional circumstances it can only act on medical evidence—is to appoint a Receiver who may be a relative or friend, a solicitor or Bank Trustee, or in many cases the Official Solicitor of the Supreme Court. The Receiver is invested by the Court of Protection with various powers of acting on behalf of the patient, and must render an account of his stewardship.

It is quite often supposed that the need for the jurisdiction of the Court of Protection and the appointment of a Receiver in a patient who is manifestly incapable of managing his affairs, can be avoided by getting the patient to give a Power of Attorney. But if a patient is incapable of managing his affairs, it would seem that, rightly or wrongly, he cannot in law give a valid power of attorney. Further, a Power of Attorney, which may be valid when given, is revoked by the patient becoming incapable.

It is the duty of the family or hospital doctor to inform the relatives when the time has come for the appointment of a Receiver. The relatives should be told to consult a solicitor or write direct to the Chief Clerk of the Court of Protection, Store Street, London, W.C.1.

A patient placed under the care of the Court of Protection does not have to remain so permanently. If his mental state improves the order can be rescinded by an Order Determining Proceedings.

A word may be added about the Lord Chancellor's Visitors, who are not officers of the Court of Protection but are appointed by the Lord Chancellor, and who have been described as the 'eyes and ears' of the Court of Protection. Their function is to visit patients who are, or who are thought to be, incapable of managing their affairs and to report to the Court either generally on their mental capacity and welfare, or more specifically on any matter on which the Court may require information, such as the testamentary capacity of the patient. The medical visitors have certain statutory rights, such as requiring the production of medical records; and any interference in the carrying out of their duties is an offence punishable by imprisonment.

(2) Testamentary capacity

This is not an uncommon question in examinations, and is quite often an important practical problem. The medical man should satisfy himself on the following essential points: Does the patient (a) understand the nature of a Will; (b) the effect of a Will; (c) appear to have a reasonable knowledge of his estate and has he any delusions thereon; (d) has he the capacity to appreciate which dependants, relatives or friends might reasonably be entitled to his bounty; (e) has he any delusions which would *per se* cause him to omit any person or persons as beneficiaries, who otherwise might reasonably have been included; (f) has he any delusion which would cause him to make a gift which he might not have made in the absence of such delusion; (g) does he appear to understand the importance attached to his act; (h) if the medical practitioner sees the draft of the Will, do the bequests appear to him to be reasonable?

A patient who is compulsorily detained may possess testamentary capacity and one who is not may not. In summary, to have testamentary capacity a man must understand the nature of a Will, he must be able to understand the extent of his property, and he must be able to form a proper judgment as to the nature of the claims on his bounty.

A medical practitioner asked to advise as to testamentary capacity should show by his report that he has considered each of these three essentials, and if he is not given the necessary particulars, he should refuse to advise until he is properly instructed.

Recent legislation, by part III of the Administration of Justice Act, 1969, gives the Court of Protection power to make a will, or make a codicil to an old will, on behalf of a patient under its jurisdiction. The court would of course need medical evidence to show that the patient himself lacks testamentary capacity, and the doctor must be prepared to give his reasons as well as an opinion.

(3) Divorce

Insanity can be a reason for divorce and for nullification of a marriage. A petition for divorce may be presented on the ground that the respondent is 'incurably of unsound mind and has been continuously under care and treatment for a period of at least five years immediately preceding the presentation of the petition'

(Matrimonial Causes Act, 1937). 'Under care and treatment' means either compulsory detention or informal stay provided the latter follows directly on a period of compulsory detention. An important amplification of what is meant by being incurably of unsound mind was given in a recent judicial decision (Whysall v. Whysall): '. . . if in the light of medical knowledge at the time of the inquiry it is said that the patient's mental state is such that the best that can be hoped for is discharge to conditions where he will not be required to manage himself or his affairs but will live an artificial existence protected from the normal incidents and problems of life he will properly be termed incurable.'

Nullification of a marriage may take place if either party was at the time of the marriage of unsound mind, or a mental defective, or subject to recurrent fits of insanity or epilepsy. The condition of such a decree is that the petitioner was at the time of the marriage ignorant of the facts alleged. The petition has to be filed within a year from the date of marriage. With regard to nullification no details about the type or degree of insanity have as yet been laid down; at any rate, to have been compulsorily detained is not the only necessary condition.

TERMINATION OF PREGNANCY

By the Abortion Act of 1967 a pregnancy may be terminated by a registered medical practitioner if two registered medical practitioners are of the opinion, formed in good faith:

1. (a) that the continuance of the pregnancy would involve risk to the life of the pregnant woman, or of injury to the physical or mental health of the pregnant woman or any existing children of her family, greater than if the pregnancy were terminated; or (b) that there is a substantial risk that if the child were born it would suffer from such physical or mental abnormalities as to be seriously handicapped.

2. In determining whether the continuance of a pregnancy would involve such risk of injury to health as is mentioned in paragraph (a) of subsection (1) of this section, account may be taken of the pregnant woman's actual or reasonably foreseeable environment.

The practitioners concerned must fill in a 'green form' (Certificate A) which is sent to the Department of Health and Social Services. The operation must be carried out only in National Health Service hospitals, or in private hospitals or nursing homes approved after inspection as being suitable.

This act has raised many problems. The phrasing . . . 'injury to the physical . . . health of the pregnant woman' is open to the interpretation that any pregnancy may be terminated, as the risks of early abortion in skilled hands are less than the risks of pregnancy, labour, and the puerperium. The psychiatric aspects 'injury to the . . . mental health' taking into account 'the pregnant woman's actual or reasonably foreseeable environment', is a problem because it is so difficult to define mental health. In patients who have had serious depressive illnesses associated with childbirth in the past, or who are schizophrenic, there is general agreement that termination of pregnancy is helpful if the woman does not want the child. There is also general agreement to terminate in those women with low incomes and large families, often of dull intelligence and socially incapable, in whom each extra child depresses the general level of the family's well being and the mother's health. In these cases sterilisation should also be considered.

The problematical cases are those who present in the largest numbers: namely women who do not want the baby, are not mentally ill, may or may not have some abnormality of personality, and are unhappy. They are often single, feel very distressed, and are sure that their present life situation is unsuitable for having a child. These women would be unlikely to become seriously mentally ill if they went through with the pregnancy, but would be generally unhappier and under greater stress, their whole lives made more difficult and distorted perhaps. It is also probable that many of them would end up happily accepting the baby, but when they are pleading for termination this possibility seems remote. The fact that termination is so freely available in most places, and that there is so much pressure towards abortion alters the situation; as do current views about over-population. People put up with something inevitable, and make an effort to adjust gracefully; but attitudes change as opportunities appear.

The *published* evidence on the effects of termination of pregnancy suggests that it has few undesirable after effects, in that marked guilt and depression do not develop as often as used to be thought, and most of the women are pleased, and happier. A sizeable proportion become pregnant again soon, and go to term; while a few again ask for termination. In this country cases in whom termination is refused mainly go elsewhere, as it is available on demand in practice at the private abortion clinics. Follow up studies abroad do not show any increase in serious mental illness, and most cope adequately. It is generally recognised that suicide in pregnancy is rare, although often threatened.

The present situation is that society has, through Parliament, expressed its views, but has left the termination of pregnancy on psychiatric grounds dependent on the moral and emotional attitudes of the individual doctors concerned, rather than on any reference to an accepted body of professional knowledge and opinion.

Bibliography

A small selection of books useful to the student

PSYCHOLOGY

Introduction to psychology, 6th ed. Hilgard E R, Atkinson R C, Atkinson R L 1975. Harcourt Brace Jovanovich Inc., New York
A very readable and informative book

PSYCHOPATHOLOGY

Psychopathology. Kraupl-Taylor F 1966. Butterworth, London
Clinical psychopathology. Schneider K 1959. Grune & Stratton, New York
New introductory lectures on psycho-analysis. Freud S 1948 (Trans. Sprott). Hogarth Press, London

CLINICAL PSYCHIATRY

American handbook of psychiatry, 2nd ed. Arieti (ed) 1974. Basic Books, New York
A very large six-volume compendium, useful for reference and browsing

Clinical psychiatry, 3rd ed. Mayer–Gross W, Slater E T O, Roth M 1969. Bailliere, Tindall and Cassell, London
Although outdated, contains much valuable clinical description

Companion to psychiatric studies, 2nd ed. Forrest A, Affleck J, Zealley A (eds) 1978. Churchill Livingstone, Edinburgh

Organic psychiatry (the psychological consequences of cerebral disorder). Lishman A 1978. Blackwell Scientific Publications, Oxford
A modern classic

Fears and phobias. Marks I M 1969. Heinemann, London

Psychiatric disorders in old age. Whitehead T 1979. HM and M Publishers, Aylesbury
A short but useful guide to doctors and others concerned

Recent advances in clinical psychiatry, No 2 & No 3. Granville-Grossman K L 1976 & 1979. Churchill Livingstone, Edinburgh
Review articles, with detailed lists of references

Contemporary psychiatry. Silverstone T, Barraclough B (eds) 1975. Royal College of Psychiatrists and Headley Bros Ltd, London

A collection of review articles from the British Journal of Hospital Medicine, a journal which has regular useful reviews of psychiatric topics

Alcoholism Kessel N, Walton H 1965. Penguin, London

TREATMENT
PHYSICAL METHODS

An introduction to physical methods of treatment in psychiatry, 5th ed. Sargant W W, Slater E T O 1972. Livingstone, Edinburgh

Drug treatment in psychiatry, 2nd ed. Silverstone T, Turner P 1978. Routledge & Kegan Paul, London

The use of drugs in psychiatry. Crammer J, Barraclough B, Heine B 1978. Gaskell Books (Royal College of Psychiatrists), London

PSYCHOTHERAPY

An introduction to the psychotherapies. Bloch S (ed) 1979. Oxford University Press

Introduction to psychotherapy. Brown D, Pedder J 1979. Tavistock, London
   These books do not, despite their titles, cover the same ground

Handbook of psychotherapy and behaviour change. Bergin A E, Garfield S L (eds) 1971. Wiley, New York
   (Especially the chapter on 'The Evaluation of Therapeutic Outcomes', Bergin, A E)

Behaviour therapy in clinical psychiatry. Meyer V, Chesser E S 1970. Science House Inc., New York

Persuasion and healing. Frank J D 1961. Johns Hopkins Press, Baltimore

CHILD PSYCHIATRY

Basic child psychiatry, 3rd ed. Barker P 1979. Crosby Lockwood Staples, London

MENTAL HANDICAP

Mental handicap. Kirman B, Bicknell J (eds) 1975. Churchill Livingstone, Edinburgh

PSYCHOSOMATICS

Brain mechanisms and behaviour, 2nd ed. Smythies J R 1970. Blackwell, Oxford

Modern trends in psychosomatic medicine No 3. Hill O (ed) 1979. Butterworth, London
   Volumes 1 and 2 are also worth reading

SEXUAL PHYSIOLOGY AND THERAPY

Human sexual response. Masters W H, Johnson V E 1966. Little Brown, Boston

Human sexual inadequacy. Masters W H, Johnson V E 1970. Churchill, London
   These books have been extremely influential

HISTORY OF PSYCHIATRY

History of psychiatry. Ackerknecht E H (Trans. Wolf S) 1969. Hafner, New York

Three hundred years of psychiatry. Hunter R A, MacAlpine I 1963. Oxford University Press, London

The former gives an overall view; the latter a more detailed and vivid account from British historical documents

Index